DEFENDING THE LION CITY

The Armed Forces of Asia

Series editor: **Professor Desmond Ball**, Strategic and Defence Studies Centre, Australian National University

This groundbreaking series is the first to examine the military capabilities of nations in Asia. Spanning the arc from Pakistan in the west to the Russian Far East in the north, each book provides a succinct survey of each service of the armed forces, including territorial and paramilitary formations. Written by military and defence strategy experts from around the world, the books assess the role of the armed forces in relation to national defence and security policy, and their social, political and economic functions. Up-to-the-minute research is drawn upon to present, in many cases, the first unclassified accounts of nations' defensive and offensive capabilities, as well as the ambitions of sectors within the armed forces establishments.

The Armed Forces of Asia series

Forthcoming titles

DEFENDING THE LION CITY

THE ARMED FORCES OF SINGAPORE

TIM HUXLEY

ALLEN & UNWIN

For my parents

Allen & Unwin
83 Alexander Street
Crows Nest NSW 2065
Australia
Phone: (61 2) 8425 0100
Fax: (61 2) 9906 2218
Email: info@allenandunwin.com
Web: www.allenandunwin.com

National Library of Australia
Cataloguing-in-Publication entry:

Huxley, Tim, 1956–
  Defending the Lion City: the armed forces of Singapore.

  Bibliography.
  Includes index.
  ISBN 1 86508 118 3.

  1. Singapore—Armed Forces. 2. Singapore—Defences. I. Title.
  (Series: Armed forces of Asia).

355.3095957

Set in 10/12 pt Trump Mediaeval by DOCUPRO, Sydney
Printed by SRM Production Services Sdn Bhd, Malaysia

10 9 8 7 6 5 4 3

Foreword

The minuscule island-state of Singapore is exceptional in a number of respects, especially in its economic accomplishments. A further striking expression of that exceptionalism has been in its government's provision for defence. Singapore stands out within Southeast Asia for the absolute and relative size of its defence budget, for the technological sophistication of its armed forces and for its model of military mobilisation. In addressing these and related topics, Dr Tim Huxley has provided the first comprehensive and scholarly account of the origins, evolution and institutional experience of Singapore's defence establishment. He brings to this subject some two decades of assiduous research based on fieldwork within Southeast Asia and involving a thorough scouring of available source materials.

At issue in this meticulous study is why Singapore, which has never experienced armed attack or an explicit threat of force since independence, should engage in defence provision well beyond that of any regional neighbour. Indeed, Dr Huxley points out that Singapore is probably the most densely defended state anywhere. He explains the strategic perspective that informs such defence provision as well as the corresponding strategic doctrine based on registering a credible deterrent capability towards its closest neighbours, in particular. He also provides a detailed account of the evolution of the country's separate services since an unanticipated independence and their roles in the order of battle, as well as an important analysis of civil–military relations in which the non-involvement in politics of serving officers contrasts with the political role assumed by select senior counterparts on retirement from active service.

Dr Huxley notes that Singapore's defence policy is transparent but that its defence doctrine is relatively opaque given its sensitivity in regional context. He has overcome the difficulties in collating data arising from that sensitivity in an admirable way. He has also written an authoritative and sympathetic account of Singapore's defence practice. He points out that without the deterrent provided by Singapore's armed forces, the vulnerable island-state lacking in territorial strategic depth would have been at the mercy of its neighbours. He adds that it would be difficult to overstate the extent to which strong defence has provided 'necessary assurance not only to Singapore's population but also to local and foreign investors so that they can continue to prosper in security'.

This study also raises an important question about the mettle of the leadership of Singapore's armed forces, which arises from the country's political culture. He asks, are they bureaucrats or are they warriors? An ability to maintain a credible deterrent, irrespective of available hardware, will depend on the answer to this intriguing question.

Michael Leifer
London School of Economics and Political Science

Contents

Tables, figures and maps

Glossary of acronyms and abbreviations

AA	Anti-Aircraft
AAM	Air-to-Air Missile
ABRI	*Angkatan Bersenjata Republik Indonesia* (Armed Forces of the Republic of Indonesia)
ACCORD	Advisory Council on Community Relations in Defence
ACMR	Air Combat Manoeuvring Range
AD	Armament Depot
ADB	Air Defence Brigade
ADSD	Air Defence Systems Division
AEW	Airborne Early Warning
AFAS	Air Force Advanced School
AFB	Air Force Base
AFC	Armed Forces Council
AFCP	Armed Forces Command Post
AFSB	Air Force Systems Brigade
AFSC	Air Force Systems Command
AFV	Armoured Fighting Vehicle
AHP	Analytical Hierarchy Process
AMDA	Anglo-Malayan Defence Agreement
AMRAAM	Advanced Medium-Range Air-to-Air Missile
AMS	Airfield Maintenance Squadron
AMT	Acquisition Management Team
ANZUK	Australia, New Zealand and United Kingdom
ANZUS	Australia, New Zealand and the United States
AOAS	Army Officers' Advanced School
AOR	Army Operational Reserve
AOS	Allied Ordnance of Singapore
APC	Armoured Personnel Carrier

APEC	Asia Pacific Economic Cooperation forum
APMT	Asia Pacific Mobile Telecommunications
APV	Anti-submarine Patrol Vessel
ARF	ASEAN Regional Forum
Arty	Artillery
ASEAN	Association of Southeast Asian Nations
ASEM	Asia–Europe Meeting
ASMB	Aircraft Systems Maintenance Base
ASW	Anti-Submarine Warfare
ATCCS	Artillery Tactical Command and Control System
ATEC	Army Training Evaluation Centre
ATV	All-Terrain Vehicle
AVLB	Armoured Vehicle Launched Bridge
BCTC	Basic Combat Training Centre
BMT	Basic Military Training
BSLC	Basic Section Leader Course
BTEC	Battalion Training Evaluation Centre
C^3	Command, Control and Communications
C^3I	Command, Control, Communications and Intelligence
C^4I	Command, Control, Communications, Computer-processing and Intelligence
CARAT	Cooperation Afloat Readiness and Training
CD	Civil Defence
CDF	Chief of Defence Force
CEB	Combat Engineers Battalion
CEO	Chief Executive Officer
CET	Combat Engineer Tractor
CEV	Combat Engineer Vehicle
CGS	Chief of the General Staff
CIQ	Customs, Immigration and Quarantine
CIS	Chartered Industries of Singapore
CMPB	Central Manpower Base
CNB	Changi Naval Base
CNRI	Combat Net Radio Interface
CNTB	Changi Naval Training Base
COMLOG WESTPAC	Commander, Logistics Group, Western Pacific
COSCOM	Coastal Command
COTS	Commercial Off-The-Shelf
CPC	Coastal Patrol Craft
CPF	Central Provident Fund
CPX	Command Post Exercise

CR	Civil Resource
CRISP	Centre for Remote Imaging, Sensing and Processing
CRM	Civil Resource Mobilisation
CSO	Command, Control, Communications, Computer and Intelligence Systems Organisation
DAB	Divisional Air Defence Artillery Brigade
DAG	Defence Administration Group
DCP	Defence Cooperation Programme
DMO	Defence Material Organisation
DPD	Defence Procurement Division
DPG	Defence Policy Group
DRD	Directorate of Research and Development
DSO	Defence Science Organisation
DSTA	Defence Science and Technology Agency
DTG	Defence Technology Group
ELINT	Electronic Intelligence
EOB	Electronic Order of Battle
EOD	Explosive Ordnance Disposal
EU	European Union
EW	Electronic Warfare
Ex	Exercise
FATEP	Field Artillery Training Evaluation Programme
FDS	Field Defence Squadron
FIBUA	Fighting In Built-Up Areas
FPDA	Five Power Defence Arrangements
FTS	Flying Training School
GDP	Gross Domestic Product
GNP	Gross National Product
GPC	Government Parliamentary Committee
GPC–DFA	Government Parliamentary Committee—Defence and Foreign Affairs
GRC	Group Representation Constituency
GSB	General Supply Base
HDB	Housing and Development Board
HUMINT	Human intelligence
IADS	Integrated Air Defence System
ICJ	International Court of Justice
ICT	In-Camp Training
IDF	Israeli Defence Force
IDSS	Institute of Defence and Strategic Studies
IFV	Infantry Fighting Vehicle
ILS	Integrated Logistic Support

IMF	International Monetary Fund
IMS	Institute of Marine Systems
IMW	Institute of Maritime Warfare
INTERFET	International Force for East Timor
INTO	Institute of Naval Technology and Operations
IPPT	Individual Physical Proficiency Test
ISD	Internal Security Department
ISR	Intelligence, Surveillance and Reconnaissance
IT	Information Technology
ITQ	Invitations To Quote
ITT	Invitations To Tender
JDA	Japan Defence Agency
JID	Joint Intelligence Directorate
JOPD	Joint Operations and Planning Directorate
JSF	Joint Strike Fighter
JTC	Joint Training Committee
KAH	Key Appointment Holder
LAYE	Learn As You Earn
LEO	Lands and Estates Organisation
LORADS	Long-range Radar And Display System
LST	Landing Ship Tank
LSV	Light Strike Vehicle
MAAF	Malayan Auxiliary Air Force
MAF	Malaysian Armed Forces
MBT	Main Battle Tank
MCM	Mine Countermeasures
MCMV	Mine Countermeasures Vessel
MCP	Malayan Communist Party
MCV	Missile Corvette
MGB	Missile Gun Boat
MHA	Ministry of Home Affairs
MID	Ministry of the Interior and Defence
MILES	Multiple Integrated Laser Engagement System
MINDEF	Ministry of Defence
MLRS	Multiple Launch Rocket System
MNF	Malayan Naval Force
MoU	Memorandum of Understanding
MP	Member of Parliament
MPA	Maritime Patrol Aircraft
MSD	Military Security Department
NALCOM	Naval Logistics Command
NAS	Naval Officers' Advanced School
NATO	North Atlantic Treaty Organisation

NCC	National Cadet Corps
NDU	Naval Diving Unit
NE	National Education
NFTC	NATO Flying Training in Canada
NMTB	Naval Maintenance and Transport Base
NS	National Service
NSF	National Serviceman Full-time
NSmen	National Servicemen
NTRACOM	Naval Training Command
NTU	Nanyang Technological University
NUSAF	Non-Uniformed Singapore Armed Forces
OA	Operational Analysis
OCS	Officer Cadet School
ODE	Ordnance Development and Engineering
ORD	Operationally Ready national service Date
OSB	Ordnance Supply Base
PAP	People's Action Party
PC	Patrol Craft
PCG	Police Coast Guard
PDF	People's Defence Force
PERISTA	*Perkembangan Istemewa Angkatan Tentera* (Armed Forces Special Expansion Programme)
POL	Petrol, Oil and Lubricants
PRC	People's Republic of China
PSTAR	Portable Search and Target Acquisition Radar
PV	Patrol Vessel
QRA	Quick Reaction Alert
R&D	Research and Development
RAAF	Royal Australian Air Force
RAF	Royal Air Force
RBAF	Royal Brunei Armed Forces
RCL	Recoilless gun
RECORD	Committee to Recognise the Contribution of Operationally Ready National Servicemen to Total Defence
REDCON	Readiness Condition
RMA	Revolution in Military Affairs
RMN	Royal Malayan Navy
RMNVR	Royal Malayan Navy Volunteer Reserve
RN	Royal Navy
ROC	Republic of China
ROD	Run-Out Date
ROVERS	Reservist On Voluntary Extended Reserve Service

RPO	Resource Planning Office
RSAF	Republic of Singapore Air Force
RSN	Republic of Singapore Navy
RSS	Republic of Singapore Ship
SA	Singapore Artillery
SAe	Singapore Aerospace (STAero after 1995)
SAB	Singapore Armoured Brigade
SADA	Singapore Air Defence Artillery or School of Air Defence Artillery
SADC	Singapore Air Defence Command
SAE	Singapore Automotive Engineering (ST Automotive (STA) after 1995)
SAF	Singapore Armed Forces
SAFRA	Singapore Armed Forces Reservists' Association
SAFTI	Singapore Armed Forces Training Institute
SAI	Singapore Aircraft Industries
SAM	Surface-to-Air Missile
SAMCO	Singapore Aircraft Maintenance Company
SAR	Search And Rescue or Singapore Armoured Regiment
SAS	SAF Advanced School
SAVER	Savings and Early Retirement plan
SCDF	Singapore Civil Defence Force
SCE	Singapore Combat Engineers
SCSC	Singapore Command and Staff College
SCTS	Systems Command Training School
SDC	Sea Defence Command
SDI	Singapore Defence Industries
SEATO	South-East Asia Treaty Organisation
SEEL	Singapore Electronic and Engineering Limited
SIA	Singapore International Airlines
SIB	Singapore Infantry Brigade
SID	Security and Intelligence Division
SIGINT	Signals Intelligence
SIMLAB	Simulation system for Land Battle
SingTel	Singapore Telecom
SIR	Singapore Infantry Regiment
SISPEC	School of Infantry Specialists
SITEST	Situational Test
SLOC	Sea Line of Communication
SLORC	State Law and Order Restoration Council
SMC	Singapore Maritime Command
SMF	Singapore Military Forces

SNVF	Singapore Naval Volunteer Force
SOF	Special Operations Force
SPF	Singapore Police Force
SPDC	State Peace and Development Council
SRBM	Short-Range Ballistic Missile
SSE	Singapore Shipbuilding and Engineering (Singapore Technologies Shipbuilding and Engineering (STSE) after 1995)
SSSO	Senior Specialist Staff Officer
ST	Singapore Technologies
STA	Singapore Technologies Automotive
STAero	Singapore Technologies Aerospace
STEngg	Singapore Technologies Engineering
STIC	Singapore Technologies Industrial Corporation
STSE	Singapore Technologies Shipbuilding and Engineering
SWBTA	Shoalwater Bay Training Area
TASC	Tactical Air Support Command
TBM	Tactical Ballistic Missile
TCS	Trunk Communications System
TD	Total Defence
TRADOC	(Army) Training and Doctrine Command
UAV	Unmanned Aerial Vehicle
UK	United Kingdom
UMNO	United Malays National Organisation
UN	United Nations
UNTAET	United Nations Transitional Administration in East Timor
US *or* USA	United States of America
USAF	United States Air Force
USN	United States Navy
USNO	United States Navy Office
USSR	Union of Soviet Socialist Republics
VDS	Vickers Defence Systems
WO	Warrant Officer
WTO	World Trade Organisation
YFC	Youth Flying Club

Preface and acknowledgements

This book represents the culmination of many years' work on the Singapore Armed Forces, dating from the early 1980s and my doctoral research at the Australian National University on the ASEAN states' threat perceptions in relation to Indochina. During the course of that research it became clear to me that Indochinese developments by no means wholly explained the huge effort which Singapore was putting into building up its military strength, and this stimulated an interest in the republic's defence policy and strategic outlook. Subsequently, this interest intensified into fascination during my time in the republic as a Fellow at the Institute of Southeast Asian Studies, from 1985–87.

Many individuals have assisted my long-term research on Singapore's defence policy and armed forces. Without their help, it is unlikely that I could have written this book. The late Gerald Segal, then editor of *The Pacific Review*, did much to encourage my work on Singapore by publishing my subsequently infamous article entitled 'Singapore and Malaysia: A Precarious Balance?' in 1991. Gerry was later Director of the Economic and Social Research Council's Pacific Asia Programme which, from 1995–97, funded my wider research on East Asian security, with substantial spin-off benefits for my simultaneous, more specific work on Singapore. Grants from the British Academy's South-East Asian Studies Committee also funded some of my research on the defence policies of Southeast Asian states, including Singapore.

I am especially indebted to Professor Victor 'Terry' King, formerly Director of South-East Asian Studies and subsequently Pro-Vice Chancellor at the University of Hull, for constantly encouraging and facilitating my research in general and my work on this project in particular. Sally Harris, Research Fellow in the

Department of Politics and Asian Studies, has consistently provided extraordinarily useful research assistance. During our period of collaborative research when he was a postgraduate student at Hull in 1995–96, the Singaporean journalist David Boey contributed substantially to my knowledge of the subject. Numerous colleagues, students and friends in the UK, Southeast Asia and Australasia have provided me with pieces of information and nuances of interpretation which have found their way into this book.

I am grateful to the series editor, Des Ball, for giving me this opportunity to contribute a volume to the Armed Forces in Asia series. The series coordinators at Allen & Unwin, Ann Crabb and Karen Penning, have indulged my rather hesitant progress towards completion of the manuscript, and I thank them for their tolerance.

The maps were helpfully prepared by my colleague Jean Michaud, using the cartographic database developed by Professor Rodolphe de Koninck and Yves Brousseau of Laval University in Quebec.

Finally, I must thank my family for their forbearance while I have been writing this book. My wife, Pauline, has read and commented on drafts of most of the chapters; I have greatly appreciated her helpful suggestions. This volume is dedicated to my parents, who met in Singapore at a time when its present-day status as a highly prosperous, technologically sophisticated, independent state with modern, powerful armed forces would have seemed an utterly incredible notion.

Introduction

We are here in Southeast Asia for better or for worse and we are here to stay, and our policies are designed to ensure that we stay peacefully in Southeast Asia in accord and amity with our neighbours but with a right to decide how we order our lives in our own house . . . any act, any programme, and decision which will help to secure a more enduring future for ourselves and our progeny in this region must be pursued whatever the sacrifice.

Lee Kuan Yew, Singapore's Prime Minister,
in Parliament, 14 December 1965[1]

The SAF is an armed force; it is not a civilian corporation. Its mission is to defeat its enemies, ruthlessly and completely. It is an instrument of controlled fury, designed to visit death and destruction on its foes . . . soldiers must have steel in their souls . . . must learn in war to kill and not flinch, to destroy and not to feel pity, to be a flaming sword in the righteous cause of national survival.

Brig.-Gen. Lee Hsien Loong, Singapore Armed Forces Chief of Staff
[General Staff], at his sending-off parade on retirement from active
military service, Khatib Camp, 18 September 1984[2]

Singapore, a small Southeast Asian city-state with an area of 648 sq km and a population of almost four million (of whom 3.2 million are citizens or permanent residents), is remarkable in many ways. Most importantly, it is a rare example of a former colonial territory which, since gaining independence, has prospered rather than merely survived. Notwithstanding widespread criticism (especially, but by no means entirely, from outside) of its authoritarian domestic political arrangements, since separation from Malaysia in 1965 Singapore has maintained not only a high degree of social cohesion—itself unusual in an ethnically diverse state surrounded by larger and sporadically unstable multi-ethnic countries—but has also achieved outstanding economic success. Rapid sustained growth (averaging 8.7 per cent between 1990 and 1996), deriving to a large extent from its government's relentless efforts to direct the economy into higher value-added, more highly technological and more capital- and knowledge-intensive activities, gave Singapore Asia's highest, and the world's fourth highest (after Switzerland, Japan and Norway), per capita GDP by 1997. While income distribution is far more unequal than is the case in North America, Western Europe, Australasia or Japan, Singapore's economic success has nevertheless yielded tangible economic prosperity and social wellbeing for the majority of its citizens.

The region-wide economic recession which began in 1997 certainly affected Singapore, reducing growth from 8 per cent in 1997 to 1.5 per cent in 1998 and creating unemployment. But the city-state was not so badly affected as its neighbours, and its advantages, particularly in terms of its geographical position, its highly educated workforce and its pragmatic, technocratic and forward-looking political leadership, ensured that its recovery was more rapid than elsewhere in Southeast Asia: the economy grew by 5.4 per cent in 1999 and was expected to expand by more than 6 per cent during 2000.

Singapore's defence policy and armed forces are also exceptional in Southeast Asia. Ever since 1965, the republic's political leaders have stressed (some, probably unjustifiably, would say over-stressed) Singapore's particular vulnerabilities—its small size, lack of natural resources, ethnic diversity and location between much larger neighbours. The pessimistic, quintessentially Realist precepts of Lee Kuan Yew and other 'Old Guard' leaders of the ruling People's Action Party (PAP) have dominated Singapore's regional and international outlook: the first 'fundamental principle' of its foreign policy is that 'as a small state, Singapore has no illusions about the state of our region or the world'. The second principle is that 'Singapore must always maintain a credible and deterrent military defence as the fundamental underpinning for an effective foreign policy'. There are other vital ingredients in Singapore's foreign policy, particularly an emphasis on promoting 'good relations with . . . immediate neighbours in all spheres' and a related commitment to regional cooperation through the Association of Southeast Asian Nations (ASEAN). In addition, since the end of the Cold War there has been a greater emphasis on Singapore behaving as a international 'good citizen', especially by supporting the role of the United Nations.[3] Nevertheless, it is clear that building up the capabilities of the Singapore Armed Forces (SAF) has played and continues to play a central role in the Singapore government's efforts to ensure security in the face of perceived external threats. While western countries' defence policies have largely ceased to focus on national survival since the Cold War's end, Singapore's government has not felt itself to be in this luxurious position—indeed, it stepped up its defence effort during the 1990s.

Singapore's defence policy is remarkable in several ways:

- through the Total Defence (TD) strategy it attempts to provide a degree of security from enemy attack unmatched elsewhere except perhaps by Sweden and Switzerland: overall, Singapore is probably the most densely defended state in the world;
- it involves the wartime mobilisation of human and other resources on a scale probably matched only in Israel, the European neutral states and the remaining Asian communist states;
- in contrast to most other Southeast Asian states, the SAF has focused on developing capabilities for offensively-oriented conventional warfare rather than internal security operations and territorial defence;
- the SAF's development has necessitated per capita defence spending exceeded (in 1998) only by Israel and Qatar;
- the local defence industry and defence science organisation provide a degree of support for the armed forces which is unparalleled in Southeast Asia, adapting, developing and producing a broad spectrum of defence equipment for specific national requirements;
- an extraordinarily wide range of bilateral defence links has been established in Southeast Asia, the wider Asian region and globally in order to develop and train the SAF; and
- despite Singapore's close security and defence links with western governments and armed forces, many details of its military equipment, organisation and capabilities remain shrouded in secrecy.

In many spheres of the social sciences, Singapore is probably the most intensively researched piece of real estate in the world. But despite their distinctive features, Singapore's remarkable defence policy and armed forces have gone largely unnoticed outside—and to some extent even within—Southeast Asia. Though Singapore's earlier military history has been closely investigated,[4] and a number of Singaporean postgraduate students have written dissertations at British and other overseas universities on Singapore's post-1965 defence policy and armed forces, little has been published on these latter themes. My own previous work on Singapore's defence strategy in relation to Malaysia and on its evolving military capabilities has not provided a full picture of the SAF. This book aims to provide a more comprehensive assessment of the development and contemporary status of the SAF, locating it in the broader contexts of the city-state's foreign policy, defence policy and strategy, civil–military relations and defence–industrial capabilities.

Producing a detailed analysis of the SAF is by no means a straightforward task. It is not as difficult as researching the armed forces of a state with a closed political system, for example China or Vietnam, but it is not as simple—particularly in terms of securing reliable sources—as investigating a western state's military capabilities. Singapore's government is formally democratic, but it tightly controls the release of information relating to security and defence matters. Little detailed official information regarding the SAF has been made available in consolidated or coherent form.

Though there has been a series of officially sponsored 'coffee table books' on branches of the SAF, some of which have contained occasional useful titbits of information, most of these publications are essentially Ministry of Defence (MINDEF) public relations documents, with the twin aims of bolstering public support for conscription and reservist service and promoting recruitment of regular officers and NCOs. These publications' historical background concerning the evolution of the SAF is rather thin and there is no official history of the SAF.[5] Since the 1990s, MINDEF has occasionally released defence information papers—most recently, in February 2000, *Defending Singapore in the 21st Century*—but these have been unimpressive and unrevealing by the standards of those produced by western governments, or Asian states such as India, Japan and South Korea.

Nevertheless, over the years official sources have cumulatively revealed a good deal about the SAF's evolving force structure, equipment, training, personnel and international links. Although independent coverage of national defence policy and the SAF has remained off-limits for the state-controlled mass media, useful data has been released through the SAF's monthly journal, *Pioneer*, the individual services' own monthly magazines, frequent press releases (now available on MINDEF's website) and defence ministers' parliamentary statements.

While these official sources have helped to build up a picture of Singapore's contemporary armed forces, such a picture would be incomplete without the use of unofficial sources. Many aspects of the SAF have remained 'under wraps', primarily because of the Singapore government's wish not to exacerbate neuralgic relations with the city-state's neighbours. MINDEF has been consistently less than frank in statements regarding the SAF's order of battle and equipment, not to mention the threat assessments which underlie Singapore's defence policy and strategy. So I have also drawn on my discussions—dating back to the 1980s—with informed observers of the Singapore defence scene, notably local and foreign journalists, diplomats and defence attachés. Most Singaporeans (particularly the majority of the adult male population who have direct experience of the SAF through the National Service system) are cautious when discussing local defence matters, particularly with foreigners, but the anonymity provided by the Internet has helped to break down some of this reserve: Net discussion groups such as soc.culture.singapore have provided some interesting revelations.

This book begins with a brief survey in Chapter 1 of the evolution of Singapore's defence arrangements from the late 1950s and, particularly after the separation from Malaysia in 1965, in the context of the city-state's political development. This first chapter also looks at the evolution of the three branches of the SAF during the 1970s and 1980s.

Chapter 2 examines the Singapore government's defence policy—summed up in the notion of Total Defence—and how the evolution of the republic's threat perceptions, which have been dominated by concerns over its immediate neighbours, have influenced its military strategy. The following chapter investigates Singapore's defence command and control arrangements, in terms both of the way in which the government shapes defence policy and how command and control is exercised over and within MINDEF and the SAF. Chapter 3 also looks at MINDEF's communications and information infrastructure, including its use of satellite systems, and at intelligence collection and analysis.

Chapter 4 probes the development of the SAF's personnel policies, in relation to full-time national service, reservists and regular personnel. This chapter considers the challenges which the SAF has faced from a declining national birth rate and a booming civilian economy, and touches on the handling of ethnic and gender issues within the SAF.

Chapters 5, 6 and 7 detail the evolution of the three services' organisation, equipment, logistic support, training and mobilisation procedures, and assess the SAF's capabilities at the turn of the century. Increasingly these capabilities have depended on locally developed or modified equipment. Chapter 8 tackles the issues of defence procurement, military research and development (R&D) and the defence industry.

The focus of Chapter 9 is on the extraordinarily wide range of regional and international defence connections which MINDEF and the SAF have cultivated, particularly during the 1990s. The final chapter assesses the unique characteristics of Singapore's civil–military relations, through which senior military officers increasingly have become integrated into the heart of the republic's political and administrative establishment. The conclusion weighs up the SAF's strengths and weaknesses, and looks to the challenges which the SAF may face in the early years of the twenty-first century.

1

The Singapore Armed Forces' origins and early years

When the Malayan Federation became independent in 1957, Singapore remained a British colony although it had effectively formed part of a political, economic and military unit with Malaya since the nineteenth century. Not only were Singapore's naval and air bases still important to Britain as a strategic foothold in Southeast Asia, but for both racial and political reasons the Malay-dominated government of the newly-independent Federation was unenthusiastic about the prospect of absorbing the island's largely Chinese population.

Nevertheless, efforts were made to move Singapore towards self-government. As in the rest of Malaya during the 1950s, both the British and moderate local politicians saw greater democracy as a necessary instrument with which to undermine the appeal of the Malayan Communist Party (MCP), which since 1948 had fought a political and military struggle against the colonial power with the aim of establishing a unitary Malayan Socialist Republic, including Singapore. During the mid- and late 1950s Singapore experienced intense political struggle which pitted anti-colonial political parties against both the British and each other. One of the leading local political organisations was the People's Action Party (PAP), established in 1954 on the basis of a coalition between English-language educated nationalist intellectuals (led by Lee Kuan Yew) and left-wing trade unionists. A third element of the political struggle involved conflict between the PAP's moderate and pro-communist elements. Nevertheless, the PAP won the May 1959 general election resoundingly and Lee Kuan Yew became Prime Minister at the head of a PAP government when Singapore was granted internal self-government in June 1959.

MERGER WITH MALAYSIA: DEFENCE IMPLICATIONS

During the early 1960s, the PAP leadership (which had long-term ambitions to play an important and eventually dominant role in wider Malayan politics) used as its principal political theme the idea that Singapore should only become independent by joining an enlarged Malayan Federation. The PAP placed great emphasis on the notion that Singapore was economically, politically and strategically unviable on its own. Drawing an obvious lesson from the Japanese conquest of Malaya and Singapore in 1941–42, the PAP stressed that, in military terms, 'Singapore and the Federation are one unit'.[1] In the view of the PAP leadership, dominated intellectually and politically by Lee Kuan Yew, an independent Singapore could ultimately find itself in a geopolitically uncomfortable position, similar to that of Israel. While the Federation's leaders had initially rejected the idea of absorbing Singapore, the PAP argued that it was unlikely that they could accept the existence of an independent, largely Chinese-populated and probably communist-influenced Singapore with equanimity because of the threat that it would pose to Malaya's political and racial stability.

At this time the PAP's proposed solution to Singapore's internal security and defence needs was merger with the Malayan Federation. Forming a larger political unit with the Federation, where the communist threat had effectively been eliminated by the late 1950s and which had become independent in 1957 under a fiercely anti-communist government, would ensure that pro-communist forces would not be allowed to take control in Singapore. In the long term, Singapore would be defended against external threats by the federal armed forces, to which it would contribute both finance and personnel. While there seems to have been little detailed PAP thinking on this matter, Lee Kuan Yew expected that ultimately an expanded Federation's army would need between 15 and 20 battalions.[2] (On merger in 1963 it deployed nine regular infantry battalions, including two from Singapore, as well as artillery and reconnaissance regiments and smaller support units.)[3] But there was no serious expectation that the larger Federation, including Singapore, would need to accept the major share of responsibility for defending itself against external threats in the near to medium term. In October 1957, three months after Malaya became independent, the Anglo-Malayan Defence Agreement (AMDA) had come into force. Under AMDA, Britain promised to help Malaya develop its armed forces, while

Malaya would permit Britain to maintain bases and forces on its territory. Malaya and Britain agreed to cooperate in taking 'all necessary action' in the event of an armed attack on Malaya or any of Britain's remaining territories in the Far East (Singapore, North Borneo, Sarawak, Brunei and Hong Kong). While even as early as 1961 there were indications that economic difficulties and a refocusing of British foreign policy on Europe might eventually force Britain to reevaluate its overseas military commitments, there was no serious expectation that it would withdraw its defence umbrella from Malaya in the foreseeable future.[4]

So in the early 1960s it appeared that Singapore's main contribution to its own defence and that of the Malayan Federation, even after the proposed merger, would continue to be through the provision of facilities for British forces, particularly naval dockyards and air bases. Britain had originally built up Singapore's military infrastructure—most notably its massive naval base and coastal defences—during the 1920s and 1930s as the lynchpin of its military presence in the Far East. Though the ignominious loss of this supposedly impregnable fortress to the Japanese in 1942 had destroyed Britain's role as the dominant military power in Asia, British forces had returned to Singapore after the war. British military strength throughout Malaya had been built up during the Malayan Emergency (the campaign against the MCP between 1948 and 1960) but, after the Federation's independence in 1957, Britain's Southeast Asian military presence—which together with smaller, locally based Australian and New Zealand forces provided a Commonwealth Strategic Reserve—was concentrated in Singapore to a greater extent. This was particularly true of the air force component.[5] A large part of the rationale for maintaining substantial forces in the region derived from Britain's commitment under the 1954 Manila Pact to the South-East Asia Treaty Organisation (SEATO), but the Malayan government had made it clear during the negotiations leading to AMDA that its 'non-aligned' foreign policy precluded allowing Britain use of Malayan military bases for SEATO purposes. During the 1957–63 period such a restriction did not of course apply to Singapore, which remained under British sovereignty.

By May 1961, Tunku Abdul Rahman, the Federation's prime minister, had accepted the desirability of an eventual merger between Malaya, Singapore and the British Borneo territories. This would ensure that Singapore could not threaten Malayan security by developing into a communist-dominated Southeast Asian 'Cuba'; at the same time, the integration of the Borneo territories with their substantial indigenous populations would help to maintain the Federation's ethnic balance despite the inclusion of the Singaporean Chinese. In a referendum in Singapore in September 1962, 71 per cent of voters supported merger. With this popular mandate, two weeks after Singapore became independent in September 1963 the PAP took the city-state into the Federation of Malaysia, which also now included North Borneo and Sarawak. In the run-up to merger, AMDA was renegotiated to cover the whole of the larger Federation, including Singapore. There was considerable debate over whether Britain's use of its Singapore bases would now be subject to the same restrictions as those in peninsular Malaya. While the Malaysia Agreement of July 1963 specified that the bases could be used for 'the preservation of peace in South-East Asia' as well as the defence of Malaysia and the Commonwealth,[6] it was clear that the Malaysian government expected to hold a veto over their use for SEATO purposes.

SINGAPORE'S FORCES AND MERGER

Singapore joined Malaysia on special terms, under which it had more autonomy (including its own prime minister) but smaller financial obligations than the other states. Defence, though, like internal security became a federal responsibility, and Singapore's own local military units were subsumed within Malaysia's armed forces. Though substantial British and Commonwealth forces remained in both peninsular Malaysia and Singapore, the Federation was gradually expanding its own military capability. As early as May 1963 the federal army established the 4th Malaysian Infantry Brigade in Singapore to take over control of locally raised regular and volunteer military units from the Headquarters, Singapore Military Forces (SMF).

Although external defence had remained a British responsibility after Singapore achieved self-government in 1959, the colonial power had provided financial and practical support for the development of the city-state's own small (but not insignificant) defence force. Until 1957, the SMF had comprised a collection of volunteer reserve units (including infantry, armoured, artillery, field engineer, electrical and mechanical engineer, signals, transport and women's elements).[7] These units traced their origins back to the Singapore Volunteer Rifle Corps, set up in 1854, and their forerunners had helped suppress the 1915 Singapore Mutiny by Indian sepoys and had fought against the Japanese invasion in early 1942. Between 1954 and 1956 the Singapore Volunteer Corps' personnel were supplemented by part-time conscript National Servicemen, some of whom later became SMF 'regulars' as the nature of the force changed in the late 1950s. During the 1950s certain local politicians—notably David Marshall, leader of the Labour Front and briefly chief minister in 1956–57—had pressed for the creation of locally recruited regular army units as the basis for the armed forces of a future independent Singapore. As a result, the Singapore Infantry Regiment (SIR) was established in 1957 and, by the time of merger, there were two SIR battalions.[8] As part of a military aid package provided to Malaysia at the time of merger, Britain agreed to finance the equipping of the second SIR battalion.

The Singapore authorities had also developed local naval forces. The Singapore Division of the Malayan Royal Naval Volunteer Reserve (originally established in 1934 as the Straits Settlements Royal Naval Volunteer Reserve), operated small coastal patrol vessels and was transferred to the command of the Royal Malaysian Navy Volunteer Reserve (RMNVR) at the time of merger. In 1948, the government of colonial Singapore had raised the regular Malayan Naval Force (MNF) as its contribution towards the defence of Malaya. The MNF became the Royal Malayan Navy (RMN) in 1952 and when the Federation became independent in 1957 the RMN was transferred to its control, although Kuala Lumpur did not assume full financial responsibility until 1959.[9] However, the RMN's headquarters and main base remained at Woodlands on Singapore's northern shore. In 1963, merger temporarily resolved this anomaly.

At one time, Singapore's volunteer units had included an air element. The wartime Straits Settlements Volunteer Air Force was revived in 1950 as the Singapore Wing of the Malayan Auxiliary Air Force (MAAF), which ultimately included a flying squadron operating in the training and light reconnaissance roles and a fighter control squadron. However, with the end of the Malayan Emergency the Singapore Wing was disbanded in 1960.[10]

Before the formation of Malaysia, the various Singapore military units' training and operational roles were largely limited to internal security and other low-intensity duties. During the Emergency, volunteer elements served in Malaya 'assuming those duties which allowed the Regular Police to perform the more active roles of jungle patrolling'.[11] By 1961, the SIR's first battalion (1 SIR) was playing a particularly important role in internal security, assisting Singapore's police to counter communist-instigated strikes and disturbances.[12] MNF (subsequently RMN) and RMNVR Singapore Division vessels conducted anti-terrorist, anti-piracy, anti-smuggling and fishery protection duties in close cooperation with the customs department, immigration authorities and Marine Police. The MAAF Singapore Wing was also involved in operations against the MCP during the Emergency.

Merger led to Singapore's military units—now part of the Malaysian armed forces—being deployed in more challenging roles. The British remained in overall control of the conduct of operations to defend the Federation against Indonesian incursions during *Konfrontasi* (Confrontation), Indonesia's attempt between 1963 and 1966 to destabilise Malaysia, which the Sukarno regime alleged to be a neo-imperialist project. Britain also contributed the bulk of the operationally useful forces, as was particularly obvious in Borneo, the principal focus of the low-intensity Indonesian offensive.[13] Nevertheless, between 1964 and 1966, the two SIR battalions saw action during Confrontation. The second battalion (2 SIR) was deployed in Johor from November 1964 to June 1965 against Indonesian infiltrators, 30 of whom it killed while losing nine of its own men. After two months of 'jungle training-cum-operational duty' in Perak (near Malaysia's border with Thailand), 1 SIR was sent to Sebatik Island off the coast of Sabah (formerly North Borneo) to defend it against Indonesian incursions between November 1964 and April 1965.[14] Confrontation also necessitated the mobilisation of RMNVR Singapore Division reservists for full-time service, with a patrol vessel being allocated to seaward defence patrols in the Singapore Straits during 1964.[15]

SEPARATION FROM MALAYSIA

Singapore's role as a state within Malaysia was short-lived. A wide array of problems relating to constitutional issues, political differences (particularly over the PAP's efforts to become a major player in wider Malaysian politics through its 'Malaysian Malaysia' campaign), racial tensions, and personal rivalry between Tunku Abdul Rahman and Lee Kuan Yew surfaced soon after merger. The Tunku seriously considered 'repressive measures' by the federal government—including the detention of the PAP leadership and the imposition of direct rule from Kuala Lumpur—though Lee Kuan Yew has argued that the Federation's dependence on the British, Australian and New Zealand defence umbrella would have precluded this option in practice.[16] During 1965, the two leaderships secretly attempted to renegotiate their constitutional relationship. At one stage a confederal arrangement, whereby Kuala Lumpur would retain control of Singapore's defence and foreign affairs, was considered. Ultimately, though, Singapore's government was forced to agree that complete separation was the only feasible solution if an intensification of bilateral tension was to be avoided.

The Tunku was greatly concerned over the defence implications of separation and insisted that, subsequently, 'Singapore was to make an adequate contribution to our joint defence and enter into a defence agreement with Malaysia'; moreover 'no treaty was to be entered into which would contravene the objectives of that agreement'.[17] According to Lee Kuan Yew, more specific Malaysian suggestions were: there should be a joint defence council; all Singapore forces should be under a joint command for operational purposes and the federal government should assist in training them; and Singapore should provide an infantry brigade and be responsible for patrolling its own waters. It was clear that the Malaysian government wished to continue exercising considerable control over Singapore's defence. Attempting to reassure Kuala Lumpur that it had no great military ambitions, Lee Kuan Yew's government indicated that it could not afford to support armed forces consisting of more than 'four battalions and some patrol boats'[18]—in other words, more or less the forces (including volunteer units) which it had contributed to the Federation on merger.

On 9 August 1965 the negotiated separation was announced and Singapore declared itself a sovereign republic. Article V of the separation agreement covered defence issues: Singapore and Malaysia agreed to 'enter into a treaty on external defence and mutual assistance' providing that several conditions were met: establishment of a Joint Defence Council; Malaysia would assist Singapore with external defence and Singapore would provide military units for this purpose; Singapore would allow Malaysia 'to continue to maintain the bases and other facilities used by its military forces within Singapore and will permit . . . use of these bases . . . for the purpose of external defence'; and both sides would undertake not to enter into treaties with third parties which might be 'detrimental to the independence and defence of the territory of the other party'.[19] These provisions seemed to lay the foundations for continuing extremely close bilateral defence links but, in practice, such ties did not endure for long after separation.

Separation caused not only the birth of an independent city-state of Singapore, but also—after a slight time-lag—the city-state's own defence policy and armed forces. Initially, however, there was little change to the status quo. The second SIR battalion was deployed operationally to Sabah for six months from August 1965, as had been planned before separation. The 4th Malaysian Infantry Brigade headquarters remained in Singapore, and it continued to control the SIR battalions as well as a Singapore-based Royal Malay Regiment battalion.

On separation from Malaysia, Singapore was hardly defence-less against external threats, given not only the close defence relationship with Malaysia, but also the massive British military presence. Separation meant that AMDA no longer applied to Singapore and thus there was no formal agreement covering the continued British military presence but, in August 1965, there was no expectation that it would be withdrawn or even reduced significantly in the short to medium term. Indonesia's Confrontation continued and Singapore still provided Britain's regional military headquarters and main base for operations in support of Malaysia. But though the British presence provided defence against Indonesian aggression, and would have served at least to complicate politically any Malaysian attempt to interfere with Singapore's new sovereign status, Singapore's leadership needed urgently to consider how Singapore could start taking responsibility for its own defence and internal security. Continuing intimate military links with Malaysia—particularly the stationing of federal forces in Singapore and the subordination of Singapore military units (principally the two SIR battalions) to the Malaysian command structure—had the potential to compromise or at least complicate the new state's efforts to establish a separate national identity.

At the time of separation there were already indications, which Lee Kuan Yew and the Singapore leadership probably quickly become aware of, that the Federation intended to make life difficult for Singapore. Singapore depended on Malaysia for the bulk of its water supplies and—according to Lee Kuan Yew's memoirs—the Tunku indicated to third parties that his government was willing to use this vulnerability to influence independent Singapore's foreign policy. Writing in the 1990s, Lee Kuan Yew claimed that the Malaysian leaders 'thought they could station troops in Singapore, squat on us and if necessary close the Causeway and cut off our water supply'.[20] Lee was particularly concerned that some of Singapore's key installations were guarded by Malaysian troops.[21] The Malaysian expectation was apparently that an independent Singapore—particularly if subjected to such pressures—might ultimately prove unviable, leading it to acquiesce in remerger on Kuala Lumpur's terms. This was almost certainly an unrealistic expectation, given the fundamental nature of the bilateral tensions which had led to separation.

INDEPENDENT SINGAPORE'S ARMED FORCES

Following separation, Singapore immediately established a Ministry of the Interior and Defence (MID) under Lee Kuan Yew's close political associate Dr Goh Keng Swee, who had been the State's finance minister since 1959. Goh, who had some military experience as a wartime NCO in the Volunteers, his permanent secretary George Bogaars and a small team of civil servants, senior policemen and army officers moved quickly to bolster the strength of Singapore's security forces. The new government saw internal and external security as 'very closely interwoven',[22] and MID controlled the police as well as the armed forces. Indeed, initially the police were counted as *part of* the armed forces. At this early stage, the government saw maintaining internal security as the primary role of the armed forces, including the military units, in view of the Malaysian government's withdrawal of Federal Reserve Unit (police riot squad) personnel.[23]

An immediate problem was that the only regular elements of Singapore's new armed forces, the two SIR battalions, included approximately 700 troops who were not Singapore citizens.[24] The second battalion (2 SIR) had been formed in 1962–63 on the basis of a Malaya-wide recruitment campaign and 195 personnel from the federal army had been drafted into the SIR units in May 1963 to bring them up to full strength, particularly in terms of providing sufficient NCOs. A smaller proportion of SIR officers were Malaysians but they included the two battalions' commanding officers. Many other officers were British loan personnel.

In late 1965 and early 1966, many non-Singaporean troops transferred from the SIR to the Malaysian army. Aside from the question of citizenship, there was an ethnic overtone to this exodus: the SIR rank and file were disproportionately Malay, while Singapore's population was 75 per cent Chinese with Malays constituting only around 15 per cent of the total. After separation, many Malay soldiers, even those originally from Singapore, preferred not to serve in the armed forces of a state which the

Chinese would inevitably dominate politically as well as socially. The new government apparently did nothing to encourage Malays to continue their military careers in the SIR. The return of some 300 Singapore personnel from the federal army only partially compensated for this depletion of the battalions' ranks.

Apart from expanding police recruitment rapidly (with particular emphasis on building up Singapore's own police Reserve Units in order to ensure internal security), MID's initial response to the weakness of independent Singapore's security forces was to 'develop a small well-equipped, highly trained and mobile defence force comprising a small nucleus of regulars backed by a large part-time volunteer citizen force'.[25] Primarily because of financial constraints, it was envisaged that the regular force would be no larger than a brigade. In October 1965, the government called for volunteers for a part-time reservist force which would have an eventual strength of at least 10 000. At the end of the year Singapore's parliament passed laws establishing both the Singapore army and the volunteer People's Defence Force (PDF).

Beginning in early 1966, MID mounted Operations Boxer and Boxer II, involving stepped-up recruitment and recruit training to boost regular personnel strength rapidly. By the end of the year, more than 1100 new regular soldiers recruited in Singapore had been trained, restoring the SIR and mobilised Volunteer infantry and artillery battalions almost to full strength.[26] In February 1966 MID established the Singapore Infantry Brigade to take control of the SIR battalions and the volunteer units from the Federation's 4 MIB. The Malaysian commanding officers of the SIR battalions were also replaced in early 1966, one by a Singaporean Volunteer and the other by a seconded British officer.[27] Meanwhile, by March 1966, 3200 Singaporeans 'from every walk of life' had volunteered for the PDF and were training in battalion-strength units on a part-time basis at five depots.[28] To set an example, a number of PAP ministers and members of parliament enrolled in the PDF and paraded in uniform on National Day in August 1966. To train officers and NCOs, in February 1966 the Singapore Armed Forces Training Institute (SAFTI) was established, initially in a vacant primary school. Its first commandant, Colonel Kirpa Ram Vij, was a seconded senior civil servant who had held junior officer rank in the SMF. In the late 1960s and early 1970s specialist training schools for artillery, armour, combat engineers, signals and other various support arms were set up within SAFTI.

To assist the transition from the meagre military resources inherited from Malaysia to a credible national army, particularly in terms of establishing operational and training doctrine, Dr Goh's team quickly decided that foreign military advice was vital. Rejecting the obvious choice of asking Britain for advisers (supposedly mainly out of fear that this might lead to long-term dependence) and after failing to receive helpful responses from Switzerland (which suggested that Singapore should dispense with armed forces altogether), India and Egypt, an agreement was reached whereby Israel would supply a small military mission consisting of eight officers in the first instance. The Israeli team arrived before the end of 1965 and remained in Singapore until April 1974; at its peak in 1969 it was 45–strong. This Israeli military mission played a particularly important part in developing training syllabuses and in directly training SAF instructors at SAFTI.[29]

TOWARDS A CITIZEN ARMY

There is no doubt that the Israeli link profoundly influenced the development of the SAF, particularly in its early stages. This influence was evident in the crucial decision during 1966 to transform the SAF from a relatively small force of regulars supplemented by volunteer reservists into an Israeli-style mass citizen force based on conscription and long-term compulsory reservist service. A confidential Defence Plan was finalised by September 1966, almost certainly with Israeli advice, and envisaged the army's expansion to 12 battalions within a decade, an objective which could only be achieved through conscription.[30]

Subsequent developments confirmed the need to expand the army. Indications from London during the second half of 1966 that Britain would soon substantially reduce its forces in Southeast Asia as a result of the end of Confrontation and the UK's deteriorating economic position were an important influence. At the governing Labour Party's conference in October 1966, a resolution was carried which called for the government to withdraw militarily from Malaysia and Singapore by 1969–70. Britain's Defence White Paper in February 1967 confirmed a decreasing emphasis on the region, and a supplementary White Paper the following July announced that forces in Singapore and Malaysia would be approximately halved by 1970–71 and withdrawn altogether by the mid-1970s. This decision was taken despite efforts by Lee Kuan Yew, Tunku Abdul Rahman and the Australian premier to postpone the British withdrawal from the region.[31] While the Singapore government's immediate concern was the economic impact of the rundown of Britain's military bases (which directly employed 40 000 workers and contributed approximately 20 per cent of Singapore's GNP),[32] anxiety over the security implications of the likely changes in Britain's role permeated the atmosphere in which the decision to introduce universal national service was taken in late 1966. Simultaneously, the escalating conflict in Vietnam accentuated the Singapore government's concern over deteriorating regional security.[33]

Meanwhile, the defence relationship with Malaysia had crumbled, partly due to the evaporation of the Indonesian threat to both parties with the end of Confrontation and partly because of differing interpretations of Article V of the separation agreement, providing further impetus for a more robustly independent national defence policy. A critical point of contention concerned Malaysia's continued stationing of troops at Temasek Camp in Singapore. By February 1966, this camp was needed to accommodate 2 SIR on its return from operational duties in Sabah. The Malaysian government claimed that Article V gave Malaysian troops the right to remain in Singapore in a mutual defence role, and that Singapore was responsible for accommodating such forces. Feeling that it was being treated as a junior partner in the defence relationship with Malaysia, in March 1966 Singapore withdrew from the Combined Defence Council and the Combined Operations Committee.[34] This marked the end of significant institutionalised bilateral defence cooperation between the two states although the Five Power Defence Arrangements (FPDA), set up in 1971 as a limited replacement for AMDA following the withdrawal of most British forces from the region, provided a multilateral context for continuing contacts including joint exercises.

Additional factors behind the decision to create a citizen army included the difficulty of recruiting sufficient volunteers to build up the strength of both the regular army and the PDF as Singapore's economic circumstances improved during 1966; by mid-1967, the return of Malaysian troops, recruitment problems and the diversion of regulars to training duties had reduced 1 and 2 SIR to a total of four companies.[35] Moreover, the PAP believed that national service could perform a vital nation-building role by providing young Singaporeans from different classes and ethnic groups with a common experience which would inculcate national consciousness, discipline and a sense of social responsibility.[36]

All these factors contributed to a government decision, announced in November 1966, that with effect from 1 January 1967 all new male civil servants and statutory board employees of military age would undergo compulsory military training. The first batch of civil servants were trained by the two SIR units for three months in early 1967. Having introduced the idea of conscription, in late February 1967 the government tabled a parliamentary bill establishing universal National Service for 18-year-old male citizens and permanent residents, as well as civil servants and students. In the first year, this would mean an intake of 18 000 conscripts, who would mostly serve on a part-time basis (up to eight hours' weekly during basic training) in the PDF, the unarmed Vigilante Corps or Police Special Constabulary. There was to be a reserve commitment of 12 years following basic training. Approximately 10 per cent of the total (mainly the better-educated) would be conscripted full-time for two years (or three years in the case of officers), followed by ten years' reservist service.[37] Under this scheme, approximately 600 national servicemen were inducted into the army in August 1967 and, together with more than 200 civil servants conscripted as a result of the previous November's announcement, formed new third and fourth battalions of the SIR. Many of the officers for these units were drawn from SAFTI's first batch of Israeli-trained graduates.[38]

In 1967, the government's attitude was that Singapore could not afford to provide two years of full-time military training for all conscripts. According to Dr Goh, 'this kind of thing is guaranteed to make us bankrupt'.[39] However, Britain's announcement in January 1968 that because of persistent economic difficulties it intended to bring forward its full military withdrawal from Singapore and Malaysia to the end of 1971 necessitated the acceleration of plans for the SAF's expansion. Representations from Lee Kuan Yew had influenced the British government to amend its plans to withdraw all forces by March 1971. Although most forces were pulled out by December 1971, the election of a Conservative administration in 1970 meant that Britain continued stationing a much-reduced force in Singapore until 1976.[40] Nevertheless, in early 1968 it was clear that within four years Singapore would have to take full responsibility for its own defence. As a result, defence spending was increased substantially between then and 1972 and, with the *Enlistment Act* of 1970, two to two-and-a-half years of full-time army service became the norm for National Servicemen. This change in policy provided the basis for the rapid expansion of the SAF's order of battle, particularly its reservist component. By the end of 1969, there were six full-time infantry battalions organised in two brigades, supported by artillery, armour, combat engineer and signals units. A further infantry brigade controlled four part-time PDF battalions, which were allotted an internal security role.[41] By the beginning of the 1970s, the first full-time National Servicemen conscripted under the 1967 *National Service (Amendment) Act* had passed into the reserves: three reservist SIR battalions appeared in the 1971 National Day Parade; another three had been raised by the end of 1972.[42]

INTERNAL SECURITY: A FADING CONCERN

Although Singapore's small size and urbanised terrain ruled out any threat from the sort of insurgency seen in Malaya and other parts of Southeast Asia, in the early years after independence its government was intensely concerned with internal security problems. In the late 1960s it even envisaged the army as well as the police element of the SAF playing a key, direct role in maintaining domestic stability in the face of potential challenges from both ideologically and racially inspired troublemakers.

In February 1963 Singapore's Internal Security Council (a joint enterprise between the British, the Singapore government, and the Malayan Federation) implemented 'Operation Cold Store' to detain more than a hundred left-wing political, trade union and student activists, including half of the core leadership of the communist-aligned opposition party, the *Barisan Sosialis* (Socialist Front). Operation Cold Store had severely undermined the main political opposition and neutralised the most important potential internal security threat even before Singapore merged with Malaysia later in 1963. However, though the *Barisan* lost much of its remaining political credibility by boycotting Singapore's parliament when it reconvened after separation in December 1965 and refusing to contest the 1968 general election, it was not quite dead as a political force. It retained the ability to mobilise Chinese-medium students and schoolchildren against the government on a range of issues, including the imposition of National Service, provoking riots in 1967–68.

Riots—often between ethnic groups—had been an occasional feature of life in Singapore since the nineteenth century; indeed violent clashes between Hokkien and Teochew clans in 1854 had led to the establishment of the Singapore Volunteer Rifle Corps. More recently, during the 1950s and early 1960s racial issues had flared into public disorder and violence. In July and August 1964 two bouts of communal disturbances involving Chinese and

Malays had left 36 dead and 563 injured. In the circumstances of the mid- and late 1960s, it was reasonable to expect that there might be a need to call upon Singapore's army to deal with renewed outbreaks of large-scale communal violence, particularly in view of the continuing tension with Kuala Lumpur and the evidence that senior figures in UMNO (United Malays National Organisation, the dominant party in the Malaysian government) had helped to instigate the 1964 disturbances.[43]

When race riots broke out in Kuala Lumpur and other urban areas of peninsular Malaysia following UMNO losses in the May 1969 general election, the Singapore government's concern over the possibility of renewed communal violence proved to be fully justified. The disturbances quickly spilled into Singapore and the entire SAF, including only part-trained officer cadets from SAFTI, was mobilised to assist police Reserve Units to maintain order.[44]

However, during the 1970s and 1980s a focus on external defence rather than internal security distinguished the SAF from the armed forces of almost all other Southeast Asian states (with the partial exception of Vietnam): although other Southeast Asian armed forces attempted to build credible conventional warfare capabilities following the Indochinese communists' victories in 1975, it was not until the 1990s that they moved away significantly from their long-standing concentration on counter-insurgency.

Several factors (apart from the pressing need to build a credible conventional military capability because of the British withdrawal), contributed to the almost complete shift in the SAF's attention away from internal security. In the first place, the diminution of internal security threats, primarily as a result of Singapore's economic success, helped to undermine the appeal of both pro-communist and communalist extremists. By the beginning of the 1970s, Singapore was enjoying an economic boom, including full employment, despite the impact of the withdrawal of the British military presence. Although the MCP staged numerous bombings and arson attacks in Singapore in 1970–71 following its return to armed struggle in 1968, these were mainly small-scale incidents. Maintaining internal security and stability in the face of perceived communist and communalist threats remained on the Singapore government's agenda even during the 1980s,[45] but the final cessation of the MCP's armed struggle in 1989 downgraded the significance of internal security as an acute concern. Although the government continued to see domestic security as a vital underpinning for national security and as recently as the early 1990s perceived internal security threats deriving from

Singapore's ethnic heterogeneity as well as from foreign (particularly western) cultural influences and low-intensity liberal political dissidence, by 1994 it felt sufficiently confident to claim that 'Singapore is free from internal subversion and insurrection'.[46]

Second, there was an efficient domestic security intelligence organisation (the Internal Security Department (ISD)), backed up by rigorous legislation aimed at curbing subversion. The government has not hesitated to use these coercive instruments to nip in the bud any political dissidence thought to represent an incipient security threat—as when the *Internal Security Act* was invoked to arrest alleged communists on five occasions between 1974 and 1980 and against 'Marxists' in 1987–88. However, during the 1990s political measures and less extreme legal provisions proved sufficient to control internal political threats.

Third, the government built up the police Reserve Units (later known as the Police Task Force) and Gurkha Contingent to replace the Malaysian police Reserve Unit withdrawn after separation. The British-officered Gurkhas, controlled by the police, were seen as particularly valuable in controlling potential communal disturbances because of their 'complete impartiality'.[47]

In organisational terms, the SAF's prioritisation of external defence was reflected in the division of MID into two new ministries in August 1970: the Ministry of Defence (MINDEF) and the Ministry of Home Affairs (MHA), the former controlling the SAF and the latter the police and ISD.[48] Although SAF units continued to participate in internal security exercises with the police until at least 1986[49] (and possibly more recently), by the early 1970s the SAF's internal security role had become essentially peripheral to its main task of defending Singapore against external threats.

THE ARMY'S EXPANDING ORDER OF BATTLE

The army continued to grow rapidly during the 1970s. By 1972, when the bulk of British forces had been withdrawn, there were already 12 infantry battalions (including six reservist units), organised under infantry brigades and divisions. The first two full-time higher formations were the 2nd and 3rd Singapore Infantry Brigades (2 SIB and 3 SIB), established in 1968 and 1969 respectively. These brigades were initially grouped under an organisation codenamed 'Area 3 Command', but in late 1972 the pretence was dropped and this formation was revealed as 3rd

Division.[50] By 1976 there were three reservist brigades, sufficient to form the first reservist division (6th Division); a second (9th Division) was established in 1978. The People's Defence Force (PDF) infantry battalions, which until 1971 included part-time conscripts as well as second-line reservists, were initially organised under 1 SIB, but later under PDF Brigade Groups.

Specialist, elite infantry units were also formed. The SAF Regular Battalion, set up in late 1969, was more accurately re-styled the 1st Commando Battalion in 1971. The Commandos took in their first conscripts in 1973, and the reservist 10th Commando Battalion was created in the mid-1970s. In 1978, 7 SIB (originally established in 1975 as the third active infantry brigade under 3rd Division) was converted into an elite infantry formation, composed of two Guards battalions—comprising fitter-than-average infantrymen—as well as the two Commando units. In 1980, 7 SIB gained a third Guards battalion and relinquished control of the Commandos.

Although the infantry has always constituted the army's largest element, the rapid development of other branches was also a priority. The SMF artillery unit had become the first Singapore Artillery battalion by 1967. Another four active artillery battalions had been formed by 1973. The first artillery National Servicemen were inducted in 1968 and passed into the reserves in 1970.[51]

The SAF first established an armoured capability in the form of the Vehicle Commando Unit in 1968. Light tanks from this unit took part in the 1969 National Day parade and, in early 1970, these were used to form the first Singapore Armoured Regiment battalion. By 1971 two armoured personnel carrier (APC) battalions had also been established. An armoured brigade was formed in 1970, conducting its first full-scale exercise in late 1971. The first reservist armoured brigade was created in 1977.[52]

The first combat engineer unit, specialising in field engineering (laying and breaching minefields, demolition, construction of fixed bridges, field fortifications and obstacles, and opening of combat routes), began training its initial batch of conscripts in late 1968. By 1973, there were three additional combat engineer battalions, equipped and trained respectively for river-crossing, bomb disposal and as armoured engineers.[53]

Other elements of the army during its earliest years included signals units, which were formed from 1966, the Transport Division and the Provost Unit (both also established in 1966) and the SAF Medical Services (created in 1968).

The army in the 1980s

By the 1980s, the army's expansion, in terms of manpower and the establishment of units, had effectively ceased. A demographic trough reduced the size of annual National Service intakes drastically over the decade but, with the introduction of a 13-year reservist training cycle in 1983, there were sufficient reservist units to fill out the planned order of battle. As a result, some active armour and artillery units were disbanded.[54] The principal formations were the three divisions, one active and two reservist. According to MINDEF, each consisted of three infantry brigades, one divisional reconnaissance battalion, four artillery battalions (one division-level with 155 mm howitzers and three at brigade-level with 120 mm mortars), a field artillery target acquisition battery, an air defence artillery battalion (administratively part of the air force, but under army operational control), a combat engineer battalion, a divisional signals battalion, and a divisional support command (providing logistical, mainte- nance and medical support). This represented the composition of the divisions on mobilisation. In peacetime, however, they were not organised as combined arms formations and only the divisional signals battalion and support command were administered by the divisional headquarters.[55] Additional non-divisional units included the two Commando battalions, two armoured brigades (one active and one reservist, each comprising three battalion-strength armoured battle groups and a self-propelled 120 mm mortar battalion), one independent armoured battalion with light tanks, four combat engi- neer battalions, one signals battalion (under MINDEF command) and the PDF Command (split into 1 PDF Command and 2 PDF Command in 1985), consisting of seven brigade groups.[56]

THE NAVAL AND AIR FORCE BUILD-UPS

Because of the continuing presence of substantial British forces during the 1960s, MID had felt able to focus its original efforts on expanding Singapore's army. But with the announcement in 1967 of Britain's plans to withdraw its forces, which would potentially denude Singapore of naval protection and air cover, urgent consid- eration was given to developing the SAF's naval and air components.

The navy's beginnings

On separation, Singapore had inherited the RMNVR's Singapore Division, which MID took over and renamed the Singapore Naval

Volunteer Force (SNVF). In September 1967, when the SNVF was retitled again, this time as the Sea Defence Command (SDC), it was still an insignificant force of less than 400 volunteer and mobilised volunteer personnel, operating just two small patrol vessels. But over the next several years it was transformed: in November 1967 a School of Maritime Training was established; in March 1968, naval cadets were sent overseas for officer training; and, three months later, six fast patrol craft were ordered. In December 1968, the SDC was re-styled yet again, becoming the Singapore Maritime Command (SMC). Although the SMC began inducting National Servicemen in November 1969, it was less dependent than the army on conscripts and reservists.[57] In 1974, the SMC transferred from its temporary lodgings at Pulau Belakang Mati (now Sentosa) to a more permanent naval base on Pulau Brani, another small island to the south of Singapore.

Singapore's lack of geographical depth and its dependence on maritime trade render it intrinsically vulnerable to attack from the sea,[58] and the acquisition of not only the fast patrol craft but also six missile-armed fast attack craft (known as Missile Gun Boats or MGBs) and two coastal minesweepers during the early 1970s represented an attempt to provide a basic maritime defence capability. The SMC also procured six ex-US Navy landing ships, tasked primarily with supporting the army's overseas training deployments. The SMC became the Republic of Singapore Navy (RSN), a separate service, in 1975.

In the first instance, the navy was primarily concerned with coastal defence and, during the mid- to late 1970s and early 1980s was preoccupied with low-intensity security concerns—particularly turning away Vietnamese 'boat people'. Years of patrolling Singapore's territorial waters, in close collaboration with the Marine Police and the air force, consumed the navy's resources and delayed its further development.[59] Between the mid-1970s and the early 1990s, the only additions to the navy's order of battle were a dozen small coastal patrol craft (delivered in 1981) to bolster inshore capabilities.

From the late 1970s, however, pressure from senior naval officers led to planning for expanded naval responsibilities and capabilities. Although Singapore's limited territorial waters and lack of an exclusive economic zone meant that its maritime interests were limited compared with those of most other Southeast Asian states, its extreme dependence on external trade suggested that the RSN should exercise a task beyond mere coastal defence. Thus the navy was assigned the task of defending

Singapore's sea lines of communication (SLOCs) and, as part of a subsequent expansion programme, in 1983 it was decided to buy six 600-tonne German-designed missile corvettes, five of which were built locally. The corvettes, equipped with sonars and torpedoes, gave the RSN its first anti-submarine warfare capability and were commissioned in 1990–91. It was also decided to upgrade the MGBs' capability, most importantly by equipping them with longer-range anti-ship missiles.[60]

From Air Defence Command to Air Force

Singapore's air arm had to be built from scratch. Although official Singaporean publications convey the impression that planning for an air force did not begin until early 1968 (after Britain's accelerated military withdrawal was announced), the first Defence Plan prepared in 1966 outlined an ambitious proposal for an air arm based on a core of 40 Hunter fighters and a strike force of 12 Canberra bombers, all to be acquired second-hand from the British Royal Air Force (RAF). Other planned equipment at this early stage included light aircraft, helicopters, surface-to-air missiles (SAMs) and other anti-aircraft defences.[61]

Nevertheless, the British withdrawal announcement—which sounded the death-knell for the RAF's Far East Air Force and its fighter, bomber, photographic and maritime reconnaissance, transport, helicopter and SAM squadrons at three major air bases in Singapore—did provide the impetus for more concrete planning within the framework provided by the original Defence Plan. In 1968, the nucleus of an Air Staff was formed within MID and with British assistance began planning the recruitment of pilots and groundcrew, as well as the establishment of radar and SAM units. The aim was to establish a credible air defence capability by the time of the RAF's planned departure at the end of 1971. In September 1968, the Singapore Air Defence Command (SADC) was set up; at about the same time, the first recruits—fixed-wing pilots, technicians and air traffic controllers—were sent to Britain for training. Helicopter pilots were trained in France. In March 1969, a School of Technical Training opened. Initially, the SADC had only one aircraft (borrowed from the local flying club), which was used for selecting potential pilots to be sent overseas for training. But during 1969 the delivery of eight Cessna 172 primary trainers from the United States allowed the SADC to establish its own Flying Training School (FTS). Eight Alouette III helicopters were delivered from France in 1969, forming the SADC's first operational unit. These were followed during 1970–71 by 16 Strikemaster jet trainers, 20 Hunter fighter ground-attack aircraft, 28 Bloodhound SAMs and 35mm anti-aircraft guns, all purchased from Britain.[62] From its inception, the SADC was largely a professional force, but small numbers of National Servicemen were trained as technicians and anti-aircraft gunners.[63]

Singapore's air arm continued its rapid expansion through the 1970s. By 1972, the SADC had taken control of all RAF facilities on the island, including the air defence radar station at Bukit Gombak as well as the airfields at Seletar, Tengah and Changi. It also took over the Royal Naval Air Station at Sembawang, which became a helicopter base. New aircraft continued to arrive. Italian-built SF260 trainers were delivered to the FTS in 1972. In the same year, 27 more Hunters from Britain allowed the formation of a second fighter squadron. Also in 1972, MINDEF purchased more than 50 ex-US Navy A-4 Skyhawks to provide a strike capability: these aircraft were thoroughly modernised to A-4S standard, including the fitting of new navigation/attack systems and heavy cannon, before delivery to Singapore in 1974–76 to equip two new squadrons. Most of the modernisation work on the A-4s was completed in Singapore by a local subsidiary of the US company, Lockheed. Six Skyvan light transports from Britain equipped another squadron from 1973; a second transport unit was formed with four much larger C-130B Hercules supplied by the United States in 1977. From 1977, UH-1H 'Hueys', also from the United States, re-equipped the helicopter squadron; another helicopter unit was formed with ex-US Army UH-1Bs before the decade's end. Nine additional Strikemasters were acquired from South Yemen and Oman for the expanding jet flying training programme and in 1979, the Republic of Singapore Air Force (RSAF, as the SADC had become in 1975) received 21 F-5E and F-5F radar-equipped interceptors armed with AIM-9J Sidewinder air-to-air missiles (AAMs).[64]

The RSAF's order of battle and operational capabilities expanded still further during the 1980s. The Skyhawk strike force grew following a 1980 decision to purchase another 70 ex-US Navy airframes, which were shipped to Singapore for rebuilding as A-4S1s by the government-owned Singapore Aircraft Maintenance Company. As a result, the RSAF was able to establish a third Skyhawk squadron in 1984. A major A-4 upgrade programme, initiated in 1984 and completed in the early 1990s, involved installation of new engines and avionics to create A-4SU and TA-4SU Super Skyhawks.[65]

Other new arrivals during the 1980s included T-33A jet trainers, to supplement the Strikemasters as the training task
expanded. Between 1984 and 1988, Italian-built S211 trainers
replaced both the Strikemasters and the T-33As. Fifteen additional
F-5E/Fs allowed the formation in 1985 of a second squadron
operating these types. Extra C-130s more than doubled the
strength of the main transport squadron. Five KC-130 in-flight
refuelling tankers (four of them converted from existing transport
aircraft) substantially extended the operational range of the A-4
and F-5 combat aircraft. The helicopter fleet grew to three squadrons with the delivery of 22 Super Pumas, most of which were
assembled locally, for both transport and search and rescue roles,
as well as seven AS350s for training and at least 30 additional
Hueys. Israeli-made Scout unmanned aerial vehicles (UAVs) were
introduced during the mid-1980s to provide short-range reconnaissance in support of army operations.[66]

The most important developments in the RSAF during the 1980s,
though, were in the air defence sphere, following a major capability
review in the late 1970s.[67] New SAMs (the medium-level Improved-
Hawk, the low-level Rapier and the RBS-70) transformed Singapore's
ground-based air defence capabilities. In 1985, MINDEF ordered a
first batch of eight multi-role F-16 fighters, which were signed over
to the RSAF in early 1988 but kept in the USA for training purposes
until early 1990. The delivery of four E-2C airborne early warning
and control aircraft in 1987 dramatically extended the RSAF's
warning time of impending air attack from the 'few minutes'
provided by ground-based sensors to at least 20 minutes.[68]
Organisational changes also contributed to a more effective air
defence: the Singapore Air Defence Artillery (SADA) was established
in 1979 as an RSAF command responsible for SAM and anti-aircraft
gun units; Air Force Systems Command (AFSC), set up in 1983,
centralised control over ground-based long-range radar and command and control facilities.

CONCLUSION

Until separation from Malaysia in 1965, it had never been an
ambition of the PAP to take responsibility for the city-state's
defence. It had been expected that Singapore's defence needs
would be taken care of both by the Malaysian federal armed
forces (which included components originally raised in Singapore)
and by a continuing major British military presence. However,

separation forced Singapore to develop its own armed forces, particularly in view of the new city-state's need to assert its sovereignty in the security sphere. In the first instance, these forces were based on the small regular and reservist army which was repatriated from Malaysian control. But, by late 1966, a combination of recruitment problems, Israeli advice, the breakdown in the defence relationship with Malaysia, the need for a nation-building institution and—most importantly—forebodings over the uncertain future of Britain's role had persuaded Singapore's government to create a much larger citizen army based on universal but mainly part-time conscription. Britain's withdrawal plans, announced in July 1967 and accelerated from January 1968, led Singapore to increase its defence spending, to expand full-time conscription so that within several years it became the norm, and to create a semi-regular navy and a largely professional air force. In the late 1960s and early 1970s, all three branches of Singapore's armed forces expanded rapidly and the fundamental features of the SAF were established. Prominent amongst these features was a clear focus on external security, despite the SAF's initially assigned internal security responsibilities. All three services continued to grow during the 1970s and 1980s. However, during this period the air force—which provided the city-state with early warning capabilities and long-range striking power to compensate for its lack of strategic depth—clearly benefited most from Singapore's expanding defence effort.

2

Defence policy, threat perceptions and strategy

The 'twin pillars of our defence policy', according to Singapore's defence ministry, 'are diplomacy and deterrence'.[1] Diplomacy—aimed particularly at fostering equable relations with neighbouring states, based on 'open and frank communication', 'due regard for international law' and cooperation in areas of common interest—is seen as key to ensuring security against external threats. Singapore has used diplomacy not only to encourage a favourable regional balance of power but also to maintain an open global and regional trading regime, which it sees as vital for East Asia's peace as well as prosperity.[2] To these ends, Singapore has participated extraordinarily actively in international organisations and institutions at global (UN, WTO), regional (ASEAN, ARF) and inter-regional (APEC, ASEM) levels.

DETERRENCE THROUGH TOTAL DEFENCE

Officially, 'Singapore's defence philosophy is not built on the premise of an existing external threat',[3] but rather on maintaining and developing a deterrent capability aimed at preventing threats from arising in the first place. Singapore's 'deterrence strategy' is operationalised through Total Defence (TD), a concept first enunciated in 1984 to 'unite all sectors of society—government, business and the people—in the defence of the country'.[4] According to the government, Military Defence is only one of TD's five components, the other elements being Psychological Defence, Social Defence, Economic Defence and Civil Defence, each the responsibility of a government department other than MINDEF.[5] Repeated public information campaigns have been used to propagate the TD concept.

Psychological Defence, motivated by governmental concern that Singapore's population—composed largely of descendants of relatively recent immigrants, with increasing numbers of first-generation newcomers from other parts of Asia—might lack the moral fibre to resist external aggression, aims to develop 'the collective will of Singaporeans to stand up for their rights, to protect what is theirs and to be left in peace to progress and prosper in their own way', thus bolstering their 'commitment to the nation and their confidence in its defence and future'.[6] Psychological Defence is operationalised primarily through the National Education (NE) programme, which seeks to convey five 'messages':

- 'Singapore is our homeland. This is where we belong.'
- 'Singapore is worth defending. We want to keep our heritage and our way of life.'
- 'Singapore can be defended. United, determined and well-prepared we shall fight for the safety of our homes and the future of our families and children.'
- 'We must ourselves defend Singapore. No one else is responsible for our security.'
- 'We can deter others from attacking us. With Total Defence, we can live in peace.'[7]

Initially, NE was part of the training programme for SAF conscripts. However, the government's realisation in the mid-1990s that few Singaporeans were aware of crucial formative national experiences such as the racial riots of 1964 and separation from Malaysia in 1965, let alone the horrors of the Japanese occupation,[8] led to the introduction of an NE element into the school history curriculum. Trainee teachers must go through a Programme for National Education, including visits to military units.[9] Since 1998, schools have marked Total Defence Day annually on 15 February (the anniversary of the British surrender of Singapore to Japanese forces in 1942).

Social Defence is intended to bolster Singapore's social cohesion in the face of centrifugal tendencies deriving from its population's ethnic, religious and linguistic diversity, thus depriving potential aggressors of opportunities to exploit such differences, and is implemented in the TD context through the NE programme, which emphasises the importance of building a tolerant multi-cultural society in the interests of inter-racial harmony. However,

since independence many key Singapore government policies—
particularly in such areas as education and housing—have been
aimed at this goal of maintaining and strengthening social
cohesion.[10]

Psychological Defence and Social Defence have sometimes
fulfilled a parallel role not directly related to defence against
external threat, by providing justifications for the suppression of
liberal dissent in the domestic political arena. For example, in
May 1988—at a time when it was embroiled in controversy over
the arrest of political dissidents—the government claimed that
'foreign elements' were attacking Singapore's 'psychological and
social defences' in the belief that these were the republic's 'weak
links'.[11]

The main aim of *Economic Defence* is to ensure that Singapore's economy 'will not collapse during war or under the cloud
of war'. There are contingency plans to enable factories and offices
to continue functioning 'when manpower and equipment are
mobilised for war'. Under the Civil Resource (CR) requisitioning
programme, the private sector will be expected to share 'its
material and manpower resources' with the civilian and military
authorities in time of crisis or war. In addition, both government
agencies and the private sector are required to stockpile 'essential
items needed for the smooth running of the country during an
emergency'. For example, after the Iraqi invasion of Kuwait in
1990 Singapore's government ensured that oil was stockpiled in
the face of a looming shortage.[12] It is understood that, with
rationing, Singapore's food stockpiles could provide for six months'
consumption.

The objective of *Civil Defence* is to 'protect civilian lives,
lower the casualty rate, minimise damage to property and pave
the way for a return to normalcy' in the event of war. Singapore's
'small size, the high density of its population and the close
proximity of civilian residential areas to military installations'
render its civilian population highly vulnerable and Civil Defence
aims to give 'citizens the confidence, capability and readiness to
meet any emergency'. Civil Defence is also intended to reassure
'citizen soldiers fighting at the frontline' that every effort has been
made to protect their families and homes. The highly-trained
Singapore Civil Defence Force (SCDF) includes regular, conscript,
reservist and volunteer personnel, and peacetime exercises 'such
as food, water and fuel distribution, blood collection and shelter-
ing' prepare civilians so that they will react 'instinctively and in
an orderly manner' during a crisis.

Military defence

Though the government claims that all elements of TD are essential, Military Defence—based on the armed forces' capabilities—provides the core of Singapore's deterrent and of its capacity to defeat aggressors if deterrence fails. Key elements of Singapore's military defence policy, made explicit in government statements, include high defence spending, a system of universal military service, operational readiness for all likely eventualities, the maintenance of technological superiority over potential adversaries in terms of defence systems, the development of integrated and balanced forces and defence diplomacy. MINDEF has also emphasised the importance of working with other government departments to develop defences against 'non-traditional threats' such as terrorism, cyber-attacks and chemical warfare.[13]

Singapore's defence spending has increased by leaps and bounds since the establishment of the SAF, from approximately US$12 million in 1967 to more than US$4 billion annually in the late 1990s. For much of the 1990s Singapore's military expenditure roughly approximated that of its much more larger fellow Southeast Asian states, Indonesia, Malaysia and Thailand. However, in stark contrast to these other Southeast Asian states, which reduced their defence spending drastically in the late 1990s because of the regional recession which began during 1997, Singapore increased its defence budget by 13 per cent (in local currency) in the 1998–99 financial year and held it at roughly the same level in 1999–2000 and 2000–2001.[14] According to Singapore's defence minister, the city-state had to demonstrate that it was prepared to commit resources to defence 'in good times and bad' in order to maintain the confidence of its citizens and foreign investors.[15]

While Singapore's defence spending has increased substantially over the last three decades (see Table 2.1), the government has always been aware of the danger of provoking a regional arms race with its Southeast Asian neighbours. For this reason, and to ensure that building up the SAF did not damage the economy, shortly after independence the government decided to cap defence spending at 6 per cent of GDP.[16] Although defence spending slightly exceeded this level at the time of the British military withdrawal in 1971–72 and again during a recession in 1985–86, Singapore's subsequent rapid economic growth meant that, during the 1990s, military expenditure was generally contained within the 4–5 per cent of GDP range. Given the government's record of

Table 2.1 Singapore's defence budgets and actual defence spending, 1966–2000

Year	Defence budget (S$m)	Actual defence spending (S$m)	Actual defence spending as %age total gov't spending	Actual defence spending as %age GDP
1966	42	36	6.8	1.1
1967	48	37	6.3	1
1968	64	85	12.1	2
1969–70	229	218	19.8	3.4
1970–71	259	257	21.3	4.4
1971–72	470	461	23.7	6.8
1972–73	573	483	30.6	5.9
1973–74	514	487	23.1	4.8
1974–75	531	524	21	4.2
1975–76	580	556	18.6	4.2
1976–77	718	670	23.2	4.6
1977–78	909	875	26.6	5.5
1978–79	954	945	27.1	5.3
1979–80	998	996	24.7	4.9
1980–81	1270	1267	25.2	5
1981–82	1498	1496	21.9	5.1
1982–83	1700	1608	23.1	4.9
1983–84	1989	1529	18.5	4.2
1984–85	2263	2103	20.1	5.3
1985–86	2411	2361	22.3	6.1
1986–87	2239	2152	18.8	5.5
1987–88	2354	2205	14.4	5.1
1988–89	2624	2461	21.2	4.8
1989–90	2916	2779	21.2	4.7
1990–91	3468	3338	23.5	4.9
1991–92	3700	3440	21.5	4.6
1992–93	4109	3793	23.9	4.7
1993–94	4335	3946	24.1	4.2
1994–95	4679	4227	28.1	3.9
1995–96	5627	5373	27.9	4.4
1996–97	5686	5878	21.4	4.5
1997–98	6121	6865	28.9	4.8
1998–99	7286	n.a.	est. 31.4	est. 5.2
1999–2000	7300	n.a.	est. 27.1	est. 5.1
2000–2001	7400	n.a.	est. 25.5	est. 4.5

Sources: Singapore Government, *Financial Statements for the Financial Year*, 1966–1993/94; Singapore Government, *The Budget for the Financial Year*, 1994/95–1997/98; International Monetary Fund, *Government Finance Statistics Yearbook 1998* and *International Financial Statistics Yearbook 1998*; *Straits Times*, 26 February 1999; Singapore Government, Ministry of Finance website; International Institute for Strategic Studies, *The Military Balance 1999–2000*.

Notes: 1. The budget and spending figures include both oprating and development finance,
2. The 1966–68 figures are for calendar years, the 1969–70 figures for the 15-month period from 1.1.69–31.3.70; subsequent figures are for financial years commencing on 1 April.
3. The figures for 1966–1970/71 are for the armed forces component of Ministry of the Interior and Defence (MID) operating finance combined with the overall figures for MID development finance (most of which was allocated to the armed forces).

pragmatic policy adjustment in other areas, though, there can be little doubt that it would exceed the 6 per cent cap if it felt this to be necessary (in the event, for example, of a dramatic deterioration in the regional strategic environment at the same time that Singapore's economy was contracting).

Singapore's sustained high defence spending has funded continuous improvements to its military capabilities: by procuring increasingly sophisticated and expensive equipment, building extensive modern infrastructure, funding large-scale overseas training programmes, and providing generous renumeration for the SAF's vital core of professional officers and enlisted personnel. However, there have been simultaneous efforts to ensure that defence funds are spent effectively. There is great emphasis within the SAF on improving productivity, and MINDEF claims that decentralised financial systems have led to more efficient use of operating budgets by the services and individual units.[17]

Conscripts and reservists, respectively NSFs (National Servicemen Full-Time) and NSmen (National Servicemen) in SAF parlance, constitute the great majority of Singapore's military personnel. While the SAF might well have found sufficient professional personnel to operate its air and naval components, given Singapore's small population and the characteristically dynamic condition of its economy since the late 1960s, it would not have been possible to develop an army significantly larger than the brigade-strength force inherited from Malaysia in 1965 without universal compulsory military service. Indeed, even maintaining the strength of that limited force proved impossible in the immediate aftermath of separation. Following full-time National Service, NSmen complete a 13–year training cycle, including several weeks of In-Camp Training (ICT) in most years, with the result that a total of almost 300,000 'operationally ready' reservists is available for recall at any time.

The SAF prides itself on its operational readiness, which is critical in view of Singapore's lack of geographical strategic depth. Active and reservist units' readiness for war is evaluated regularly. A range of forces is on permanent 20-minute standby for operations. Mobilisation of NSmen can bring the SAF to a war footing in approximately six hours and selected reservist units are mobilised, using the mass media, several times a year. The mobilisation of civilian resources needed by the SAF is also rehearsed.[18]

Singapore's government has striven to ensure that its armed forces retain their technological superiority over regional counterparts.

Technology is seen as a force multiplier which can at least partially compensate for some of Singapore's disadvantages such as its lack of strategic depth and the SAF's reliance on conscripts and reservists. The SAF's equipment is continually enhanced, both through procurement of new systems from foreign suppliers and through upgrading existing hardware locally—a process in which both the local defence industry and MINDEF defence scientists play vital parts. Local industry and MINDEF's Defence Technology Group have also developed a range of indigenous defence equipment, including small arms, artillery, armoured fighting vehicles and naval vessels. Since the late 1980s, MINDEF has been committed to exploiting new information and communications technologies to give the SAF a 'strategic edge' over likely adversaries in the area of C³I (Command, Control, Communications and Intelligence).[19] These efforts have capitalised on Singapore's overall technological and industrial sophistication; the related high educational levels of most SAF personnel (including NSFs and NSmen) have facilitated the introduction of more complex systems.

MINDEF has emphasised the importance of ensuring that the development of the SAF's various branches proceeds synergistically. In the mid-1980s a Joint Staff was created and, since the 1990s, the Integrated Warfare concept has provided the basis for a doctrinal framework which attempts to integrate the three services' capabilities. Joint-service exercises are held routinely.[20] Organisational changes within the army have provided the basis for more effective combined arms operations.

SINGAPORE'S THREAT ENVIRONMENT

Having governed since 1959 without interruption, even by Southeast Asian standards the PAP has enjoyed an exceptionally lengthy tenure. The party has been responsible for the republic's security since 1965 and its leadership's strategic outlook and threat perceptions have consequently dominated the making of Singapore's defence policy and strategy. Specific threat perceptions aside, PAP ministers have repeatedly expressed concern over the security implications of the city-state's innate vulnerabilities and weaknesses.[21] Assessing these 'constraints' in 1987, Lee Kuan Yew asserted that Singapore 'cannot count on springing back on our feet if we are knocked off balance' and that Singapore is 'peculiarly vulnerable'.[22] This concern has provided the overarching framework for the development of Singapore's external security policies since the late 1960s.

Structural vulnerabilities

Unique demographic and geographical factors have conferred distinct economic advantages on Singapore. The island's location at the geographical centre of Southeast Asia and astride important trade routes allowed it to develop its economic role as an entrepôt during the colonial period, when it became a vital commercial link between Southeast Asia and the rest of the world. Since separation from Malaysia, the virtual absence of natural resources in Singapore has forced the government to develop a diversified and highly successful economy based on manufacturing and services as well as international trade. At the same time, in contrast to other Southeast Asian governments, the PAP administration has not had to contend with the problem of an impoverished and rapidly growing rural population. Singapore's highly urbanised population, composed predominantly of the descendants of ethnic Chinese immigrants, has provided an energetic workforce as well as financial and trading links with Chinese communities elsewhere in the region.

However, these same factors also carry strategic disadvantages. Singapore is an island city-state with a resident population of only 3.2 million sandwiched between much more populous neighbours—Malaysia (population 22 million) and Indonesia (220 million) (see Figure 2.1). The relatively small size of Singapore's population has promoted a sense of vulnerability while at the same time limiting the scale of its armed forces. Incidents such as Iraq's invasion of Kuwait have served to highlight the Singapore government's concern over the inherent insecurity of small statehood.[23]

A complete lack of natural resources and the continuing importance of its entrepôt role—Singapore's annual international trade is three times as large as its GDP, and its port has consistently been the world's busiest since 1986—have enforced extreme dependency on the outside world. Singapore still relies on Malaysia for the bulk of its water supply; virtually all its fuel and most of its food is imported. Moreover, Singapore and its territorial waters are entirely surrounded by the territorial waters of Indonesia and Malaysia: the city-state has no access to the high seas, on which it depends for 85 per cent of its trade, other than through these neighbours' waters.[24] Serious disruption of Singapore's physical links with the outside world would threaten

Figure 2.1 Singapore and its sub-regional locale

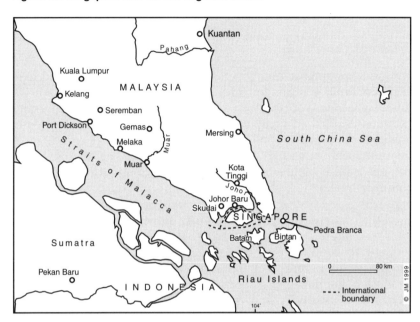

not just its economic wellbeing: its very survival as an independent nation would be at stake. Singapore is also vitally dependent on foreign investment: any significant decline in new investment in the manufacturing sector by foreign multinationals because of loss of confidence in the republic's stability or security would seriously damage its economic health. Similarly, foreign confidence is crucial to the continuing success of Singapore's increasingly important financial and banking sector.

Singapore's extremely small land area means that the republic has no territorial strategic depth: it cannot yield territory to an aggressor with the expectation of later regaining it. Singapore's population and its civilian and military infrastructure are necessarily highly concentrated and thus vulnerable to physical attack, further weakening Singapore's overall strategic position.

Singapore's location in a geopolitically and ethnically complex, and potentially unstable, region has accentuated its government's external security concerns. Singapore's population is 77 per cent Chinese in a region where this ethnic group has traditionally been distrusted because of its supposed political loyalties to the Chinese motherland, envied for its material wealth, and consequently often persecuted, exacerbating Singapore's sense of vulnerability. Singapore's ethnic and religious make-up, which includes a 14 per cent Malay Muslim minority, affects its security in another, related sense. Malaysia and Indonesia both have Muslim majorities and Chinese minorities; the spread of Malaysia's 1969 race riots to Singapore demonstrated the potentially dangerous linkage between developments in these neighbouring countries and communal relations within Singapore. Although increasing prosperity between the 1970s and the mid-1990s helped to subdue communal tensions in all three states, there have been no grounds for assuming that altered economic or political circumstances might not destabilise relations between ethnic Chinese and indigenous communities.

Singapore and the regional balance of power

In the light of this collection of peculiar vulnerabilities, Singapore has always been less reserved than other Southeast Asian states in acknowledging the usefulness—indeed the centrality—of balance-of-power mechanisms for maintaining both its own and regional security. Indeed, an appreciation that its interests are best served by preventing the regional dominance of any power 'which might in consequence be able to challenge its independence' has been a fundamental aim of Singapore's foreign policy since the late 1960s.[25] As Lee Kuan Yew said in 1966, it was vital for Singapore to have 'overwhelming power' on its side.[26] This balance-of-power approach has operated at two levels: Singapore has endeavoured not only to prevent Indonesia and Malaysia from dominating its immediate locale; the republic has also worked to forestall any 'adverse change in the overall regional balance'.[27] Singapore's horizons for maintaining a favourable overall regional balance of power were originally restricted to Southeast Asia but, recognising the increasing power and international assertiveness of China, and potentially Japan, following the end of the Cold War, its interest expanded during the 1990s to subsume the wider East Asian region. At the grand regional level, Singapore's small size and limited diplomatic influence and military capacity have forced it to base its balance-of-power strategy principally on borrowing political and military strength from extra-regional powers.[28] However, at the more immediate sub-regional level, particularly in relation to its immediate neighbours, Singapore has relied to a much greater extent on its own resources.

In contrast to Indonesia and Malaysia, which have argued in

favour of a regional security system managed by regional states (though they have themselves tentatively indulged in balance-of-power strategies from time to time), Singapore's leaders—remembering their city's subjugation by the Japanese during the Second World War as well as Indonesia's aggression during the 1960s, and ever-conscious of their city-state's inherent vulnerabilities—have feared that the implementation of such a policy would open the way to the domination of smaller Asian states by larger ones.[29] Soon after independence Singapore made clear its support for the maintenance of the regional *status quo* based on a multi-polar balance of power, and has subsequently sought to develop mutually valuable relations with as wide a range of powers as possible. During the Cold War, this included the development of economic relationships with both China and the Soviet Union, with the aim of giving these states as well as the western powers and Japan a 'tangible stake in the prosperity, security and integrity of Singapore'.[30]

However, despite a brief period of non-aligned posturing aimed at cementing links with other post-colonial states in the immediate aftermath of separation from Malaysia, since the late 1960s Singapore's leaders—and particularly Lee Kuan Yew, the most influential architect of its foreign policy—have repeatedly expressed anxiety that the declining military presence and involvement of the western powers (pre-eminently the United States) in Southeast Asia and, during the 1990s, East Asia as a whole endangers the stability of the regional balance. Singapore's government has consistently been concerned that the gradual decline of western influence might provide opportunities for other large powers—particularly China and until its demise in 1991 the Soviet Union—to assert themselves in the region, potentially threatening Singapore's freedom. Singapore's way of life (characterised by 'a relatively open, non-communist society based on merit, competition and social justice') and, even more importantly, its economy have always been primarily oriented to the West.[31] The city-state's government pursued an explicitly anti-communist internal security policy between the 1960s and the 1980s, because of the threat perceived from the MCP and its local political allies, and ideological distrust undoubtedly helps to explain its attitude towards the major communist powers during the Cold War, notwithstanding the simultaneous development of economic relations with them. But anti-communism by no means totally accounts for Singapore's persistent anxiety over challenges to the existing regional order. This was demonstrated by its concern with the potentially adverse regional impact of China's growing power and assertiveness during the 1990s despite the fact that communist ideology clearly no longer motivated the foreign policy of the People's Republic.

From Singapore's viewpoint, the late 1960s and 1970s brought potentially adverse changes to Southeast Asia's political and military configuration. President Nixon's 1969 Guam Doctrine outlined a reduced direct US commitment to the region's security. The Paris Peace Agreement of 1972 led to the withdrawal of US combat forces from South Vietnam and ultimately to communist victories there and in Cambodia in 1975. Vietnam was united under a communist regime, as was Laos. USAF units were finally withdrawn from Thailand in 1976. Singapore had lent both rhetorical and material support for the US war effort in Indochina since 1967, but these developments—which held the potential to increase the regional influence of China and the Soviet Union—provoked the city-state into playing a more active role in regional balance-of-power politics. Most importantly, whereas Singapore's support for the Association of Southeast Asian Nations (ASEAN) had been lukewarm during the grouping's early years, from 1975 it began to appreciate that the Association might be a useful vehicle for expressing political solidarity amongst Southeast Asia's non-communist states in response to the region's new circumstances.[32]

In late 1978 Vietnam—apparently emboldened by its increasingly close strategic relationship with the Soviet Union—invaded and occupied neighbouring Cambodia. Singapore viewed this development as seriously disturbing the regional equilibrium, being particularly concerned that Cambodia's subjugation was part of a wider pattern of Soviet-orchestrated aggression.[33] Moreover, Vietnam's action set an unhealthy precedent for the security of small states, repudiated ASEAN's 1976 Treaty of Amity and Cooperation (which had sought to establish a code for peaceful inter-state relations in the region) and threatened Thailand's security. For these reasons, throughout the 1980s Singapore took a leading role in maintaining ASEAN's hard line towards Vietnam's domination of Cambodia. In essence, ASEAN's strategy—which Singapore's political leaders and diplomats at times appeared to lead—involved constructing a diplomatic *entente* including China as well as the West, aimed at preventing international recognition of the Vietnamese-backed Cambodian regime and at sustaining the Cambodian resistance.

Singapore and the major powers

These developments during the 1970s and 1980s led Singapore to see the United States as a vital component of an emerging quadrilateral balance of external influences on Southeast Asian security, also involving China, the USSR and Japan. Fearing that the United States might lack the stamina to sustain its commitment to Southeast Asian security following the defeat of anti-communist forces in Indochina, Singapore sought to build military cooperation with Washington in order to delay the attenuation of its regional security role. Despite frictions over issues ranging from trade relations and human rights to the supply of military equipment, the foundations for a close bilateral strategic relationship were established.

Singapore's belief in the continuing importance of the United States' regional security role was undiminished at the end of the Cold War, indicating again that ideological antipathy did not fully explain the republic's concern over the potential regional ascendancy of possibly less benign major powers. Since the USSR's demise, Singapore's leaders—particularly successive defence ministers—have repeatedly emphasised the crucial importance for East Asian regional security of a stable triangular relationship between the United States, China and Japan.[34] Singapore views a continuing substantial US military presence in East Asia as a vital constraint on not only China's regional behaviour but also the potential remilitarisation of Japan's foreign policy.[35] Whereas during the 1970s and 1980s, Singapore had relatively little opportunity to promote rather than merely encourage the United States' regional security engagement,[36] the prospect of the withdrawal of US naval and air forces from the Philippines (and hence from Southeast Asia) allowed the republic tangibly to facilitate Washington's continued regional military presence by providing expanded access for American ships and aircraft.

However, Singapore's positive outlook on the United States' regional role did not imply that it would support future strategies aimed at 'containing' China in the event of a hardening strategic confrontation between Washington and Beijing. Indeed, during the Taiwan Straits crisis in early 1996, Lee Kuan Yew encouraged both Washington and Beijing to act with restraint in conducting their bilateral relations, and stressed his view that the United States should not alienate China by pressing too hard on trade issues. Lee also emphasised his great concern that an American effort to contain China might in the longer term divide East Asian states into antagonistic camps according to their attitude towards the People's Republic.[37] Such a development would place Singapore in a particularly uncomfortable position. Despite its clearly western-inclined positions on many international issues, for domestic political reasons it is extremely unlikely that Singapore could ever take the side of the United States and Taiwan in a future conflict with China. Similarly, Singapore's membership of ASEAN does not mean that it could easily support directly-involved ASEAN partners if they decided to offer military resistance to any Chinese attempt to dominate the South China Sea. Particularly since the profit motive replaced communism as the guiding ideology of the People's Republic, most Singaporean politicians, officials, business people and opinion-formers would find it difficult to conceive of China as a threat. While the US government and armed forces may well see defence relations with Singapore primarily in terms of their contribution to balancing China, Singapore's government sees their utility more in terms of maintaining regional stability in general terms, while also bolstering the island's security in the face of more local security concerns.

The Five Power Defence Arrangements

Though the United States has played a much more important part than other western states in Singapore's balance-of-power thinking since the late 1960s, the republic has also supported intensified security cooperation under the aegis of the Five Power Defence Arrangements (FPDA), established in 1971 as a partial substitute for AMDA with Singapore, Malaysia, the United Kingdom, Australia and New Zealand as members. The initial underlying rationale for the Arrangements was that the defence of Malaysia and Singapore remained indivisible and that they still faced certain common potential threats: most importantly, a revival of Confrontation in the event of a reversion to a politically radical leadership in Indonesia, and the possibility of a major escalation in the MCP's campaign of violence against both governments. While the nature of the threats they face has changed, the notion that the defence of Malaysia and Singapore is indivisible has persisted.

The Arrangements were facilitated by the election in 1970 of a Conservative government in Britain, which decided to retain a military presence, albeit considerably reduced, in Singapore after 1971 (see Chapter 1). From 1971, residual but not insignificant Commonwealth 'ANZUK' forces, totalling around 7000 personnel in the first instance, remained in Singapore under bilateral arrangements with the republic, but Australia pulled out its infantry battalion in 1974, all British units had left by 1976 and New Zealand withdrew its battalion in 1989. Australia continued to base Mirage fighter aircraft at Butterworth in Malaysia, with a small detachment in Singapore, until 1988. Since then, the Australian presence has been reduced to a small permanent detachment at Butterworth consisting of maritime patrol aircraft and an infantry company, with F/A-18 fighters deployed for several months annually.

While the FPDA is fundamentally a consultative arrangement, involving no automatic commitment by the extra-regional members to defend Singapore and Malaysia, and although most of the extra-regional partners' forces have been withdrawn from Singapore and Malaysia, it still oversees a range of multilateral military activities. The Integrated Air Defence System (IADS), set up in 1971, has continued to provide an Air Defence Operations Centre for peninsular Malaysia and Singapore at Butterworth; it has a small permanent multinational headquarters commanded by a senior Australian officer. Each FPDA member assigns air defence units to the IADS: in Singapore's case these include two fighter squadrons and a SAM unit. Every year there are several joint air exercises involving Malaysian and Singaporean forces, as well as annual air and maritime manoeuvres in which some or all of the extra-regional partners participate.

In the early 1980s, following the Vietnamese invasion of Cambodia and the Soviet Union's establishment of a strategic toehold in Vietnam, Singapore, like the other FPDA members, supported an Australian initiative to resuscitate the Arrangements which, notwithstanding small-scale exercises, had essentially lain dormant during the 1970s. The most obvious indications of the upgrading of FPDA activities were the larger-scale annual 'Starfish' maritime exercises which commenced in 1981. However, Singapore has sometimes indicated impatience with the slow pace of efforts to intensify cooperation within the FPDA. In 1980–81, Foreign Minister S. Rajaratnam argued the need for an 'intermeshing of defence capabilities' or at least a 'military understanding' between the FPDA powers, other Southeast Asian states, Japan and the United States.[38] In 1989 Brigadier-General Lee Hsien Loong, then Second Minister for Defence (Services), argued that FPDA forces should train together more often, place greater emphasis on joint service operations and establish a combined staff as a 'stand-by' organisation which could be activated during

a crisis.[39] The most important obstacle to realising these suggestions for enhancing the FPDA's role was the attitude of Malaysia,
which 'played a relatively low-key, constraining role'.[40]

Like its support for the United States' regional military role,
Singapore's enthusiasm for the Arrangements has not diminished
during the strategically uncertain period since the end of the Cold
War, with its ministers continuing to press for intensified FPDA
activities.[41] In 1997, Defence Minister Tony Tan argued that 'without the FPDA there will be a loss of confidence and stability in
this part of the world' and that the Arrangements were 'a deterrent to aggression'.[42]

Part of the FPDA's significance for Singapore is undoubtedly
its contribution—minor but not insignificant—to maintaining a
favourable overall regional balance of power. As Defence Minister
Yeo Ning Hong said in 1992, the FPDA is 'an important element
in the network of regional security arrangements'.[43] While its
argument in the early 1980s for the FPDA to be somehow linked
more closely to the United States' regional military role did not
win favour, Singapore has valued institutionalised security cooperation with Australia and (at least until the breach in ANZUS
during the mid-1980s) New Zealand partly because their close
alliance with Washington provided an indirect security link to the
United States.[44] The FPDA has also been important for Singapore
in the sense of providing a context for sustaining and, during the
1990s, expanding bilateral defence relations with Australia and
New Zealand. However, from its beginnings the FPDA has also
served more localised purposes for Singapore by providing a neutral forum for continued defence cooperation and security-related
confidence building with Malaysia despite repeated strains in
bilateral relations, and by providing a potential counterweight to
any long-term revival of a coercive Indonesian foreign policy.

Singapore's own growing military capability has facilitated
efforts to encourage a favourable regional balance of power since
the late 1960s in two main senses. In the first place, possessing
its own armed forces provides Singapore with a vital prerequisite
for credible diplomacy in relation to friendly powers. Although
Singapore is not engaged in any formal alliances, its evident
ability to share the burden of regional defence strengthens its
hand when attempting to persuade extra-regional powers to maintain or enhance their regional security roles. Without possessing
fairly sophisticated capabilities, it would be difficult and perhaps
impossible to engage either the United States or the extra-regional
FPDA powers in militarily significant cooperation. Moreover, the

existence of a significant market for defence equipment—by the late 1990s the largest in Southeast Asia—provides an additional incentive for these extra-regional powers to cooperate with Singapore on defence and security. Second, the availability of high-grade local military infrastructure—particularly air bases and naval dockyards—which has been maintained and developed primarily for the SAF, allows Singapore to accommodate visiting US (and, incidentally, Australian, New Zealand and British) forces without the need for any significant expenditure on fixed facilities by friendly powers. At the same time, Singapore is able credibly to claim that it has not allowed foreign military bases on its soil, thereby placating neighbouring Indonesia and Malaysia.

Sub-regional tensions

The conflicts in Indochina and the Soviet–Vietnamese alliance formed important elements of the regional strategic backdrop against which the SAF was developed between the late 1960s and the late 1980s. PAP leaders sometimes pointed to Indochinese developments as vindications for Singapore's defence programmes,[45] and Singapore's defence spending increased rather more rapidly than usual both in 1976 and 1977 (following the 1975 communist victories) and between 1979 and the mid-1980s (after the Vietnamese invasion of Cambodia) (see Table 2.1). Concerns over the Soviet–Vietnamese alliance may have influenced the development of some aspects of the SAF force structure, particularly in the air defence sphere.[46]

However, the potential danger from immediate sub-regional neighbours (primarily Malaysia, but also Indonesia) was always at least as important a security concern for the PAP leadership as Indochinese developments and was probably a more important driver of Singapore's military build-up, even during the Cold War period.

In the early 1990s, some outside observers argued that Singapore and its neighbours, Malaysia and Indonesia, together constituted an increasingly cohesive economic and geopolitical community, drawn together by not only economic complementarities but also by common security interests, particularly in the maritime sphere. Some saw the emergence of a distinct and potentially divisive interest group within ASEAN,[47] or alternatively viewed the three states as the incipient driving force—'a provisionally emerging regional security core'—within a still cohesive ASEAN.[48] However, such analyses tended to underestimate the significance of tensions between these states and the potential for conflict between them. The concept of a 'Malay archipelago complex' including the three states, together with Brunei, and characterised as much by competition and latent conflict as by cooperation was closer to reality.[49] Within this often tense subregional environment, Singapore has used conventional diplomacy and economic instruments to manage its relations with Malaysia and Indonesia, but military deterrence has also played a central— if obscured—role.

Clear evidence that the Singapore leadership's concern over external communist threats was not the only important influence on the republic's external security policies was provided by the continuing expansion of Singapore's defence effort during the 1990s, although the end of the Cold War had fundamentally changed the wider regional strategic environment. By the beginning of the decade, Vietnamese troops had been withdrawn from Cambodia, Soviet military aid to Vietnam had ceased and Soviet naval and air force deployments to Vietnamese bases were being reduced substantially. Yet in 1991, Defence Minister Yeo Ning Hong emphasised that, despite the end of the Cold War, Singapore would not reduce its current level of defence spending or shorten the period of conscription.[50] In fact, far from reducing military spending, between 1990 and 1998, Singapore approximately doubled its defence expenditure in real terms. While it could credibly be argued that Singapore's phenomenal economic growth and prosperity during the early and mid-1990s meant that its government could well afford to spend more on defence, and that it was logical to do this because of increasing regional strategic uncertainty—particularly in terms of the withdrawal of US forces from the Philippines in 1992—the scale of the increased spending suggested more tangible security concerns. The maintenance of Singapore's defence effort even during the economic recession of the late 1990s served to underline this point.

Singapore's perennially unstable relationships with its immediate neighbours indicate clearly the sub-regional locus of its most pressing external security concerns. The city-state's often problematic relations with Malaysia and Indonesia derive to a considerable extent from ethnic factors: Singapore is a Chinese-dominated state in the midst of the Malay world, where nationalism has often been expressed in anti-Chinese terms.[51] Partly with the intention of reducing the potential for conflict with Malaysia and Indonesia, after 1965 Singapore's government asserted a multiracial national identity and avoided close political identification with either the

People's Republic of China (PRC) or the Republic of China (Taiwan). Participation in ASEAN and efforts to build stable and mutually profitable bilateral links with Indonesia and Malaysia have also played key roles in this strategy of cementing the republic's identity as an acceptable member of the Southeast Asian community of states. However, Singapore has never been able to mitigate entirely the sub-regional political complications accruing from its perceived Chineseness. Though Indonesia and Malaysia have also prospered, the widespread jealousy of the wealth of many ethnic Chinese in the region has sometimes translated into resentment of Singapore's outstanding economic success since 1965. Moreover, the strengthening of Singapore's Chinese identity during the 1990s, resulting from a renewed domestic emphasis on Chinese language and culture as well as closer relations with the PRC—especially in the economic sphere—since the establishment of diplomatic links with Beijing in 1990, has tended to heighten negative regional perceptions of Singapore.

Singapore's determination to defend and assert its national sovereignty—deriving originally from the PAP leadership's experience of union with Malaysia in 1963–65 and Indonesia's simultaneous attempt to assert sub-regional hegemony—has also complicated relations with Indonesia and Malaysia. In the early years after separation, relations with Malaysia remained cool, as Singapore demonstrated a willingness to resist Malaysian pressure on a collection of relatively minor issues. Singapore's execution in 1968 of two Indonesian marines convicted of terrorist offences committed during Confrontation soured relations with Jakarta. Moreover, Singapore was unnerved by the warmth of the initial *rapprochement* between Kuala Lumpur and Jakarta in the aftermath of Confrontation. In 1971 Singapore, ever sensitive to any threat to its seaborne trade and its role as a regional shipping centre, refused to acquiesce in Indonesia's and Malaysia's joint challenge to the traditional legal status of the Straits of Malacca and Singapore.[52] These and other tensions help to explain Singapore's attempts during the late 1960s and early 1970s to develop 'a range of countervailing external relationships' in order to balance its obvious continuing economic dependence on, and political and strategic vulnerability within, its immediate region.[53] Following the collapse of anti-communist forces in Indochina, since the mid-1970s Singapore has devoted greater energy towards developing cooperative relations with Malaysia and Indonesia but, at the same time, has consistently demonstrated unwillingness to compromise on any issues where it has assessed its sovereign prerogative or economic interests to be at stake. Singapore's difficult relations with Malaysia and Indonesia have reinforced its government's distrust of regional security formulas resting on the exclusion of extra-regional powers; indeed, its sub-regional security concerns have contributed to its support for both the United States' engagement and the FPDA.

While there can be little doubt that Singapore has developed its military capabilities with the primary aim of deterring Malaysia and Indonesia from interfering with its vital interests, the republic's leaders have taken care to avoid pointing directly at either neighbour as a source of threat. The city-state's government has taken the view that 'to name an enemy is to make an enemy', recognising that Singapore cannot afford to live in a permanent state of hostility with its larger neighbours, on which it depends not only for a good part of its long-term economic prosperity but also for day-to-day necessities—most importantly Malaysian water. Moreover, open hostility would also imperil Singapore's domestic communal relations and adversely affect the inflow of foreign investment. Certainly, from the late 1980s onwards, back-bench PAP Members of Parliament and local newspaper columnists have sometimes highlighted sub-regional threats to Singapore's security, particularly from Malaysia. However, government ministers have seldom referred to such threats other than obliquely. Brigadier-General Lee Hsien Loong's reference in 1987 to the need to avoid forcing Malay SAF soldiers to choose between loyalty to their 'nation' (Singapore) and to their religion (Islam) represented an atypically pointed assessment.[54]

Although Lee Kuan Yew claimed in his 1987 SAF Day speech that his government did 'not consider our neighbours in Southeast Asia to be threats', he did indicate a concern with 'irrational and extremist forces' in Southeast Asia.[55] The worst-case sub-regional scenario from Singapore's viewpoint, drawing on its experience during the mid-1960s, has been that an ultra-nationalist or fundamentalist Muslim regime might take power in Malaysia or Indonesia, and that Singapore might find itself the victim of a neighbour's aggressive foreign policy aimed at overturning the sub-regional political *status quo*. A variation on this theme is the fear that domestic political instability and violence in either neighbour, particularly if it involved conflict between Muslim indigenes and ethnic Chinese, could spread to Singapore.

However, even relatively stable Indonesian and Malaysian governments have sometimes made life difficult for Singapore. A crucial explanation for Singapore's often uncomfortable relations with its neighbours—in particular, Malaysia—is the relationship between domestic politics and foreign policy in these countries. Singapore has often found itself an easy target for criticism by Malaysian—and, since 1997, Indonesian—politicians seeking a scapegoat in the face of their own domestic social, political and economic problems. This influence was especially clear in terms of the pressure felt during the 1980s and 1990s by the Malaysian government both from within the ranks of its leading constitutent party, the United Malays National Organisation (UMNO), and from opposition Malay nationalist and Muslim movements. Notably, the most serious downturns in independent Singapore's sub-regional bilateral relationships (with Malaysia in 1986–87 and with both Malaysia and Indonesia in the late 1990s) have occurred in the context of economic recessions and accompanying political turmoil in the republic's neighbours. While Singapore's government may have derived domestic political benefits from adopting uncompromising postures in relation to disputes with neighbours, there is considerably less evidence that it has felt compelled to 'play to the gallery' to the same extent as its less secure Malaysian and Indonesian counterparts.

Malaysia: the most likely adversary?

An upbeat assessment of the relationship between Singapore and Malaysia since 1965 might stress that each has generally remained conscious of the need to avoid policies or actions which might seriously jeopardise the other's political or social stability (especially in a communal sense), that there has been substantial bilateral cooperation across a wide range of mutual interests and that common membership of ASEAN has helped to mitigate bilateral tensions. The bilateral economic relationship has continued to be important for both sides: trade between Singapore and Malaysia has remained substantial, as has Singaporean investment in Malaysia. At the end of the 1990s, Malaysia and Singapore were each other's second-largest trading partners, and Singapore was Malaysia's fourth-largest investor. Malaysia continues to supply Singapore with more than half of its water, as well as much of its food. Personal connections between the two states have remained strong: an estimated 60 000 Malaysians are employed in Singapore, which remains Malaysia's largest source of visitors. Singaporeans make over one million visits monthly to the nearest Malaysian city, Johor Baru.[56]

Singapore and Malaysia have also cooperated on many aspects of security. After 1965, links between the two states' internal security organisations were maintained. Malaysia's Marine Police and Singapore's Police Coast Guard have collaborated against low-intensity maritime threats such as piracy and illegal immigration. Although the Malaysian infantry battalion was withdrawn from Singapore in 1966, Malaysia's main naval base was Woodlands in Singapore until the late 1980s when it was replaced by new facilities at Lumut in Perak. Even then, the Malaysian navy's recruit training school was at Woodlands until 1997. Malaysia's and Singapore's armed forces have cooperated extensively in the context of the FPDA. At times there has also been bilateral military cooperation outside the FPDA, including naval and army exercises. Singapore has stressed its recognition of the continuing indivisibility of the two states' defence.[57]

However, while the two states have remained highly inter-dependent economically, socially and in security terms, Singapore's relations with Malaysia have simultaneously been characterised by considerable tension and mutual distrust. Indeed, this is the most sensitive and unstable relationship between any pair of ASEAN members. While the bilateral nexus has been character-ised by prickliness since 1965, stresses and strains in the relation-ship have been particularly pronounced since the mid-1980s. In November 1986, Israeli President Herzog's official visit to Singapore triggered anti-Singapore demonstrations in Malaysia and political controversy lasting several months. In February 1987 Brigadier-General Lee's attempted justification of restrictions on the role of Malays in the SAF outraged Malay politicians across the Causeway, who since 1965 have tended to see themselves as the protectors of Singapore's Malay population. In October 1987, a senior Malaysian defence intelligence officer revealed that an SAF assault boat had recently intruded into a riverine area of southern peninsular Malaysia. Subsequent reports suggested that this incident was but one of many in recent years: Malaysian officials claimed that 'Singapore baits Malaysian armed forces regularly by sending their soldiers into Malaysia, without warning, on routine training exercises'.[58]

Compared with the severe disruptions of 1986–87, bilateral relations were generally relatively stable and productive for an extended period between 1988 and 1996, following a reconcilia-tion between Lee Kuan Yew and Malaysian premier Mahathir Mohamad in October 1987. Examples of intensifying cooperation included the January 1988 agreement covering the supply of

Malaysian natural gas while confirming the continued supply of water to Singapore, the staging of bilateral army exercises for the first time in May 1989, establishing the trilateral Singapore–Johor–Riau economic 'growth triangle' (involving Indonesia as a third partner) in 1990, agreement in March 1994 to construct a 'second crossing' between Johor and Singapore to supplement the existing Causeway, the inauguration of the Singapore–Malaysia Defence Forum in January 1995 and agreement on the two states' maritime territorial boundary in July 1995. .

However, security-related issues continued to disrupt bilateral relations, particularly between late 1989 and 1992. In August 1989, Singapore's government announced its willingness to host US military facilities, provoking criticism from its Malaysian counterpart.[59] At the end of the year, Malaysia arrested nine alleged spies and accused them of selling military secrets to 'a fellow ASEAN member' (evidently Singapore); this was not the first time that Malaysia had apprehended spies working for Singapore.[60] Soon afterwards, Kuala Lumpur closed its airspace to aircraft of the Singapore Flying College and Singapore Flying Club, which had allegedly been conducting photographic reconnaissance over 'strategic places'.[61] As a result of these incidents, but also apparently partly because of Malaysian suspicions regarding closer defence cooperation between Singapore and Indonesia,[62] in March 1990 Kuala Lumpur suspended all bilateral military exercises with Singapore: thus, after the initial two joint army exercises during 1989, no more were held until April 1992. In August 1990, Singapore's deputy prime minister and defence minister, Goh Chok Tong, caused new offence in Malaysia by comparing Singapore's geopolitical vulnerability with that of recently-invaded Kuwait. The relationship's sensitivity was highlighted again in August 1991 when Singapore responded to the largest ever Malaysian–Indonesian bilateral military exercise, *Malindo Darsasa 3AB*—held in the nearby Malaysian state of Johor and culminating in the dropping of paratroops on Singapore's National Day—with a large-scale military mobilisation.[63] Following a decision apparently made in 1991 after the Singapore government proposed to triple the rent it charged for the facility, in November 1992 Malaysia's defence minister announced that, in 1997, the Malaysian navy would close its Woodlands training base.

Other contentions manifested themselves in chronic rather than acute form. Most importantly, during the 1990s, there was simmering disagreement over ownership of the island of Pedra Branca (Pulau Batu Puteh) and its Horsburgh Lighthouse at the eastern entrance to the Singapore Strait. After lying in abeyance since the late 1970s, the issue resurfaced in 1989 and again in 1991–92 when Singapore prevented Malaysian fishing boats from approaching the island. Although in 1994 the Malaysian and Singapore prime ministers agreed in principle to refer the dispute to the International Court of Justice (ICJ), by the end of the decade no firm agreement had been reached on how to proceed. Another chronic problem involved repeated allegations that Singaporean military aircraft habitually intruded into Malaysian airspace.

From mid-1996, relations between Singapore and Malaysia deteriorated significantly. Ironically—in the light of the subsequent economic crisis in Malaysia—a growing appreciation by Singapore's government of the potential implications for the city-state of its neighbour's rapid economic development apparently contributed to the incident which triggered this deterioration. In the mid-1990s, because of Malaysia's phenomenal economic success, and the appearance of growing compatibilities not only in the economic sphere but also in terms of convergent security interests with respect to wider regional issues, there was a growing conviction among Singapore's leaders that the republic needed to develop a 'new paradigm' for sub-regional economic and political relations. There was concern not only over Singapore's declining economic advantages over Malaysia, but also the long-term costs of an adversarial bilateral strategic relationship.[64]

It was in this context that in June 1996 Lee Kuan Yew suggested that Singapore might ultimately need to consider 'remerger' with Malaysia. Rather than underlining the logic of pursuing closer relations, Lee's proposal hardened the Malaysian government's attitude towards Singapore, particularly in view of his suggestion that Malaysia would need to meet certain conditions—notably in terms of fostering socio-economic meritocracy—if remerger was to be possible. In essence, this position seemed to represent a reversion to Lee's arguments during the 1960s for a 'Malaysian Malaysia'. In August 1996, Prime Minister Goh Chok Tong's apparent use of the remerger idea as a 'bogey' with which to encourage Singaporeans to maintain their economy's competitive edge further soured relations, setting the scene for renewed tension in late 1996 and early 1997 over alleged airspace intrusions, the development of Malayan Railway land in Singapore, Lee Kuan Yew's comments in a legal affidavit on the prevalence of crime in Johor and Singapore's desire to secure guaranteed long-term water supplies from Malaysia. The last was a vital concern for Singapore in view of its rapidly expanding demand for water (by almost

5 per cent annually during the 1990s) and the limited supplies obtainable from domestic reservoirs. In mid-1997, backbench PAP MPs warned that the two countries' relationship might 'plunge . . . without warning' and that Singaporeans were 'sick and tired of Malaysian threats to cut off Singapore's water supply'.[65]

At the same time, despite occasional indications to the contrary, bilateral military cooperation remained superficial and trouble-prone, reflecting the continuing deep distrust between the two governments and their defence establishments. Though Singapore's defence minister Lee Boon Yang had claimed in 1995 that its establishment 'raised bilateral defence relations to a new plane',[66] no more was heard of the Singapore–Malaysia Defence Forum after its second meeting in March 1996. The army exercises lapsed once again after July 1996.

Apparently recognising the dangers inherent in deteriorating bilateral relations, given the wider context of the growing impact of the regional economic crisis, including the potential for instability in Indonesia, the Singapore and Malaysian prime ministers met five times in early 1998. In February, they agreed to step up economic cooperation, pursue negotiations on the supply of water to Singapore (in the context of a Malaysian agreement not to truncate the flow on the expiry of the two existing water agreements in 2011 and 2061), accelerate efforts to resolve differences over the development of Malayan Railway land and resume negotiations over referral of the Pedra Branca dispute to the ICJ.[67] Within weeks, however, there was renewed disagreement over the water issue, which had become a critical concern for Malaysia as well as Singapore in the light of a severe water shortage in the peninsula: water rationing was imposed in parts of Kuala Lumpur in March 1998.[68] In July 1998, the Malayan Railway land dispute revived when Malaysia claimed the legal right to retain its Customs, Immigration and Quarantine (CIQ) checkpoint at the Singapore railway terminus.[69] As relations declined to their lowest point since 1986–87, in August Malaysia's premier warned Singapore 'Don't take for granted our goodwill . . . Take heed' and claimed that the government was studying a proposal by his party's youth wing to 'freeze' new ties with Singapore.[70] In response, referring to Singapore's water supply, many in his audience shouted *'Potong! Potong! Potong!'* ('Cut! Cut! Cut!').[71] Soon afterwards, speaking on Singapore's National Day, Malaysia's information minister argued that his country should 'regain full control' over parts of its 'land, sea and air space given to Singapore to manage' since 1965.[72]

These developments during 1998 took place against the background of profound economic crisis in Malaysia and a simmering dispute within its government over how best to foster recovery, which culminated in the sacking and subsequent arrest of Deputy Premier Anwar Ibrahim following the imposition of capital and currency controls in early September 1998. The Malaysian government's wish to direct controversy away from these acute domestic problems at least partially explained the subsequent further deterioration of relations with Singapore. On the same day that the new economic policies were declared, Malaysia announced that it would not participate in FPDA exercises scheduled for October. Though Malaysia justified this unprecedented withdrawal on the ground of recession-induced economic stringency, its defence minister admitted that tension with Singapore had contributed to the decision.[73] In mid-September, the publication of the first volume of Lee Kuan Yew's memoirs, which blamed UMNO politicians for Singapore's separation in 1965, sparked an angry response from Dr Mahathir and other current UMNO leaders. Malaysia then decided to impose tight restrictions on the entry of Singapore's military aircraft into its airspace for training and search and rescue operations.[74] While local Malaysian residents' concerns were cited to justify this decision, in reality it reflected official Malaysian displeasure over Singapore's supposedly recalcitrant behaviour.[75] An incident a week later illustrated the high tension by then pervading the relationship, when Malaysia delayed permission for a Singaporean rescue helicopter to transit its airspace *en route* to a crash site at sea after an accident involving a British helicopter participating in a bilateral UK–Singapore naval exercise. In November 1998, Malaysia's defence minister threatened to deploy fighter aircraft in the event of airspace infringements by Singaporean aircraft.[76]

Because of their economies' interdependence, Malaysia's capital and currency controls affected Singapore adversely. However, Singapore's leaders refrained from criticising Malaysia's economic policy. Indeed, in November 1998 it became clear that, in exchange for agreement on the water issue, they were willing to provide funds which Malaysia desperately needed to recapitalise its banking sector and underwrite its growing budget deficit.[77] In mid-December, though, the Malaysian prime minister declared that his government no longer needed Singapore's financial assistance and that all outstanding bilateral issues would be dealt with 'as a package'.[78] Singapore then emphasised that it would not yield to Malaysia on matters such as the CIQ issue, which it viewed as a matter of sovereignty.[79]

While Malaysia's ruling coalition won the November 1999 General Election, the loss to the Islamic Party of significant numbers of federal parliamentary seats, as well as control of the Terengganu state government, further weakened its domestic position and increased the premium on adopting a hardline position in relation to Singapore. Though Singapore's threat of legal action forced Kuala Lumpur to capitulate on the 'Clob' issue (concerning Singapore-owned shares frozen by Malaysia since September 1998) in February 2000, there was no sign of movement towards settling other bilateral problems. But it seemed unlikely that even resolution of all outstanding disputes would bring about long-term harmony. The nub of the matter is that the particular bilateral contentions are symptoms rather than causes of major structural tensions which have been embedded in the bilateral relationship since 1965, due to the two states' ethnic compositions and their governments' divergent political visions. These differences can probably only be ameliorated in the long term with renewed economic prosperity. Domestic political change in either or both states could improve the relationship (in the event of a convergence of political style through the rise of more liberal leaderships on both sides of the Causeway, for example) but, alternatively, it could further complicate it (if, for instance, a more assertively Islamic or nationalist government came to power in Malaysia). In the meantime, despite the instability of its nexus with Malaysia, Singapore's government has maintained an upbeat rhetorical stance—stressing the potential of a 'win–win' relationship based on equal partnership for mutual benefit—while continuing to prepare for the worst.[80]

Indonesia: a secondary concern

Although Singapore's relations with the New Order regime during the 1980s and 1990s were characterised by collaboration in many areas, including particularly close links between the SAF and the Indonesian armed forces (ABRI), Indonesia has never ceased to be a security concern for the city-state and the SAF's deterrent capabilities have been developed with Indonesia in mind as well as Malaysia.

During the late 1960s and early 1970s it was commonplace for observers to portray Singapore as 'a Chinese nut in a Malay nutcracker'. The new state's political relations with both Indonesia and Malaysia were less than comfortable, while there appeared to be a fraternal cosiness in relations between Singapore's two immediate neighbours following their post-Confrontation reconciliation. By the end of the 1980s, however, there had been a fundamental realignment in the triangular relationship between Indonesia, Malaysia and Singapore. Relations between Indonesia and Singapore warmed considerably, while a gulf developed between Indonesia and Malaysia. While this realignment was manifested mainly in political and economic terms, it also had strategic overtones.

A range of issues, but most notably large-scale Indonesian illegal immigration into Malaysia, clashes of economic interest and poor personal relations between Prime Minister Mahathir and President Suharto contributed to the souring of relations between Kuala Lumpur and Jakarta in the late 1980s. Simultaneously, there was a significant change in the Suharto regime's view of the relative importance of its relationships with Malaysia and Singapore. The Indonesian administration was apparently impressed with Singapore's political stability, while valuing its role as an investment source, a trading partner and an important service centre for the business interests of Jakarta's political, military and bureaucratic elite. During the 1990s, Singaporean investment in Indonesia expanded rapidly. In 1991, Singapore's government committed itself to developing a major industrial park on Pulau Batam, as well as tourist and industrial infrastructure on nearby Pulau Bintan, both in the Riau Islands to the south of the city-state (see Figure 2.1). Singapore's growing economic ties with Riau provided the impetus for the establishment in 1990 of the Singapore–Johor–Riau growth triangle, partially intended to soothe Malaysian irritation at the growing closeness of Singapore–Indonesia ties.

Singapore also developed closer security relations with Indonesia, to Malaysia's displeasure. From the viewpoint of Indonesia's military commanders and, particularly, General Benny Murdani (commander-in-chief, 1983–88 and defence minister, 1988–93), Singapore's security was closely linked to Indonesia's, with the result that there was a marked upswing in defence relations after 1983, when Murdani took command.[81] There were also security overtones in bilateral agreements signed in 1992–93 in which Indonesia agreed in principle eventually to supply Singapore with up to 1000 million gallons of water per day from Riau province, this arrangement potentially reducing the city-state's dependence on Malaysian supplies. (However, even at the end of the 1990s, water from Indonesia had not begun to flow, in part because of squatters' occupation of water catchment areas on Pulau Bintan).[82]

Despite their apparent warmth, uneasiness persisted beneath the surface of Singapore–Indonesia relations during the 1990s. Singapore is acutely aware that, like most of Malaysia, the city-state falls within the geopolitical zone sometimes referred to as *ASEAN kecil* (small ASEAN), which senior Indonesian officers view as being of particularly vital importance for Indonesia's security. The essence of this Indonesian security concept is that no hostile outside power should be allowed to establish a physical presence within 1500 km of Jakarta. While this might be reassuring for Singapore, in the unlikely event of a threat to itself from a major power, and provides Indonesia's rationale for pursuing bilateral defence cooperation, it is not altogether comforting in the sense that a future Indonesian regime less well-disposed towards Singapore might view its security interests in its sub-regional 'buffer zone' as justifying interference with Singapore's political or economic freedom of action. Even Murdani, who was instrumental in developing Indonesia's relations with Singapore, ruffled feathers there in 1994 when he emphasised that the city-state lay within Jakarta's sphere of strategic interest; he also suggested that Indonesia and Malaysia could become 'more aggressive and less accommodating' if Singapore's relations with China became significantly closer.[83]

Singapore's economic connections with Indonesia were based primarily on links with the larger country's ethnic Chinese. But broader political links and security cooperation during the 1980s and 1990s were built on the foundation of ties between the SAF and ABRI. Growing political estrangement between ABRI leaders and President Suharto (highlighted by Murdani's removal from office in 1993), together with the concomitantly increasing political clout of observant Muslims in the Jakarta government (some of whom resented not only Singapore's economic success but also its close links with Israel), resulted in slightly cooler government-to-government relations. Relations between ABRI and the SAF remained close, however, and economic cooperation continued. In 1997, Indonesia's state oil company Pertamina agreed to supply Singapore with natural gas from the West Natuna offshore field, in quantities sufficient to replace that provided from Malaysia under a contract due to expire in 2007.[84]

By the mid-1990s there was considerable anxiety on Singapore's part regarding the likely trajectory of Indonesia's political development and its implications for bilateral relations and the regional security environment. It was becoming increasingly evident that although Suharto was likely to leave the political stage before the end of the decade, there was no clear political succession mechanism. There was particular concern over the possible impact of growing social tensions, heightened by the corruption and nepotism which pervaded the later years of the New Order, on the political succession. A long-standing Singapore government fear was that the succession to Suharto could bring to power a radical leadership which might destabilise the comfortable bilateral relationship built up under the New Order.[85]

The economic crisis of 1997 brought dramatic political changes and deteriorating relations with Jakarta sooner than Singapore had expected. The Singapore government's diplomatic activism in late 1997 and early 1998 underlined its acute concern over the impact of the crisis on Indonesia: Prime Minister Goh visited Suharto three times, encouraging him to accept International Monetary Fund (IMF) assistance despite the conditions attached to this aid. After the first meeting in October 1997, Singapore offered Indonesia US$5 billion in soft loans to supplement the proposed IMF aid programme, intervened—unsuccessfully—to support Indonesia's currency, proposed a Finance Guarantee Scheme to help Indonesian exporters and provided humanitarian aid. Demonstrating Singapore's wish to broaden its previously rather narrow Indonesian links to include emerging political and social forces, rice and medicines were supplied for distribution through Indonesia's two main Muslim organisations as well as the government and armed forces.[86]

Despite Singapore's efforts to maintain stable relations with its neighbour, Indonesia's economic and political crisis during 1998–99 seriously undermined bilateral ties. In February 1998, Senior Minister Lee Kuan Yew offended B.J. Habibie, then research and technology minister, by suggesting that if the 'market' was uncomfortable with the Indonesian parliament's choice of vice-president in March, the Indonesian currency would be further weakened: it was clear that Lee was referring to the possible election of Habibie, whose ascendancy was seen in Singapore as potentially destabilising because his power base among Muslim intellectuals and his economic nationalism both implied an anti-Chinese and possibly anti-Singapore disposition.[87] Ultimately, Habibie not only became vice-president in March but succeeded to the presidency in May, after Suharto was forced to step down following large-scale demonstrations against his regime which destroyed his support within the political establishment. As expected, Habibie's rise to Indonesia's political apex damaged bilateral relations. The rigorous conditions which Singapore wished to impose in connection with its proposed credit line fuelled Habibie's resentment, which derived partly from his belief that Singapore had attempted to frustrate some of his grandiose development plans, including those for an international airport on Batam and the construction of nuclear power stations. In August 1998, Habibie claimed Singapore was 'pro-active in a negative direction' and famously referred to the city-state as a mere 'red dot' on the map.[88] In February 1999, Habibie alleged that Singapore was a country of 'real racists'.[89]

Issues relating to Indonesia's ethnic Chinese minority further complicated relations. The brutal treatment of Indonesian Chinese during the May 1998 Jakarta riots, especially the apparent complicity of Indonesian military elements in these atrocities, provoked widespread public outrage as well as governmental concern in Singapore. Large numbers of Chinese fled Indonesia at the time of the riots, many seeking temporary refuge in Singapore. Annoyingly for Habibie's government, they also transferred substantial funds—which might otherwise have assisted Indonesia's economic recovery—to Singapore's banks. Jakarta's irritation with Singapore's role was evident in March 1999, when one of Habibie's close advisers referred to it as a 'Chinese enclave'.[90]

These tensions by no means totally disrupted bilateral relations. The SAF maintained its links with ABRI and the change of government did not prevent joint exercises from continuing as normal. The SAF also helped to distribute Singapore's humanitarian aid, as well as engaging in joint civil action programmes with ABRI.[91] Collaborative anti-piracy patrols involving the Indonesian and Singaporean navies were increased.[92] In July 1998 and January 1999 agreements were signed which confirmed Indonesia's willingness to supply Singapore with natural gas from Natuna in return for Singapore's investment in the project's infrastructure.[93] Singapore hoped that the gas deal could be a model for a similar arrangement involving water supplies.[94]

Yet Singapore's government remained deeply apprehensive over the potential impact of continuing economic recession, social dislocation and political instability in Indonesia. Suharto's ousting had heralded a new and essentially unwelcome era in bilateral relations, in which Singapore's interests might not be accommodated as easily as they had been under the New Order. While Singapore attempted to establish links with a wider range of Indonesian political forces in advance of the June 1999 parliamentary election,[95] the city-state had no significant influence over the future of its giant neighbour. The government's hope was that the election would produce an Indonesia 'focussed internally on growth and externally on ASEAN' in the best interests of Singapore and the region.[96]

Throughout 1999 and into early 2000, calls for secession in many outlying Indonesian provinces and escalating violence in many of these areas (including the Riau Islands, the closest Indonesian territory to Singapore), suggested that renewed stability was only one of a number of possibilities for Indonesia's short-to medium-term future. The military-inspired débâcle in East Timor following the UN-sponsored referendum in August 1999, and the subsequent international intervention there, reinforced forebodings over Indonesia's stability and cohesion. Although the formation of the Gus Dur–Megawati government in October 1999 allowed a thaw in relations with Singapore, which in January 2000 announced a four-point plan to assist Indonesia's economic recovery,[97] calls for a referendum on independence in Aceh and intensified intercommunal strife in Maluku soon afterwards provoked renewed fears of instability and even concerns that Indonesia might disintegrate.[98] There was a growing perception in Singapore that its sub-regional geopolitics had returned full circle to the situation of the late 1960s, in which the city-state was sandwiched between two unstable and potentially threatening neighbours.

SINGAPORE'S STRATEGY

While most elements of Singapore's defence policy are to a greater or lesser degree transparent, its defence *strategy* is relatively opaque. Official statements emphasise Singapore's 'non-directional deterrence'. This, however, belies the fact that the interaction of Singapore's innate vulnerabilities, historical experiences and contemporary relations with sub-regional neighbours have generated a national military strategy reflecting acute concerns over fairly precise threats.

Singapore's complex and sometimes tense relations with its immediate neighbours have provided its defence strategy's core rationale: the maintenance of a sub-regional balance of power in maritime Southeast Asia based on deterrence by Singapore's national military capabilities. In some circumstances, regional or extra-regional associates might supplement these national military resources, but Singapore has planned its defence primarily on a self-help basis. Indeed, the government has always viewed self-reliance as the *sine qua non* of Singapore's defence, calculating that no external assistance could be expected if Singapore failed first to demonstrate the willingness and ability to defend itself.[99] In the early years of independence, however, the government sometimes conveyed the impression that the SAF was essentially a holding force, necessary to provide token resistance until Singapore's friends came to the rescue. But during the 1970s, particularly in view of the scaling down of FPDA partners' military presence in Singapore to little more than symbolic Australian and New Zealand contingents, and the concurrent build-up of the SAF, increasingly it became both necessary and realistic to think in terms of self-reliant defence.

The evolution of Singapore's strategy

While the SAF's capabilities remained rudimentary, defensively oriented and based on an infantry-dominated army during the early years after separation, Singapore used the analogy of a 'poisonous shrimp' (small, but indigestible by predators) to describe its military strategy. The idea was that any aggressor would find that the costs of attempting to invade and occupy Singapore outweighed any conceivable benefits. How the SAF would have defended Singapore was never specified precisely, though the assumption was presumably that it was likely that Singapore-based UK, Australian and New Zealand forces would support its resistance to direct military intervention (whether from Malaysia, Indonesia or other sources).

The 'poisonous shrimp' concept remained Singapore's *declaratory* strategy even during the 1980s. Indeed, as late as 1991 a government manifesto on Singapore's future likened the republic to a 'small fish' needing to swim in 'shoals' for security, but argued that it 'should be like the poison shrimp with bright colours to warn others of the poison we carry'.[100] However, with the encouragement of Singapore's Israeli military advisers, as defence funding increased rapidly during the late 1960s and early 1970s, the SAF's organisation, training, doctrine and equipment inventory were developed to provide the foundations for the only strategy which made sense if Singapore, bearing in mind its peculiar geostrategic vulnerabilities, was to base its deterrent on national military resources: strategic pre-emption of potential adversaries (primarily Malaysia). Yet it was not until after the 1984 launch of Total Defence that it was officially acknowledged that Singapore's core strategy had moved away from its original concept. According to Brigadier-General Lee Hsien Loong, then Chief of Staff (General Staff), the 'poisonous shrimp' strategy was deficient in that it offered Singapore merely a choice of 'suicide or surrender' because of its implication that the SAF would fight an ultimately unwinnable war on its own territory. In Lee's view, the city-state needed a strategy which conveyed the message 'I may not completely destroy you but you will have to pay a high price for trying to subdue me, and you may still not succeed'.[101]

Though official statements have never referred explicitly to the SAF's offensive capabilities, let alone to its pre-emptive strategy, by the 1990s they were emphasising the need for the SAF to achieve a 'swift and decisive victory' over aggressors.[102] Probably the clearest statement came when Minister of State for Defence Matthias Yao spoke in 1997 of the need to give any aggressor a 'knock-out punch in round one'.[103] But still he did not admit that Singapore might throw the first punch.

Singapore's geopolitical circumstances and the nature of its armed forces' equipment, organisation and training indicate heavy doctrinal emphasis on the offensive as part of a pre-emptive deterrent strategy, but over time this strategy has become more sophisticated and flexible. Since the 1980s, developments in infrastructure and training such as the 'hardening' of air bases and C^3 sites, construction of an underground ammunition depot, as well as exercises involving use of highways as auxiliary runways or under simulated biological and chemical warfare conditions, have indicated that the SAF has aimed to develop sufficient resilience to absorb an aggressor's first strike. The growth of Singapore's civil defence capability has supported this objective. These developments have significantly widened Singapore's crisis options, by reducing the compulsion to strike first. This could be beneficial in two ways: first by allowing for a margin of error in assessing an adversary's intentions (if the adversary struck first, it need not imply total disaster for Singapore); second, Singapore could intentionally decide to absorb the first wave of an enemy's offensive in order to gain political advantage (its subsequent counter-attack would more clearly constitute self-defence in the eyes of the international community). It is hard to imagine that any regional adversary could feel sufficiently confident to strike first, though, in view of Singapore's obvious preparations for such a contingency and its ability to hit back, hard.

However, the greater sophistication of Singapore's strategic posture during the 1980s and 1990s—particularly the new emphasis on civil defence—may also have reflected fears that the SAF might be unable to deter certain types of threats. For example, from the late 1970s MINDEF developed plans for contingencies which might have arisen from the presence of Soviet forces in Vietnam, such as Soviet air attacks in retaliation for any Singaporean intervention in defence of Thailand, or in the event of a wider conflict between the rival superpower-led coalitions.[104]

By the early 1980s, Singapore's growing military capabilities enabled it to begin to think in terms of limited power projection in the wider Southeast Asian region as well as deterrence through pre-emption within its immediate sub-region. MINDEF prepared contingency plans for the deployment of SAF ground forces and probably also strike aircraft, possibly in conjunction with Malaysian and Indonesian contingents, to assist in the defence of Thailand in the event of a large-scale Vietnamese incursion across the border from Cambodia. Indeed, although such a Vietnamese onslaught never eventuated, SAF Commandos are known to have familiarised themselves with the Cambodian border region by participating in Thai army patrols there during the 1980s.[105]

There has also been a significant maritime dimension to the SAF's power projection capability. Following the navy's acquisition of missile corvettes, in 1993 the Chief of Navy claimed that it was 'not inconceivable' that, in the event of conflict over the Spratly islands, the Fleet would escort 'our merchant ships' in the South China Sea.[106] The navy evidently expected to protect Singapore's SLOCs as far as 1000 miles from home. However, this was obviously not the whole story: securing Singapore's vital maritime trade in the event of a regional conflict would require the navy to protect not only Singapore-registered and -owned vessels but also other merchant ships serving Singapore. This could probably only be achieved through close collaboration with the navies of regional and extra-regional allies and associates.

A scenario for war with Malaysia

While it is clear that the SAF is sufficiently flexible in terms of its organisation, equipment and doctrines to be useful in a wide variety of national security contingencies, its capabilities have been refined with specific contingencies in mind: these envisage above all the possibility of war with or in Malaysia, though Singapore's defence planners have undoubtedly also considered possible conflicts with or in Indonesia. These contingencies have been played out repeatedly in SAF staff college exercises since the late 1960s.

The central assumption of Singapore's strategic thinking is that an invasion of southern peninsular Malaysia, either with or without the Malaysian government's acquiescence, might be necessary to ensure the city-state's security by forestalling a repeat performance of the successful Japanese offensive of 1942, which had demonstrated the extreme difficulty of defending Singapore once an enemy had secured control of the island's landward hinterland. During the late 1960s and 1970s Singapore's defence planners considered the scenario of an upsurge in the MCP's insurgency overwhelming Malaysia's security forces, which would then require assistance to prevent a communist takeover.[107] In the 1980s, thought was given to the prospect of helping to defend Malaysia against Vietnamese aggression.

Always more credible from the Singapore government's viewpoint, however, were scenarios in which conflict with Malaysia would be triggered by political instability there (resulting perhaps from advances by Islamic political forces) leading to widespread communal violence or interference, by governmental or nongovernmental forces, with Singapore's vital water supply from Johor. In such circumstances, Singapore's government might judge direct military intervention in the Malaysian peninsula to be necessary—in order to protect fleeing ethnic Chinese refugees or to secure control over the water pumping stations.

To make intervention possible, the SAF would need to disable the Malaysian armed forces with a brutal and fearless pre-emptive offensive, or at least to retain the capability to execute such an offensive after absorbing an initial Malaysian onslaught. Probably in conjunction with electronic attacks on the Malaysian armed forces' communications and sensors (such as radars), the SAF would first attempt to establish air superiority by devastating the Malaysian air force on the ground (in the first few hours of any conflict), before mounting further air strikes against other military targets. Singapore's army would then seize the initiative on the ground, with Commandos—infiltrated by air and sea—and helimobile Guards units securing the Malaysian side of the Causeway (in Johor Baru) and the 'second-link' bridge (to the south-west of Johor Baru). Combined arms forces, most importantly armoured battle groups equipped with light tanks and other AFVs, would then cross into Johor and conduct a rapidly paced advance into the peninsula, supported by Guards battalions and their associated

RSAF transport helicopter squadrons. RSAF strike aircraft and armed helicopters would provide close air support.[108]

The navy would play a significant role in any Singapore–Malaysia conflict. Amphibious landings, using the Singapore navy's large fleet of landing craft, would position elements of the Singapore army's 21st Division—a semi-elite rapid deployment force—on Johor's coast. But the primary role of Singapore's navy would be to prevent Malaysian interference with its vital maritime trade, by using its Mine Countermeasures Vessels (MCMVs) to keep the Singapore Straits and their approaches safe for merchant shipping and by protecting SLOCs in the Singapore and Malacca Straits and perhaps further afield. The navy would also secure the maritime flanks of the thrust into Malaysia against interference by the Malaysian navy and deter intervention by other interested powers' navies. It could, in addition, be used offensively to interdict maritime communications between peninsular and East Malaysia,[109] in order to prevent the deployment of reinforcements from Sabah and Sarawak while simultaneously complicating the Malaysian government's strategic calculations in view of the relative fragility of its political dominance over these far-flung states. Disruption of Malaysian trade might also be considered.

Just how far Singapore's army might advance into peninsular Malaysia is unclear, although informed observers have spoken of the SAF aiming to establish a 'Mersing Line', implying seizure of a zone approximately 80 km deep into Johor. There would be a clear strategic rationale for halting the SAF's advance at this line: such an operation would secure Singapore's water-pumping stations at Skudai and Kota Tinggi, while providing substantial strategic depth (particularly important in view of the potential threat to Singapore from Malaysian 155 mm artillery). At the same time, the SAF would not be encumbered with occupying an area with a huge Malay population: Johor is not densely populated compared with Melaka or the Kuala Lumpur-Kelang-Seremban-Port Dickson conurbation, and at the same time it is relatively heavily populated by ethnic Chinese. Moreover, large numbers of Singaporeans own property and live in southern Johor, and the state's economy is heavily integrated with that of Singapore.

The potential reaction of regional neighbours and ASEAN partners would be a key question in the event of any outbreak of war between Singapore and Malaysia. Since the warming of relations between Singapore and Jakarta during the 1980s, there have been grounds for calculating that Indonesia might remain neutral in a conflict between Singapore and Malaysia. Nevertheless, concerns over a potential *rapprochement* between Indonesia and Malaysia have not disappeared, as was evident in the large-scale SAF mobilisation in August 1991.

Although Singapore–Indonesia ties cooled in the late 1990s, particularly after the overthrow of Suharto in 1998, relations between Indonesia and Malaysia have not noticeably improved. Briefly in 1998, after Habibie became Indonesian president and before Malaysian Deputy Premier Anwar was dismissed and arrested, it seemed that an alliance between these leaders, both self-consciously Islamic intellectuals, might lead to close relations between Jakarta and Kuala Lumpur.[110] The removal from the political scene of both Habibie and Anwar has negated this prospect, but concerns over potential strategic cooperation between Indonesia and Malaysia have not disappeared, forcing Singapore to think in terms of deterring and, if necessary, preventing Indonesian military intervention in the event of conflict with Malaysia.

It is likely that Singapore's air and naval capabilities would indeed act as a powerful deterrent in case Jakarta was tempted (perhaps as the result of domestic political pressures) to intervene on Malaysia's side. Despite its massive geographical size, population and natural resources, even during the boom years of the New Order Indonesia's defence budget was never adequate to fund a significant power projection capability. Indonesia's small and technologically limited armed forces have remained thinly spread, with their best units committed to counter-insurgency campaigns in East Timor, Irian Jaya and Aceh. Since 1998, Indonesia's armed forces have been severely stretched to maintain law and order throughout the archipelago in the face of mounting political and inter-ethnic unrest, and have no spare capacity for regional adventurism.

Related to the issue of the triangular relationship between Singapore, Malaysia and Indonesia is the question of Brunei's political and strategic position. Like Singapore, Brunei has encountered serious difficulties in its bilateral relations with Malaysia, which the Sultanate declined to join in 1963. Contentious issues include Brunei's territorial claim to the Limbang River Valley which separates the mini-state's two enclaves on the coast of Sarawak. Although there has been an uneasy *détente* with Malaysia since the early 1980s, Brunei's relations with Indonesia have improved more significantly. Moreover, since the 1970s Brunei has developed extremely close military, as well as political and economic, ties with Singapore. There is no publicised, formal defence agreement between Brunei and Singapore, but the SAF rotates conscript and reservist infantry battalions through its jungle warfare school in Brunei, and joint exercises involving Singaporean strike aircraft supporting combined ground forces may be intended at least partially as notice to Malaysia that Brunei can expect military support from Singapore if its security is seriously threatened. If conflict erupted between Singapore and Malaysia, Brunei's military links with Singapore could raise fears in Kuala Lumpur over the potential for a 'second front' in East Malaysia.

In 1997, one leading Malaysian defence analyst alleged that Singapore's 'forward basing' in other regional states, made possible by training arrangements, 'stirs suspicion'.[111] Such suspicions have led some observers to suggest that Singapore's close relations with Thailand, including substantial military cooperation, imply that Bangkok might take the city-state's side in the event of a Singapore–Malaysia conflict, perhaps by allowing the use of Thai air bases to attack Malaysia. But while Bangkok's relations with Kuala Lumpur were often tense during the 1990s, giving rise to such speculation, it seems unlikely that Thailand—particularly under a liberal, civilian government—would risk the costs of becoming needlessly involved in a war with Malaysia.

Political objectives of Singapore's strategy

Assuming that Singapore's offensive and quite possibly pre-emptive strategy would be militarily successful (and this is by no means a foregone conclusion) raises the question of what *political* outcome Singapore would hope for in a conflict with Malaysia. Long-term occupation of Malaysian territory would be an extremely hazardous undertaking in the face of not only a predictable international outcry (though this might be muted if Singapore did not strike first), but also the likelihood of protracted resistance from remnants of the Malaysian armed forces supported by the Malay population in the occupied territory. Relations with Indonesia, the West and Japan would, at best, have been complicated. The confidence of local and foreign investors in Singapore's economy might be seriously damaged. There would probably be a hostile reaction from elements of Singapore's own 450 000-strong Malay community. By throwing the SAF into action against Malaysia, Singapore might effectively transform itself into the 'Israel' of Southeast Asia.

The key to understanding Singapore's strategy, though, is that the SAF's clear capability to inflict severe damage on Malaysia (by implication creating serious political and economic repercussions for Singapore) is not intended to be used. The capability is a deterrent—a sort of regional 'doomsday machine' intended to manipulate Singapore's regional threat environment by forcing neighbouring states to treat the city-state with a degree of respect and caution which might otherwise be absent. Indeed, the nature of Singapore's strategy—and the dangers implicit in pushing too hard on issues of vital interest to Singapore—are apparently well understood in Malaysian government circles. Malaysian cabinet members have sometimes signalled their recognition of the danger of conflict and their wish to avoid it. In 1992, Malaysia's foreign minister stressed that the alternative to settling the Pedra Branca dispute using diplomacy was war, which Malaysia did not want.[112] In 1998, after announcing the ban on Singapore's military aircraft from using Malaysian airspace, the Malaysian defence minister declared that 'Malaysia would not easily go to war with Singapore'.[113] Moreover, despite recurrent bilateral tensions, the Malaysian government has always ensured that Singapore's water-pumping stations and pipelines in Johor are not physically interfered with, despite calls by Malay nationalist and Muslim organisations in both 1986 and 1998 for the supply to be cut off.

The Singapore–Malaysia military balance

A central assumption in Singapore's contingency planning for a war against Malaysia (based on strategic pre-emption) must be that the SAF is a superior force compared with the Malaysian Armed Forces (MAF). However, it was only during the 1980s that the military balance between Singapore and Malaysia moved decisively in the former's favour, making an offensive strategy a realistic option for the SAF.

By the 1990s, the SAF's quantitative and qualitative superiority over the MAF was well-entrenched. (Table 2.2 compares Singapore's military strength with that of Malaysia and Indonesia.) In 2000, the potential fully mobilised strength of the SAF stood at 350 000.[114] By comparison, the MAF totalled only about 145 000 personnel, although 105 000 of these were regulars. Singapore's army formations, most importantly three combined arms divisions (each including integral armour and artillery) and a rapid deployment division, are coherent and highly offensively oriented, in contrast to their Malaysian equivalents which, during the

Table 2.2 Singapore, Malaysia and Indonesia: strategic comparisons, 2000

	Singapore	Malaysia	Indonesia
Population (millions)	3.2	22	220
%age Ethnic Chinese	77	27	3
Defence expenditure (US$bn)			
1996	4.0	3.6	est. 4.7
1997	4.1	3.4	est. 4.8
Defence budget (US$bn)			
1998	4.4	2.1	0.9
1999	4.2	2.3	1.5
2000	4.3	2.3	1.1
Conscription	2–2.5 yrs	None	None
Total armed forces	350 000	145 000	700 000
	(incl. 275 000+ reservists)	(incl. 40 000 reservists)	(incl. 400 000 low-grade reservists)
Combat aircraft (locally-based)	120	65	65
Hardened air bases	Yes	No	No
Airborne early warning aircraft	4	0	0
In-flight refuelling aircraft	4	2	2
Main battle tanks	60	0	0
Light tanks	350	26	300
Other armoured fighting vehicles	1000	1200	630
Heavy artillery	108	12	5
Naval anti-ship missile launchers	120	72	76
Submarines	3	0	2

Sources: The Military Balance 1999–2000 (London: International Institute for Strategic Studies, 1999), supplemented by author's data base.

1990s, remained dispersed thinly throughout peninsular and East Malaysia and were only beginning to develop combined arms capabilities. One of the SAF's crucial strengths lies in its armoured force, which includes 350 locally upgraded AMX-13SM1 light tanks as well as a smaller number of modernised Centurion MBTs: the Malaysian army, possessing a mere 26 light tanks itself, has little anti-tank capability. The SAF also has a clear advantage in artillery, with more than 100 long-range 155 mm guns clearly outclassing Malaysia's 12 similar weapons and its larger numbers of short-range 105 mm artillery.

Singapore has a crucial military advantage in its air force: now the largest in maritime Southeast Asia and potentially the most effective in the whole ASEAN region, it deploys almost as many combat aircraft as its Malaysian and Indonesian counterparts combined. In-flight refuelling tankers and early warning aircraft act as force multipliers, and a dense air defence system includes several types of SAM. Singapore lacks the major surface combatants deployed by Malaysia and Indonesia, but its navy nevertheless deploys more anti-ship missiles (on corvettes and fast attack craft) than any of its Southeast Asian counterparts. It is also developing submarine and amphibious capabilities.

More important than these mainly quantitative indicators of the SAF's capabilities are qualitative factors. Though the SAF lacks combat experience, its soldiers are highly-educated, well-trained and technically proficient. Even its reservists take part in overseas exercises regularly and there is persistent pressure on units to improve their operational readiness. The SAF's overall technological sophistication, particularly in terms of its superior C⁴I and high-quality logistical support from local defence industry, together with heavy investment in infrastructural development, the high levels of remuneration for regular personnel and the synergistic relationship between the three services all yield important military advantages over Malaysia or any other potential Southeast Asian military adversary.

By comparison, the MAF suffers from several important deficiencies. Most fundamentally, Malaysia's armed forces have since the early 1970s become effectively an occupational niche reserved for the Malay population: in contrast to the SAF which relies on universal conscription, the MAF is hardly a national institution. A related problem is that the MAF found it difficult to recruit adequate numbers of high-quality personnel during Malaysia's economic boom in the 1990s, with the result that keeping key weapons systems (such as combat aircraft) operational has often proved problematic.

Another contributory reason for Malaysia's military weakness relative to Singapore has been the MAF's traditional orientation towards counter-insurgency. Serious efforts to develop effective conventional warfare capabilities only began in 1979 with the the Armed Forces Special Expansion Programme (Perista). An economic slowdown in 1984 led the government effectively to freeze the MAF's modernisation. When the economy revived in the late 1980s, the modernisation programme was resuscitated, most importantly by signing a Memorandum of Understanding (MoU) covering defence procurement from Britain.

Diverse threat and non-threat factors have influenced efforts to reorientate the MAF towards external defence. These factors included concern over the potential threat from Vietnam (in the late 1970s and early 1980s), apprehension over China's assertive strategic posture in relation to the South China Sea, the availability of funds, the government's desire to maintain the army's apolitical professionalism, and a desire to develop Malaysia's defence industries as part of the overall national industrialisation project.[115] However, although Singapore has never constituted such a serious security threat in the view of Malaysian politicians and defence policy-makers as Malaysia has from Singapore's viewpoint, many recent and potential improvements in the MAF's capabilities have almost certainly been intended partly as responses to Malaysia's military weakness in comparison with Singapore.

Equipment ordered under the MoU with Britain included 28 Hawk light fighters, air defence radars and associated C^3 facilities, Starburst portable SAMs, two heavily-armed missile frigates and the 'Defence Operations Room' C^3I network.[116] During the 1990s, Malaysia also acquired much defence equipment outside the MoU's ambit, including eight F/A-18D and 18 MiG-29 combat aircraft, and four Italian-built corvettes. While the Malaysian army did not benefit to the same extent as the other two services from this round of re-equipment, in 1994 it began a major reorganisation aimed at enhancing its capacity for conventional warfare. Initially, this included the transformation of two infantry brigades into combined arms formations, one forming the core of a planned division-strength rapid deployment force and the other a mechanised brigade.

In many respects, though, the MAF's capabilities did not develop as quickly as expected during the 1990s. Most importantly, when the economic recession forced the suspension of large-scale re-equipment and other MAF development plans in 1997, many army requirements were still outstanding: it still required large numbers of MBTs and armoured infantry fighting vehicles, new 105 mm and 155 mm artillery, new low-level SAMs and attack and utility helicopters. Moreover, there had been little progress towards building two long-planned major infrastructural projects for the army—a combat training base at Gemas, straddling the states of Negeri Sembilan, Johor and Melaka, and a Special Forces base at Mersing on Johor's east coast—which could ultimately substantially reinforce Malaysia's defences in the south of the peninsula. Other major procurement programmes suspended because of the recession involved AEW aircraft, additional combat aircraft and submarines.

By late 1999, Malaysia's economic recovery was prompting considerable speculation concerning defence equipment likely to be purchased under the Eighth Malaysia Plan (2001–2005). While acquisitions may include new armoured vehicles, additional fighter aircraft and submarines, some expensive planned purchases (such as attack helicopters and AEW aircraft) were still unlikely to be funded.

Singapore's response to Malaysia's defence modernisation

In March 1978 Goh Keng Swee, then Singapore's deputy prime minister and defence minister, argued that the republic did not want to arm herself 'to the teeth' for fear of starting 'an arms race in our part of the world'.[117] This concern that the SAF's build-up should not be counterproductive has permeated Singapore's defence planning from its earliest stages, and helps to explain the '6 per cent of GDP' cap imposed on defence spending as well as MINDEF's reluctance for Singapore to be seen to be the first state in the region to acquire new types of major military equipment. Furthermore, because of its concern not to transform potential military adversaries into real ones, Singapore has never expressed publicly its forebodings over the development of the MAF's conventional warfare capabilities.

Nevertheless, between the late 1980s and mid-1990s, it appeared that the MAF's developing conventional capabilities might considerably undermine Singapore's existing military superiority. Because of its concern over the implications of Malaysia's 1988 MoU with Britain, in 1989 Singapore mounted a major intelligence operation to secure details of Malaysian defence planning.

Some Malaysian equipment purchases during the 1990s certainly complicated Singapore's own military planning. If properly protected on the ground, Malaysia's F/A-18D strike aircraft could offer an implicit threat of damaging retaliation for any Singaporean attempt at military pre-emption. At the same time, Malaysia developed a more credible national air defence system, threatening to reduce the likely effectiveness of pre-emptive air strikes by Singapore. In addition, the Malaysian army's acquisition of Eryx anti-tank missiles may have upgraded its ability to slow down a Singaporean armoured assault. At the same time, in stark contrast to the SAF's almost total lack of operational experience, during the 1990s Malaysia's army improved its combat readiness through deploying units on international peacekeeping operations in Cambodia, Somalia and Bosnia.

If Singapore had not taken these developments seriously in planning its own defence posture its deterrent might eventually have lost credibility, possibly giving Kuala Lumpur greater leeway in the use of levers such as its control of a large part of the city-state's water supply. But it was never likely that Singapore's leadership would allow any such situation to develop. During the 1990s, the 'SAF 2000' force modernisation project emphasised the importance of maintaining and enhancing the SAF's technological advantages, particularly by developing advanced C^3, ISR (Intelligence, Surveillance and Reconnaissance) and ILS (Integrated Logistic Support) capabilities. Simultaneously, many of the SAF's equipment procurement programmes have appeared to be aimed at blunting the likely impact of the MAF's modernisation. For example, since the early 1990s the SAF's acquisition of missile-armed helicopters has increased the vulnerability of Malaysia's new mechanised and armoured forces. The perceived need to counter Malaysia's MiG-29s and their long-range R-77 AAMs has largely motivated Singapore's efforts to secure AIM-120 AMRAAM missiles for its F-16 fighters.[118] An expanding anti-submarine capability will reduce the impact of Malaysia's eventual procurement of submarines. Singapore's own submarines threaten Malaysia's expanding fleet of frigates and corvettes.

The recession of the late 1990s led to some relaxation in this interactive military procurement. The fact that Singapore's defence spending for 1999–2000 and 2000–01 was held at almost the same level as in 1998–99, indicating that some defence programmes are being stretched over longer timeframes, may have reflected not only the recession's impact on Singapore's economy, but also its already evident effects on Malaysia's defence programmes. While the SAF still suffers from some important weaknesses in relation to the Malaysian armed forces, particularly in terms of its reliance on conscripts and reservists and its lack of operational experience, the differential impact of the recession can only highlight the credibility of Singapore's military deterrent.

New Indonesian scenarios

During the 1990s Indonesia's growing prosperity, technological capacity and aspirations to develop well-equipped, modern armed forces capable of projecting power meant that Singapore could not dismiss its giant neighbour's long-term military potential. ABRI's reported interest in 1992 in acquiring Russian-built Scud SRBMs,[119] combined with Jakarta's plans for civilian nuclear power plants, provoked concern in Singapore that Indonesia might become capable of deploying weapons of mass destruction. In July 1997, ABRI announced an order for advanced Su-30 comb at aircraft from Russia. However, major cuts in ABRI funding, due to the recession, forced the cancellation of this and other contracts, and at the end of the decade the bilateral military balance still strongly favoured Singapore.

Though the recession's political and social fall-out implies that it is still unlikely that Indonesia could become a source of conventional military threat in the short- to medium-term, since 1997 Singapore's security environment to the south has been considerably less predictable than at any time since the 1960s. Indeed, it seems possible that the Indonesian archipelago could generate a variety of unconventional and low-intensity, but nevertheless serious, threats. Some of these threats—such as environmental problems caused by the failure of attempts to prevent the burning of Indonesian forests—are not amenable to military solutions. Others, though, could involve the SAF: possibilities include a major exodus of ethnic Chinese and other persecuted minority groups as refugees, large-scale migration in search of economic opportunities (or even food if Indonesia fails to recover from its recession), and extensive piracy (with possibly disastrous environmental consequences) if law enforcement agencies become ineffective. In 1999, there were already signs of an increase in piracy, with 66 ships attacked in Indonesian waters during the first nine months of the year, more than double the figure for the same period in 1998.[120] At the same time, Singapore was also beginning to consider seriously the possibility that intensifying centre–periphery and Muslim–Christian strains might lead to Indonesia's disintegration, with potentially extremely dangerous consequences for the city-state.

Singapore's investments in the nearby Riau islands (the closest of which, Batam, is only 20 km away) could be threatened in the event of civil strife; at the same time these islands could become jumping-off points for refugees and illegal immigrants heading for Singapore, as well as bases for pirates preying on commercial shipping entering and leaving Singapore. In July 1999, inter-ethnic violence erupted on Batam. In January 2000, a dispute between dispossessed local people and the developers of a tourist resort led to demonstrators besieging the Bintan Industrial Park, managed by the Singaporean government-linked Sembcorp conglomerate and the locus for considerable Singaporean investment. This incident led Singapore's government to warn Jakarta that it should protect the interests of foreign investors. In February 2000, a major conference of Riau's local politicians concluded with a vote favouring secession from Indonesia. While separation from Indonesia remained unlikely, it was clear that Jakarta would need to reform fundamentally its relationship with Riau, amongst other peripheral provinces, if it wished to maintain Indonesia's national cohesion.[121]

Because of the likely impact on the city-state's security and economic interests, it would be unacceptable from Singapore's perspective for the Riau islands to descend into chaos.[122] While the Indonesian security forces contained the problems on Bintan in early 2000, there is clear potential for a larger-scale 'complex emergency' in the Indonesian islands to Singapore's south, which might *in extremis* require some form of military intervention. The potential need to defend Singapore's interests in Riau had been considered as far back as 1993 (and possibly even earlier),[123] but potential military operations to the south were necessarily figuring more prominently in Singapore's strategic thinking by 1999. In practical terms this new focus vindicated the emphasis during the 1990s on building up the SAF's maritime, amphibious and rapid deployment capabilities. However, changes in doctrine and training may also be necessary to equip the SAF to deal effectively with the low-intensity challenges—potentially including chronic inter-ethnic violence and large-scale refugee outflows—which could in the worst case increasingly pervade the sub-regional security environment.

CONCLUSION

The reality of Singapore's defence strategy is at odds with its declaratory posture of non-directional deterrence. Though Singapore's own military capability has undoubtedly also served the objective of encouraging the continued engagement of extra-regional powers (most importantly the United States, but also the non-Southeast Asian parties to the FPDA) in Southeast Asian regional security, the primary role of the SAF has been to maintain a favourable sub-regional balance of power in maritime Southeast Asia. Because of the structural tensions in sub-regional relations, and especially because of Singapore's dependence on Malaysian water supplies, the SAF has always been primarily concerned with deterring interference with its vital interests by Kuala Lumpur. Though initially characterised as akin to the defence mechanism of a 'poisonous shrimp', during the 1970s the SAF began to develop capabilities for pre-emptive offensive operations. Since the 1980s, Singapore's deterrent posture has become more flexible, with a growing capacity to absorb an adversary's first strike. The expansion of the SAF's capabilities has also allowed the development of a power projection strategy, particularly in terms of protecting Singapore's SLOCs.

Without the deterrent provided by the SAF, Singapore would have been at the mercy of its neighbours, particularly Malaysia, to a far greater extent. It would have been a 'political football' subject to kicking whenever domestic problems indicated a scapegoat might be useful; its own political, economic and social stability would have been seriously endangered. It would be difficult to overstate the extent to which strong defences have provided necessary reassurance not only to Singapore's population but also to local and foreign investors that they can continue to prosper in security.

Since the late 1980s, Singapore's government has striven to reduce the city-state's vulnerabilities. For example, it has attempted to lessen dependence on Malaysian water by seeking alternative supplies from Indonesia and by investing in desalination plants.[124] It has also tried to increase national food security by securing guarantees of emergency rice supplies from Thailand, while planning to increase dramatically local production of fish and vegetables.[125] Moreover, in the mid-1990s, there appeared to be genuine interest in constructing a new, less conflictual pattern of relations with Malaysia.

Singapore also realises that military power is not the appropriate instrument for dealing with every challenge to its interests. Its military capabilities are only marginally relevant to threats deriving from regional environmental degradation (the SAF might help to reduce marine pollution by policing regional waters, but can do little to prevent the air pollution caused by Indonesian forest fires) and of no use when fighting for an open international trade regime, which is crucial for Singapore's wellbeing. Recognising the reality of regional and global interdependence, during the 1990s Singapore's foreign policy has made greater use of the city-state's 'soft power' based on its economic and ideational strengths, while engaging more fully in the activities of the UN and other international institutions. The government has stressed the importance of regional confidence-building mechanisms, particularly the ASEAN Regional Forum (ARF). Nevertheless, mainly reflecting continued governmental concern over its unpredictable locale, the emphasis on building up the SAF's capabilities continued relentlessly.

The regional recession underlined both the persistent significance of unpredictable sub-regional relations to Singapore's security and the continued perceived relevance of military means to managing such concerns.[126] Though the recession's drastic implications for other Southeast Asian states' defence spending and procurement increased Singapore's sub-regional military advantages, the economic downturn also generated profound social and political instability in Indonesia and Malaysia, injecting new wariness into Singapore–Indonesia relations and further complicating an already tense Singapore–Malaysia relationship. Indonesia's new instability has increased the likelihood of potential SAF operations to the city-state's south, but has also raised the issue of whether the SAF is sufficiently prepared for the sort of 'complex emergency' which might arise there in the context of prolonged economic and political disarray or disintegration around Indonesia's periphery.

3

Command and control

Singapore inherited some military units and personnel when it separated from Malaysia in 1965 and assumed control of substantial defence infrastructure following the British military withdrawal in the early 1970s, but the SAF's command and control mechanisms had to be constructed from scratch. Throughout independent Singapore's existence, the PAP government has considered defence a core policy area, not only because it has been seen as vital to the city-state's existence, but also because of its demands on the national budget and the need to prevent the armed forces from presenting any sort of political challenge.[1] Consequently, Singapore's core leadership has consistently taken a close interest in the SAF's development. The PAP's firm hold on power throughout the city-state's life has led to tightly concentrated political control of defence policy-making and to notable continuity in defence policy, reflected in the steady, uninterrupted build-up of the SAF's capabilities since the late 1960s.

POLITICAL CONTROL OF DEFENCE POLICY

As in other areas of Singapore's public life, it is evident that the PAP leadership—and in particular its small core of key personalities—has always exercised untrammelled authority over the defence ministry and the SAF. Under Lee Kuan Yew's 'Old Guard' leadership between 1965 and the early 1980s, the PAP government's inner Cabinet or 'Team' consisted of Lee Kuan Yew, Goh Keng Swee (who was defence minister from 1965–68 and again from 1972–80), S. Rajaratnam (responsible for Foreign Affairs until 1984) and Toh Chin Chye.[2] As long as the 'Old Guard' led

Singapore, the 'Team' dominated policy-making in all key areas, including defence, holding frequent meetings 'to discuss important issues that were eventually to come before one of the three institutional policy-making forums'.[3] These three policy-making forums were the PAP's Central Executive Committee, the Cabinet and the Defence Council.

Important defence matters were discussed in the full Cabinet, and a rather less central Cabinet member (Lim Kim San) held the defence portfolio from 1968 to 1972, but it was the 'Team'—particularly Lee Kuan Yew and Goh Keng Swee—which made the key decisions. Goh provided much of the intellectual and doctrinal framework for Singapore's emerging defence policy in the late 1960s and early 1970s but, as on many important matters, Lee exercised paramount authority over important defence issues. Examples include Lee's decisions to acquire surplus Bloodhound missiles from Britain at the time of the UK's military withdrawal and to restrict the potentially politically counterproductive expansion of army training areas.[4] The Defence Council brought together the defence minister, his permanent secretary and senior SAF officers to discuss policy matters in a formal context but, given the then pervasive sense of urgency and the small number of relevant personalities, it seems likely that many of Singapore's early defence policy decisions were taken in an *ad hoc* and relatively informal fashion by Lee, Goh, Lim (from 1968–72) and Permanent Secretary George Bogaars. This core group of policy-makers would draw on expert military advice from senior SAF officers whenever necessary, before their decisions were presented to the Defence Council and the Cabinet for formal approval. More detailed policy-making, including formulation of the original Defence Plan which guided the armed forces' development in the late 1960s and early 1970s, was the responsibility of the team of bureaucrats and SAF officers led by Bogaars and the first three Directors of General Staff, successively Brigadier-Generals Tan Seck Khim, Kirpa Ram Vij and T. J. D. Campbell. Like many of the SAF's early senior officers, none of these men was a military professional.[5]

During the SAF's early years, Singapore's defence ministers—though themselves in practice informally subject to Lee Kuan Yew's veto power—exercised huge authority over the armed forces. Indeed, until the advent of legislation extending the powers of Singapore's president in 1990, the *Singapore Armed Forces Act* allowed the defence minister to appoint, promote and dismiss the SAF's senior officers without the knowledge, let alone approval, of the prime minister or Cabinet. As Cabinet minister Brigadier-General Lee Hsien Loong remarked during the debate on the new legislation in 1988, 'No other country does it like this'.[6] Lee Kuan Yew's extremely close working relationship with his early defence ministers (particularly Goh) helps to explain the degree of authority over military matters which he delegated to them.

In the late 1960s, Goh Keng Swee even appeared in uniform as a senior military officer, highlighting his role as the SAF's effective commander-in-chief and underlining the lack of sufficiently senior local professional officers to assume the higher command of the SAF.[7] In the early years, many of Singapore's senior military officers were seconded civil servants or policemen, or foreign loan personnel. In 1971, Lee Kuan Yew spoke publicly of the desperate shortage of sufficiently qualified and capable people to run Singapore and of the government's aim to 'produce a general within the next three to five years'.[8] Indeed, it was not until 1974 that a Singaporean professional officer, Brigadier-General Winston Choo, was appointed as Director of General Staff, subsequently becoming successively Chief of the General Staff, and Chief of Defence Force (CDF). The fact that Choo led the SAF for 18 years until he retired from active service with the rank of Lieutenant-General reflected not only his own competence and reliability but also a continuing shortage of suitable officers for promotion to senior rank. Singapore's naval commander between 1975 and 1985, Colonel Khoo Eng An, was locally born but he had served 27 years in Taiwan's navy before returning to the city-state.

As the SAF grew during the 1970s and 1980s, and as the government moved beyond the early phase of crisis decision-making in security and other policy areas aimed at ensuring national survival in an unstable regional environment, defence policy-making became increasingly bureaucratised. Singapore's defence policy-making processes are relatively opaque compared with those of western countries but it is known that, since 1987, MINDEF decision-making in areas as diverse as military operations, combat analysis, logistic support, resource planning, finance, manpower and systems acquisition has increasingly been derived from Operational Analysis (OA), a quantitative management technique. One application of OA has been the generation of detailed plans for military responses to a wide variety of security contingencies and crises. The SAF's rapid and extremely successful response to the hijacking by terrorists of Singapore Airlines flight SQ117 in 1991 was reputedly derived from such 'scenario planning'. OA is also likely to have significantly influenced the major structural review commenced by MINDEF in 1988, which produced the overall force development plan referred to as SAF 2000[9]—together with more detailed plans for the individual services (Army 2000, Navy 2000, Air Force 2000) and the army's various combat branches—designed to guide the upgrading of the armed forces' capabilities during the 1990s.

Despite this bureaucratisation of defence policy-making, however, MINDEF like other areas of government remained closely subservient to political direction. To the present day, key defence policy matters—such as Singapore's regional and international defence links, major procurement programmes and National Service issues—have continued to receive specific attention from the prime minister and his closest political associates. During the 1980s, however, a series of developments brought important changes to the administration of Singapore's defence policy. Most importantly, the PAP leadership began to undergo a major transition, as Lee Kuan Yew initiated the succession to his 'Old Guard', with significant implications in terms of changes in the personalities involved in making defence policy and controlling the SAF. The top leadership 'team' which had dominated the government since 1959 still centred on Lee Kuan Yew, but younger politicians—Ong Teng Cheong, Goh Chok Tong and Lee's own son, Brigadier-General (BG) Lee Hsien Loong—had by the end of the 1980s replaced the other key Old Guard players. Though Goh Keng Swee remained in the Cabinet as deputy prime minister and education minister until 1984, he had relinquished the defence portfolio in 1979. Since Goh left MINDEF, the defence minister's job has been divided between at least two (and sometimes three) Cabinet members, who have been assisted by at least one minister of state or parliamentary secretary. While this primarily reflects the ever-expanding range of defence activities and the increasingly large budgets under defence ministers' supervision, it may also indicate Lee Kuan Yew's concern not to let political control of defence policy and the armed forces fall into the hands of any single member of the untested successor generation of PAP leaders.

Goh Keng Swee's immediate replacement as defence minister was Howe Yoon Chong, but he was shadowed by Goh Chok Tong, a former bureaucrat selected as a leading member of the PAP second-generation leadership. Lee Kuan Yew evidently saw experience in defence as vital for his potential successor as prime minister: Goh Chok Tong was appointed senior minister of state in MINDEF in 1977, second defence minister (as well as health minister) in 1980, and defence minister in 1984. He subsequently held the defence portfolio until 1991, as well as being first deputy prime minister (1984–90) and, ultimately, prime minister (from 1990). Other second-generation politicians assigned major roles in MINDEF were Yeo Ning Hong, whose 13-year service there culminated in three years as defence minister (from 1991–94) and Lee Boon Yang, second defence minister from 1991–94 and defence minister, 1994–95.

Simultaneously, the fruition of the SAF Scholarship scheme (which offered accelerated promotion to an elite of highly educated young officers)[10] saw senior serving or reservist SAF officers appointed to important positions in MINDEF as both politicians and bureaucrats. A prime example is BG Lee Hsien Loong—who as a professional army officer had played an important role in developing the SAF's capabilities (particularly in artillery and joint-service cooperation) during the late 1970s and early 1980s[11]— who took on appointments in MINDEF as political secretary (1984–85), minister of state (1985–87) and from 1987–90, as second minister for defence (Services), though he was concurrently trade and industry minister from 1986. Within MINDEF, Lee was particularly concerned with fostering joint-service planning and coordination. While he gave up his secondary defence portfolio in 1990 on being appointed second deputy prime minister, Lee's formal link with MINDEF was restored briefly from July 1994 to June 1995 when he was given the task of 'overseeing' the ministry, following the resignation of the highly experienced defence minister Yeo Nin Hong. As the first senior SAF officer to be inducted into the Cabinet as a member of the contemporary leadership triumvirate with his father and Goh, and as the politician widely seen in Singapore as Goh Chok Tong's likely successor as premier, Lee Hsien Loong has played a crucial role in ensuring that the government understands the needs of the SAF and vice versa.

In 1994, another retired senior SAF officer—former naval chief Commodore (later Rear-Admiral) Teo Chee Hean, who had previously been 'groomed to be the Chief of Defence Force'[12]—left active service for politics and was appointed senior minister of state in MINDEF. Teo subsequently became second defence minister in 1986. Like Lee Hsien Loong, Teo has acted as a pivot linking the government and the SAF. By the late 1990s the armed forces were well-represented in the Cabinet by four ministers who were former senior regular officers (Lee Hsien Loong, Teo Chee Hean, George Yeo and Lim Hng Kiang).[13]

Moreover, since the late 1980s senior serving and reservist officers have sometimes been appointed to key policy-related posts in MINDEF. For example, in the late 1990s one of the ministry's two permanent secretary posts was held by a reservist Colonel, Peter Ho Hak Ean. A former naval commander, Rear-Admiral Richard Lim, was designated to become deputy secretary (Technology) during 2000.[14]

However, although serving and reservist or retired SAF professionals may have increased their influence over the formulation of detailed defence policy, this does not imply that a military interest group within the government and administration had taken control of defence policy and the SAF. Firm political control over defence policy-making has been maintained through a series of political and administrative checks and balances. Most significantly, the existence of a team of PAP politicians holding defence portfolios has balanced the influence of former SAF professionals on defence policy within the government. Crucially, the post of defence minister has consistently remained in the hands of civilians without professional SAF backgrounds.

The government has also ensured the maintenance within MINDEF—despite the rising influence of senior military or ex-military figures—of a caucus of reliable senior civil servants possessing long experience of the defence sector. During the 1980s and 1990s, Lim Siong Guan (MINDEF's permanent secretary from 1981 to 1994) and Eddie Teo (a long-serving MINDEF intelligence officer promoted to became permanent secretary (Defence) in 1994) were notable examples.[15]

The government has given Singapore's president some authority in the area of defence, providing an additional check on the defence establishment. In 1988, Goh Chok Tong—then first deputy prime minister and minister for defence—admitted during the parliamentary debate on the proposal for a more powerful, elected presidency, that:

> I can tell you I am most uncomfortable at the authority which I have as Minister of Defence . . . I don't feel comfortable because the potential for abuse is that it is very easy for a potential mischief-maker, who is a Defence Minister, to build up the military behind him . . .[16]

Because of such concerns, when legislation concerning the elected presidency was introduced in 1990 it gave the president the right to veto candidates for appointment as Chiefs of Defence Force, Air Force, Army and Navy as well as other members of the Armed

Forces Council (AFC).[17] This represented a refinement of the *modus operandi* of governmental control over the SAF: it was unthinkable while the PAP remained in power that the elected president could be other than a figure drawn from or extremely close to the party's core leadership.

Prime Minister Goh Chok Tong further bolstered his government's control over MINDEF and the SAF in August 1995 when he brought Dr Tony Tan—a political heavyweight who during the 1980s had sometimes been seen as a potential premier but who had stepped down from the Cabinet in 1991—back into the government as deputy prime minister and minister for defence. Apparently wary of the dangers—particularly in financial terms—of senior SAF officers gaining undue or unchallenged influence over defence policy-making, one of Tan's first initiatives as defence minister was to set up an Institute of Defence and Strategic Studies (IDSS), attached to Nanyang Technological University (NTU). IDSS was intended to provide postgraduate education for MINDEF civil servants in strategic and defence studies and to supply the government 'with alternative viewpoints on the regional strategic situation and security environment'.[18] This initiative underlined the almost total lack of informed debate over defence matters outside the bureaucracy, despite a fairly high level of detailed military knowledge among the general population as a result of universal conscription.[19] Local journalists' coverage of defence matters has been stymied by a combination of MINDEF's tight controls on the release of information and the government-controlled media's reluctance to publish stories or analysis relating to local defence issues, other than the ministry's press releases. The prosecution of journalist Ho Kwon Ping in the early 1970s after he wrote a report on Singapore's local manufacture of M-16 rifles illustrates the dangers inherent in attempting to cover defence matters in an independent fashion.[20] Local academics have been reluctant to conduct research on Singapore's contemporary defence, except in anodyne fashion, for similar reasons.

Since the 1980s, the government has allowed carefully vetted nominees from outside MINDEF and the SAF privileged insights into defence activities and a limited degree of influence over defence policy-making. PAP backbench MPs—all by definition highly loyal to the party leadership—have exercised such a role through the Government Parliamentary Committee (GPC) system, established in 1987 as a result of the government's recognition of a rising demand for checks on its unbridled freedom, and of the need to enliven Singapore's parliament which, because of the PAP's near-monopoly of representation, has not constituted a forum for significant debates over policy since 1965. Apart from their quota of MPs, these GPCs include academics and representatives of major employers as 'resource panel members'. The GPCs, intended to 'look into the major subjects of ministry portfolios',[21] include one concerned with defence and foreign affairs (GPC-DFA). Though the GPC-DFA has not investigated policy issues with a fraction of the assertiveness and attention to detail which characterises its counterparts in the West, it has nevertheless helped to foster a knowledge of and interest in defence issues within the broader parliamentary PAP. Indeed, by the late 1990s government backbenchers were beginning to ask fairly probing defence-related questions in parliament. For example, during the 1998 Committee of Supply debate on the defence budget, one MP asked a series of questions drawing attention to significant short-comings in MINDEF's procurement procedures.[22]

Some of the GPC-DFA's activities (such as visits to SAF units) are carried out in tandem with the Advisory Council on Community Relations in Defence (ACCORD), a body established by the government in 1984 with the aims of increasing 'support and recognition' for conscript and reservist SAF personnel, while creating 'awareness and understanding among the general public of their roles'. ACCORD also provides 'feedback to Mindef on new policies and programmes'.[23] As well as visiting units and exercises, the Council meets every three months to discuss MINDEF policies and programmes. RECORD (Committee to Recognise the Contribution of Operationally Ready National Servicemen to Total Defence) and RECORD II were similar bodies convened in 1990 and 1995 respectively with the more specific objective of recommending improvements to reservists' conditions of service.

ACCORD, RECORD and RECORD II have been composed of not only senior executives from local employers, but also educators, trade unionists and media representatives. They have constituted the main channels through which Singapore's wider community has been able to influence defence policy.

COMMAND AND CONTROL WITHIN MINDEF AND THE SAF

According to official statements, MINDEF 'provides the policy directions, managerial and technical support' for the SAF,[24] but the institutional relationship between the political leadership on the one hand, and MINDEF and the armed forces on the other has never been clearly defined publicly. However, the AFC, which was established by the 1972 *Singapore Armed Forces Act* as 'the highest policy-making body which oversees the administration of the Armed Forces', is the formal channel through which the government exercises its control over routine decision-making on defence matters. The AFC's membership consists of the defence minister, any other ministers who have been assigned to assist him, the MINDEF permanent secretary or secretaries, the CDF, the three single-service Chiefs and as many as four other members appointed by the president.[25] Full details of the AFC's membership have not been revealed, but the additional members are probably Cabinet members with military backgrounds and senior MINDEF figures such as the Director of Joint Staff. The AFC has legal as well as administrative responsibilities: it can, for example, convene a senior disciplinary committee to try senior officers summarily, quash decisions of summary trials, order retrials and refer cases to subordinate military courts for court martial.[26]

Though the Defence Council has not been mentioned offficially in recent years, substantial anecdotal evidence suggests that this body, rather than the AFC, has remained the locus for top-level decision-making on major strategic, defence and security matters. The Defence Council is believed to meet quarterly, possibly 'back-to-back' with the AFC. The membership of the two councils is overlapping but not identical. The Defence Council, chaired since 1998 by the prime minister (though previously by Senior Minister Lee Kuan Yew), includes ministers and permanent secretaries from the ministries of Home Affairs, Foreign Affairs and Information and the Arts, as well as the CDF and senior intelligence officers. Decision-making in time of national crisis or war is the responsibility of the Defence Council's Executive Group, chaired by MINDEF's permanent secretary and composed of senior officials, though under the direction of the defence minister. The Defence Council is understood to have a permanent secretariat located inside MINDEF.[27]

Beneath the AFC is MINDEF, which has two distinct components (see Figure 3.1). The policy-making side of MINDEF, staffed by a mixture of civil servants, serving SAF officers, and Non-Uniformed SAF (NUSAF) personnel, is organised into three 'functional groups' under two permanent secretaries who report to the minister for defence. Under the permanent secretary (Defence), the Defence Policy Group (DPG) 'formulates and coordinates' policy regarding international defence links, public communications,

Figure 3.1   Ministry of Defence (MINDEF) organisation, 2000

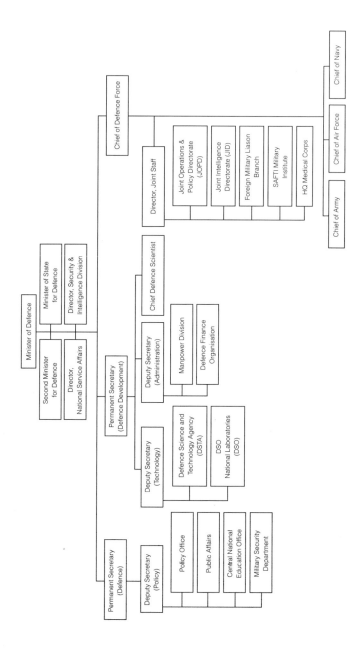

national education and security intelligence. The permanent secretary (Defence Development) exercises authority over:

- the deputy secretary (Administration), whose Defence Administration Group (DAG) 'looks after the manpower, financial and administrative' aspects of MINDEF and the SAF.
- the deputy secretary (Technology), who oversees the technological development of MINDEF and the SAF. Until recently, this role was mainly the responsibility of the Defence Technology Group (DTG), which was charged with 'defence research and development, acquisition, modification, upgrade and maintenance of weapons systems', *matériel* planning and stockpiling. However, in March 2000, most of DTG and some elements of DAG were restructured into the Defence Science and Technology Agency (DSTA). The DSTA is a semi-autonomous statutory board, with the permanent secretary (Defence Development) as its chairman, and the deputy secretary (Technology) as its chief executive. The deputy secretary (Technology) is also responsible for the DSO National Laboratories, a corporatised non-profit research organisation affiliated to the DSTA.
- the chief defence scientist, who advises on and supports defence technological development.[28]

Most of these MINDEF branches, including DSTA, are located in the ministry's high-rise Defence Technology Towers building in Depot Road, although the policy and public communications elements of DPG are accommodated in MINDEF's main building at Gombak.

MINDEF also fills the role of armed forces headquarters, with the CDF, a three-star officer, heading the ministry's General Staff and commanding the SAF. CDF's small but extremely important joint-service staff, under the Director, Joint Staff consists principally of the Joint Operations and Planning Directorate (JOPD) and the Joint Intelligence Directorate (JID). The Joint Staff and the three single-service headquarters staffs are located at Gombak.

From the beginning, the SAF was a highly integrated force, at least in administrative terms. In 1968 the SAF's naval and air components were named the Singapore Maritime Command (SMC) and Singapore Air Defence Command (SADC) respectively, emphasising their subordinate status. Though the SADC, at least, clearly had an important part to play in Singapore's strategy even in the early 1970s, the SAF at this time was a heavily army-dominated organisation. In 1968, all three branches of the SAF began wearing the same green uniforms (a practice which was discontinued in the early 1970s) and adopted the same, army-based system of ranks. More importantly, the Director, General Staff and subsequently the Chief of the General Staff (CGS) exercised authority over the naval and air elements as well as the SAF's much larger land forces. However, as the size, capabilities and responsibilities of the SMC and SADC grew, they emerged in 1975 as separate services—the Republic of Singapore Navy (RSN) and Republic of Singapore Air Force (RSAF). Nevertheless, the CGS remained the overall commander, with senior members of his staff—successively the Deputy Chief of the General Staff, the Chief of Staff-General Staff and the Deputy Chief of General Staff (Army)—effectively acting as army commanders. Even in the mid-1980s, the CGS and one or two other senior army officers were the only serving general officers; the air force and navy commanders were both only colonels.

With the continuing growth of the navy and air force, in 1990 the SAF's higher command was fundamentally reorganised: the CGS post was redesignated Chief of Defence Force (CDF), and the new appointment of Chief of Army replaced that of Deputy Chief of General Staff (Army).[29] Each service was subsequently com-manded by a one-star or two-star officer, with his own staff, including manpower, intelligence, operations, logistics, plans and training departments. These measures substantially increased the status of the RSAF and RSN and, in 1995, an RSAF officer, Major-General Bey Soo Khiang, was appointed CDF—the first non-army officer to hold the post. This move underlined the fact that the RSAF could no longer be regarded as a junior service within the SAF, given the vast expenditure during the 1980s on equipment for the air force, and the service's vital role in Singa-pore's strategy.

While the SAF's early emphasis on integration was 'aimed at achieving unified command and control, unified and coordinated doctrine',[30] this integration was not manifested to any significant degree in doctrinal, let alone operational, terms. However, during the 1980s and 1990s efforts were made to increase operational coordination between the SAF's various combat elements with the aim of creating synergistic combined arms and joint-service capa-bilities. In this connection, following an unsuccessful experiment with various joint-service committees during 1982, the Joint Staff was created as a permanent element of the General Staff in 1983. As well as coordinating joint operations, the Joint Staff sets priorities and provides central direction for the SAF's development (ensuring that the three services work towards common objectives) and apportions limited personnel and financial resources.[31] Holding 'joint' posts such as Director JOPD or Director JID, or heading departments within these directorates, soon became a vital part of the necessary career structure for the SAF's most successful rising officers.

The Director, JOPD was the effective head of the Joint Staff, a position formalised in 1999 when the one-star incumbent was concurrently appointed Chief of Staff, Joint Staff and promoted to Major-General, indicating the importance of the post. By then the Joint Staff also shared control of part of the Manpower Division and the Resource Planning Office with DAG and DTG respectively.[32]

SINEWS OF COMMAND AND CONTROL: COMMUNICATIONS AND INFORMATION SYSTEMS

Singapore's small physical size and technological sophistication facilitate the republic's military communications, the vital physical means of transmitting command and control, which have developed in tandem with the SAF's combat capability. The SAF's Communications and Electronics Department was established in 1966 and reorganised to become HQ Signals in 1982.[33]

The fact that Lieutenant-General Winston Choo, the SAF's commander from 1974 to 1992, was a former Chief Signals Officer may have helped to maintain the high profile of the Signals formation. In the early 1990s, MINDEF identified communications technology as a 'key area in which to improve professional expertise and knowledge', and initiated studies to increase transmission capacity to enable greater volumes of information to be transferred using existing frequencies and channels. A Communications Technology Interest Group was formed to promote the sharing of relevant knowledge between MINDEF, local industry, academic institutions and foreign defence agencies.[34]

This aggressive attitude towards the exploitation of new technology led to substantial improvements in Singapore's defence communications during the 1990s. Within the army, divisional signals capabilities were revolutionised with the introduction of the Trunk Communications System (TCS) in 1990–91. TCS replaced the previous point-to-point radio relay system used since 1972, providing secure diallable access to all other users in the area and supporting data as well as voice communications. Mobile radio users in the field can communicate with TCS users through the Combat Net Radio Interface (CNRI) facility. This 'quantum jump' brought much greater flexibility and versatility to the army's communications at both tactical and operational levels.[35] Lighter, more compact signals equipment has allowed greater mobility, reducing the vulnerability of tactical communications systems.[36]

Although primarily an army formation, deploying battalions with front-line divisions, SAF Signals also includes a strategic tri-service unit (1st Signals Battalion) tasked with maintaining communications between MINDEF's semi-underground site at Gombak in the middle of Singapore and operational commands, formations and units of all three branches of the SAF.

In 1991, as part of efforts to improve the SAF's Integrated Warfare capabilities, MINDEF requested proposals for a conceptual plan for a Singapore-wide command, control, communications and intelligence network, based on microwave and fibre-optic channels and including links to air and maritime surveillance assets.[37] Although details remain scant, it is believed that DTG's Command, Control, Communications, Computer and Intelligence Systems Organisation (CSO) developed such a network, and that it is focused on an Armed Forces Command Post (AFCP, which includes the General Staff Operations Centre together with its naval and air force counterparts) located deep underground in MINDEF's Gombak facility.[38] According to MINDEF, a 'computerised command and control system provides up-to-the-minute updates of the battlefield situation, including the disposition of friendly and hostile forces'.[39]

The AFCP's air element, run by Air Force Systems Brigade (AFSB), provides a full picture of the air situation, integrating data from ground-based radars and Hawkeye AEW and control aircraft. The navy's Coastal Command contributes a central sea surveillance facility, using data from shore-based military and civilian radars, ships at sea and shore-based electronic and signals intelligence.[40]

Singapore's growing involvement in satellite communications has clear military applications, especially in relation to the operational command and control of the SAF when deployed beyond home territory. The republic's first communications satellite was a joint project between Singapore Telecom (SingTel) and Taiwan's Chungwa Telecom, agreed in 1995 and launched from French Guiana in August 1998. The ST-1, built by the Anglo-French Matra-Marconi company, is designed for both broadcasting and telecommunications (including data, telephony and multimedia) purposes, with its thirty Ku-band and C-band transponders shared equally between Singapore and Taiwan. The satellite's 'footprint' covers 'the whole of Asia'.[41]

In 1998 SingTel withdrew from a second communications satellite joint venture, the Asia Pacific Mobile Telecommunications (APMT) project, which also involved Singapore Technologies and four Chinese companies; under a 1996 contract the US company Hughes Space Communications International was to build the satellite itself.[42] Although Singapore Technologies took over SingTel's stake, in April 1999 APMT terminated its contract with Hughes after the latter was unable to secure an export licence for the programme 'in a timely manner', following allegations regarding China's exploitation of 'civilian' satellite technology—specifically citing its links with APMT—for military purposes.[43]

A third satellite programme, involving local satellite technology developed at NTU, was announced in 1998. In April 1999, a 350-kilogram mini-satellite designed jointly by NTU and the University of Surrey in the UK was launched from the Russian space base at Baikonur in Kazakhstan. This low-orbiting satellite passes over Singapore every 90 minutes. It carries NTU-designed components in a package referred to as the Merlion Communications Payload, and is being used to research 'faster ways of moving data with less distortion'. The next phase will involve a 100-kilogram micro-satellite 'fully designed and built' at NTU and scheduled for launch in 2002. This will be the first of a planned 'equatorial belt' of Singaporean micro-satellites, ultimately providing Singapore (and other users located close to the equator) with round-the-clock access to clearer and faster satellite communications.[44]

During the 1990s MINDEF also invested heavily in cutting-edge information technology (IT) for command and control purposes. Speaking in 1990, Brigadier-General Lee Hsien Loong, then second defence minister (Services), claimed that IT had the potential to provide the SAF with a 'strategic edge' over an opponent. He foresaw IT applications including computer-based tools and staff aids to assist SAF commanders and staff officers in operational planning and decision-making.[45] CSO has played a central role in monitoring, acquiring and integrating relevant new technologies. 'Commercial-off-the-shelf' (COTS) computer technology has been widely exploited: for example, Defence Minister Tony Tan claimed in 1996 that Singapore was 'among the leaders in the world in using [COTS] computers in real-time command and control systems', particularly in the integration of air defence sensors and weapons systems for the RSAF's Air Defence Systems Division (ADSD).[46] New technology has impacted on tactical as well as strategic command and control; for example, in the late 1990s the artillery introduced the battalion-level Artillery Tactical Command and Control System (ATCCS) to compute and manage firing data more accurately and rapidly.

Doctrinal implications

These advances in Singapore's application of communications and information technology, much of it deriving from the republic's own thriving high-technology industrial base, have profound implications not only for the future of Singapore's military command and control, but also for the SAF's operational doctrine in broader terms. The SAF's command and control have in the past tended to be rigid and strictly hierarchical, with effective authority concentrated at the higher levels of MINDEF and the SAF, and have been characterised by a reluctance to delegate authority to middle-level and junior commanders. For example, RSAF squadron commanders have hitherto been able to exercise little operational initiative compared with their Australian or British counterparts. The SAF's lack of organisational flexibility has been reinforced by not only the political and administrative system—which has tended not to reward individualism or creativity—but also by the local cultural milieu. According to one young middle-ranking army officer (the commander of a Guards battalion), the SAF could gain an edge over opponents by adopting the German military philosophy of *Auftragstaktik*, involving considerable decentralisation of command and control, and greater expectations of initiative on the part of lower-level commanders and even individual soldiers:

> Our Asian heritage has unfortunately . . . put too much premium on the value of 'face'. We are exceedingly hierarchy-conscious to the extent that constructive criticism is extremely rare from bottom-up. It will take much time and deliberate effort to dispel the fear of . . . subordinates to speak up if they think their superiors are in the wrong, and for the latter to accept constructive criticism.[47]

This officer effectively identified the military component of a broader problem with which Singapore's political leaders were grappling at the end of the 1990s: how to encourage Singaporeans to be more creative in order to retain and enhance the city-state's competitive advantages. As in other areas of competition, it is evident that in the defence field technological superiority alone is not sufficient for Singapore to come out on top. New information and communications technology, though, is likely to stimulate the development of new command and control doctrines. In 1999 the RSAF's Chief of Staff, Brigadier-General 'Rocky' Lim, pointed out that, by providing rapid access to more information, the latest IT applications increase the pressure for decision-making at lower levels in the chain of command. According to Lim, this 'could change your entire doctrine of air warfare'.[48] The influence of intensified interaction (most importantly the RSAF's long-term training programmes in the United States, Australia and France) with western armed forces, which already practice more decentralised command and control, may also push MINDEF and the SAF to delegate operational authority to lower levels of command more effectively.

INTELLIGENCE COLLECTION AND ANALYSIS

MINDEF is responsible for the collection and analysis of Singapore's external intelligence, an essential prerequisite for effective command and control decision-making. While Singapore's intelligence organisations are necessarily small in comparison with those of its larger neighbours, they are generally highly efficient and effective, particularly in terms of technical intelligence collection and assessment. The primary strategic intelligence organisation is the Security and Intelligence Division (SID), which is headed by a senior civil servant or one-star SAF officer and has approximately 500 staff. As well as acting as Singapore's interlocutor with the secret intelligence agencies of friendly countries, its activities include extensive human intelligence (HUMINT) operations in other Southeast Asian countries, most importantly Malaysia. On occasion, target states' counter-intelligence agencies have compromised such operations, temporarily undermining bilateral relations. One example was the major SID HUMINT operation that was mounted in the late 1980s with the aim of discovering details of Kuala Lumpur's defence procurement programmes: while this successfully penetrated the Malaysian defence ministry and secured considerable amounts of classified material for Singapore, it also led to the arrest of nine alleged spies.[49] In the mid-1990s, Australian defence and intelligence officials claimed that, following a serious but unspecified 'incident', Canberra became alarmed over apparent Singaporean efforts to collect intelligence on Australian defence capabilities.

SID also coordinates and manages Singapore's signals intelligence (SIGINT) activities. SIGINT sources include several land-based Signals battalions, one of which took over the former Australian wireless interception facility at Kranji in 1974, which had 'provided a comprehensive coverage of military, diplomatic and commercial communications across Indonesia, Malaysia, Thailand, China and the Indochinese countries'.[50] There is no reason to suppose that the facility's coverage has been any less extensive under Singapore's control. SIGINT collection systems are also deployed on RSAF aircraft and RSN vessels, and the Singapore Telecom radio receiving station at Yio Chu Kang probably also contributes SIGINT data.[51] According to Australian defence analyst Desmond Ball:

> Some of Singapore's SIGINT capabilities, especially the systems acquired from Israel over the last decade but increasingly also some designed and developed indigenously by [DTG] and Singapore Technologies [ST], are among the most advanced in the world. Overall, it amounts to a sophisticated capability which provides Singapore with strategic COMINT concerning its neighbours (Malaysia and Indonesia); HF DF/ocean surveillance information, including a very detailed picture of the maritime traffic in the Straits and waters surrounding Singapore; a comprehensive picture of the electronic order of battle (EOB) of its neighbours; and the most advanced electronic warfare (EW) capability in Southeast Asia.[52]

Furthermore, SID is presumed to be responsible for managing the analysis of imagery received from the satellite ground station operated by the National University of Singapore's Centre for Remote Imaging, Sensing and Processing (CRISP), which became operational in 1995. CRISP routinely downloads images from European, French and Canadian satellites, including the French Spot-4, launched in March 1998.[53] CRISP's role in monitoring marine pollution and forest fires in the region has received wide publicity, but its defence intelligence role has not been acknowledged officially. However, the 10-metre resolution of these images is sufficient to generate militarily useful information on the location of ships, armoured vehicles and aircraft. Ultimately, Singapore may be able to rely to a large extent on its own satellites for the collection of intelligence imagery. The NTU–University of Surrey mini-satellite launched in 1999 carries 10-metre resolution cameras, which were reportedly returning 'spectacular' imagery within weeks of launch, and the projected NTU micro-satellites are intended to have a remote-sensing as well as a communications role. However, a joint project with Israel (which has reportedly already provided satellite imagery on a commercial basis) may eventually give Singapore its most effective space-based surveillance capability. Under an agreement signed in June 2000, Singapore will fund further development of Israel's Ofeq series of satellites, advanced versions of which will eventually be operated by MINDEF.[54]

The second major intelligence agency within MINDEF is the Joint Intelligence Directorate (JID), which is analogous to Australia's Defence Intelligence Organisation. JID, which is headed by a one-star officer reporting directly to CDF, is principally concerned with intelligence analysis and assessment and with coordinating the intelligence activities of the three services. Working with CSO, during the 1990s JID developed INSIGHT, a system which enables 'efficient and effective means of information gathering, processing, retrieval as well as timely dissemination' in support of SAF operations.[55] Each of the single-service headquarters includes an intelligence department, mainly concerned with the analysis of tactical intelligence. The Military Security Department (MSD) is concerned with counter-intelligence operations within MINDEF and the SAF.[56] As a result of their Cyberspace Security Project, MINDEF and the SAF have developed countermeasures which respond automatically to attacks on their computer systems.[57]

Intelligence activities are authorised, supervised and coordinated by the Security and Intelligence Committee (SIC), a standing committee of the Defence Council chaired by the defence minister.[58]

CONCLUSION

Singapore's most powerful political leaders have taken an extremely close interest in the development of the SAF since the 1960s, and have closely supervised both the defence ministry and the armed forces. Although the input from senior SAF officers into defence policy has increased since the 1980s, the government has taken measures to ensure that MINDEF and the SAF remain under its strict control. Within the SAF, command and control has traditionally been rigidly hierarchical, but during the 1990s the exploitation of new communications and information technology, among other factors, began to challenge this paradigm.

Because of the constraints imposed by Singapore's small population and lack of strategic depth, during the 1980s and 1990s the republic has increasingly invested its growing defence budgets in high-technology systems, placing great emphasis on improving command, control, communications, computer-processing and intelligence (C^{4}I) capabilities. Singapore's military establishment has also begun to make some of the organisational and doctrinal changes required to fully exploit the advantages offered by this new technology, particularly in terms of emphasising joint service operations, planning and intelligence. These developments will help ensure that Singapore retains key military advantages over potential adversaries for the foreseeable future.

4

Personnel

Though Singapore's defence ministers and senior military officers have made much of the SAF's need to exploit modern military technology in order to compensate for its manpower constraints, when fully mobilised the SAF is, by regional standards, an impressively large organisation. Despite Singapore's small population, the SAF's total mobilised personnel strength of 350 000 far exceeds the military manpower of Australia (90 000), Malaysia (150 000) the Philippines (150 000) and even outnumbers that of Japan (290 000). In contrast to these examples, though, only a relatively minor proportion of the SAF's strength is composed of active personnel. Of the total of 350 000 personnel, approximately 20 000 are regular officers and NCOs, 40 000 are conscripts (officially referred to as Full-Time National Servicemen or NSFs), and the remainder are reservists (known as Operationally Ready National Servicemen or NSmen).

FULL-TIME NATIONAL SERVICEMEN

Highlighting the fact that conscripts and reservists provide the great bulk of Singapore's military personnel strength, as well as performing a significant nation-building role, in 1995 Defence Minister Tony Tan claimed that National Service (NS) was the 'very basis for Singapore's continued existence as an independent nation-state'.[1] Under the *Enlistment Act* of 1970, all Singapore citizens and permanent residents become liable for National Service (always referred to simply as NS in Singapore) on reaching the age of 16½, and are required to serve two or two-and-a-half years of full-time service, followed by up to 40 days of reservist service annually until the age of 40, or age 50 in the case of officers.[2] Citing the time taken to learn how to operate increasingly sophisticated weapon systems and other equipment and the need to develop the operational readiness of large formations, as well as the danger of eroding the confidence of both Singaporeans and foreign investors in Singapore's security, the government has repeatedly and steadfastly resisted suggestions (particularly from opposition politicians) that the period of full-time National Service should be reduced.[3]

Singapore's majority Chinese population is culturally predisposed to deprecate soldiering as an occupation. According to a popular Chinese adage: 'One never uses good iron to make nails; good sons do not become soldiers'. Soldiering was traditionally seen as an occupation for Malays and members of the criminal classes. Moreover, as Defence Minister Howe Yong Chong admitted in 1979, during the early years of NS 'harshness and abuse' had occurred in SAF establishments 'in spite of every effort by MINDEF to eradicate them'.[4] For these reasons, during the late 1960s and 1970s, the government had to work hard to convince Chinese Singaporeans—conscripts, their families and the wider community—that NS was vital for the nation's security and prosperity.[5] It was especially difficult in the early NS years to find suitable candidates for officer training (which increased the NS period for the individuals concerned from two to three years). This problem necessitated the imposition of two-and-a-half years of mandatory NS for all conscripts with 'A' levels or higher educational qualifications.[6] In 1978, a sociological investigation of NS revealed the depths of many NSFs' lack of motivation.[7]

In 1983, Defence Minister Goh Chok Tong highlighted a public opinion survey revealing that four in ten respondents felt that NS was 'a waste of time'. In Goh's view, the government's 'message' was 'not getting across'.[8] Ultimately, though, after heightened efforts by the government during the 1980s to promote public support for its defence policy—not least through the Total Defence concept—by 1990 the Chief of Defence Force felt able to claim that the average NSF was entering the SAF 'with a positive attitude and with the intention of making the best of his time in the armed forces'.[9] In 1992 Defence Minister Yeo Ning Hong remarked that there had been a 'dramatic change' in Singaporeans' attitude towards NS.[10] By this time, sons were following in the footsteps of fathers and NS was universally—if often grudgingly—accepted as a necessary rite of passage.

Enlistment for NS normally takes place at age 18, though every year approximately 1000 draftees (mainly those who have left school before completing 'A' levels) are allowed to enlist early as 16- or 17-year-olds.[11] Small numbers of potential NSFs are exempted from service on medical grounds; even smaller numbers are barred for security reasons. In the early years of NS, exemptions were allowed on the ground of the economic hardship of potential conscripts' dependent families, but this excuse is no longer accepted: a Financial Assistance Scheme is available in such cases.[12] Conscientious objection has never constituted a ground for exemption, and there are no 'soft' alternatives to military service such as community work. Every year, small numbers of conscientious objectors (38 in 1997) are tried and imprisoned. Most or all are members of the Jehovah's Witnesses, banned in Singapore in 1972.[13] Although most NSFs are directed towards the SAF, approximately 15 per cent of each cohort are required to serve in the police or the civil defence force.

The impact of a declining birth rate

During the 1970s, there were considerably more NS registrants than the SAF could use. At the start of the decade the annual cohort of 18-year-olds numbered 22 000, of whom only 11 000 (generally the fittest and academically brightest) were called up for NS. Of these 11 000, only around 6000 were taken into full-time SAF service; the rest were assigned to part-time service in the People's Defence Force, Special Constabulary and Vigilante Corps.[14] The annual number of NS registrants (including many who, for one reason or another, might not be suitable for service in the SAF) peaked at 32 000 in 1976. But during the 1980s and 1990s, the SAF's requirements expanded at the same time that the size of the overall 18-year-old cohort declined (to 20–22 000 by the late 1990s).[15] As a result, the SAF saw its annual NSF intake fall from 20 000 in the early 1980s to 15 000 in the late 1980s and early 1990s and a mere 13 000 by 1993.[16] This decline in the NS cohort's size, noted with concern by Goh Keng Swee as early as 1978,[17] reflected the PAP government's success in reducing Singapore's birth rate drastically between the mid-1960s and mid-1980s.

By the mid-1980s, this trend was provoking alarm in the government, with cabinet minister BG Lee Hsien Loong warning that Singapore faced 'calamitous consequences'—a shortfall in the number of men needed to defend Singapore—unless something was done to reverse the declining birth rate.[18] The government's response in 1987 was to adopt a pro-natalist New Population Policy including tax incentives to encourage better-off families to have more children, thus dispensing with its previous emphasis on family planning. The message changed from 'stop at two' to 'have three, or more if you can afford it'. Although this new policy contributed to an increased birth rate from the late 1980s, it will not yield increased numbers of NSFs until 2005 at the earliest. Large-scale immigration of permanent residents (numbering 30 000 annually by 1997) has meanwhile boosted the population, but has not contributed significantly to the pool of 18-year-olds available for NS. Fearing the negative economic (and possibly political) impact of increasing the length of NS, the government chose to use smaller NSF cohorts more efficiently.

NSFs, most of whom are inducted into the armed forces in four main batches annually, are posted by the SAF's Central Manpower Base (CMPB) to military vocations (combat, technical or service) primarily on the basis of their medical fitness, physical characteristics and educational qualifications. Efforts are also made to allocate NSFs to units located as closely as possible to their family homes. Officers and NCOs are selected from among those NSFs with stronger academic qualifications. This allocation and selection process is largely computerised.

Since the mid-1990s, MINDEF has made particularly strenuous efforts to ensure the optimal use of NSFs, taking into account not only the shrinking of the annual cohort, but also the increased educational level of conscripts—by 1997, 60 per cent possessed or were destined for post-secondary education, compared with only 22 per cent in 1982.[19] The main initiatives adopted by 1996–7 were:

- commercialisation of non-combat support services, such as supply bases and catering, reducing the demands on NSF manpower. In addition, some support services were assigned to female regular personnel, non-uniformed SAF personnel and civilian MINDEF employees;
- utilisation of technology to minimise manpower requirements. To this end, weapons and other equipment were modernised, MINDEF emphasised research and development to enable the SAF to benefit from technologically advanced weapons, and the use of simulators and computer-aided instruction was stepped up;
- a restructuring of the army order of battle, with smaller formations and units maintaining their firepower and combat effectiveness with upgraded equipment;

- improvement of administrative productivity, through the use of computers and office automation systems;
- improvements to Basic Military Training (BMT), especially in terms of reducing the attrition of otherwise combat-fit NSFs through training injuries. The systems for selecting officers and NCOs were also renovated;
- refinement of the medical classification system to allow the assignment to certain combat posts (as headquarters signallers, for example) of NSFs who would previously have been classed as unfit for combat duties (approximately halving the previous annual figure of 3500 SAF NSFs who could not be given combat roles);
- the provision of more challenging roles and responsibilities for NSFs. For example, NSF armoured vehicle drivers are now cross-trained as mechanics to allow them to repair their own vehicles. Some NSFs are now trained as middle-level 'specialists' (as NCOs other than Warrant Officers are known in the SAF).[20]

These improvements followed an earlier initiative to cope with the increasingly apparent negative impact of Singapore's increasing affluence on the physical fitness of NSFs. After the failure of efforts during the 1980s to improve the fitness of schoolboys before they enlisted,[21] it was decided in 1990 to lengthen BMT for obese recruits from three to five months, in order to allow the eventual allocation of more such servicemen (who already constituted roughly 10 per cent of the total NSF intake to the SAF) to combat units.[22] This Obese Recruit Training Programme was broadly successful by 1993, with approximately 1400 men or 70 per cent of the programme's intake being deployed in combat units and some even being selected for officer training. In 1997, by which time the regular BMT period had been cut to 10 weeks, the special variant of BMT was reduced to 16 weeks, with continuing 'obese training' integrated into the remainder of overweight recruits' full-time NS period.[23]

The main components of BMT are drill, basic weapons training, physical training, fieldcraft and National Education, and it is conducted (according to a particular NSF's vocation) by either the Basic Military Training Centre (BMTC), or by a combat unit. Under the 'mono-intake' system, introduced in the early 1980s, recruits allocated to infantry, artillery, armour, combat engineer and commando units train together as battalion- or company-sized groups from their first day to the end of their full-time NS.

They then pass into Operationally Ready National Service (the reserves) *en bloc*. NSFs (such as those destined for signals, logistics, air force and navy units) who are not trained under the mono-intake system proceed either to their units or to specialised training after completing BMT.

Reducing apprehensions

Under the Direct Enlistment Scheme, introduced in 1997–98, most NSFs report directly to their units for BMT, rather than to CMPB. This scheme is intended primarily to reassure NSFs' parents that their sons were 'in good hands', thus reducing their apprehensions about NS.[24]

One major cause of such apprehension on the part of NSFs and their families has been the occasional deaths and much more frequent injuries which inevitably occur as part of a large-scale military training programme. Over the years, MINDEF and the SAF have become increasingly sensitive to the need for not only high levels of safety-consciousness in training and exercises, but also for adept handling of public relations in the aftermath of such accidents, because of the protracted difficulties it has faced in convincing the city-state's population that NS is vital for Singapore's defence and—indirectly—prosperity. Though NS is accepted as a fixture of Singapore life, the death or injury of conscripts in peacetime training is widely perceived as unacceptable. In the words of Deputy Prime Minister and Defence Minister Tony Tan, speaking after two serious accidents in early 1997 triggered a review of safety guidelines and a three-day suspension of training exercises, 'any accident is one accident too many for the SAF'. However, the drawback to this concern with avoiding casualties is that it may constrain SAF training to the extent that it undermines potential combat effectiveness.[25]

Since the 1980s, MINDEF has also devoted substantial resources to improving provision for dealing with the small proportion of NSFs (around 2 per cent of the total) who suffer from significant psychological and emotional problems. On occasion, disturbed NSFs have committed suicide or, more rarely, turned their weapons on other servicemen. The SAF's Psychological Medicine Branch is responsible for NSFs with psychological problems, most of whom come to the SAF with a previous history of mental ailments, although a minority (roughly 100 annually) develop difficulties after enlistment, mainly due to stress.[26] Less serious problems are dealt with by the SAF's Counselling Centre, originally set up in 1976 as the Social Work Branch with the primary role of counselling drug abusers. The Counselling Centre provides a 24-hour telephone helpline, a team of professional counsellors and trains regular SAF personnel as unit-level para-counsellors. In addition, the army maintains 'grief counsellors' on permanent stand-by.[27]

Beyond Basic Military Training

The SAF places great emphasis on identifying leadership potential among its NSFs, as there are insufficient regular personnel to provide other than the most senior commanders for most active units. After four weeks of BMT, recruits are put through a three-day Situational Test (SITEST) which assists selection of NSFs with leadership potential for further training as specialists or officers: other factors taken into account are appraisals by platoon commanders and peers, educational attainment and the candidate's record of extra-curricular activities at school.[28] After completing BMT, all those selected as specialists (approximately one-third of the total) take the 10-week Basic Section Leader Course (BSLC) at the School of Infantry Specialists (SISPEC). At the end of this course, trainees are promoted to Corporal. Those destined to become section leaders in infantry and Guards units remain at SISPEC for the 11-week Advanced Section Leaders' Course: this culminates in a nine-day exercise including a helicopter assault and a beach landing.[29] Those selected for other army combat branches proceed from BSLC to 11-week special-to-arms Specialist Continuation courses. After 21 weeks of post-BMT training, specialists are assigned to their units. During the 1990s, the role of NSF specialists widened to include positions traditionally held by regulars, such as Platoon Sergeants and Assistant Chief Clerks of units.[30]

One in every 15 NSF recruits, including the top 10 per cent of Specialist trainees (who are 'creamed off' at the end of BSLC), are selected for officer training. As part of the effort to foster an integrated SAF, officers of all three services are trained at the Officer Cadet School (OCS), part of the SAFTI Military Institute opened in 1995 to subsume the original SAFTI and the SAF's advanced officer training schools. The course involves an 11-week tri-service term, a 'service term' of eight weeks (during which cadets are introduced to the practices and traditions of their respective services) and a 23-week 'professional term' (aimed at developing service specialisations).[31] On commissioning, NSF army officers are typically appointed platoon commanders in operational units. The top 10 per cent of NSF officers are allocated to the Company Tactics Course to prepare them for posts as company and battalion commanders during their reservist service.[32]

NSFs in the navy and air force

The great majority of military NSFs are directed towards the army, but the navy and the air force also make use of conscript personnel. Indeed, as these services have expanded since the 1980s, so NSFs have come to constitute increasingly important components of their personnel strength.

By the mid-1990s, all naval vocations were open to NSFs, a far cry from the early 1970s when their role was largely restricted to manning Ferry Transport Units. By the mid-1970s, conscript sailors had begun to be drafted to patrol craft and missile gunboats, and by 1987 were allowed to join the elite Naval Diving Unit. NSF officers have been commissioned into the navy since 1974.[33]

NSFs' role in the air force has developed rather more tentatively, largely because of the particularly specialised and time-consuming training necessary for most of its personnel. Small numbers of NSF technicians were trained in the early 1970s, but this scheme was discontinued in 1974. When a ground-based air defence element was added in 1971, NSFs were transferred from the army to man a battalion equipped with 35 mm anti-aircraft artillery, but between 1972 and 1980 this unit was not under the control of the air force, which thus included no conscripts during the 1974–80 period. However, from 1980 considerable numbers of NSFs were allocated to the air force, following the establishment of the Singapore Air Defence Artillery (SADA) as a subordinate command including all ground-based air defence units. In 1984, the air force established its own small infantry force, the Field Defence Squadrons, based on conscripts and reservists. During the 1980s and 1990s, NSFs took on increasingly diverse roles in the air force (as air crew specialists in helicopter and transport squadrons, and as air operations specialists in air traffic control and fighter direction units, for example); commissioned NSFs were trained as Air Operations and Communications Officers. Taking advantage of the technical qualifications possessed by some NSFs, in 1995 the air force began to employ NSFs as aircraft technicians again.[34]

National service as nation-building device

The SAF is far from being the only institution which the PAP government has used for nation-building purposes: in particular,

Singapore's school system clearly plays a crucial part. Singapore's leaders, though, have always stressed that the SAF—as a conscript-based military institution—provides not only the basis for national defence but also has an important social role to play. Indeed, in 1979 Defence Minister Howe Yoon Chong argued that Singaporeans 'should look upon national service as a continuation of the social transformation' which had been taking place since their city obtained self-government in 1959.[35] It was envisaged that National Service would 'contribute towards the creation of a cohesive society by providing the opportunity for young men of diverse ethnic, religious and cultural backgrounds to live, learn and work closely together'.[36] According to Cabinet minister Brigadier-General George Yeo, the SAF is one of the city-state's 'social distilleries' which produce 'our Singapore essence', enabling Singapore 'to remain different and separate from the world outside'.[37] The National Education programme is used to strengthen NSFs' understanding of Singapore's history and strategic circumstances, but the more general experience of full-time NS also has an impact. In the words of one young NSF officer, 'NS makes you feel that you are important to the country, that the country needs you . . .'.[38]

At the same time, NS was intended to imbue conscripts with 'attributes such as discipline, hard work, perseverance and commitment to excellence'.[39] Moreover, many NSFs with weak academic backgrounds have benefited from educational programmes run within the SAF, both in terms of acquiring technical skills and by improving their English-language fluency. The emphasis on the physical fitness of not only NSFs, but also reservists, has made a long-term impact on the health of the male population as a whole. Initially, conscription served an additional social role in the sense of reducing unemployment by removing large numbers of young men from the labour market periods of two to two-and-a-half years, but by the early 1970s, Singapore's economic boom meant that this role was counterproductive because it exacerbated an extremely tight labour market.

By the end of the 1990s, more than 500 000 men had passed through NS. There seems to be little doubt that they have contributed substantially to the international reputation of Singapore's workforce for discipline, efficiency and flexibility. More specifically, in its early years NS may have played an important part in breaking down the aversion of Singaporeans to technical education and 'hand-dirtying' blue collar work, thereby facilitating Singapore's industrialisation during the 1970s.[40] It has also helped to bring

Singaporeans—and particularly Chinese Singaporeans—of all
social classes together in a common experience.[41]

However, the SAF has faced considerable challenges in terms
of helping to integrate Singapore's culturally and ethnically diverse
society. Language issues have proved particularly problematic. In
the late 1960s and early 1970s, the army was forced to create
separate 'Hokkien platoons', when it found that many of its early
ethnic Chinese NSFs spoke only that dialect, and could not
understand either Malay (the national language, used for drill
purposes) or English (used for instruction).[42] By the mid-1970s, the
government's bilingual education policy, under which all
schoolchildren learn both English and their 'mother tongue' (Mandarin Chinese, Malay or Tamil) was supposed to be producing
school leavers fluent in both languages. However, even as late as
1983, the Commanding Officer of one army unit spoke of his
struggle 'to create a proper English-speaking environment in his
camp'.[43] More recently, it has become evident that the bilingual
policy has 'Sinicised' Singaporean society, producing a new generation of Chinese NSFs, many of whom feel more comfortable
speaking Mandarin than English. In some cases, the result has
been the exclusion of non-Chinese NSFs from social interaction
with their Chinese peers.

Malays in the SAF

Even more importantly, though, national service as implemented
in the late 1960s and 1970s contributed directly and substantially
to the alienation of Singapore's largest ethnic minority from the
PAP government and the Singaporean state. The government's
wish to increase the proportion of Chinese in the SAF to reflect
better Singapore's ethnic make-up combined with an instinctive
distrust of Malay personnel in the armed forces (because of
independent Singapore's dominant threat perceptions) to produce
a policy under which virtually no Malays were conscripted into
the SAF between 1969 and 1973; at the same time regular Malay
soldiers were removed from combat posts, early retirement was
encouraged and promotional prospects curtailed.[44] Goh Keng
Swee, then deputy prime minister and defence minister, justified
this policy as necessary in the interests of a fairer ethnic distribution in the SAF.[45] Whatever the reasons behind it, this policy
substantially reduced the military role of a community which,
under British rule during the 1950s and 1960s, had taken to
soldiering in the Singapore Infantry Regiment with enthusiasm.

Indeed, the Malay community had come to rely on uniformed service as a source of employment and income: in 1957 almost 20 per cent of male Malay workers were employed in the armed forces or police.

The policy of excluding Malays from NS, together with their reduced opportunities for regular military careers, had severe economic and social implications. Malay youths, who were neither called up for NS nor officially exempted, were often unable to find long-term employment or apprenticeships because of employers' fears that they might be required to undertake military service at short notice. Moreover, the *National Service (Amendment) Act* of 1967 forced employers in some sectors to employ only discharged national servicemen. Apart from fostering a generalised sense of alienation amongst Malay youths and their families, by forcing the youths into an irregular lifestyle exclusion from military service may have contributed to widespread heroin abuse and, in some cases, criminality.[46]

Although limited conscription of Malays into the SAF recommenced in 1973, restrictions on their placement in certain militarily critical areas persisted. These limitations on Malays' role in the SAF acquired a high profile following BG Lee Hsien Loong's comments on the issue in February 1987. Clearly referring to the possibility of conflict with Malaysia or Indonesia, Lee's main point was that the government's concern over the danger of Malay personnel in the SAF suffering from divided loyalties if they ever had to fight fellow Muslims explained the continuing restrictions on their military employment.[47] However, in responding to criticisms of his speech from Malay community leaders and politicians in Singapore as well as from Malaysia, Lee pointed out the progress that had been made in terms of widening opportunities for Malays in the SAF since the 1970s. According to Lee, since 1985 all eligible Malays had been called up for NS, the proportion of Malays in the SAF had doubled since 1977, they were being posted more widely within the armed forces and more were being trained as officers, including some who were given local training awards for university study. But Lee also claimed that greater Malay participation in the SAF could only be allowed incrementally, as the Malays became more fully integrated into the mainstream of Singapore's society: he explicitly denied that there was any 'chicken and egg problem'.[48]

Since the late 1980s, concern over the impact on the SAF of a lower national birth rate has helped to ameliorate discrimination against Malays, both in NS and military employment more generally:

because of the manpower shortage, every potential serviceman is a vital resource. During the 1990s, Malay NSFs were still disproportionately directed towards the police and civil defence force, but were increasingly allocated to the SAF.

Within the SAF, however, Malays were still generally not given high levels of security clearance and were posted less than proportionately to combat vocations.[49] Although the first Malay pilot received his 'wings' in 1992, there were still few Malays in the professional cadre of the air force. While this apparent discrimination was partially explained by the lower than average educational attainment of many young Malays, comments by Lee Kuan Yew in late 1999 underlined his own—and possibly the government's—continuing distrust of Malays in the SAF.[50]

RESERVISTS

Each year the SAF's active units disgorge a large number of NSFs—approximately equal to the number inducted for full-time NS—who become reservists or 'operationally-ready national servicemen' (NSmen) as they are known officially, each liable for up to 40 days of in-camp training (ICT) annually. During the 1970s, reservist numbers increased rapidly, from a mere 3000 in 1972 to 150 000 by 1980. By the end of the 1990s, the NS system, together with the smaller but still significant outflow of regular personnel, had generated a total of more than 500 000 reservists, although almost half of these had reached the end of their obligatory service (at the age of 50 for officers or 40 for other ranks). The army relies on reservists to provide the great bulk of its fighting strength, and the other two services probably could not sustain high-intensity operations for my length of time without the vital additional manpower provided by their NSmen.

Although reservist numbers grew rapidly as early NS intakes reached their 'run-out date' (ROD) during the 1970s, SAF reservists were in many cases unfit, poorly motivated, badly led and ill-trained. ICT sessions were neither well-planned nor taken seriously and facilities for reservists were inadequate.[51] Many reservists were concerned that their civilian careers might suffer because of their military training commitments, fearing that colleagues exempt from NS and reservist service—because they were female, recent immigrants or physically unfit—would gain unfair advantages over them. In the late 1970s and early 1980s, these problems greatly concerned the government and resulted in several initiatives which sought to enhance reservists' contribution to the SAF's capabilities. In the first place, in 1979 Defence Minister Howe Yoon Choong announced that reservists would be provided with facilities to enable them to maintain their physical fitness; the following year, MINDEF introduced the Individual Physical Proficiency Test (IPPT), which all reservists would be required to take twice annually. Reservists who failed the IPPT were required to undertake a seven-day Residential Training (RT) programme. In 1991, extended 10-day RT became mandatory for reservists who had failed or missed two successive IPPTs.[52]

Upgrading reservists

The Reservist Upgrading Scheme, introduced in 1980, sought to improve the training and skills of all reservists through comprehensive changes to ICT syllabuses, together with courses to prepare reservist officers and NCOs more effectively for their leadership roles. Crucially, promising officers could be selected—during reservist ICT as well as full-time NS—for grooming for eventual posting to senior command and staff positions referred to as 'key appointments'. Usually after two three-year tours in relatively junior battalion or brigade staff posts, the best reservist officers would be sent (if their employers released them) on the full-time seven-month Singapore Command and Staff College (SCSC) course, or the largely part-time Reservist Officers Staff Course (ROSC). During the 1990s, the ROSC was restructured into two separate streams: the Reservist Command Course (RCC) and Reservist Staff Course (RSC).[53] After taking these courses, NS officers would be eligible for appointment as battalion commanders or senior staff officers at brigade level. A related development was that such reservist key appointment holders (KAHs), who also included Regimental Sergeant-Majors, would be required to serve a 16-year reservist training cycle.[54] Moreover, under the Reservist On Voluntary Extended Reserve Service (ROVERS) scheme, KAHs have been encouraged to extend their training cycle beyond the mandatory 16 years and to serve for longer than the statutory 40 days per year. In 1987 new legislation regularised the position of such personnel, particularly in terms of protecting their civilian employment.[55] In compensation for their additional input, KAHs were granted a Special Reservist Appointment Allowance and other incentives (such as the same access as regular SAF personnel to reduced-rate holidays). In 1991, some KAHs were granted an additional Reservist Command Allowance.[56]

Largely with the intention of maintaining the size of the army's order of battle in the face of contracting NS intakes, in 1983 a new 13-year reservist training cycle replaced the previous 10-year cycle (which included five ICTs) for most reservists. The new cycle included nine 'high key' years, in which ICT lasts for at least a week (usually two to three weeks), and four 'low key' years involving no more than six days' training (but often only IPPT tests). In 1985, three-day ICTs, involving refresher training at a new Basic Combat Training Centre (BCTC), were introduced in all years of the cycle for the 75 000 or so active reservists in infantry and armour units.[57] By the end of the 1990s, of the nominal total of approximately 300 000 reservists, perhaps 180 000 were still working through their 13-year training cycles; the remainder were on MINDEF's Reserve List and had no peacetime training obligation.[58]

By the mid-1980s, then, the calibre of SAF reservists had improved markedly. Reflecting the success of fitness courses organised in conjunction with the SAF Reservists' Association (SAFRA) and the the People's Association, almost half of the reservists taking their IPPT in 1985 performed sufficiently well to be exempted from their second test that year.[59] Training facilities had improved and active personnel were more cooperative. Reservist officers noted improved morale among their men during ICT.[60]

The most dramatic change in reservist policy came at the beginning of 1994, when the very notion of 'reservists' was officially discarded. In announcing this radical change, Defence Minister Yeo Ning Hong spoke of the 'wrong connotation perpetuated by the term "reservist"'. In fact, despite a continuing widespread misconception that reservists were not frontline troops, servicemen who had completed their full-time NS were 'battle-ready, combat-ready, war-ready, operationally-ready', Yeo claimed. To stress SAF reservists' front-line status, while at the same time not applying a term which might be construed as 'unduly aggressive', MINDEF chose to re-style them 'Operationally Ready National Servicemen' (NSmen).[61] At the same time, reservist units became known as 'National Service units'. Subsequently, 'Operationally Ready National Service Date' (ORD) replaced ROD as the term signifying the end of an NSF's full-time NS. This new reservist terminology was linked to the major restructuring of the army in 1994–95, which brought the wholesale integration of active and NS units within the same divisions.

Societal support and recognition for reservists

The government has made strenuous efforts since the late 1970s to strengthen societal support for reservists' role in defending Singapore. Reinforcing suggestions which had been aired by ministers and senior civil servants since 1979, in 1981 the government announced that it intended to 'create a direct nexus between the advancement of a citizen as a soldier and his advancement as a civilian, and vice versa'.[62] Reservists were encouraged to use their military ranks in civilian life, and employers were provided with reports on their employees' performance during ICT, which would—or so it was hoped—influence their non-military careers. In practice, though, this rather crude attempt at social engineering fell flat. Employers remained unconvinced that military skills were transferable to the workplace, most continuing to view their reservist employees' absence for several weeks of ICT every year as irksome and unnecessary. While some reservists whose civilian careers had prospered expected additional confirmation of their social status through promotion in the reserves, the SAF was reluctant to reward part-time servicemen who in many cases had shown little enthusiasm for their military duties.

However, the relationship between reservists' military and civilian lives remained an issue of concern to the government, which ultimately addressed it in a more thorough and sensitive fashion. Recognising that reservists' civilian employers need to understand the importance of their employees' military commitments, since the mid-1980s MINDEF has attempted—with considerable success—to strengthen its cooperation with them. Developments have included the direct notification to employers of their employees' ICT schedules, expanding the scale of employers' visits to units to watch 'their' reservists training and the inauguration of a Best Employer's Award.[63] The Office Support System, which provides fax machines in reservist training centres, has enabled white collar reservists to remain in contact with their offices during ICT. By the early 1990s, many major employers, in both public and private sectors and including foreign multinationals, were actively supporting rather than merely accommodating reservist training: by carrying out their own in-house mobilisation exercises; by not requesting deferment of ICT for employees; by encouraging reservists to attend upgrading courses; and by providing fitness training facilities.[64] The fact that many of Singapore's senior managers were themselves reservists facilitated such collaboration.

In its efforts to recognise and reward reservists' contributions during the 1980s and 1990s, MINDEF relied heavily on ideas proposed by ACCORD, RECORD and RECORD II, all of which included employers' representatives. The most important recommendations derived from RECORD II's report in 1996. Some of the main suggestions, all of which were accepted by MINDEF, were for:[65]

- 'asset enhancement schemes', giving NSmen 'top-ups' for their CPF (compulsory state savings) accounts and access to additional discounted shares in privatised utilities;
- expanded and improved recreational facilities;
- monetary rewards for marksmanship;
- early release from ICT and faster promotion for reservists who perform well;
- recognition of the best NS units in an annual awards ceremony; and
- an institutionalised dialogue between MINDEF and employers on NS matters.

While the long-term commitment of time and energy to part-time military training, often to the detriment of family life and careers, is unlikely ever to be popular, these and other initiatives—which have been implemented within the broad framework of Total Defence—have gone a long way towards making reservist service more acceptable from the viewpoint of individual NSmen, their employers and the broader community.

One other problem related to reservists, though, may prove more difficult to resolve. According to Tony Tan, the SAF has 'to take into account that more young men would be living and working outside Singapore' as efforts to develop a 'second wing' to the economy, based on internationalising Singaporean enterprises, come to fruition. This phenomenon has obvious implications in terms of training and mobilising NSmen living overseas, who may include significant numbers of officers and NCOs. In 1996, MINDEF saw this complication as 'manageable so far', but acknowledged that increasingly it had 'to be factored into the training regime'.[66]

REGULAR PERSONNEL

The problem of maintaining a sufficiently large and well-trained core of professional NCOs and officers to train and manage

Singapore's large conscript and reservist army, and to provide the majority of its peace-time air force and naval personnel, has preoccupied the city-state's defence planners since the late 1960s. While periods of economic difficulty (for example, the mid-1980s and 1998) have provided short-term relief,[67] Singapore's usual condition of economic buoyancy has made recruiting and retaining regulars an uphill struggle. This is despite the fact that such personnel are salaried throughout their initial six-year contracts, including their first two-and-a-half years' service (during which time they would only have received token allowances as NSFs).

The SAF employs approximately 4–5000 uniformed regular officers and around 15 000 Warrant Officers and specialists. To maintain these levels it needs to recruit around 600 new officers and 2000 specialists annually out of an NS intake of 13 000. In other words, it must aim to retain one-fifth of each NS cohort as regular personnel. In order to make this a practical proposition in a socio-economic environment which has been transformed since the 1960s by expanding educational opportunities and rising incomes, MINDEF has been forced to offer its regulars increasingly attractive terms of service. It has also been necessary to widen opportunities for female personnel.

Singapore's military scholars

At the apex of the SAF's regular personnel are those officers who have benefited from government scholarships for higher education. In 1971 the government, recognising the critical importance of securing a fair share of the 'brightest and best' of Singapore's young men to provide the armed forces' future staff officers, in the face of not only strong competition from the private sector and the civil service but also the disdain with which the Chinese have traditionally regarded soldiering, inaugurated the SAF Overseas Scholarship scheme. Under this scheme, six to ten officers are selected annually from 'the cream of the officer cadet national servicemen'[68]—principally on the basis of academic merit—for sponsorship through tertiary education in British and, since the 1990s, US universities. Having already trained at and graduated from SAFTI's OCS alongside their NSF and regular contemporaries (though in a discrete unit, Delta Company), they are paid a full officer's salary while studying, as well as maintenance and book allowances. Most of them read for first degrees in engineering, a subject of clear relevance to their military careers in the SAF's high-technology environment, though some have studied economics, management or politics. Since the late 1990s, some have been permitted to extend their period of study to take Master's degrees.[69] Some SAF Overseas Scholars (typically, one or two annually) are simultaneously awarded the even more prestigious President's Scholarship. By 1999, a total of 206 SAF Overseas Scholarships had been awarded.

Slightly lower down the hierarchy of SAF educational awards, in terms of status, are the rather more numerous Merit Scholarships for overseas study, approximately 12 to 15 of which are awarded annually.[70] In total, almost as many SAF Overseas and Merit Scholarships are awarded every year as there are entrants to the government's elite civilian Administrative Service.[71]

On their return to Singapore, Scholars—who accumulate seniority while studying and are made Captains one year after graduation—are 'bonded' to the SAF for a minimum of eight years, although most serve for longer periods. Many, particularly the Overseas Scholars, have been promoted rapidly in the course of what have been—by international standards—short military careers. This rapid career advancement has generated controversy within the SAF's officer corps, and more widely, over the implications of promoting officers whose educational achievements may exceed their military experience and competence. By 1982 three out of the four original 1971 SAF Overseas Scholars had already reached the rank of Lieutenant-Colonel.[72] Such rapid advancement was facilitated by Scholars' automatic inclusion in the 'Wrangler' scheme, which MINDEF had inaugurated in 1973 with the objectives of identifying and grooming the SAF's future leadership. Approximately 10 per cent of SAF officers, all below the rank of Colonel and selected on the basis of performance or educational achievement, were included in the scheme.[73] However, by 1981 it was apparent that there were serious shortcomings in the Wrangler scheme: 'some officers who entered the Wrangler List on the basis of their scholastic achievements did not subsequently prove themselves in performance . . . Officers continue to remain in the Scheme despite mounting evidence that they are not capable of holding senior appointments'.[74] It was also reported that:

> [R]apid advancement of younger, educated officers has had negative effects . . . morale has been damaged among older professional officers as younger, less experienced people are moved above them. In the SAF . . . many older officers have either been pushed aside or have retired. Experience . . . has had to yield to brains and technology. Even among the younger

professional officers, there is an air of uncertainty engendered by the number of rapid shifts and promotions.[75]

Because of these problems, in 1982 MINDEF revised the Wrangler scheme's implementation, so that assessments of officers' performance and potential 'would be done for all officers, whether Wranglers or non-Wranglers, at the same rank . . . using the same criteria and standards of assessment'.[76]

Recognising that the SAF needed to attract more high-quality school leavers to officer careers, particularly as combat officers in the army, and that more highly educated officers would benefit the armed forces by providing 'leaders of high calibre who can think, plan and innovate at a high level of sophistication', in the early 1980s MINDEF began to provide far wider opportunities—through the Overseas Merit Scholarships, Academic Training Awards, Local Study Awards and the University Cadet Pilot Training Scheme—for officers to study at university. It also became possible for serving middle-ranking and senior as well as junior officers to take degree courses.

The proportion of graduates among SAF officers increased steadily during the 1980s and many non-Scholar officers continued to attain high rank. However, tensions between Scholars and non-Scholars within the officer corps persisted; indeed, by the early 1990s, this problem had crystallised into the labelling of non-Scholar officers as 'Farmers', a jocular reference to the traditional Chinese social hierarchy in which scholars (mandarins) were at the apex, above (in descending order) farmers, merchants and soldiers. Scholars now dominated the SAF's upper echelons: one estimate suggested that by 1991 as many as two-thirds of Majors, Lieutenant-Colonels and Colonels were Scholars.[77] By 1993, seven out of the SAF's 12 most senior officers (Brigadier-General or higher) were Scholars.[78]

Responding to dissatisfaction among Farmer officers with the SAF's promotion policies,[79] in March 1995 Rear-Admiral Teo Chee Hean (then an acting Cabinet minister and senior minister of state for defence) addressed senior army officers, arguing that Scholar–Farmer differences should not be allowed to polarise the officer corps. Teo claimed that the SAF was prepared to develop and promote any officer who performed well and demonstrated potential: simply being a Scholar did not guarantee automatic advancement. Indeed, according to the minister, there were some SAF Scholars who had proved unsuccessful as officers.[80]

Rewarding the officer corps

By the mid- and late 1990s the main cause of dissatisfaction among SAF officers was not that Scholars received preferential advancement, but that the SAF's terms of service were no longer attractive compared to those offered by other employers. While full-time and reservist NS were accepted as necessary evils, Singapore still lacked any substantial military tradition and its government had to work increasingly hard to recruit and retain professional officers.

Singapore's government tried, throughout the 1980s and 1990s, to ensure that SAF officers were sufficiently well-rewarded financially. In 1982, MINDEF stated its 'intention that SAF officers should get 20 per cent more than their counterparts with similar qualifications and seniority' in comparable posts in the Civil Service.[81] As well as remunerating its officers competitively, increasing numbers of them have been promoted to high ranks by Singaporean standards. Until the late 1980s, the SAF's officer promotion policy was conservative: in 1987, only three serving officers held the rank of Brigadier-General or higher and there were no more than 15 full Colonels. By 1999, though, there were 20 Generals or Admirals of various grades and approximately 50 Colonels.[82] In 1998, more than 1000 officers—approximately a quarter of the total—were promoted in rank or grade.[83]

Even these policies were not sufficient to provide the officers which the SAF needed. The armed forces operate a 'Keep SAF Young' policy—under which most officers have to leave the armed forces by the age of 40 or 45—in the interests of maintaining an energetic and innovative military leadership and, more to the point, of providing opportunities for fairly rapid career progression, though this risks diluting the reservoir of experience among senior officers. From the viewpoint of officers who are forced to retire in their early forties, there is also a major drawback in that they have to find second careers for the remainder of their working life. The most senior officers—particularly Scholars—generally move effortlessly into rewarding and lucrative posts in the public (or, to a lesser extent, private) sectors, but less highly educated middle-ranking combat officers (mainly army Captains and Majors) have sometimes found difficulty in securing suitable employment. This is despite various programmes organised by MINDEF to ease their transition to civilian life, including the recruitment of such officers as teachers and 'operations managers' for government schools.[84] Partly because of this long-term insecurity, as well as the discomforts of military life compared with civilian employment, during the 1990s two-thirds of regular officers preferred to leave the SAF to seek civilian employment at the earliest opportunity (after six years' service) rather than pursue a longer military career.[85]

MINDEF's recognition of the problem of retaining SAF officers led to several initiatives to improve their pay and other benefits during the mid-1990s, culminating in Defence Minister Tony Tan's announcement in 1997 of a new career structure and 'compensation package' to be introduced the following year. The main innovations were SAVER (the Savings and Early Retirement Plan, a generous 'financial buffer' to ease retirement for career officers, geared to rewarding those who serve at least two six-year contracts), and extended salary ranges for long-serving and effective Majors and Lieutenant-Colonels. Other changes included greater openness in the management of officers' careers, such as providing more feedback on an individual's performance.[86] A new 23-year 'Route of Advancement' was introduced as the norm, largely replacing the existing 25-year career structure (which was retained only for pilots and officers attaining the rank of Colonel).[87]

Advanced training for officers

Graduation from command and staff courses is vital for most SAF officers aiming to advance their careers beyond the rank of Captain. All of the SAF's advanced training for officers is conducted at SAFTI, where the SAF Advanced School (SAS) trains officers for intermediate level command and staff appointments.[88] Each component of SAS conducts a variety of short courses, including:

- Army Officers' Advanced School (AOAS)—Company Tactics Course, Advanced Infantry Officers Course, Battalion Tactics Course;
- Naval Officers' Advanced School (NAS)—Naval Junior Officers' Course, Naval Warfare Officers' Course;
- Air Force Advanced School (AFAS)—Air Force Officers' Advanced Course, Air Liaison Officers' Course.

AFAS also provides the Tri-Service Staff Course, which is conducted six times a year for a total of up to 240 officers, and is aimed at furthering the SAF's Integrated Warfare capability.[89] The Singapore Command and Staff College (SCSC) trains 160 more senior officers annually on its eight-month Command and Staff

Course, which is intended to prepare them for Lieutenant-Colonel grade appointments.[90]

Non-uniformed SAF personnel

One career route adopted by many officers (and specialists) forced to retire as a result of the 'Keep SAF Young' policy has been to join the Non-Uniformed SAF (NUSAF) scheme. This scheme was introduced in 1987, initially to ease the shortage of officers by allowing retiring military personnel to continue working for MINDEF and the SAF in administrative positions until the civil service retirement age of 60. Soon, though, the SAF was also advertising for recruits from outside the military and the scheme was expanded to accommodate additional retiring uniformed officers in 1995.

NUSAF officers are subject to military discipline rather than to Public Service Commission conditions of service, but are not required to meet some of the normal requirements (particularly in terms of fitness) for SAF officers. They are paid more generously than civil servants, but not as well as uniformed SAF officers. They quickly came to fill many appointments within MINDEF, as well as in service headquarters and certain military units, particularly in the areas of finance, purchasing, logistics, personnel and legal services. In its early years, the scheme suffered from teething problems, with some newly-recruited NUSAF officers experiencing difficulties in adapting to a military working environment, and in relation to their lack of status compared with uniformed officers. Nevertheless, during the 1990s the scheme expanded, so that by mid-decade there were several thousand NUSAF personnel, acccounting for 22 per cent of regular officers and 12.5 per cent of regular specialists and Warrant Officers. The eventual aim is for as many as 40 per cent of all regular officer posts (in other words, most administrative appointments concerned with non-operational matters) to be filled by NUSAF officers.[91]

Ethnicity, religion and the officer corps

The government's post-independence objective of ensuring that the SAF's ethnic make-up more accurately reflected the predominance of the Chinese in the population is clear from the present composition of the officer corps. Indeed, the highest echelons of the armed forces, mainly composed of men recruited in the 1970s and early 1980s, are almost exclusively filled by ethnic Chinese officers: of the 70 most senior officers (Colonels and higher) listed in 1999, only one was not Chinese.[92] This contrasts with the situation in the 1980s, when there were more non-Chinese senior officers including Indians, Eurasians and even a Malay: by the late 1990s these men had retired and had largely been succeeded by ethnic Chinese officers.

However, Indonesia's President Habibie missed the mark when, in early 1999, he accused Singapore of racism, claiming that Malays 'could never be military officers' there. As Malay organisations in Singapore were quick to point out, there were many Malay officers in the SAF. One local Malay youth group produced a list of 15 such officers holding the ranks of Major and Lieutenant-Colonel.[93] During the 1990s, members of this new generation of Malay officers were appointed to command positions in combat as well as logistic and training units, including one of the active infantry battalions.[94] While it is clear that Malays and other ethnic minorities are still grossly under-represented among higher-ranking officers, since the mid-1980s the overall shortage of officer candidates has implied that the SAF can ill-afford to discriminate on racial grounds. Consequently, the proportion of non-Chinese officers recruited has increased, with some even receiving SAF Merit Scholarships. Over the next decade, a number of these officers may be promoted to senior ranks, although the over-representation of ethnic Chinese officers is likely to persist.

Though ethnic minorities are under-represented in Singapore's officer corps, in 1994 opposition politician Tang Liang Hong, whom the government subsequently portrayed as a Chinese racial chauvinist and successfully sued for defamation, claimed that Christians (who numbered 14 per cent of Singapore's total Chinese population) were over-represented within the armed forces ('. . . our Ministry of Defence, our Chief of General Staff, our Army, our Air Force, our Navy, are basically headed or led by mostly Christians') as well as other parts of the state apparatus.[95] While Tang's claim may have exaggerated the true situation, anecdotal evidence suggests that many senior officers are indeed Christians. However, given the westernised, English-speaking, middle-class cultural milieu from which the majority of SAF officers are drawn, this is unsurprising.

Non-commissioned officers

The problems which have complicated officer recruitment, particularly Singaporeans' increasing education and prosperity, have also affected efforts to sustain recruitment of NCOs. Whereas in the 1960s (when only around five per cent of school-leavers progressed to tertiary education) and 1970s the SAF could recruit adequate numbers of NCOs from those whose education had not progressed beyond 'O' levels (who needed, in many cases, to leave school early in order to contribute to their family's income), by the late 1990s more than 60 per cent of Singaporeans were progressing to higher education at diploma (Polytechnic) or degree (University) level. The proportion is expected to rise to 70 per cent by 2005. The annual pool of school-leavers with only 'O' levels— the main source of NCO recruits since 1982—contracted from 10 000 in 1990 to less than 4000 by the end of the decade.

From the mid-1980s, MINDEF adopted a range of initiatives to boost NCO recruitment and retention in the face of rising educational attainment and a tight employment market. The Learn As You Earn (LAYE) scheme, introduced in 1984, played on increased educational aspirations among even less academically inclined Singaporeans by allowing regular combat NCO recruits with disappointing 'O' level results to study at the SAF Education Centre, with a view to improving their grades while simultaneously undertaking BMT and receiving regular soldier's pay.[96] The Joint Polytechnic–SAF Diploma Scheme, established in 1986, offers sponsorship through three-year engineering diploma courses for technical NCO recruits to all three services.[97] In the case of the air force, it was intended that NCOs sponsored under this scheme would 'form the backbone' of the maintenance workforce.[98] Under the 'Warrant Officer and Specialist 21 Development Master Plan', announced in 1997, a similar joint scheme involving the Institute of Technical Education was established.[99]

In 1990, the SAF abandoned its previous reliance on 'O' level school-leavers as the source of regular combat NCOs and began to focus on attracting NSF holders of 'A' levels and diplomas under the Enhanced Combat NCO Scheme. The aim was to recruit one-third of combat NCOs—some of whom would subsequently be sponsored through management courses—by this route.[100] The 'A' Level Study Programme, set up in 1991, was essentially a more academically advanced version of the LAYE scheme.[101]

Restructuring the NCO Corps

In 1992, the SAF fundamentally restructured its NCO Corps in order to provide its increasingly highly educated members with more challenging and rewarding careers. The Corps was divided into a Corps of Warrant Officers (WOs) and a Corps of Specialists, the latter including the former Staff Sergeant, Sergeant and Corporal First Class ranks. Additional ranks were created within each Corps in order to allow for 'more frequent and visible upgrading'.[102] Following the restructuring, able WOs and specialists could expect to be promoted approximately every three years.

Although some WOs (about five per cent of the total) had previously held appointments normally assigned to commissioned officers—such as Platoon Commander—after the restructuring this became a much more common phenomenon and partially compensated for the officer shortage. WOs were recognised as equivalent in status to junior officers up to the rank of Captain and, by the mid-1990s, in some cases their pay had been increased to equal that of Majors. In 1999, 13.5 per cent of WOs were holding officer appointments, including some staff and training posts established for Majors.[103] As WOs took on more officers' posts during the 1990s, so some of the less-demanding, traditional roles of junior regular NCOs were delegated to NSF specialists.

Enhanced training and educational opportunities have supported the increased status and expanded role of WOs and specialists. A tri-service Joint Warrant Officers' Course was inaugurated in 1992 to act as a bridge between the two new Corps. The SAF has also sponsored selected WOs and specialists through higher education under the Defence Technology Training Award and the SAF Diploma Studies Award.[104] Many WOs were sent for specialised courses originally intended for officers. The most senior WOs continued to be trained as Regimental Sergeant-Majors, who were increasingly seen by the SAF as units' personnel managers.[105]

Throughout the 1990s, MINDEF attempted to pay regular NCOs competitive salaries, based on the notion of paying premiums over pay for near-equivalent non-military occupations. Pay scales are re-assessed regularly, and bonuses for re-engagement as well as 'market adjustment allowances' supplement basic pay. The SAF has also maintained its competitive edge as an employer by offering long-term job security through a 20–25-year career structure. However, while many support and technical NCOs acquire transferable skills during their SAF careers, the prospect of transition to a civilian occupation on retirement has worried many combat NCOs. In response, MINDEF has attempted to overcome such anxieties through special retirement gratuities, the Pre-Release Employment Programme (under which ex-SAF personnel continue to receive half-pay during their first six months of civilian employment) and pre-retirement training programmes. In addition, the number of NUSAF officer posts open to regular WOs was expanded in the mid-1990s.

These measures were evidently insufficient and, in March 2000, a new 'career plan' for WOs and specialists came into effect. The key element was a two-stage career: after ten years as a specialist, successful NCOs will be offered the chance to stay on as a WO to a new, later retirement age of 55 (rather than 50). All specialists will be paid a lump-sum gratuity after their initial ten years' service, as well as benefiting from a new renumeration system known as the Premium Plan.[106]

While taking up NUSAF officer positions is an option for some retiring WOs, mobility between NCO and officer rank has otherwise remained rather limited despite the greater responsibilities assigned to many WOs during the 1990s and the similar educational backgrounds of many NCOs and officers. Apart from the selection for officer training of the top 10 per cent of SISPEC graduates, the other main route for transfers to uniformed officer status is from amongst ex-NSF specialists studying at local universities, who are eligible to apply for the Local Study Award, involving SAF sponsorship followed by officer training and six-year terms as regular officers.[107]

WOMEN IN THE SAF

Although all NSFs and all but a negligible portion of reservists are men, female service personnel have formed an increasingly significant part of the SAF's regular personnel strength since the mid-1980s. By 1990, there were approximately 4000 female personnel (equivalent to around 20 per cent of the total number of regulars), and their numbers have probably increased since then. This is not the result of any commitment to an equal opportunities policy, but rather of the realisation that 'the recruitment of women allows males to be released for frontline combat duties'. At the same time, MINDEF recognises that employing women in the SAF helps to 'improve the quality of its regular corps'.[108]

Women have served in the SAF since the mid-1960s. Originally, they were essentially restricted to administrative roles such as clerks, store personnel, telephonists and library assistants, and none undertook BMT until 1970. Others have served in the SAF Medical Corps, particularly as volunteer reservist doctors and nurses. During the 1980s, however, the profile of women in the

SAF was raised considerably, despite the fact that their recruitment was temporarily cut back during the economic recession of 1987, when it was easier to recruit males.[109] The most important innovation during the 1980s was the decision, in 1986, to follow the Israeli practice of training women as combat instructors.[110] Subsequently, two batches were trained each year, and 56 female combat instructors were teaching in the schools of infantry, signals, armour, artillery, engineering and military medicine by 1990.[111] The majority of these initial combat instructors had already been serving in administrative roles, but since then most have been recruited directly. Women also entered the SAF's technical vocations: in 1988, the Joint Polytechnic–SAF Diploma Scheme was opened to women aspiring to be army technicians.[112] In 1987, a woman was promoted to the highest NCO rank, Senior Warrant Officer, for the first time.[113]

A handful of female officers was trained in the late 1960s, but it was not until 1972 that women went through OCS on a regular basis. Since 1978, female officer candidates have been put through a 12-month course (including BMT) with 'G' Company at OCS. As was the case with female NCOs, women officers took on more diverse roles during the 1980s, some being trained as combat instructors. However, there were still less than 200 female officers in the early 1990s, these including 39 per cent employed as 'manpower' (personnel) officers, 17 per cent who were NUSAF staff and 20 per cent who were still officer cadets.[114] It was not until the late 1990s that some female officers were tentatively assigned to combat roles, such as radar officers in the artillery.[115]

In 1992, MINDEF announced that women would henceforth be eligible for the award of SAF Merit Scholarships and, since 1993, several female Merit Scholars have been sent under SAF sponsorship to overseas universities every year. The aim is that these Scholars will eventually 'hold key policy implementation posts at departmental level in the service HQs and Joint Staff'.[116] Until recently, however, few female officers were promoted beyond the rank of Captain, and it was not until 1997 that one took the Command and Staff Course.[117] In 1999, for the first time, two women were promoted to Lieutenant-Colonel.[118]

The air force has trained a small number of women pilots since 1979. None have been allowed to fly combat aircraft, but several have been posted to operational transport and helicopter squadrons.[119] Others have been trained as flying instructors, and one has commanded the Air Grading Flight. Women also serve in the air force as air operations officers and specialists, engineering officers, aircraft technicians and safety equipment technicians (amongst many other vocations), and with anti-aircraft missile and gun squadrons as Air Defence Weapons Specialists and Air Defence Artillery Officers.

In the navy's case, women were confined to administrative, technical and service vocations until 1990. In the early 1990s, a first batch of female combat specialists was trained and the first female combat officers graduated. Initially, these female specialists were posted to operations and communications centres—and to the Tactical Training Centre as instructors—but, like their officer counterparts, they were soon going to sea, in the first instance for day-trips on board coastal patrol craft and missile gun boats.[120] New naval vessels, such as the Endurance-class landing ships, however, have been built with separate accommodation to allow the routine deployment of female personnel at sea. By 1997, there were approximately 250 women in the navy; the long-term goal is to increase the proportion of women to about 15 per cent or 1400–1500.[121]

Though the SAF has opened more roles to female personnel since the 1980s, National Service for women is not a likely prospect despite the problems caused by a smaller cohort of 18-year old males and declining fitness levels. Indeed, the government's position in the late 1990s was remarkably consistent with that of 20 years previously: while the possibility was not ruled out, neither was it seen as other than a long-term option. In 1978, Goh Keng Swee claimed that 'the need to introduce national service for women still exists but need not come about in the near future';[122] in 1998, Minister of State for Defence Matthias Yao argued that there was 'no immediate need to consider the option of enlisting women for national service'.[123] The main stumbling block seems to be that while there might be some support in the wider community for conscripting women in non-combatant roles, there is no social consensus in favour of women being conscripted for combat duties, the very area where extra NSF personnel would be useful.

CONCLUSION

Not without reason, Singapore's defence ministers and senior military officers have often claimed that the SAF's servicemen and women are its most valuable asset. Accordingly, MINDEF has directed tremendous energy and substantial resources towards solving Singapore's military personnel dilemmas during the 1980s and 1990s. Continual public relations campaigns, in the context of Total Defence, as well as initiatives to reward NSmen in concrete terms, have contributed to the widespread acceptance of full-time National Service and reservist service as necessary evils by a society which lacks any substantial military tradition. More effective training, more efficient deployment of NSF manpower and less discrimination against ethnic Malays have largely compensated for the declining numbers and poorer physical condition of school leavers. Reservists' operational readiness has been improved through the 13-year training cycle and efforts to cultivate KAHs.

Mainly because of Singapore's economic success, recruiting regular officers and NCOs has been a perennial problem. However, generous educational awards, coupled with virtually continuous reviews of pay, and faster promotion, have all helped to maintain the attractiveness of military careers *vis-à-vis* civilian alternatives. Allowing women access to an increasingly wide range of roles, including combat training posts in operational arms, has also helped to ease the shortage of regulars.

The very nature of Singapore's military personnel, however, raises questions about the SAF's likely effectiveness in time of war. In particular, it could be argued that too much attention is paid to academic criteria and not enough to leadership qualities in the selection and promotion of the SAF's regular officers, many of whom are essentially bureaucrats, overly oriented towards securing financial rewards and comfortable second, civilian careers, rather than warriors. Criticisms could also legitimately be made regarding the quality and motivation of the army's conscript and reservist units. Overall, there may be good reasons for doubting the durability of the SAF's morale if faced with professional and possibly battle-hardened adversaries, even if the latter are relatively ill-equipped and poorly-educated. Nevertheless, given the constraints imposed by the nature of Singapore's society and economy, it is hard to envisage how military personnel issues could have been handled more effectively.

5

Singapore's army

Since they were established in the late 1960s, Singapore's armed forces have expanded their capabilities almost exponentially. Using defence budgets which have usually increased in real value year-on-year, the SAF's three services have procured ever more sophisticated and effective equipment. At the same time, their organisation, doctrine and logistic support have been refined continually. Training and exercises have become increasingly realistic, extensively exploiting overseas training opportunities and links with foreign armed forces. Operational readiness is taken extremely seriously and is tested through frequent mobilisation exercises and unit evaluations. The 1990s saw particularly impressive improvements in the SAF's capabilities, funded by large increases in defence spending and guided by SAF 2000, a planning blueprint adopted in 1988 as the result of a major force structure review.

Under Army 2000, a single-service derivative of SAF 2000, army doctrine stressed offensive combined arms operations and the conduct of a '24-hour battle'. But this interest in modern, high-intensity, high-technology warfare did not detract from the army's efforts to maintain core capabilities for jungle warfare and fighting in built-up areas (FIBUA),[1] reflecting the nature of the most likely environments in which it could have to fight. The Army 21 'vision' (the successor to Army 2000 launched in April 1999) has apparently added a new emphasis on deploying information capabilities, deriving from the 'integration of command, control, communications and sensor systems', sufficient to achieve 'dominant battle-field awareness'.[2]

ARMY RESTRUCTURING

With the combined aim of increasing the SAF's operational effectiveness while using military manpower more efficiently, the army was fundamentally reorganised during the late 1980s and early 1990s. This reorganisation, driven by Army 2000, involved at its most basic level reducing the size of individual units. New anti-tank weapons, light machine-guns and grenade launchers introduced since the early 1980s allowed infantry sections to be reduced from nine to seven men.[3] Moreover, by 1990 infantry battalions had been reduced from four to three rifle companies: together these developments cut their strength from 800 to 600 men. Armoured units' manpower went down from 840 to 730.[4] Artillery and combat engineer units were also reduced in size. Introducing the FH88 155 mm howitzer allowed artillery gun crews to be reduced from 12 to eight men.

Even more importantly, the reorganisation introduced genuine (as opposed to nominal) combined arms divisions. These new divisions' headquarters would command all their units even in peacetime, taking responsibility for their training and operational readiness. Each division lost one of its infantry brigades, but gained an armoured brigade. The reservist armoured brigade, 8 SAB, was converted into an active formation and joined 3rd Division, which became the first combined arms division in March 1991. Also in 1991, two new reservist armoured brigades were created: 54 SAB (allocated to 6th Division) and 56 SAB (for 9th Division).[5] Among other changes, each division also acquired an artillery group consisting of howitzer, mortar and locating units. As a result of the reduction in unit sizes, these new formations had a strength of 14 000, compared with 18 000 men in each old-style division.

Another extremely significant dimension to the 1991 restructuring involved creating two new divisions, the 21st and 25th. Ostensibly, these were Army Operational Reserve (AOR) divisions, holding formations composed of brigades which had completed their 13-year reservist training cycle and lacking the combat support units of the new combined arms formations.[6] The 25th Division was indeed an AOR 'paper division', having been allocated several time-expired reservist brigades. However, 21st Division's AOR status camouflaged its real role as a rapid deployment force built around three Guards brigades, one active (7 SIB) and two reservist. Of these three brigades, one

Figure 5.1 Singapore Army organisation

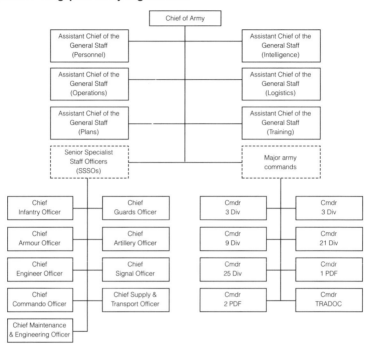

trains in an airmobile role with air force helicopter units, and another in amphibious operations with naval fast transport craft.

The next phase of the restructuring, implemented in January 1995, involved integrating reservist and active units within each combined arms division, to create three co-equal formations, each built around a core consisting of two infantry brigades (one composed of two active and one reservist battalions, and one controlling three reservist units) and an armoured brigade (with one active and two reservist battalions). This phase, which followed the 1994 re-styling of reservists as NSmen, reflected a recognition that reservist (now 'NS') units—particularly those composed of personnel who had recently completed their full-time service—could be just as effective as active units composed of conscripts and a sprinkling of regular officers and NCOs.[7] The new divisions each had a strength of 13 000 personnel, of whom 2500 were active.[8] Table 5.1 provides details of the major army formations and their constituent units. Figure 5.1 shows the army's organisation and senior command and staff appointments.

Table 5.1 Major Singapore Army formations, 2000

Divisions	Constituent brigades and units
3rd Division (combined arms)	3 SIB (2 SIR, 5 SIR, 187 SIR) 5 SIB (3 × NS SIR) 8 SAB (1 × NSF SAR, 2 × NS SAR) 3 DIV ARTY HQ (21 SA, 2 × NS SA) 3 DA Bn 3 DISCOM (3 DSMedB, 3 DSMaintB, 3 DSSB)
6th Division (combined arms)	2 SIB (1 SIR, 4 SIR, 1 × NS SIR) 9 SIB (3 × NS SIR) 54 SAB (1 × NSF SAR, 2 × NS SAR) 6 DIV ARTY HQ (1 × NSF SA, 2 × NSF SA) 6 DA Bn 6 DISCOM (6 DSMedB, 6 DSMaintB, 6 DSSB)
9th Division (combined arms)	10 SIB (3 SIR, 6 SIR, 188 SIR) 12 SIB (3 × NS SIR) 56 SAB (1 × NSF SAR, 2 × NS SAR incl. 432) 9 DIV ARTY HQ (1 × NSF SA, 2 × NSF SA) 9 DA Bn 9 DISCOM (9 DSMedB, 9 DSMaintB, 9 DSSB)
21st Division (supposedly 'AOR': actually RDF)	7 SIB (2 × NSF GDS, 1 × NS GDS) 13(?) SIB (3 × NS GDS) 15(?) SIB (3 × NS GDS) 21 DIV ARTY HQ (?) 18 DA Bn 21 DISCOM
25 DIV (AOR)	6(?) SIB, 11 SIB, 14(?) SIB, 17(?) SIB
32(?) DIV (mechanised or armoured)	4 SAB possibly earmarked
1st People's Defence Force Command	23, 24, 28, 30, 31 SIB (may not all be current)
2nd People's Defence Force Command	21, 22, 25, 26, 27, 29, 32 SIB (may not all be current)

Acronyms and abbreviations:
AOR = Army Operational Reserve
DA Bn = (Air) Defence Artillery Battalion
DISCOM = Divisional Support Command
DSMaintB = Direct Support Maintenance Battalion
DSMedB = Direct Support Medical Battalion
DSSB = Direct Support Supply Battalion
GDS = Guards Battalion
NSF = National Service Full-time (conscript)
NS = Operationally Ready National Service (reservist)
SA = Singapore Artillery battalion
SAB = Singapore Armoured Brigade
SAR = Singapore Armoured Regiment battalion
SIB = Singapore Infantry Brigade
SIR = Singapore Infantry Regiment battalion
? = designation not certain

The People's Defence Force (PDF)

The two PDF Commands are essentially second-line reservist light infantry divisions, composed largely of less fit and less well-educated NSmen together with other reservists who may not have served in combat units during their full-time National Service. PDF units were originally exclusively concerned with home defence, emphasising FIBUA, static defence of key points and coastal protection but, by the mid-1980s, their war role had been expanded to include route protection and counter-partisan duties on enemy territory.

In keeping with this role expansion, PDF nomenclature changed: in the early 1990s, the former 'PDF battalions' were designated as Singapore Infantry Regiment battalions, and the 'PDF Brigade Groups' became Singapore Infantry Brigades. During the 1990s, the two PDF Commands possibly controlled as many as 12 such brigades in total.

Non-divisional combat forces

The reorganisations of 1991 and 1995 left one armoured brigade, 4 SAB, outside the divisional structure, prompting speculation that it had been earmarked to form the core of a planned mechanised formation, sometimes referred to as 32nd Division.[9] However, if this division was indeed established during the 1990s, at the decade's end it remained under wraps.

Other non-divisional units include the Commando units, special forces trained in parachute and amphibious infiltration to allow reconnaissance and sabotage missions behind enemy lines.[10] The active 1st Commando Battalion is a large unit including as many as five companies, some of which comprise only regular personnel. A detachment is stationed on the disputed islet of Pedra Branca. Following their conscript service, Commando NSFs are fed into the 10th Commando Battalion. Because of the high fitness requirements, Commando NS involves only six years of ICT, but the training regime is intense and includes quarterly parachute jumps to maintain proficiency.[11]

The Commandos also have a counter-terrorist role, demonstrated in a highly professional manner when they stormed a hijacked Singapore Airlines aircraft in 1991, killing the four hijackers and rescuing all the passengers unharmed.[12] The Special Operations Force (SOF), an independent Commando unit responsible for this operation, was established in 1984, though its existence was not publicised until 1997.[13]

Army logistic and medical support

Close attention has been paid to developing the army's capability to provide combat support for its operational formations. As in the other services, computerised systems are used extensively to administer army logistics, ensuring the availability of supplies and maintenance for operational units.

Each front-line division, including 21st Division, includes a Divisional Support Command (DISCOM) consisting of supply, maintenance and medical battalions, respectively responsible for:

- providing petrol, oil and lubricants (POL), food, water, ammunition and essential equipment;
- recovery and repair of vehicles and equipment; and
- casualty evacuation and treatment.

On operations, these battalions are deployed in company strength in Brigade Support Areas.[14]

Second-line medical support is provided by three battalion-strength Combat Support Hospitals (formerly known as Field Hospitals), staffed by NSmen and volunteer doctors and nurses, and able to provide support for division-sized forces.[15] The General Support and Maintenance Battalion is tasked with providing depot-level support for SAF (in practice, mainly army) vehicles, in war as well as peace.[16]

In war, three Transport Battalions would operate the supply chain between the DISCOMs and the main logistics bases, namely:

- the General Supply Base (GSB, which subsumes the former General Equipment Base, POL Base and General Equipment Maintenance Unit);
- the Ordnance Supply Base (OSB) and its Sub-Bases throughout Singapore (which are responsible for storing and maintaining the army's weapons); and
- the Ammunition Base.

GSB and OSB were commercialised in 1993–94 as part of the drive to make more efficient use of SAF manpower, with the result that Chartered Materials and Services (a Singapore Technologies subsidiary) took over the storage and distribution of SAF equipment.[17] It can be assumed that the army, like the other services, would receive wholehearted support from Singapore Technologies in the event of crisis or war.

Following a series of studies since the early 1990s, in 1999 construction work started on a large-scale underground facility at Mandai in the centre of the island. When completed in 2003, this facility will store a 'significant proportion' of the SAF's ammunition, freeing 300 hectares of land currently used by the Ammunition Base for other purposes, while providing greater protection from enemy attack.[18]

ARMY EQUIPMENT

MINDEF's expenditure on army equipment has hardly been profligate. Many of the early major weapons systems (particularly armour and artillery) were purchased second-hand, subsequently upgraded and kept in service to the present day. A wide range of lesser items has been built under licence and, increasingly, locally developed equipment is answering the army's requirements. Equipment has been absorbed into service gradually and deliberately with the result that, since the late 1960s, the army's firepower and general capabilities have improved incrementally, though extremely significantly.

Infantry

As early as the mid-1960s, US-manufactured 5.56 mm M-16 rifles (also known as AR-15 Armalites) were purchased to replace the SIR's Belgian FN FAL 7.62 mm weapons. The new rifles were shorter, lighter and generally more suitable for use by the then mainly relatively slightly-built SAF soldiers.[19] In the late 1960s, Chartered Industries of Singapore (CIS) began producing the M-16S1 under licence, and the weapon has remained standard equipment for the Infantry, Guards, Armour and Commandos.

The locally produced SAR 80 and SR 88A, both Armalite developments, were taken into limited SAF service during the 1980s but were never adopted by front-line combat units. However, in the early 1990s the Combatman 2000 study (an element of Army 2000) defined a requirement for a New Generation Rifle: as a result in 1999 the radically new SAR 21, developed jointly by CIS, MINDEF's Defence Technology Group and the army, began at last to replace the M-16.[20] The new rifle features an in-built laser-aiming device and optical scope. Other innovations in the pipeline include body armour for every infantryman, while face/helmet-mounted displays may be introduced to enhance infantry command and control and situational awareness.[21] To increase its capability to fight a 24-hour battle, since the 1980s the army has also invested heavily in image-intensification devices for the infantry.[22]

Weapons in widespread use with infantry sections include the CIS Ultimax 100 5.56 mm light machine-gun (known as the Section Automatic Weapon (SAW) in SAF service), licence-built Armbrust 300 m-range light anti-tank weapons (known as the LAW or Crossbow in the SAF) and M203 40 mm grenade launchers. The Steyr SSG 69 was introduced in the late 1980s as a sniper weapon, replacing the Carl Gustav 63. In addition, by 2000, several specialised versions of the SAR 21 rifle, including light machine-gun, grenade launcher and 'Shap Shooter' variants, were about to enter service.[23]

Heavier locally produced support weapons include CIS 50MG 50 mm heavy machine-guns, FN MAG 7.62 mm general-purpose machine-guns, Israeli-designed Soltam 60 mm and 81 mm mortars and the locally developed CIS 40GL 40 mm grenade launcher. Larger, longer-range anti-tank weapons are the usually jeep-mounted Swedish-designed Carl Gustav 84 mm and M-40A1 106 mm recoilless guns (RCL). From 1990, infantry battalions also acquired two km-range Milan anti-tank missiles, which intially supplemented and then began to replace the 106 mm RCL.[24] In the late 1990s, four km-range Rafael NT-S Spike missiles were purchased from Israel to replace the 106 mm guns. MINDEF claimed that the technologically advanced Spike was effective even against explosive reactive armour.[25]

In 1997–98, the army purchased a first batch of Australian Defence Industries Flyer light strike and reconnaissance vehicles (LSVs) for use as platforms for anti-tank weapons (including Spike) and the 40 mm automatic grenade launcher. A second batch of LSVs, bringing the total procured to 79, was reportedly ordered in 1999 and it is expected they will become standard equipment for Guards and infantry units' support companies.[26]

Artillery

The Singapore Artillery was originally equipped with British 25-pounder guns inherited from the Singapore Volunteer Artillery on separation from Malaysia. By late 1966, plans had been formulated for the procurement of 120 mm mortars as well as 155 mm howitzers. The mortars came into service from 1971: 120 mm tubes were mounted on V-200 and later M113 armoured personnel carriers (APCs) to provide a self-propelled mortar battalion. Three types of 155 mm artillery came into service during the 1970s: 45 Israeli M-68s in 1971; approximately 20 refurbished, second-hand M-114s from the USA in 1976; and around 40 Israeli M-71s in 1979.[27] A dozen Soltam 160 mm heavy mortars were introduced in 1980.

The emphasis on 155 mm artillery continued during the 1980s and 1990s with the introduction of the locally developed FH-88 in 1989, the upgraded M-71S in 1993 and the FH 2000 (a longer-range, 52-calibre version of the FH-88) in the mid-1990s. By the end of the 1990s, more than 100 of these modern guns were in service, and the older M-68s and M-114s had been withdrawn from use. The early 1990s also saw procurement of the SAF's first 105 mm artillery in the form of 37 French Giat LG1 Mk1 light guns: these were deployed with the new 21st Division. Later deliveries of LG1s may have brought the total in service to at least 60.[28]

The artillery also uses a range of target acquisition equipment. The US-manufactured 15 km-range TPQ-36 locating radar was introduced in the early 1970s, supplemented from 1991 by the larger, 30 km-range TPQ-37.[29] Other key items include the Position Azimuth Determining System (a push-button surveying device) and a field artillery meteorological system.

Reports in the late 1980s indicated that the artillery was planning to acquire the devastatingly effective Multiple Launch Rocket System (MLRS) from the USA.[30] However, purchasing the MLRS would have introduced a dramatic new capability into the region and the proposal was, ultimately, shelved.

The artillery's next major procurement will involve a significant quantity of lightweight, airportable 155 mm guns, which may be produced under licence locally.[31] It is understood that in 1998 MINDEF selected the British-designed Vickers Ultralightweight Field Howitzer (the choice of the US Marine Corps the previous year), and that as many as 105 of these weapons may be purchased.

Armour

Beginning in 1969, the SAF acquired 200 French-built AMX-13 light tanks. These were Model 51s armed with a 75 mm gun and were supplied from surplus Israeli and Indian stocks; in the early 1980s France supplied an additional batch of 150 tanks.[32]

Most of the SAF's Armour formation might be more accurately described as mechanised infantry: most of its battalions, usually referred to as 'armoured battle groups', each include three times as many APCs as tanks. In 1968, MID ordered the Cadillac Gage Commando 4 × 4 wheeled APC, which was supplied in two main variants, the V-150 and V-200. The V-200, mounting a 90 mm gun, was developed especially for the SAF.[33] Initially equipping reconnaissance battalions, by the 1990s the 250 Commandos in service were mainly used as platforms for SAMs and by second-line units such as the PDF and the RSAF's field defence squadrons.

In 1974, the SAF also took delivery of its first M113 APCs, although no official mention of these was made until 1986, by which time 600 were in service.[34] Though most sources indicate that approximately 720 M113s were acquired, subsequent deliveries may have brought the total to more than 1000.[35] The majority of these APCs have been allocated to active and reservist armour battalions (most of which include 39 M113s alongside 12 AMX-13s), but others have been configured for use as mortar carriers, armoured engineer vehicles, command and control vehicles and ambulances.[36]

In 1975, the SAF purchased 63 British-built Centurion Mk3 and Mk7 main battle tanks (MBTs) from India.[37] These were later supplemented by a second batch acquired from Israel in 1993–94, bringing the total to at least 80 and possibly as many as 100. Singapore's Centurions have all been modernised, with Israeli assistance, to the standard of the Israeli Defence Force's Upgraded Centurion, featuring new main guns, diesel engines and—probably—reactive armour. These modernised Centurions are known as Tempests in SAF service. Although some were used for training in Taiwan, most are stored in Singapore, ready for operational use if necessary. In the mid-1990s, Centurions were withdrawn from Taiwan, but six were deployed to Brunei.[38] Apparently for fear of provoking controversy with Singapore's neighbours, Mindef has never admitted that the SAF operates MBTs.

It was reported during the 1980s that the SAF also kept a small number of M-60 MBTs, acquired second-hand from the US Army, in Taiwan. Moreover, some sources indicated that 'large numbers' of these heavy tanks were stored underground in Singapore.[39] These reports may have confused the M-60 with the Centurions. Nevertheless, in 1992 it was reported that the SAF was evaluating the M-60A3, with a view to acquiring a small number from US Army surplus stocks to replace the Centurions.[40] However, quite apart from concerns over the possible reaction of Singapore's neighbours to such a purchase, continuing doubts regarding the suitability of the regional terrain and infrastructure (especially bridges) to sustain MBT operations apparently prevented this purchase from proceeding. The Cadillac Gage Stingray, a much lighter tank, was also evaluated.[41]

During the 1980s and 1990s, upgrade programmes improved the operational effectiveness of the AMX-13s and 300 of the M113s, while extending their service life. The modernised AMX-13SM1 began to enter service in 1988, followed by the M113 Ultra from 1998. The M113 upgrade was particularly significant, in that the Ultra's firepower was significantly improved over that of the basic APC. Two variants have been produced: the OWS (overhead weapon system) Ultra with a 25 mm Bushmaster cannon, and the 40/50 Ultra with a 40 mm automatic grenade launcher and 0.5 inch heavy machine gun.[42]

In the early 1990s, the SAF acquired additional tracked armoured vehicles in the form of 22 AMX-10P mechanised infantry fighting vehicles and 22 AMX-10PAC90 fire support and tank-destroyer vehicles. The SAF has referred to the latter, armed with 90 mm guns, as 'multi-mission tanks'. These French-built amphibious vehicles were all allocated to 46 SAR as part of the new 21st Division. Reports in the early 1990s indicated that the SAF had also purchased AMX-10RC 6 × 6 wheeled armoured reconnaissance vehicles as well as additional AMX-10Ps and PAC90s, but these have remained unconfirmed. At the very least, it seems likely that a small number of AMX-10RCs were acquired for evaluation alongside the PAC90 and the Swedish Hägglunds CV90. The army also tested less heavily armed reconnaissance vehicles such as the tracked Wiesel and the Panhard VBL.[43]

By the mid-1990s, however, it was clear that MINDEF intended the SAF to rely increasingly on local industry to supply its armour requirements. This trend was first evident in the AMX-13 and M113 upgrade programmes and was confirmed in 1997 when the SAF unveiled a locally designed and built tracked infantry fighting vehicle (IFV), developed secretly since 1989. This vehicle has been produced in two versions—the Bionix 25 and the Bionix 40/50—their armament similar to the two variants of the M113 Ultra. By mid-1999 the Bionix was fully operational in an active armour unit, 42 SAR, which deployed 40 of the 40/50 variant alongside 13 Ultras and 12 AMX-13s. Between 300 and 500 Bionix vehicles will be produced in total, replacing those M113s not upgraded to Ultra standard. Bionix variants such as armoured recovery and command post vehicles may be produced.[44]

It was reported in 1997 that the SAF's future tank options had been narrowed down to a requirement for a light tank with a 105 mm gun. It seemed possible that the new tank, intended to replace the venerable AMX-13SM1s, would be built locally using the automotive components or even the chassis of the Bionix.[45]

Combat Engineers

Because of the likelihood of Singapore's army being involved in operations across the Johor Straits and rivers in southern peninsular Malaysia in the event of war, the Singapore Combat Engineers possess a considerable inventory of water-crossing equipment: tactical floating bridges, rafts and ferries, line of communication bridges, and locally-made assault boats. There are also self-propelled tactical bridges (the German-manufactured 26-metre MAN GHH Leguan, introduced in the early 1990s) together with a dozen US-supplied M-60 AVLB armoured bridge-layers. In early 2000, MINDEF ordered an unspecified number of self-propelled German-made Eurobridge systems.[46]

Since 1972, the Combat Engineers have operated a small number of M-728 combat engineering vehicles, specialised variants of the M-60 MBT fitted with a dozer blade and a 165 mm demolition gun. During the 1990s, the addition of 36 Royal Ordnance FV180S Combat Engineer Tractors (CETs) supplied from the UK improved the capability of armoured engineering units dramatically. Importantly, the CET is relatively light and easily deployable.

Field engineering units use specialised M113 variants both for the mechanical laying of bar-mines during the construction of anti-tank obstacles and as mine-ploughs. Equipment used for breaching enemy minefields includes Bangalore torpedoes and the Viper mine clearance system. Explosive ordnance disposal devices include the Mark 8 Plus Wheel Barrow, a remotely-controlled robot.

Logistic vehicles

The army uses a wide range of unarmoured 'B' class vehicles, mostly of European origin, in logistic and support roles. The earliest trucks acquired by the SAF in the 1960s and 1970s were Bedford R-type 3-tonners and Mercedes-Benz 911 series. Later purchases included Mercedes-Benz Unimog series trucks, IVECO 2.5-ton and 5-ton vehicles (some with self-loading cranes), and MAN 4 × 4 (6-ton) and 6 × 6 (10-ton) prime movers. The MAN vehicles' roles include towing 155 mm artillery. Land Rover variants—particularly the Defender 110—predominate among the SAF's light vehicles and are used mainly for command and communications duties. Mercedes 230G field cars are used in a similar role and for reconnaissance.[47] A variety of Japanese-built vehicles, including Hino 6 × 6 trucks, and Daihatsu and Mitsubishi jeeps, is also in service. In 1993–94, the army received 300 Swedish-built Hägglunds Bv 206 tracked all-terrain vehicles (ATVs) in four versions: troop transport, cargo, tankers for POL or water, and signals. These unarmoured ATVs will probably be supplemented by substantial numbers of locally developed armoured All-Terrain Tracked Carriers.[48]

TRAINING FOR OPERATIONAL READINESS

Much of the responsibility for training army personnel and developing doctrine lies with the headquarters of 'formations', as the army calls its specialist corps, the more important of which are led by Senior Specialist Staff Officers (SSSOs). There are SSSOs for the Infantry, Guards, Armour, Artillery, Signal, Commando, Supply & Transport and Maintenance & Engineering formations (see Figure 5.1). Each of these formations maintains its own vocational school for training recruits, as well as a training centre for managing the ICT training of recalled NS units; the two PDF Commands maintain their own training centres for this purpose. Each formation is also responsible for developing and reviewing unit-level tactics and doctrine in its own specialist area, as well as improving operational capability through continuously reviewing unit-level organisation, weapons and equipment.

The Chief Infantry Officer and his HQ have a particularly large training task, which is divided between the following units:

- the Basic Military Training Centre (provides BMT for infantry and Guards recruits);
- the School of Infantry Specialists (trains infantry and Guards NCOs);
- the SAF Warrant Officers' School (trains senior NCOs for the SAF as a whole);
- the School of Infantry Weapons (provides training on infantry support weapons);
- the Infantry Training Centre (trains infantry and Guards NS units during their 'high-key' ICT sessions up to the seventh year of the 13-year NS training cycle); and
- the Basic Combat Training Centre (provides two-day annual refresher training in basic military skills for infantry, Guards, PDF and armour NSmen prior to their ICT).[49]

NSF unit training and evaluation

Conscript units (usually battalions, but companies in the case of formations with a relatively small number of active units such as the Combat Engineers) work through a two-year training programme. In general, BMT is followed by three months of particular-to-formation vocational training aimed at establishing company-level operational proficiency. For example, infantry and Guards NSF training includes building proficiency in FIBUA and jungle operations. The next stage involves battalion-level training and emphasises a combined arms context. This includes brigade-scale exercises, which mainly take place overseas. Exercises may involve joint-service cooperation: this is particularly true for Guards units, which work with the navy in amphibious 'coastal hook' operations, and with air force helicopters in Ex Pegasus.[50] Unit training during the 1990s stressed development of 'round-the-clock' capabilities, in some cases involving non-stop 72-hour exercises.

The Army Training Evaluation Centre (ATEC) provides quality control for NSF training. Initially established in 1990 as the Battalion Training Evaluation Centre (BTEC), with responsibility for impartially gauging the proficiency of infantry and Guards units, in 1993 its title was changed and its remit expanded to include armour and Commando units. At the same time, it transferred from the control of HQ Infantry to Training and Doctrine Command (TRADOC). ATEC assesses units on their overall physical fitness, tactics and coordination, collection and use of intelligence and competence at casualty evacuation. Having originally drawn an 'opposition force' for evaluation exercises from the unit being evaluated, from 1995 ATEC deployed its own Aggressor Company to add realism.[51] The Aggressor Company, a Guards-trained NSF unit, is trained in 'enemy' tactics: in order not to cause offence to Singapore's immediate neighbours its doctrine, equipment and uniforms are based to some extent on those of the Asian communist states' armed forces. For example, the unit's standard weapon is the AK-47 assault rifle. Artillery units are assessed under the longer-established Field Artillery Training Evaluation Programme (FATEP), which is conducted at battery, battalion and divisional artillery levels.[52]

An annual SAF-wide competition, with awards for the Best Unit in each arm of service, provides a further spur to attain high levels of operational readiness and assesses each unit's combat proficiency. The competition, introduced in 1969, assesses units on their overall combat proficiency, marksmanship, physical fitness, security, manpower management, logistics readiness, vehicle state and training safety.[53]

Following battalion-level evaluation by ATEC or FATEP, NSF units are assigned a readiness condition (REACON). Unit commanders naturally seek the highest status, REDCON-1, but how many achieve this is—understandably—a closely guarded secret. Towards the end of their biennial schedule REDCON-1 NSF units take their turn on Stand-by Duty, forming part of Singapore's first-line defences. NSF units (particularly from the infantry, Guards and armour) achieving high readiness status are often deployed for bilateral or multilateral exercises with the armed forces of Singapore's defence cooperation partners, such as other ASEAN members, FPDA powers and the United States.

NS unit training

On completing their period of full-time conscription ('achieving Operational Readiness' in SAF parlance), NSFs commence their 13-year NS training cycle, usually as part of the same 'mono-intake' unit to which they have belonged for the past two years. The NS training cycle includes nine high-key years, when whole units are recalled for training in three phases: (1) a commanders' training phase; (2) a functional training phase; and (3) a tactical training phase. During the tactical phase, NS units go through similar exercises to their active equivalents, with which they often train jointly.

During the 1990s, MINDEF made considerable efforts to increase the effectiveness of training for NS units by emphasising mission-oriented exercises, and exploiting overseas training opportunities and new training technologies.[54] As a result, the operational readiness of NS combat units—which is assessed regularly by ATEC or FATEP and in Best Unit competitions—is on a par with active units, according to MINDEF.[55] Fresh NS units may indeed be as proficient as newly trained NSF battalions and are increasingly assigned to Stand-by Duty during their ICT. Anecdotal evidence, though, suggests that the effectiveness of NS units often declines significantly several years after their ORD.

Training constraints and solutions

Singapore's army faces a fundamental obstacle in attempting to conduct training and exercises of the scale and intensity necessary for its operational effectiveness: since independence, expanding residential and industrial demands on Singapore's limited land supply have impinged on the SAF's valuable training areas. In 1967, 178 sq km were designated as manoeuvring areas; by 1991 only 23 sq km of this land remained.[56] In 1995, the army anticipated that by 2000 it would have lost roughly 50 per cent of its existing training areas in Singapore.[57]

A partial solution to this problem has been the large-scale relocation of army training and exercises overseas. The most important overseas locations, all still used intensively by both active and NS units, have been Taiwan, Brunei, Thailand and, in more recent years, Australia.[58] New training possibilities in New Zealand and South Africa were also opened up in the late 1990s. Imaginative use has also been made of 'non-traditional' areas of Singapore for training: for example, infantry units have used empty government housing blocks for FIBUA exercises and train in coastal defence on Pulau Sudong, an unpopulated island to Singapore's south, close to an air force weapons range.[59] Another innovative move has been to exploit reclaimed land: in 1997 it was announced that most army manoeuvre training in Singapore would be concentrated on new plots off Singapore's present east coast, adjoining Changi, Pulau Tekong and Pulau Ubin. By 2010 reclamation will double the area of Pulau Tekong, which will become a 'training paradise'. However, the SAF will retain its live firing areas on the west coast.[60]

At the same time, technology has partially compensated for training space restrictions in Singapore. Since the late 1980s, indoor electronic shooting ranges have allowed the use of infantry weapons against simulated targets. Simulators are also used to train anti-tank missile operators, as well as tank and artillery crews.[61] The Multiple Integrated Laser Engagement System (MILES) is used to simulate the effects of direct-fire weapons in field exercises.[62] In 1997, plans were revealed to improve MILES and integrate it with a 'battlefield instrumentation' system under which the movement of individual soldiers will be monitored using global positioning systems. Increased numbers of more sophisticated marksmanship simulators will also be acquired.[63]

Since 1998, the locally developed Simulation System for Land Battle (SIMLAB) has allowed commanders and their staff officers (up to 120 personnel at a time) to conduct computerised wargameing exercises up to divisional scale. Compared with earlier wargames, SIMLAB adds realism and challenge to command post exercises by taking into account logistical factors, such as ammunition inventories, and physical conditions such as fatigue. All aspects of exercises can be recorded, played back and assessed.[64]

Mobilisation procedure

While all three services rely on the mobilisation of NSmen to reach their full operational strength, the army depends on reservists to a far greater extent than the air force and navy. NS units make up the great bulk of the army's combat strength, and include approximately 60 infantry (including Guards), 12 artillery, eight armour, eight engineer and one Commando battalions, as well as signals, logistic and medical units. Most NS unit commanders, many brigade staff officers and even some brigade commanders are reservist officers.

Given Singapore's geo-strategic vulnerability and the SAF's resultant doctrinal stress on offensive operations, the ability to mobilise, arm and deploy the NS order of battle rapidly is essential. Having studied and adapted Israeli, Swedish and Swiss procedures, the SAF uses two types of mobilisation: silent and open. Silent mobilisation is executed discreetly, nowadays mainly through telephone and pager calls which have supplemented the previous laborious system, prevalent until the mid-1980s, which relied largely on physical delivery of mobilisation notices to reservists' homes. Before telecommunications were used for silent mobilisation, the process could take up to 24 hours, followed by another six hours to issue weapons and other equipment: far too long if potential aggressors were to be persuaded that the SAF was combat-ready.[65] The much more rapid open mobilisation system disseminates the codenames of mobilised units through radio and television broadcasts and even through messages on cinema screens. MINDEF has staged between three and six open mobilisations annually since the mid-1980s, usually without advance warning.

As authorised under the 1985 *Defence Requisition Act*, some mobilisation exercises have involved the call-up of civil resources (particularly vehicles, civil engineering equipment, vessels and light aircraft), as well as units from all three services.[66] Separate civil resource mobilisations are also held. Emergency Transportation Exercises have rehearsed the conservation of national fuel resources through rationing. Other exercises have involved water rationing for the general population.

As well as testing operational readiness, mobilisation exercises are used to communicate a deterrent message to Singapore's neighbours. They have sometimes manifestly constituted pointed responses to specific unsettling regional developments—such as the joint Indonesian–Malaysian exercise in Johor in August 1991. At the same time, they bring home to Singapore's wider population the potential need for a rapid transition to a war footing. Efforts are made to involve the families and employers of NSmen in open mobilisation exercises.

Mobilisation exercises have been used to call up whole brigades and even divisions to pre-arranged reporting centres. Having reported for duty, some NSmen are sent home; others, though, are issued with personal weapons and, on occasion, major equipment is brought out of storage. Major equipment, including armoured vehicles, is kept under protective coverings and shelters, ready for immediate use: one important depot is the massive Nee Soon Driclad Centre, which stores vehicles for 6th Division.[67] Since 1983, mobilisation exercises and ICT sessions have often been combined, with recalled NS units being sent straight into field exercises.

In 1985, the SAF claimed that 'more than 97 per cent' of reservists were reporting for duty within six hours of no-notice open mobilisation calls.[68] Legislation in 1989 reduced reservists' mandatory response time from 12 to six hours.[69] In the late 1980s and early 1990s, the use of modern telecommunications technology and improvements in public transport—especially the inauguration in 1989 of the Mass Rapid Transport System, which has stations close to a number of major army camps—helped to accelerate silent as well as open recalls. Partly to speed up mobilisation by simplifying its logistical aspects, in 1994 MINDEF decided to allow NSmen to keep personal equipment items such as helmets, webbing, water bottles and mess tins at home.[70] In 1995, it was reported that more than 90 per cent of 5000 NSmen recalled in a silent mobilisation exercise had responded within six hours.[71] Official claims that 'at the press of a button, we can field an SAF of over a quarter of a million men' and that the SAF could deploy three battle-ready divisions 'within hours' of mobilisation are probably not exaggerations.[72]

CONCLUSION

During the 1990s, fundamental reorganisation and significant reequipment under the Army 2000 modernisation programme helped Singapore's army to develop its combined arms capabilities while simultaneously establishing a rapid deployment force, despite the shortage of NSF personnel.

Compared with the air force and navy, the army has been less favoured in terms of equipment procurement, but it nevertheless benefited from a variety of programmes intended to enhance firepower and mobility. The most important of these procurement programmes included upgrading existing armoured vehicles, acquiring limited numbers of new AFVs and a substantial infusion of new artillery. What is known of the army's C⁴I systems suggests that they were substantially modernised during the 1990s and are highly effective as a result. Mobilisation and logistic support systems have been refined.

However, the most important change in the army during the 1990s was probably the upgrading of training at all levels, particularly the emphasis on training NSF units for a 24-hour, combined-arms battle and the increased stress on maintaining NS units' operational readiness after their ORD, reflecting their thoroughgoing integration into front-line divisions. Quality control mechanisms for unit operational readiness—notably ATEC and FATEP—have assumed a much greater prominence. More effective overseas training and increased use of simulators have probably more than compensated for the loss of domestic training areas.

The Army 21 development programme will see further development of the army's capabilities during the first decade of the new century. The nature of Singapore's geopolitical predicament suggests that the main emphasis is likely to remain on developing relatively light forces which can be deployed easily and quickly. Equipment procurement is likely to include acquisition of light-weight 155 mm artillery and new light tanks. MINDEF is also likely to prioritise the continued enhancement of the army's C⁴I capabilities.

In the final analysis, it must be remembered that Singapore's army will remain a citizen force, dependent for its personnel on essentially acquiescent rather than enthusiastic conscripts and reservists. However well it is organised, equipped, trained and led, it will probably continue to suffer from the weaknesses inherent in such an army.

6

The Republic of Singapore Air Force (RSAF)

The army has remained the SAF's senior service in terms of numbers of personnel and senior officers, but during the 1990s the RSAF's central role in Singapore's defence was reflected in a series of extremely expensive procurement programmes and the appointment of an air force officer as CDF in 1995.

Although RSAF doctrine emphasises air power's centrality in Singapore's overall military deterrent, public statements naturally avoid mentioning its potential role in pre-emptive operations. Instead, the air force's status as the 'first line of defence' against threats to Singapore is emphasised, together with its air defence role exercised through a multi-layered 'shield' consisting of various types of radar (including AEW), interceptor aircraft, SAMs and anti-aircraft guns. Air power is also seen as playing a key role in supporting surface forces, through interdiction (targeting hostile forces' infrastructure and supply lines), tactical strike and reconnaissance, the provision of air mobility for the army and maritime reconnaissance for the navy. Ancillary roles include search and rescue and emergency relief operations in the event of civilian disasters.[1]

Particularly in light of the limited resources at the RSAF's disposal, it is understandable that senior RSAF officers are sceptical of the notion, advanced by some western strategists during the 1990s, that air power can win conflicts on its own: they emphasise instead close integration with the other services. However, during the 1990s the RSAF has become a more assertive partner in joint operations, attempting to anticipate rather than merely react to the requirements of the army and the navy by providing these services with 'plans and options' for the use of air power.[2]

Figure 6.1 Republic of Singapore Air Force organisation, 2000

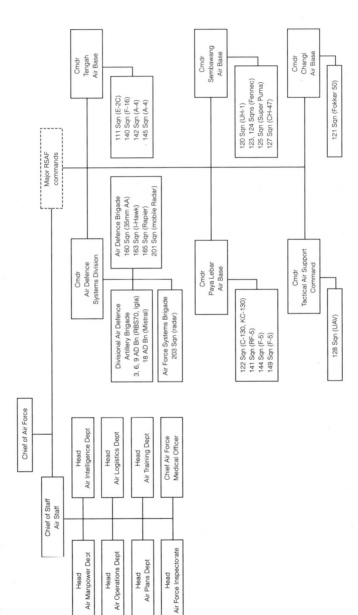

CAPABILITY ENHANCEMENTS DURING THE 1990S— AND BEYOND

During the 1990s, MINDEF made continual efforts to enhance the RSAF's capabilities in almost every operational area with the aim of maintaining and, if possible, enhancing the RSAF's technological edge over its potential adversaries.

Air defence, strike and surveillance

In 1990, the RSAF deployed seven squadrons of combat aircraft: one with F-16A/Bs (operating as a dual-role air defence and strike unit), two with F-5E/Fs (primarily in an air defence role but with secondary ground-attack capability), three with A-4SU/TA-4SU Super Skyhawks (in the strike role) and one with the remaining operational Hunters (tasked with lead-in fighter training as well as ground attack and reconnaissance). There was also one squadron with E-2C Hawkeye AEW and control platforms and another operating Scout unmanned aerial vehicles (UAVs), conducting tactical reconnaissance in close coordination with army units. With a strength of approximately 135 fighter, strike and reconnaissance aircraft, the RSAF deployed more combat aircraft than its Indonesian and Malaysian counterparts combined. This outline order of battle did not change fundamentally during the 1990s: Figure 6.1 shows the RSAF's structure in 2000. However, over the course of the decade there were extremely important developments in the RSAF's capability.

The Hunters were retired in 1993, and were replaced in 141 Squadron the following year by eight RF-5E reconnaissance aircraft, locally converted from F-5E fighters.[3] By this time, an upgrade programme for the whole F-5E/F fleet, contracted to Singapore Technologies Aerospace (STAero) in 1991, was under way. This programme, which involved significant assistance with systems integration from the Israeli Elbit company, principally involved installing a more effective radar (the FIAR Grifo F) and an up-to-date navigation/attack system in 40 F-5E/Fs (including seven extra aircraft purchased from Jordan) and was intended to result in significantly improved interception capability. In addition, the RF-5Es (which lacked radar) received the new avionics. The F-5 upgrade programme may also have involved modifications to allow the aircraft to be armed with the Israeli Python 4 short-range AAM in place of the earlier Sidewinders (and, reportedly, Python 3s).[4] Although initially intended for completion in

1996, serious problems in fitting the new radar caused delays and the programme was not completed until early 1999, with all three F-5 squadrons operational with the upgraded aircraft by April that year. The modified aircraft are expected to remain in service for a further 10 to 15 years.[5]

Even more important developments resulted from a decision to expand the F-16 force. The RSAF's interest in eventually procuring as many as 30 to 36 aircraft in the F-16 or F-18 class had been reported as early as 1984 and the original 1985 order for eight F-16s included an option to buy 12 more. However, the government's reluctance to offend Singapore's neighbours unnecessarily, combined with the feasibility of upgrade programmes for existing combat aircraft and budgetary restrictions, deferred a firm decision on additional purchases until the early 1990s.

In 1992, it was reported that long-term RSAF plans still envisaged a larger F-16 force of as many as 40 aircraft. But at this stage, only two F-16A/Bs were ordered as attrition replacements. Nine more aircraft were leased from the US Air Force for training purposes in the United States.[6] After some uncertainty over whether to purchase F-16C/Ds (which feature more powerful engines as well as a longer-range radar and enhanced strike capability) or the even more capable but considerably more expensive F/A-18s, culminating in a 'fly-off' evaluation of both types, in 1994 MINDEF announced the purchase of eight F-16Cs and ten two-seat F-16Ds. Further F-16C/Ds were ordered to equip Singapore's long-term training programmes in the United States. In 1996, the RSAF leased 12 F-16C/Ds from the US Air Force for use at Luke Air Force Base, but these were replaced in mid-1998 by a dozen aircraft leased from the manufacturer, Lockheed Martin, with an option to buy at a later date. In 1997 another 12 F-16C/Ds were purchased, to be based at Cannon Air Force Base from late 1998.[7]

Singapore's CDF did not exaggerate when he claimed in 1998 that the acquisition of F-16C/Ds marked a 'quantum leap' in the RSAF's capability.[8] The new F-16 package included AIM-7M radar-guided AAMs, giving RSAF fighters a beyond-visual-range engagement capability for the first time.[9] They may also be armed with Python 4 missiles. Following Malaysia's reported introduction of the Russian-supplied long-range R-77 missile for its MiG-29s in 1999 it seemed likely that the US government would soon allow Singapore to purchase the roughly equivalent AIM-120 AMRAAM for its F-16s.[10]

In the strike role, the F-16C/Ds can—like earlier RSAF combat aircraft—carry Maverick air-to-surface missiles (both the AGM-65E and the TV-guided AGM-65B for anti-ship strike), cluster bombs and Paveway laser-guided bombs. However, the new F-16s were also equipped with Sharpshooter navigation and targeting pods, enabling them to execute long-range precision strike missions and to 'self-designate' targets during day or night and in all weather conditions.[11] It was also reported that the ten F-16Ds had received special modifications on the production line, involving the installation of Israeli-supplied electronic countermeasures equipment. This may indicate that the new two-seat F-16s are specially equipped for missions to suppress enemy air defences.[12] By early 1999, eighteen F-16C/Ds had been delivered to 140 Squadron in Singapore. They joined the seven remaining F-16A/Bs, all of which were scheduled to have received a structural life extension upgrade by the year's end.[13]

Beginning in 1993–94, the RSAF began investigating a range of alternative new combat aircraft, with the probable intention of signing a contract around 2001 to enable the selected type to enter service from 2005. In 1998, Singapore's Chief of Air Force revealed that the RSAF would initially seek to replace its A-4s, which still provided the bulk of the strike force. In July 2000, it was announced that another 20 F-16C/Ds would be ordered to replace one squadron of A-4s as soon as 2003–4.[14] From around 2010, additional aircraft will be required to replace the F-5s. It is intended eventually to minimise the RSAF's logistical burden by reducing the number of different types of basic combat aircraft from three to two. Possibilities include the Eurofighter Typhoon, the Dassault Rafale, or options from the United States (the Block 60 version of the F-16, or the F-15E Strike Eagle) and even Russia (the Su-30). The promise of training facilities outside Singapore could be an important influence on the final choice: in the case of Eurofighter, this could involve the RSAF expanding its training in Australia.[15]

Concern over the dangers of over-dependence on a single source of equipment may bias the RSAF's selection of a new combat aircraft against choosing another US product: during the 1980s and 1990s, Washington's restrictions on the transfer of advanced defence technology (for example, F-16 software source codes in 1993–94) had sometimes irked Singapore. Nevertheless, in 1999 Singapore joined the 'concept demonstration phase' of the US-led Joint Strike Fighter (JSF) programme as an observer, the RSAF seeing the JSF as a potential long-term successor to its F-16s.[16]

Though the RSAF has not admitted to acquiring heavier or longer-range air-to-ground weapons to arm its strike aircraft, its dependence on a small number of expensive platforms and aircrew suggests that it could usefully employ a stand-off weapon such as the US-manufactured (but originally Israeli-developed) AGM-142 Popeye missile.[17] While the United States would be reluctant to introduce this class of weapon into Southeast Asia, Singapore could acquire Popeye or similar missiles from Israel.

The RSAF has also become increasingly interested in unmanned aerial vehicle (UAV) technology as a possible solution for some of its future requirements, envisaging the use of remotely piloted vehicles as manpower-efficient force multipliers which could not only increase the surveillance range of army units or naval vessels, but eventually also operate in tandem with manned aircraft in the strike role.[18] During the mid-1990s, Singapore purchased about 40 Searcher Mk2 UAVs from Israel Aircraft Industries to replace the Scout UAVs acquired from the same source during the 1980s. Following serious performance deficiencies which prevented deployment of the Searchers with the RSAF's UAV unit, 128 Squadron, until 1997, in December of that year MINDEF launched a new procurement programme involving smaller, simpler and cheaper UAVs.[19] Singapore Technologies has purchased Israeli technology to allow it to produce the lightweight Blue Horizon UAV, which is equipped with a thermal imaging sensor and could fill the RSAF requirement. It is also developing a high-altitude, high-speed reconnaissance UAV known as Firefly, which could be of interest to the RSAF—and possibly also the navy—in the longer-term.[20]

The RSAF's increasing involvement in joint-service operations was also evident in the expansion of its maritime reconnaissance role during the 1990s. As well as providing AEW and controlling both air defence and strike aircraft, 111 Squadron's E-2Cs conducted maritime surveillance and provided over-the-horizon targeting for the RSN's Harpoon anti-ship missiles. However, apart from short-range Skyvans, there were no dedicated maritime patrol aircraft.[21] In 1991, MINDEF ordered five Fokker 50 Maritime Enforcer Mk2S aircraft, which were fitted with a custom-made systems configuration and delivered in 1994–95 to 121 Squadron. In a unique arrangement, the Enforcers (known by the SAF as 'MPAs') are flown by RSAF pilots, but owned by the RSN, which provides operators for their surveillance and combat systems. Capable of flying 10-hour maritime surveillance patrols, the MPAs can be armed with air-to-surface Harpoon missiles, lightweight torpedoes and mines. However, their ASW capability is reportedly weak.[22] The MPAs can also be used for gathering SIGINT.[23]

In the late 1990s, the computing and software systems of the E-2Cs were upgraded locally to permit them to exchange tactical data with RSAF interceptor aircraft. In the longer-term, MINDEF may be interested in acquiring a more advanced and capable AEW platform such as the Boeing 737 AEW and Control Aircraft.[24]

Support aircraft

At the start of the 1990s, two RSAF squadrons were equipped with fixed-wing support aircraft: one with six Skyvans for light transport and maritime patrol, and one with five C-130 and five KC-130 Hercules for tactical and long-range transport and in-flight refuelling.

The most significant development in the RSAF's fixed-wing support force over the decade involved the acquisition of four modernised ex-US Air Force KC-135R tanker aircraft, following a contract signed in 1997. The KC-135s are intended particularly to support the RSAF's F-16s, which cannot be refuelled from the KC-130s in service since the 1980s: the new tankers will be equipped with both hose-reel pods (for refuelling A-4s and F-5s) and a 'flying boom' system (for the F-16s). Though the KC-135s' airframes date from the early 1960s, they will be re-engined before delivery to the RSAF; subsequently Singapore Technologies will install new digital avionics. The primary declared peacetime role of the KC-135s will be to service the SAF's diverse overseas training detachments and exercises by moving personnel and equipment as well as refuelling other aircraft, but their operational role clearly will be to extend the range of Singapore's combat aircraft. As MINDEF says, the acquisition of these aircraft marks 'a substantial leap' in the air force's capability. The first KC-135 is due for delivery to Singapore during 2000; two aircraft will be kept in the United States for training, but four additional aircraft may be purchased to boost the Singapore-based tanker fleet.[25]

The KC-135Rs are scheduled to 'replace' the four KC-130Bs, but these ageing Hercules may be kept in service as transports. If it is decided to retire the KC-130Bs, it is possible that new C-130Js will be purchased to maintain the size of the tactical transport force. In the meantime, at least one C-130 has been converted for SIGINT duties.[26]

While the Fokker 50 MPAs took over the Skyvans' maritime surveillance role in the mid-1990s, four utility versions of the Fokker 50 were delivered to 121 Squadron in 1994 to fill the light transport niche. These aircraft have been modified to provide endurance of up to 12 hours, allowing long-distance navigation training flights.[27]

Helicopters

In the early 1990s, the RSAF included three helicopter squadrons: one with UH-1Hs (tactical transport), one with AS350Bs (training and light observation) and one with Super Pumas (tactical transport and search and rescue (SAR)). Since then, the RSAF's helicopter force has expanded considerably and has taken on new roles. In the first place, 12 Cougars and 20 AS550 Fennecs were purchased from France in 1991–92. The Cougars (essentially Super Pumas equipped with emergency flotation gear) were allocated to 126 Squadron, which also absorbed four SAR-equipped Super Pumas from 125 Squadron. 123 and 124 Squadrons were equipped with the AS550A2 and C2 versions of the Fennec, respectively. The AS550A2s, armed with cannon and unguided rockets, are used for reconnaissance and training, replaced the AS350Bs; the AS550C2s are used in an anti-armour role with TOW-2A missiles.[28] Although the UH-1Hs had previously been fitted with door-mounted heavy machine-guns and rocket pods, the Fennecs were Singapore's first dedicated armed helicopters.

In the late 1990s, the RSAF gained a heavy-lift helicopter capability. Six CH-47D Chinooks ordered in 1994 were, according to official statements, intended for the SAR role on behalf of the local Civil Aviation Authority and to support SAF training detachments overseas. However, it was widely anticipated that this was only the first instalment of a larger order for Chinooks (which might eventually total more than 20), to be used primarily to support the army's rapid deployment force. In 1997, MINDEF ordered another six Chinooks, this time the modernised, longer-range CH-47SD version. In June 1999, it was reported that a third order, for four CH-47SDs, would soon be placed.[29] By that time, 127 Squadron had been formed in Singapore with the first three CH-47Ds delivered from the United States. However, the US-based 'Peace Prairie' training detachment was scheduled to continue on a long-term basis using helicopters leased from the manufacturer.[30]

After the RSAF had evaluated several other types of attack helicopter (particularly the Eurocopter Tiger), in March 1999 Defence Minister Tony Tan announced that eight AH-64D Apaches would be ordered. The order included 216 Hellfire 2 laser-guided anti-armour missiles as well as large numbers of Hydra-70 unguided rockets. Following protracted negotiations with Washington, in February 2000 Singapore was allowed to purchase the highly sophisticated and capable Longbow fire control radar as part of the RSAF Apaches' equipment, enabling them to designate their own targets for attack with the latest 'fire and forget' version of Hellfire. A second batch of 12 AH-64Ds may be ordered, with eventual total procurement totalling as many as 30.[31]

The RSAF's helicopters work closely with the other two services. In operational circumstances, UH-1Hs and possibly other types would be attached to army divisions. There is a particularly close link with the airmobile brigade which forms part of the army's rapid deployment 21st Division. Indeed, an 'affiliation programme' between helicopter squadrons and active Guards units was set up as early as 1986.[32] Super Pumas have provided logistic support for naval operations and, by the mid-1990s, the RSN and RSAF were considering deploying helicopters equipped for anti-submarine and anti-surface vessel roles on planned larger naval vessels. The experimental fitting of dipping sonar to a Super Puma was reported, and at one stage it seemed that MINDEF was about to order six such systems.[33] At the end of the decade, though, the RSN's requirement for six to 12 naval helicopters was still outstanding and, in an apparent effort to maximise logistical cost-efficiency, was being linked to the replacement of the RSAF's UH-1H utility helicopters.[34] This suggests the probable choice of a type such as the Sikorsky S-70, which is available in both army and naval versions.

Air defence missiles, guns and radar

In 1990, the Singapore Air Defence Artillery (SADA) deployed seven units, including three tactical air defence battalions (3, 6 and 9 SADA, of which only the first was an active unit) equipped with RBS-70 SAMs and 20 mm Oerlikon AA guns mounted on V-200 armoured vehicles under the army's operational control. There were also four squadrons for national air defence: one with towed 35 mm Oerlikon GDF AA guns, one with two batteries (totalling 16 three-missile launchers) of Improved-Hawk (I-Hawk) SAM, one with Rapier SAM and one with 32 Bloodhound II SAM. Together with the long-range radars (the ITT RS320 mobile system and the military element of the Singapore Air Traffic Control Centre, operated by 201 and 203 Squadrons respectively) and C[3] systems, the AEW aircraft and the interceptor squadrons, these missile and

AA gun units—all of which included their own search radars (such as Blindfire radars in support of the Rapiers)—formed a layered air defence system. The Bloodhounds (with a range of up to 140 km) and I-Hawks (40 km) provided long-range coverage, the 7 km-range Rapiers and 35 mm guns protected air bases against fast, low-flying aircraft, and the low-level, 5 km-range RBS-70s and 20 mm guns were deployed with army divisions and for point defence of vital military installations in Singapore.[35]

The withdrawal from service of the long-range Bloodhounds during 1990 heralded a series of major changes during the decade. 163 Squadron's I-Hawks were assigned to the FPDA's Integrated Air Defence System (IADS) in place of the Bloodhounds.[36] However, the I-Hawks lacked the older missiles' long-range capability, highlighting a long-term need for a genuine Bloodhound replacement. Although MINDEF probably does not anticipate a near-term threat from theatre ballistic missiles (TBM), despite Indonesia's reported interest in acquiring Scud SRBMs in the early 1990s, the proliferation and increasingly indigenised production of such systems in Northeast and South Asia may impinge on Singapore's calculations regarding a future long-range SAM. While a logical solution might be the eventual purchase of US-made Patriots, budgetary considerations and a wish to avoid offending China will probably militate against involvement in any US-sponsored East Asian missile defence network. An alternative to a US-made long-range SAM might be the cheaper Russian S-300 system, in which MINDEF expressed an interest in 1996.[37]

The main focus of improvements to SADA's capabilities, however, was on shorter-range systems. In 1990, the upgraded 35 mm Oerlikon AA gun was introduced, featuring an improved rate of fire and superior fire control equipment.[38] In 1992, 30 Mistral portable, low-level, 5 km-range air defence systems were purchased to provide air defence for the army's 21st Division. A new unit, 18 SADA, was formed to operate these missiles, some of which may be mounted on M-113 AFVs, in conjunction with a locally-customised version of the US-supplied P-STAR radar.[39] Another capability enhancement during the 1990s involved upgrading the Rapier systems with the improved Mk2 missile.[40] Finally, the RSAF's investigation of Russian systems led to the procurement in 1997 of Igla 5 km-range SAMs to supplement and perhaps eventually replace the RBS-70s deployed with the combined arms divisions.[41]

The long-range ground-based radars at the RSAF's disposal were replaced with new systems, substantially boosting the capability of

Singapore's air defences. In 1994, the LORADS II system, including four radars, superseded the existing long-range radar and display system which formed the core of the joint civil–military Singapore Air Traffic Control Centre at Changi airport.[42] In 1998, the FPS 117 succeeded 201 Squadron's ITT RS320 system as the RSAF's principal dedicated air defence radar. The new radar's 250 km range represents a 50 per cent improvement over that of the older system, while simultaneously increasing the probability of detecting potentially hostile aircraft. Though located in peacetime on Bukit Gombak, close to MINDEF, the FPS 117 is a mobile system.[43]

In 1995, SADA and AFSC were merged to form the Air Defence Systems Division (ADSD), with the intention of maximising synergies between the sensor and weapon elements of Singapore's ground-based air defences. ADSD consists of three subordinate brigades:

- Air Defence Brigade (ADB), controlling national ground-based air defence operations, including 201 Squadron with its mobile radar system as well as the 35 mm guns, Rapiers and I-Hawks;
- Divisional Air Defence Artillery Brigade (DAB), responsible for tactical air defence units (henceforth known as 'DA Battalions') deployed with the army; and
- Air Force Systems Brigade (AFSB), responsible for long-range airspace surveillance and air force command and control. AFSB oversees all static C^3 systems and 203 Squadron's long-range radars.[44]

Being charged with the 'operational and tactical control of all airborne aircraft',[45] AFSB's C^3 role is not restricted to air defence assets but includes controlling strike operations.

Tactical Air Support Command

In 1989, the RSAF established a Tactical Support Wing, which became Tactical Air Support Command (TASC) in 1991. TASC ranks alongside the air bases and ADSD as one of the RSAF's six operational formations and is responsible for planning, coordinating and providing air support for the army and the navy.

TASC deploys joint operations personnel and forward air control officers with army divisions, brigades and lesser units, to provide air support advice to ground commanders. Forward air controllers can call down offensive air support, identifying targets and coordinating strikes using smoke grenades and laser designators as well as voice instructions. TASC also controls the UAV-equipped

128 Squadron, a large but mobile unit whose miniature aircraft work closely with artillery and armoured units. Other TASC elements include:

- Tactical Air Control Parties, which employ personnel drawn from the Commandos as ground forward air controllers;
- the Air Terminal Company, charged with loading and unloading freight and passengers from RSAF transport aircraft; and
- the Air Photo Unit, a photographic interpretation intelligence unit.[46]

AIR FORCE TRAINING

The RSAF is widely acknowledged as the best-trained air force in Southeast Asia. Its operational fast jet pilots fly an average of between 180 to 200 hours annually, which is comparable with the figures for the most effective western air forces. However, these hours may have been reduced by approximately 10 per cent as a result of funding constraints imposed in 1998–99.[47] During the 1990s, RSAF training, particularly for strike units, especially emphasised the development of night-fighting capabilities.

At the start of the 1990s, the RSAF's flying training was carried out almost entirely from bases in Singapore, making extensive use of training areas over the South China Sea and (for low-level flying) in central peninsular Malaysia. Concerned over the increasing congestion of Singapore's airspace as it became an ever more important international air transport hub, much of the RSAF's flying training was transferred overseas during the course of the 1990s. Towards the end of the decade, Malaysia's imposition of severe restrictions on RSAF aircraft using and transiting its airspace provided an additional reason for using overseas training locations.[48] Nevertheless, Singapore-based squadrons continue to use local facilities such as the helicopter training areas in Mandai, Jurong and Pulau Tekong, and the air-to-ground weapons range at Pulau Pawai, an island 12 kilometres south of Singapore.

Some of the RSAF's most important training activities are its exercises at home and overseas with other air forces, especially those of the United States and other western countries. These exercises provide RSAF commanders and aircrew with indirect access to these foreign air forces' doctrines, which are often based on extensive combat experience. During the 1990s, joint exercises grew in scale and complexity: the most important are the FPDA's

Stardex series, Pitch Black (with Australia and the US), Commando Sling (with the US), and Cope Tiger (with the US and Thailand).

Securing sufficient pilots for the RSAF has never been easy. At the end of the 1970s, the air force was forced to almost quadruple its intake of pilot trainees to provide aircrew for its rapidly expanding order of battle at the same time that lucrative opportunities in commercial aviation were seducing many of its more experienced officers.[49] The fleet of jet trainers was expanded and expatriate flying instructors recruited from India and Taiwan on a contract basis. During the 1980s, the eyesight requirements for pilots were relaxed on two separate occasions, expanding the pool of potential trainees to include some who use spectacles or contact lenses.[50]

Under the All Jet Training system (first adopted in 1994), RSAF pilot trainees selected from candidates assessed by the RSAF's Air Grading Centre at Tamworth in Australia (where they fly commercially owned and maintained Airtrainer light aircraft) proceed to a basic phase flown on 130 Squadron's S211 light jet trainers, based at Pearce in Western Australia. Of the 200 or more potential pilots inducted for grading each year, less than 40 ultimately qualify as pilots.[51] Between 20 and 25 of these are streamed to advanced jet training (including weapons and tactical training), conducted by 150 Squadron at Cazaux in France on two-seat and single-seat A-4s. In early 2000, it was revealed that the RSAF was finalising arrangements to send six trainee pilots (together with two instructors) annually for advanced and operational flying training to the commercial NATO Flying Training in Canada (NFTC) programme, where they will fly British Aerospace Hawk 115s.[52]

The remaining trainee pilots are allocated either to 124 Squadron at Sembawang for rotary-wing training on Fennec light helicopters (followed by advanced and operational training on Super Pumas and Cougars with 126 Squadron at Oakey in Queensland) or to multi-engine training.

Ranking alongside the great expansion in the use of overseas facilities during the 1990s as a key development in RSAF training was the increasingly widespread use of simulators. In 1987, a Flight Simulator Centre equipped with F-5, A-4 and air combat simulators was commissioned at Paya Lebar Air Base. In 1995, the RSAF introduced the Israeli EHUD air combat manoeuvring instrumentation system, which can be fitted to F-16, F-5 and A-4 aircraft to allow them to simulate the use of AAMs in dogfights. The RSAF began using a commercially operated C-130 simulator in 1992 and a Helicopter Simulator Centre for training Fennec and Super Puma pilots was opened in 1994. In 1998, the RSAF acquired the world's first UAV simulator.[53] All these simulators have helped to overcome the problem of Singapore's severely restricted airspace.

RSAF ground training

RSAF ground training is conducted at three main schools:

- the Air Engineering Training Institute, which trains technical personnel;
- the Systems Command Training School (SCTS), responsible for training air operations and communications officers, and air operations specialists; and
- the School of Air Defence Artillery (SADA), which trains officers and specialists for AAM and AA gun units.

Training simulators are used extensively at SCTS (Tower and Radar Simulator) and at SADA, where a Complete Engagement Simulator trains short-range air defence missile operators.[54]

OPERATIONAL READINESS: INFRASTRUCTURE, LOGISTICS AND MOBILISATION

The RSAF's aircraft and ground-based air defence assets constitute the most obvious elements of its capability, but they would be useless without a sophisticated and resilient logistical support system, including infrastructure which is able to withstand an enemy's initial onslaught. Moreover, though regulars provide at least half of its peacetime personnel the RSAF would depend in crisis or war on mobilisation of reservists, as well as civil resources, to sustain its capabilities.

Infrastructure

By the 1990s, the RSAF operated from four air bases in Singapore: Tengah, Paya Lebar, Sembawang and Changi, the latter being an enclave at the international airport. There was also a light aircraft element at Seletar Airport. With the maturing of Singapore's deterrent strategy since the 1980s, MINDEF and the RSAF have expended great effort in 'hardening' the main facilities to protect them against enemy attacks. Tengah Air Base, home to the F-16s, A-4s and E-2Cs, has received particular attention: most importantly, underground facilities have been built to house C^3I facilities;

parking for more than 100 aircraft is provided in reinforced shelters dispersed across the base in 'loop areas', some of which extend below ground. Similar blast-proof loop areas have been built at Paya Lebar.[55] Camouflage, including the use of decoy aircraft as well as the liberal application of low-infrared-signature paint, has been used extensively at all three major bases.

At both Tengah and Paya Lebar air bases, an Airfield Maintenance Squadron (AMS) is responsible for not only peacetime base maintenance, including provision of vital power, communications, lighting and fuel, but also wartime battle damage repair of runways, taxiways and infrastructure. Each AMS includes an Explosive Ordnance Disposal (EOD) Flight tasked with defusing and removing unexploded enemy bombs.[56] At Sembawang, there is a smaller Airfield Maintenance Flight.

In the event that enemy action succeeds in disabling the runways at Tengah and Paya Lebar, the RSAF is prepared to use expressways as auxiliary airfields in wartime. The 'Torrent' series of Emergency Runway Exercises since 1986 have, on four occasions, involved the off-base deployment of A-4s, F-5s and F-16s to a 2500-metre stretch of Lim Chu Kang Road, parallel to the main runway at Tengah. Lamp-posts, decorative flora in the central reservation and other obstacles can be removed easily within several hours, transforming the road into a runway. Other major roads which can be reconfigured in this way include Tuas Road in Singapore's southwest corner, and East Coast Parkway (the main thoroughfare from Singapore's central business district to Changi). RSAF helicopters have also rehearsed off-base operations, flying from areas such as parks and golf courses.[57]

The RSAF is well aware that in time of crisis its bases and aircraft could be threatened by enemy special forces or saboteurs. In 1984, it established Field Defence Squadrons (FDSs) tasked with ground defence of the air bases and with providing infantry weapons training for all air base personnel. In the first instance, the FDS were formed from three PDF reservist infantry battalions which were transferred to RSAF control. There are now FDS at Tengah, Paya Lebar, Sembawang and Changi: basically equipped as infantry units, they also deploy V-200 APCs armed with 20 mm Oerlikon guns.[58]

Logistics

Apart from the Airfield Maintenance units, the main logistics units at air base level are:

- Air Logistics Squadrons, which service, maintain and repair aircraft, together with ground systems directly supporting flying operations;
- Ground Logistics Squadrons, responsible for on-base transport, vehicle maintenance, messing and accommodation and ground equipment supplies; and
- Flying Support Squadrons, charged with providing air traffic control, fire and rescue services and meteorological support.

ADSD possesses its own specialised logistics squadrons to support its radar equipment, missiles and anti-aircraft guns.[59]

The Aircraft Systems Maintenance Base (ASMB), formerly located at Paya Lebar and providing depot-level maintenance, was disbanded in 1993: much of its work was commercialised but some functions were delegated to the ALSs at the four air bases. However, two important centralised logistics units remain. The Air Force Supply Base operates a computerised supply system linked to three Forward Supply Depots, located at the main bases. The Air Force Armament Base controls the RSAF's munitions stockpile, which is held in three Armament Depots: 4th AD (Paya Lebar); 6th AD (Tengah); and 10th AD (Sembawang).[60]

Mobilisation

Like the army, the RSAF permanently maintains forces on stand-by: in the air force's case, air defence radars and C^3 operate around the clock and interceptors are maintained on five-minute Quick Reaction Alert. Notwithstanding this high level of readiness to deal with air threats at short notice, mobilisation of NSmen would be vital to bring the RSAF up to full wartime strength in a crisis. The RSAF has a total mobilised strength of around 13 500, this figure including 3000 regular officers and NCOs, 3000 conscripts (mostly allocated to anti-aircraft and field defence units) and 7500 NSmen. The reservists comprise not only former conscripts needed mainly to fill out the air defence artillery units and the FDSs, but also a high proportion of ex-regular personnel including aircrew and technicians required to provide a wartime 'surge' capability for flying operations: significant numbers of RSAF combat aircraft (particularly the A-4s) are not flown regularly in peacetime.

Air Defence NSmen are called up for ICT on the same basis as their army counterparts. NS technicians return to their units for two ICTs, each of 12-and-a-half days, annually. Reservist aircrew, many of whom are commercial pilots in their civilian lives, maintain their currency through frequent but short stints of ICT, although occasional 'total recalls' to squadrons are held to update NSmen on the latest developments in operational doctrine and flight safety.[61]

In time of crisis, the RSAF would also mobilise civil resources. A civil resource mobilisation (CRM) exercise involving a small number of light aircraft and helicopters, which the air force planned to use for casualty evacuation and SAR in a crisis, was held in 1987.[62] CRMs have also involved ground equipment, particularly logistic vehicles. The Airfield Maintenance Squadrons' Civil Engineering Flights depend on the wartime mobilisation of civilian equipment such as graders, loaders, asphalt cutters and roller compactors.[63]

If the RSAF has an Achilles' heel, it is due to its increasing reliance on overseas training. The training agreements with the United States, Australia, France and other countries have hugely benefited the RSAF, particularly in relation to the extensive, long-term training deployments in the United States, which allow Singaporean personnel to take advantage of some of the world's best training facilities (including the Red Flag exercise series), and to learn from extremely experienced air power practitioners. However, there were drawbacks. By 1999, almost 30 per cent of the RSAF's 300 aircraft and a similar proportion of its aircrew, together with large numbers of groundcrew, were based overseas on long-term training detachments. According to Singapore's CDF, overseas basing does not bring the RSAF's capability into question, as these forces could be redeployed to Singapore in 'a matter of weeks'.[64] But in the event of a national security crisis, this might not be fast enough. Moreover, while it would be possible to fly personnel back to Singapore in an emergency, host government restrictions could prevent the return to Singapore of crucial operational aircraft (including F-16s, A-4s, Chinooks, Super Pumas, Cougars and KC-135s), significantly weakening the RSAF's deployable order of battle. One tactical benefit, though, would be that RSAF assets overseas would be immune to an enemy's first strike on Singapore's air bases.

CONCLUSION

During the 1990s, the RSAF was the principal beneficiary of Singapore's increased defence spending and procurement, substantially expanding its capacity for air defence, strike, reconnaissance and tactical air transport operations. The most important improvements in combat capability resulted from the acquisition of the fleet of F-16C/Ds, enabling the air force to operate in the long-range all-weather precision strike role while providing the basis for a 'beyond-visual-range' air defence capability (which will be fully realised with the eventual delivery of AMRAAM missiles). The KC-135 tankers will significantly extend the RSAF's reach, facilitating not only the deployment of forces overseas for training but also extended-range operational strike, reconnaissance and air defence missions. Simultaneously, the RSAF's ability to provide useful direct support to the other two services has grown with the deployment of the Fokker MPAs, the expansion of the helicopter fleet, the establishment of TASC and the acquisition of more capable UAVs.

The wholesale relocation of much of the RSAF's training overseas during the 1990s will not only allow the air force to transcend the constraints imposed by Singapore's restricted local airspace. Training in the USA, Australia and France will benefit the RSAF by permitting direct, long-term exposure to the 'best practice' of highly professional western air forces. Nevertheless, there is a danger that the basing of such a large proportion of the RSAF's assets overseas might seriously complicate mobilisation in an emergency.

The 2000–2010 period is likely to see further significant enhancement of the RSAF's capabilities. The air force will replace its elderly A-4 strike aircraft with additional F-16s and possibly a new combat type, which may be equipped with stand-off weapons. The tanker fleet may be further expanded, and AEW capabilities upgraded. The RSAF will also expand its use of UAVs, probably not only for reconnaissance. Jointly with the navy, it will also begin operating dedicated maritime helicopters. However, the level of defence spending during the coming decade will directly affect the scale and pace of procurement for the RSAF.

7

The Republic of Singapore Navy (RSN)

After an extended period as the SAF's 'cinderella' service in the 1970s and 1980s, the RSN's capabilities expanded near-exponentially during the 1990s following decisions made both in 1983 and in 1988. The 1983 decision to expand the RSN's capabilities to allow it to protect Singapore's SLOCs led to the delivery of missile corvettes; the implementation of the Navy 2000 plan after 1988 saw the acquisition of minehunters, maritime patrol aircraft, new patrol vessels, submarines and new landing ships. Older vessels were modernised and many vessels were armed with air defence as well as anti-ship missiles. At the same time, major infrastructure has been built in the form of two new naval bases. According to the Chief of Navy, the aim is to 'develop a small but balanced navy that will meet our unique defence requirements by exploiting technology and developing a first-class training system'.[1] In 2000, a new phase of capability upgrading began with an order for six frigates.

RESTRUCTURING THE NAVY

At the beginning of the 1990s, the navy's operational arm (known as the Fleet), comprised the following units, all operating from Brani Naval Base:

- 182 Squadron (six Vosper Thorneycroft gun-armed fast attack craft, known as patrol craft or PCs);
- 183 and 186 Squadrons (12 coastal patrol craft (CPCs));
- 185 Squadron (six Lürssen TNC-45 missile-armed fast attack craft, known as missile gun boats (MGBs));

159

- 188 Squadron (six Lürssen MGB-62 missile corvettes (MCVs));
- 191 Squadron (five ex-US Navy County-class landing ships (LSTs));
- 194 Squadron (support and training vessels); and
- 195 Squadron (fast transport craft).

Naval Logistics Command (NALCOM), providing technical, engineering and logistic support for naval operations, and the Institute of Naval Engineering, responsible for training engineering and logistics personnel, were also located at Brani. Training and support units based at Sembawang, in Singapore's north, included the School of Naval Training (responsible for combat systems training), the Midshipman School (officer training) and the Naval Diving Unit (NDU, tasked with mine clearance, underwater salvage, explosive ordnance disposal and underwater demolition of navigation hazards).

Changes in this structure during the 1990s reflected the expansion of the RSN's responsibilities and capabilities. The first major organisational development of the decade saw the establishment in 1991 of Coastal Command (COSCOM) as a formation separate from the Fleet, entrusted with safeguarding Singapore's territorial waters and the conduct of all naval operations in the Singapore Straits. COSCOM took over the 12 CPCs of 183 and 186 Squadrons (which effectively operated as a single unit), as well as 12 small, recently delivered inshore patrol craft known as 'fast boats'.[2] The CPCs were only interim equipment for COSCOM and from 1993 were transferred to the Police Coast Guard.[3] COSCOM also operates a network of five coastal and island radar stations equipped with Giraffe 100 systems and is responsible for the NDU.[4]

The second stage of restructuring, in 1992, involved the division of the Fleet into two functional flotillas:

- 1st Flotilla, the navy's striking arm, controlling the PCs, MGBs and MCVs of 182, 185 and 188 Squadrons; and
- 3rd Flotilla, in charge of the support vessels of 191 and 195 Squadrons and 192 and 193 Squadrons (reservist units charged with requisitioning and operating civilian vessels in wartime).

Though the Fleet is organised in peacetime on the basis of vessel types, in wartime it would transform quickly into mission-oriented task forces. Figure 7.1 shows the RSN's organisation in 2000.

Figure 7.1 Republic of Singapore Navy organisation, 2000

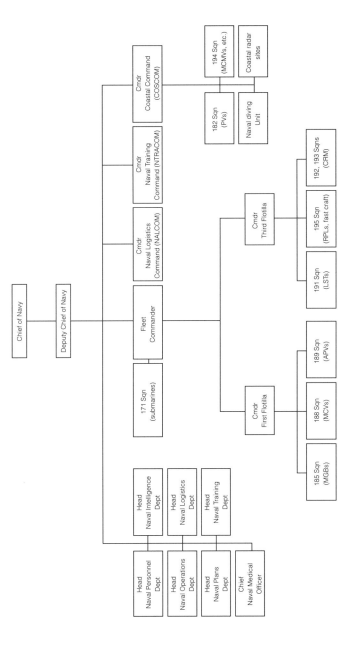

BOOSTING NAVAL CAPABILITIES

At the beginning of the 1990s, the navy was already absorbing into service the newly commissioned MCVs, while the MGBs were being substantially modernised and upgraded. Under Navy 2000, the RSN received additional new equipment which filled significant gaps in its capabilities.

Missile armament

One key aspect of the navy's capability expansion during the 1990s involved fitting anti-ship and anti-aircraft missiles to all major surface vessels. Anti-ship missiles were no novelty to the RSN: the MGBs had been armed with relatively short-range Gabriel systems since the 1970s; in the late 1980s they had been retro-fitted with much longer-range Harpoon missiles capable of hitting targets 'over-the-horizon' (with targeting assistance from RSAF E-2C aircraft and, later, the MPAs). Harpoons were also fitted to the MCVs commissioned in 1990–91. At the end of the 1990s, the RSN deployed a total of 120 anti-ship missile launchers on its MCVs and MGBs, by far the largest number of any Southeast Asian navy.

Arming its ships with air defence missiles was a new development, however. Probably influenced at least partly by the successes of Coalition aircraft and helicopters against Iraqi naval vessels during the 1991 Gulf War, in 1993 the RSN took delivery of Matra Simbad launchers and Mistral missiles. Initially fitted to MGBs (one system per ship) and the old LSTs (two systems), the Simbad/Mistral system subsequently also armed the PVs and new LSTs. In 1996, the more capable, fully-automated Barak 1 system, effective against anti-ship missiles as well as aircraft, was purchased from Israel for the MCVs.[5]

Mine countermeasures vessels (MCMVs)

Although the RSN had operated two elderly ex-US Navy coastal minesweepers since 1975, by the early 1980s their mine countermeasures equipment had been removed. RSS Jupiter, a locally built diving support vessel, commissioned in 1990, provided only a limited minehunting capability with its towed sonar.[6] Consequently, in 1991 MINDEF ordered four Landsort-class MCMVs from Sweden, each equipped with two remotely operated undersea mine disposal vehicles, with the aim of providing a capability to keep Singapore's local sea lanes, which were judged to be particularly vulnerable to mining, open in time of tension or conflict. The design of these ships was customised for the RSN, and three vessels were built locally by Singapore Shipbuilding and Engineering (SSE).[7] The MCMVs, which had all been commissioned by 1996, re-equipped 194 Squadron, which became a key component of Coastal Command.

Patrol vessels (PVs)

In 1993, MINDEF awarded SSE a contract to build 12 Fearless-class PVs. Though intended as replacements for the 46-tonne CPCs and 142-tonne PCs, at 500 tonnes the new water-jet powered ships were much larger. They were also equipped with modern C3I and navigation systems and were more heavily armed: all carried Mistral air defence missiles as well as single 76 mm guns; the first six also carried torpedoes and sonar for ASW. These initial vessels were commissioned in 1996–97 and equip 189 Squadron, which replaced 182 Squadron's PCs in the 1st Flotilla. The second batch of six PVs was commissioned in 1998, re-equipping 182 Squadron, now under COSCOM.[8]

Submarines

Confirming rumours that had circulated since the beginning of the decade, in mid-1995 Mindef confirmed that the RSN was evaluating the possibility of acquiring submarines and had sent officers to Germany for relevant training.[9] The international defence press speculated that Singapore would procure two ex-German Navy Type 206 boats, followed by four modern Type 209s, but the RSN did not pursue this option. In September 1995, Defence Minister Tony Tan announced that the navy would purchase a 'low-cost' second-hand submarine from Sweden 'as part of a package in submarine warfare'. Tan stressed that this did not imply that Singapore had decided that a submarine capability was necessary: the Swedish package 'was purely for training'.[10] The submarine in question was the *Sjöormen*, an A12 type boat launched in 1967. RSN personnel began submarine training in Sweden in 1996 and, following modernisation (including installation of new combat management systems) and tropicalisation, the *Sjöormen* was re-launched as RSS *Challenger* in September 1997.

In July 1997 Tan announced that the RSN would purchase three additional A12 boats, for delivery between late 1999 and 2001. Although Tan claimed that the aim of this additional procurement was to enable continued evaluation of the practicalities of submarine operations,[11] it was clear that the RSN was committed to building an operational submarine capability. By early 1998, the RSN was operating the RSS *Challenger* in the Baltic; training on the second submarine, RSS *Conqueror*, began in early 1999. In May 1999, RSS *Challenger*'s Singaporean crew fired a torpedo for the first time.[12] A year later, RSS *Conqueror* was deployed to Singapore, where it joined the new 171 Squadron. The Chief of Navy, Rear Admiral Richard Lim, stated in June 1999 that he expected all four submarines to attain full operational capability by 2003, if not earlier.[13]

Landing ships

The main roles of 191 Squadron's landing ships were originally to support the army's overseas training deployments, to provision other RSN ships at sea, and to provide sea training for midshipmen. By the early 1990s, however, the army's development of a rapid deployment force led to a requirement for more effective amphibious support from the navy. The strength of 191 Squadron was bolstered in 1994 with the commissioning of RSS *Perseverance*, a former British Landing Ship Logistic. While this ship usefully supplemented the capacity of the five smaller 50-year-old ex-US Navy LSTs, it only represented an interim solution.

In 1996, an order was announced for four new Endurance-class LSTs, to be built locally by Singapore Technologies Marine (formerly STSE). At 8500 tonnes, these are by far the navy's largest-ever ships and can travel at almost twice the speed of the old LSTs which they will replace, but require only half the manpower. Each new LST will be armed with a 76 mm gun and two Mistral air defence missile systems. The first two ships of the new class were commissioned in March 2000, with all four due to be operational by 2001. In anticipation of the arrival of the new ships, three of the old LSTs were decommissioned during 1998.

The potential utility of the new LSTs for amphibious operations is clear. Each has two helicopter landing pads and will be capable of moving 350 troops, 18 armoured vehicles and 20 'B' vehicles.[14] A well dock will allow fast transport craft to enter the LST for loading and unloading equipment and personnel.

Frigates

After several years of speculation regarding the next stage in the RSN's development, in March 2000 MINDEF signed a contract with the French shipbuilder, DCN, for six frigates 'to replace the six Missile Gunboats'. At 3000 tonnes, the new 110-metre multi-purpose warships, which will incorporate stealth technology to enhance their survivability and will each carry a helicopter, will hugely expand the RSN's anti-surface, anti-submarine and anti-air warfare capabilities. The first of the class will be built in France, but ST Marine will build the remainder locally. The first ship is due to be operational by 2005, the rest by 2009.[15]

As part of a joint programme involving MINDEF's Defence Technology Group, the RSN and local industry to define the C^3 technologies to be incorporated in the navy's new surface combatants (referred to by the late 1990s as the Intelligent Naval Defence Platform 21), one of the new PVs was designated a Naval Technology Evaluation Ship. A particular aim was to use technology to minimise the crew requirements of future vessels—a vital consideration in view of the RSN's extremely limited personnel numbers.[16] In consequence, though only slightly smaller than the DCN-built La Fayette-class frigates delivered to Taiwan's navy during the 1990s, the RSN's highly automated frigates will each need a crew of only 60.

Future equipment

The frigate contract may have superseded the RSN's reported interest in acquiring a class of 1000- to 1500-tonne corvettes, featuring a stealth design developed jointly with Sweden's naval industry and defence science organisation. However, it is more likely that such a programme—probably aimed at eventually replacing the existing MCVs—will continue.

The RSN is also believed to have a long-standing interest in procuring a larger helicopter-carrying vessel. However, cost and manning considerations and the ability of the new LSTs, the planned larger surface combatants and requisitioned merchant vessels to carry helicopters suggest that procurement of a specialised platform is not a high priority.

MINDEF has not released any details of its plans for the RSN's future submarine capability. However, follow-on orders for additional, modern boats are widely anticipated and it is understood that MINDEF's Defence Technology Group is involved in a project with its Swedish counterpart relating to air-independent propulsion—a key 'stealth' technology for submarines.

During the late 1980s and early 1990s, the RSN experimented with a locally produced Tiger 40 hovercraft, capable of carrying

30 troops or 2.6 tonnes of equipment, as a logistic support craft. Although the acquisition of additional ramp-powered lighters and landing craft (known as 'fast craft' in the RSN) may have been seen as a satisfactory alternative to pursuing the hovercraft option during the 1990s, in the longer-term there may still be an interest in acquiring larger air-cushion vehicles of the type used by the US Marine Corps, which are able to carry armoured vehicles.[17]

New infrastructure

With the RSN's existing infrastructure clearly inadequate in view of the navy's acquisition of larger vessels with more demanding logistics and training requirements, the process of replacing the existing facilities on Pulau Brani and at Sembawang commenced during the 1990s. A new base, built on reclaimed land at Singapore's western extremity, was opened at Tuas in 1994 (see Figure 7.2). This facility provided accommodation for the MCV and LST squadrons and most elements of NALCOM, as well as a temporary location for the Fleet Headquarters.[18] In 1997, the NDU moved into new facilities at Sembawang, where it will remain on a long-term basis.[19]

In January 1998, work began on a new base at the eastern end of Singapore. When completed, this Changi Naval Base (CNB) will fully replace Brani Naval Base, which MINDEF will relinquish for development as a container terminal. CNB will have twice the land area and five times the berthing space of Brani, as well as deeper waters (which will allow, incidentally, the docking of vessels as large as US Navy aircraft carriers). The main part of CNB, comprising the operational base and maintenance facilities, was scheduled for completion by 2000. Vessels to be based there will include the submarines. By 2003, CNB will also include a new Fleet Command Building, housing the headquarters of the Fleet and the two flotillas, as well as the Changi Naval Training Base (CNTB), which will consolidate the RSN's training facilities in one location.[20]

TRAINING DEVELOPMENTS

The organisation and content of RSN training were modified substantially during the 1990s in view of the service's new equipment and wider roles. To cope with the navy's expanding training requirements, Naval Training Command (NTRACOM) was established at Sembawang in 1994 to coordinate control of all training

Figure 7.2 Singapore: major military installations

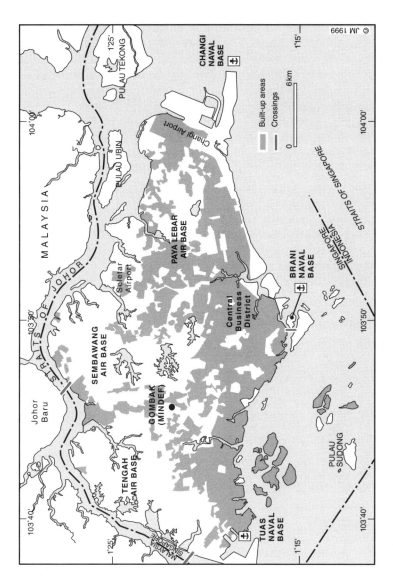

units (with the exception of the Midshipman Wing and NAS which were incorporated into the SAFTI Military Institute).[21]

As in the SAF's other two services, training simulators are being used ever more extensively by the RSN. Naval simulators include the Combat Simulation Centres, which provide complete replicas of MCV and PV combat information centres, allowing ships' warfare teams to experience a range of simulated scenarios, including some which cannot easily be created during sea exercises. Other simulators include two Tactical Training Centres (for training Principal Warfare Officers and widely used in command post exercises with other navies), trainers for the Simbad/Mistral air defence system, naval gunnery and damage control and simulators for mine disposal vehicles and minehunting sonars.[22] In 1997, the Institute of Maritime Warfare (IMW) was established to oversee the Tactical Training and Combat Simulation Centres and other computer-based naval training. During 1999, the RSN was due to extend the use of simulation dramatically, by introducing a Naval Warfare Instrumentation System, capable of 'simulating realistic combat scenarios among multiple ships and aircraft during exercises at sea'.[23]

Recognising both the higher educational qualifications of its specialist recruits and the need to contain manpower requirements as larger, more sophisticated ships were introduced, in 1997 the RSN introduced the Combat Technician scheme, intended to produce naval specialists cross-trained in operating as well as maintaining shipboard systems. To train Combat Technicians more effectively, in 1999 the RSN inaugurated two new training schools to replace the School of Naval Training and Institute of Naval Engineering. The new Institute of Naval Technology and Operations (INTO) will train specialists to operate and maintain combat systems; the Institute of Marine Systems (IMS) will train specialists in platform systems. Initially located at Sembawang, INTO and IMS will move to CNTB in 2003.[24]

Notwithstanding the increasing emphasis on simulation, sea training has remained a vital component of the RSN's efforts to maintain and enhance operational readiness. Most unilateral training has taken place in the South China Sea, where well-publicised test-firings of Mistral, Barak and Gabriel missiles during the late 1990s have clearly been partly intended to communicate a deterrent message.[25] A Naval Gunfire Support Scoring System began operating at Pulau Karu Ara, an Indonesian island in the South China Sea, in October 1999. The acquisition of Fokker MPAs has led to more intensive joint exercises with the air force, also involving A-4 aircraft operating in a maritime strike role. Vessels from the 1st Flotilla have also trained extensively with friendly navies: major FPDA exercises involving up to 100 ships have provided particularly valuable experience, according to the Chief of Navy.[26] Exercises with Australia and the United States have included the test-firing of Harpoon missiles.[27] Australian, US and Indian submarines have acted as targets in ASW exercises.

NAVAL LOGISTICS

By the end of the 1990s, NALCOM's main units were Maintenance Bases at Brani and Tuas (with 13 workshops providing base-level engineering support for Fleet and COSCOM vessels) and the Naval Materials and Transport Base (NMTB). The Command was also responsible for the Naval Logistics Computer Centre, and medical facilities and base defence squadrons at Brani and Tuas. Over the course of the previous decade, MINDEF had paid great attention to increasing the efficiency of logistic support for the RSN. An Automated Storage and Retrieval System was introduced in 1992 to optimise land and manpower utilisation: it can store up to 265 000 items, but is staffed by only 12 personnel—a saving of 103 posts compared with the previous system.[28]

Since 1990, some of the RSN's maintenance and logistic support has been commercialised and taken over by various branches of ST, the local state-owned defence industrial conglomerate, reducing naval manpower requirements in this area.[29] However, many defence industry employees are naval reservists and a high-level of support for the navy would be assured in crisis or war. Further commercialisation of NALCOM activities is planned, but handling of ammunition, logistics planning, audit and quality control will remain service responsibilities.[30]

OPERATIONAL READINESS AND MOBILISATION

Even in peacetime, RSN vessels are on permanent patrol in the Singapore Straits and further afield. They are backed up by a stand-by task force of MGBs and MCVs, all fully armed and at immediate notice for sea.[31] But as in the other two services, mobilisation would be necessary to bring the navy to a war footing.

Like the air force, the RSN does not depend on reservists to the same degree as the army. Nevertheless, more than half of its fully mobilised strength (5000 out of 9600 personnel) would be composed of NSmen, including many former regulars as well as ex-NSFs. NSmen would be particularly important for manning the base defence squadrons, 195 Squadron (fast transport craft) and 194 Squadron (COSCOM's fast boats), as well as supplementing the crews of larger vessels on extended operational missions. In 1997, the Head of Naval Plans spoke of making 'greater and better use' of reservists.[32]

One key responsibility of mobilised NSmen in a crisis would be to requisition Civil Resource (CR) craft (such as launches, tugs and lighters) for the 3rd Flotilla's 192 and 193 Squadrons, an activity rehearsed during ICT sessions.[33] An innovation in the late 1990s was the leasing of a merchant vessel, MV *Jaya Venus*, for training NSmen, who used the ship to deliver humanitarian food aid to Indonesia during 1998.[34] In wartime, CR craft would play particularly important roles as 'afloat support depots', resupplying warships on extended operations. Some naval reservist officers are master mariners and chief engineers in Singapore's merchant navy: in wartime it is likely that Singaporean-flagged merchant vessels would be operated under naval discipline to guarantee a minimum level of critical supplies despite threats to civilian shipping.

CONCLUSION

Benefiting from a substantial infusion of new ships and liberation from its previous coast guard role (which largely became a police responsibility), the RSN's capabilities for mine countermeasures, anti-submarine warfare and air defence, as well as anti-surface vessel operations, expanded considerably during the 1990s. This enabled the navy not only to patrol Singapore's immediate maritime locale more effectively, but also to project naval power further afield and to think in terms, for example, of protecting merchant vessels in the South China Sea. At the same time, the navy's new LSTs, which will work closely with RSAF transport and attack helicopters, have significantly boosted the army's rapid deployment capabilities.

During the decade to 2010, the build-up of the Singapore-based submarine squadron (and the probable procurement of modern, new-build submarines), commissioning of the new class of frigates and the development of dedicated naval helicopter operations will continue to transform the RSN's capabilities. An order for a new class of corvettes, possibly built to a radical new stealth design, is also a strong possibility. Assuming that the defence budget is able to support these programmes, the main constraint on the further expansion of RSN capabilities will be the availability of adequate numbers of suitable personnel. However, the RSN's success in getting to grips with this issue is reflected in the minimal crewing requirements of the new frigates.

8

Defence procurement, R&D and industry

Unable to deploy large standing forces because of manpower constraints, Singapore bases its military capability to a considerable extent on the possession of modern, technologically advanced defence equipment. Singapore's defence ministers have spoken explicitly of the SAF's need to maintain its 'technological edge' over potential (but undefined) aggressors—according to Yeo Ning Hong, speaking in 1994, Singapore possessed 'a superiority we must never lose'.[1] All the evidence suggests that this aim has been achieved, at least in relation to putative regional aggressors. Other Southeast Asian states such as Malaysia and Thailand spent large amounts on modern arms during the 1980s and 1990s, but they have usually not integrated this equipment into their armed forces as effectively as has Singapore. Singapore's relative success in this area derives from the nature of its procurement system and the highly developed status of its own defence industry and defence R&D organisation.

DEFENCE PROCUREMENT

Singapore directs as much as two-thirds of its defence spending—in other words, up to US$2.5 billion annually in the late 1990s—towards procurement and infrastructural development, with perhaps half of this procurement expenditure going overseas. Procurement of major equipment such as F-16 fighters, KC-135 tankers, CH-47D helicopters and submarines helps to explain the significant increase in Singapore's defence spending during the decade. During the 1990s the main foreign suppliers of Singapore's defence equipment were, in approximate order of importance: the

United States (accounting for the largest share of Singapore's defence imports, including US$2 billion worth in 1995 and 1996 alone),[2] Sweden, Israel, France, the United Kingdom and Germany. Lesser suppliers included Russia, Australia, the Netherlands, Norway, Canada and Italy. (Table 8.1 provides details of the most important contracts during the 1990s.) The remainder of Singapore's defence procurement budget is spent on locally produced equipment or upgrade programmes, mainly supplied by subsidiary companies of the government-linked Singapore Technologies conglomerate.

The 'defence creep' phenomenon

While Singapore procures minor defence equipment through a fairly transparent process, the details of more significant purchases are obscured by secrecy. As a result, despite MINDEF's evident emphasis on long-term planning for defence funding and procurement, Singapore's procurement of major items often appears hesitant and piecemeal. In part this may be explained by the need to spread expensive purchases across several years' procurement budget and the wish to test equipment in service before making a larger-scale commitment. But Singapore's government also recognises that its neighbours might feel obliged by either domestic political considerations or balance-of-power reasons to respond politically or with counter-balancing procurement to any perceived military advantages gained by the city-state.

The term 'defence creep', coined by Singaporean journalist David Boey, aptly describes the paradigm dominating the presentation of those major SAF procurement programmes which MINDEF and the government see as politically sensitive and potentially counter-productive in political and security terms.[3] The phenomenon is characterised by the initial purchase of small numbers of a particular class of weapon system, which are often based overseas for training purposes for several years in the first instance. Holdings of the system in question are then expanded after the initial publicity has subsided. The introduction of F-16 fighters typifies 'defence creep': although Singapore was the first Southeast Asian state to order the US-built fighters, the first order was for only eight aircraft, which were initially based for two years in the US. By the time these aircraft were delivered to Singapore in 1990, both Thailand and Indonesia had not only ordered but had taken delivery of their own F-16s. However, by the end of the 1990s, Singapore's F-16 fleet was the largest in

Table 8.1   Selected major defence equipment contracts with foreign suppliers, 1990–2000

Supplier	Equipment type	Role	Number	Ordered	Delivered
USA	TOW-2A	ATGW	240	1990	1991–92
France	LG1 Mk1	105 mm arty	37	1990	1991–93
France	AS532UL	Transport helo	6	1990	1991–92
France	AS550A2/C2	Armed helo	20	1990	1991–92
France	AMX-10P	AFV	22	1990	1991–92
France	AMX-10P AC90	AFV	22	1990	1991–92
Italy	Skyguard	AA radar	1	1991	1992
USA	AGM-84A Harpoon	AShM	20	1991	1993–94
Italy	Griffo F/X	Fighter radar	37	1991	1993–94
Sweden	Landsort-class	MCMV	4	1991	1993–95
Netherlands	Fokker 50	MPA	5	1991	1994–95
Israel	Hotshot	Air combat sim.	1	1991	nk
UK	Perseverance-class	Landing ship	1	1992	1992
France	Mistral	SAM	150	1992	1994–95
France	Sadral/Simbad	Naval SAM	nk	1992	1994–95
Israel	Barak	Naval SaM	nk	1992	1996
Sweden	V206	All-rerrain veh.	300	1993	1993–94
Italy	A-244/S Mod 1	Torpedo	nk	1993	nk
UK	FV180S CET	Engineer veh.	36	1993/95	1994–96
Netherlands	Fokker 50	Transport ac	4	1994	1994
Jordan	F-5E/F	Fighter ac	7	1994	1994
USA	F-16C/D	Fighter ac	18	1994	1998–99
USA	AIM-7M/AIM-9	AAM	86	1994	1998–99
USA	CH-47D	Transport helo	6	1994	1997–98
Israel	Searcher	UAV	40	1995	1997
USA	LANTIRN	Nav./attack syst.	8	1995	1998–99
Sweden	A12-type	Submarine	4	1995/97	1997–99
USA	KC-135R	Tanker ac	4	1996	1999–
USA	AGM-84A Harpoon	AShM	24	1996	nk
Russia	Igla	SAM	nk	1996	1997–99
Australia	Flyer	Light strike veh.	79	1996/98	1997–
USA	CH-47SD	Transport helo	6	1997	2000–
USA	F-16C/D	Fighter ac	12	1997	1999–2000
Israel	Spike	ATGW	nk	nk	1999–
USA	AH-64D	Attack helo	8	1999	2002–
France	nk	Frigate	1+5 lic.	2000	2005–9
USA	F-16C/D	Fighter ac	20	2000	2003–4

Sources: Bates Gill and J.N. Mak (eds), *Arms, Transparency and Security in South-East Asia*, Oxford University Press for the Stockholm International Peace Research Institute, Oxford, 1997, pp. 126–7; *The Military Balance 1999–2000* (London: International Institute for Strategic Studies, 1999), p. 174; author's database.

Acronyms and abbreviations:

AA	anti-aircraft		MP	maritime patrol aircraft
ac	aircraft		nav	navigation
AFV	armoured fighting vehicle		nk	not known
arty	artillery		SAM	surface-to-air missile
AShM	anti-ship missile		sim.	simulator
ATGW	anti-tank guided weapon		syst.	system
helo	helicopter		UAV	unmanned aerial vehicle
lic	licence-built		veh.	vehicle
MCMV	mine counter measures vessel			

Southeast Asia (although many of the aircraft were based in the US under long-term training arrangements). Other examples of procurement programmes manifesting 'defence creep' during the 1990s include the acquisition of submarines and CH-47 helicopters.

Another dimension of 'defence creep' involves the incremental upgrading of the operational capabilities of major equipment systems after they have seen several years' service. Upgrading may constitute a considerably more economic option than purchasing new equipment, but it also carries the advantage of not unduly alarming Singapore's neighbours.

The defence procurement system[4]

MINDEF's Defence Technology Group (DTG) is responsible for procuring equipment and services for the armed forces and for developing their infrastructure. Within DTG, the Defence Material Organisation (DMO) provides project management for most equipment procurement, the Command, Control, Communications, Computer and Intelligence Systems Organisation (CSO) performs a similar role in relation to C^4I programmes and the Lands and Estates Organisation (LEO) is responsible for infrastructural developments. DTG's Defence Procurement Division (DPD) prepares and issues Invitations to Tender (ITT) and Invitations to Quote (ITQ), evaluates commercial aspects of potential suppliers' bids and negotiates contracts.[5] DPD issues ITQs for low-value, 'off-the-shelf' items required by SAF units and MINDEF departments: such invitations require simply a price from companies, rather than the copious documentation demanded for the evaluation of tenders.

More important equipment is procured by tender. In the tendering process, a complex system of checks and balances, which prevents undue influence of individual elements of MINDEF and the SAF over procurement choices, is intended not only to ensure rational decision-making but also to minimise the potential for corruption. Technical and commercial considerations are evaluated separately, and are only brought together at the final stage of the process. And, crucially, the DTG will only deal and enter into contracts directly with manufacturers and suppliers, which cuts out any significant role for intermediary agents.

The procurement process is guided by the philosophy of Life Cycle Management, which is intended to ensure the reliability and maintainability of the SAF's equipment, minimise personnel required to support defence systems, reduce logistic support requirements and facilitate more effective use of the procurement budget.[6] DTG's target is that life cycle and maintenance costs should be no more than 60 per cent of the initial purchase costs of any particular procurement programme.

The procurement process involves five phases. First, an Equipment Master Plan, derived from consultation between DTG, the Joint Staff and individual service planning staffs, sets procurement priorities over a five-year period, within the context of longer-term frameworks (during the 1990s, the SAF 2000 plan) which identify the SAF's operational needs. The Master Plan provides comprehensive operational and engineering plans for all proposed new equipment, including details such as how doctrine and training might need to be modified.

In the second phase (Requirement Definition), DMO or CSO prepare a Statement of Need, covering threat definition, availability of funding and an assessment of available technology. A more detailed Statement of Requirement follows: this examines the equipment's operational uses, together with the applicability of new technology, and includes a market survey of relevant systems. The most crucial part of this definition stage, though, is the generation of a Programme Management Plan. This includes development of an 'analytical hierarchy process' (AHP) assigning weightings to relevant technical and commercial factors. Commercial factors taken into consideration include not only price and quality, but also compliance with MINDEF specifications and conditions of tender, the technical expertise of the tenderer and availability of after-sales service support (including spares and maintenance support), tenderers' performance in previous MINDEF contracts and availability of documentation (including technical data).[7] These weightings cannot be altered once set.

MINDEF does not release details of factors used in particular programmes' AHPs, let alone the weightings assigned to each factor. However, foreign suppliers are well aware that while Singapore does not specify a required percentage level of offset, DTG gives preference to foreign bidders for major contracts if they are able to enter into 'Industrial Cooperation Programmes' (ICPs) aimed at boosting indigenous capabilities through technology transfers to local defence industry. During the late 1990s, ICPs led to the local manufacture of components for F-16C/D fighters and CH-47D helicopters.[8] Where sophisticated, major equipment (including aircraft, helicopters and submarines) has been concerned, the willingness of the supplier's government to provide long-term overseas training facilities has often also been assigned significant weight.

The third phase starts with establishing an Acquisition Management Team (AMT), including representatives from the relevant service's logistic staff, within DMO or CSO. The AMT's role is to devise the technical elements of the tender documentation, and to decide—crucially—on the most cost-effective mode of meeting the requirement: by modifying an existing system, by developing a new system locally or by purchasing a new system on the international market. For programmes with low security classification, the usual procedure is for DPD to issue open tenders, which are advertised in local newspapers and through the MINDEF Internet Procurement System, launched in 1998.[9] Typical open tender equipment items include IT hardware and software and logistics vehicle spares. However, more significant open tender purchases during the late 1990s included the modification of three-tonne trucks to transport I-HAWK SAMs, body armour and spares for AMX-13 tanks.[10] The less numerous, but more important, highly classified programmes are subject to closed tendering, whereby DPD invites specific potential suppliers to submit bids.[11]

The key element of the Acquisition Management phase involves the computerised AHP evaluation of tenders using the weightings established during the Requirement Definition phase. This evaluation produces a rank order of competing tenders and DPD then negotiates a final contract with the preferred supplier. At this stage, DPD may attempt to reduce the price asked, particularly where the technical evaluation has produced two or more acceptable suppliers. Following agreement on contract terms, final approval for the purchase is sought, usually from MINDEF's Deputy Secretary (Technology). Particularly valuable contracts, or those which are politically sensitive because they provide Singapore with a new capability, are referred to the Permanent Secretary (Defence Development), ministers or even the Cabinet.

The fourth stage of the procurement process is the introduction of the equipment into service, involving building up logistic support, operational testing and, ultimately, transferring responsibility for Life Cycle Management from DTG to the service concerned. Once in service, a Logistic Management Information System monitors the equipment's performance. In the final phase, usually some years after introduction of a system into service, a 'post-implementation review' assesses its viability and may cue a new procurement cycle involving upgrading or replacement.

DEFENCE R&D IN SINGAPORE

DTG is not simply concerned with managing SAF procurement; it also links the armed forces with local defence industry and foreign sources of defence technology. According to MINDEF, the organisation's mission is to 'provide cost-effective technological solutions to enhance Singapore's defence capability'.[12] In the words of Defence Minister Tony Tan, 'DTG . . . concentrates on the conversion of the defence budget into high technology weapons, equipment and systems required by the SAF'.[13] Former Defence Minister Yeo Ning Hong's reference to DTG as 'the fourth service of the SAF' underlined its huge contribution to Singapore's defence effort.[14] The posting of senior serving SAF officers to senior DTG positions (such as Director, DMO and Director, CSO) underlines the intimacy of the armed forces' relationship with this branch of MINDEF.[15]

Apart from DPD, DMO and CSO, the DTG comprises the Lands and Estates Organisation (LEO), the Resource Planning Office (RPO) and the Directorate of Research and Development (DRD). The DSO National Laboratories, formerly the Defence Science Organisation, are also affiliated with DTG.

The broader roles of DMO and CSO

Beyond their managerial roles, DMO and CSO play much more extensive parts in procurement. DMO includes aeronautical, armament, guided weapons, land, naval and sensor divisions and collaborates extensively with local and foreign industry on:

- systems engineering and systems integration for new equipment;
- upgrading the performance and capability of existing systems;
- providing engineering support for selected weapon systems; and
- keeping abreast of relevant technology and advising the SAF on how to exploit it.

As the design authority for all MINDEF and SAF C[4] system hardware and software, as well as for simulation systems, CSO performs a similarly broad role. CSO deploys more than 400 engineers in divisions covering 'joint and army', naval, air, simulation, information, telecommunications and data communications systems. It also has an extremely active dual-use systems division, which has spearheaded the application of COTS software and hardware within MINDEF and the SAF. It has also found civil applications for defence IT systems.[16]

Lands and Estates Organisation

LEO is responsible for designing and managing the construction of defence infrastructure and, by 1997, employed more than 400 engineers, architects, researchers and technical support staff.[17] Examples of LEO projects include the construction of new military facilities (such as Jurong Camp III, Depot Road Camp, the SAFTI-Military Institute, Tuas Naval Base and the Defence Technology Towers) and the redevelopment of existing facilities (for example, the Pulau Tekong basic military training centre). LEO is responsible for ensuring that Singapore's military installations are capable of sustaining wartime operations, and emphasises the incorporation of not only 'hardened' mechanical and engineering systems, as well as water, communications and power lines, but also back-up systems for these vital utilities.[18]

LEO also functions as MINDEF's land-use planning agency. At the end of the 1990s, MINDEF and the SAF still occupied 20 per cent of Singapore's scarce land resource with camps, air bases, naval ports and training areas. A major preoccupation remains 'land optimisation' aimed at reducing this figure by building more compact camps, training facilities and storage depots. In addition, LEO manages the construction and maintenance of infrastructure for long-term SAF overseas training deployments, such as the Flying Training School at Pearce in Western Australia.

LEO is the designated 'National Authority' for protective technology, which became a new focus of activity during the 1990s. In 1998 two protective technology research centres were set up in conjunction with local universities to carry out advanced R&D on protective structures, mechanical and electrical systems able to withstand explosions and camouflage and concealment.[19] The first publicised result of this collaboration is the underground ammunition storage facility at Mandai, catering for a 'significant proportion' of the SAF's ammunition and scheduled to be operational in 2003.[20]

LEO has become heavily involved in facilitating energy and water conservation within MINDEF and the SAF as an economy measure. Examples include the use of solar power and thermal storage machines to reduce energy consumption, construction of energy-efficient 'intelligent buildings' and the development of automated washing systems for armoured vehicles and aircraft.[21]

Resource Planning Office

The responsibilities of the Resource Planning Office (RPO), which reports to the Chief of Staff, Joint Staff as well as the Director, DTG, encompass not only corporate planning for the latter, but also much wider issues:

- RPO's Joint Logistics Department is responsible for overall planning for the SAF's logistic support and sustainability and develops procedures to ensure the availability of civilian logistic, industrial and technical support for the SAF. It also assesses possibilities for the contractorisation of SAF support and logistics.
- The Defence Industry Department's role is to develop strategic plans for the build-up and sustenance of Singapore's defence–industrial capability. It also fosters technology transfer to local industries by planning and managing Industrial Cooperation Programmes.[22]

Defence Science Organisation

Fundamental research and development are mainly the responsibility of the Defence Science Organisation (DSO) which, with more than 500 engineers and scientists, is Singapore's largest R&D organisation. DSO's origins lay in the establishment in 1972 of a small but initially highly secret Electronic Test Centre. During the 1970s this body, which spawned DSO in 1977, was concerned particularly with electronic warfare, but its capabilities expanded considerably during the 1980s and 1990s.[23] The essential aim, though, has remained constant: to conduct defence-related R&D in order to improve the SAF's combat effectiveness.

In practical terms, limited resources dictate that while attempting to 'stay close to the leading edge in the basic technologies',[24] Singapore's defence R&D must target highly specific technological niches, chosen through close consultation with the SAF. These R&D niches must offer substantial potential payoffs in terms of enhanced operational capability, lie within DSO's capabilities and be assessed as worthwhile to investigate 'in-house' for reasons of secrecy or because of the lack of alternative sources of the technology in question. DSO conducts R&D in some 18 areas of interest to Mindef and the SAF:

- artificial intelligence and expert systems
- computer security
- simulation
- software engineering

- electromagnetics
- electronics design and packaging
- radar
- aeronautics
- guidance and control
- marine technology
- navigation
- communications
- signal and image processing
- electro-optics
- materials
- mechanics
- applied chemistry
- operations research.

The aim has been to provide the SAF with an edge over potential adversaries, often by upgrading systems such as missiles and radars to a technological level not accessible through off-the-shelf purchase in the international defence market. However, Singapore's defence decision-makers realise that such leads are ephemeral, and that defence R&D is a constant race to stay 'ahead of the game'.[25]

Some of DSO's most important contributions to enhancing the SAF's capabilities have involved systems integration and software development. Examples include the integration of radars, various types of SAMs and fighter aircraft with command and control elements into the air defence system during the 1980s, and the integration and capability optimisation of new sensors and weapons (such as Harpoon anti-ship missiles and Barak SAMs) for warships.

Applied chemistry became a particularly important area of research during the 1990s, focusing on technologies relevant to defensive chemical warfare, particularly the early detection and accurate identification of toxic chemicals, environmental detoxification (including purification of contaminated water), medical treatment of the effects of toxins and effective protection against chemical warfare agents for people in tropical climates. By 1998, DSO's Centre for Chemical Defence had developed a prototype automated detection device ('Toxispy'), effective for detecting even minute amounts of contaminants in water.[26] This research programme clearly has direct relevance to the security of Singapore's water supplies and to enhancing Singapore's ability to withstand a possible 'first strike' involving chemical weapons.

DSO has played a key role in exploiting as well as generating 'dual-use' technologies—in other words, technologies with both civil and military applications. In 1992, a Technology Watch programme was inaugurated, with the aim of identifying and monitoring 'key emerging technologies for application in the SAF', including 'ideas from technologically-advanced commercial sectors'. Dual-use communications technology has been used in components and subsystems for radar systems and COTS components in the DSO-developed Airborne Compute Engine, an ultra-fast military computer. Dual-use technologies have also played a key part in DSO's efforts to develop protection for the military communications and computing infrastructure against 'information attack'.[27]

The restructuring of DTG

During the 1990s, MINDEF began a fundamental restructuring of DTG's operations. The process began in 1991, when DSO was granted Executive Agency status within MINDEF, allowing it greater operational autonomy. A more fundamental change came in 1997 when DSO was corporatised, becoming DSO National Laboratories, a non-profit company affiliated with rather than part of DTG.

The aim of corporatising DSO was essentially to improve its efficiency by introducing more flexible, less bureaucratic commercial best practice in project management, sub-contracting, technological alliances, intellectual property protection and commercial ventures. In the personnel sphere, the intention was to equip DSO better to attract and retain the scientists and engineers essential to its effective operation.[28]

Corporatisation was also intended to facilitate increased cross-fertilisation of R&D with local academic and research institutes, notably the National University of Singapore, Nanyang Technological University, the Institute of Systems Science and the Institute of Information Technology. One major aim is to expand DSO's dual-use R&D, particularly in terms of making relevant technologies available for non-defence 'national missions'—for example, by offering information security expertise to the financial sector and by helping the Port of Singapore Authority to develop an autonomous guided vehicle navigation system for container handling.[29]

DSO's focus remains on defence-related R&D on behalf of MINDEF and the SAF. However, it 'can no longer be assumed that defence R&D work will automatically be contracted to DSO'.[30] When DSO was corporatised, MINDEF also established the

Directorate of Research and Development (DRD) within DTG as its R&D 'masterplanner' as well as the buyer of R&D services for the ministry and the SAF—with the option on drawing on sources outside DSO.[31]

In March 2000, the process of restructuring DTG was furthered by the devolution of almost all its functions to a new Defence Science and Technology Agency (DSTA), a more autonomous organisation which was intended to meet the SAF's demand for advanced military technology more effectively, particularly in terms of cooperating with other research organisations, both locally and internationally. The DSTA, with 2400 personnel, subsumed all of DTG, with the exception of the policy, planning and resource allocation functions of DRD and RPO: 50 personnel remained part of MINDEF in order to continue providing strategic direction for Singapore's defence R&D. The new Agency also absorbed the Systems and Computer Organisation and the Defence Medical Research Institute from MINDEF's Defence Administration Group.[32]

International collaboration in defence R&D

DTG has drawn extensively on foreign technological expertise in its R&D work and is increasingly deeply involved in collaborative projects in areas of mutual interest with foreign counterparts, with the aim of maintaining the SAF's regional lead in military technology. Much of this cooperation is highly classified. This applies particularly to Singapore's defence R&D cooperation with Israel, which is believed to include work in the areas of electronic warfare, missiles and unmanned aerial vehicles.

During the 1990s, R&D collaboration has intensified with several other national defence science establishments. Despite Washington's concerns during the 1980s that Singapore was a potentially untrustworthy end-user for high-technology military and dual-use exports,[33] US–Singapore defence–technological cooperation has gathered pace in the new context of a much closer post-Cold War bilateral security relationship. In 1999, Singapore joined the US–UK Joint Strike Fighter (JSF) programme as a 'major participant', allowing access to information regarding the programme's technological progress.[34] Though this status will not allow Singapore to influence the JSF's design, it might open the way for later industrial cooperation if the aircraft is ordered for the RSAF. The US and Singapore have also collaborated on naval stealth and on protective technology.

Collaboration with Sweden has been particularly close. Since 1994, a Swedish navy officer has served under an exchange programme as deputy assistant director in DMO's Naval Systems Project Office.[35] There is also cooperation on protective technology and chemical defence. In 1997, Singapore and Sweden established a Joint Technology Development Fund to finance joint defence R&D projects.[36] Singapore has also explored possibilities for defence–technological collaboration with Australia (a 1993 Agreement for Cooperation in Defence Science and Technology led to joint projects in military communications), France (leading to the establishment of a Joint Technology Development Fund in 1997), South Africa, the United Kingdom and Norway. In 1999, MINDEF set up a Defence Technology Office in Paris to coordinate . Singapore's defence technology cooperation with France and other EU members.[37] During 2000, Singapore was expected to enter into a defence technology exchange agreement with Germany, potentially leading to close cooperation in military aerospace.[38]

SINGAPORE'S DEFENCE INDUSTRY

DTG has provided the essential managerial and R&D underpinnings for Singapore's defence procurement, but the role of the local defence industry has been equally crucial in the local production and modification of equipment for the SAF. Singapore's national defence industry began on a small scale in the late 1960s, on the initiative of then Defence Minister Goh Keng Swee. Motivated in the first instance largely by a wish to pre-empt over-dependence by Singapore on foreign governments and arms suppliers for the SAF's basic requirements in terms of the supply of basic army weapons and ammunition, and the depot-level maintenance of equipment for all three services, Goh oversaw the establishment of a range of state-owned and -directed defence industrial enterprises during the late 1960s and 1970s.[39]

Though the early focus was on producing unsophisticated arms and on maintenance, by the 1990s the industry had developed strengths in the areas of retrofitting and upgrading (particularly of combat aircraft) and the design, development and production of artillery, armoured vehicles and small and medium-sized naval vessels. With DTG as an intermediary, the industry has collaborated widely with foreign defence companies, facilitating its growing sophistication through Industrial Cooperation Programs involving technology transfer, agreed in connection with contracts for licence production and 'off-the-shelf' purchases for the SAF. Singapore's high-technology industrial base, sophisticated and competent defence R&D organisation, and well-educated work-force have enabled it to absorb advanced defence-relevant technologies considerably more easily than other Southeast Asian states. By the end of the 1980s, Singapore's defence industry had become the most substantial, sophisticated and diverse in South-east Asia.

Government-controlled companies dominate Singapore's defence industry, but there are also numerous privately owned suppliers, many of which are local subsidiaries of multinational companies. Some of these companies are important suppliers of minor defence goods (including spare parts) and services to the SAF.

Defence–industrial growth and restructuring

Singapore's government-controlled defence sector has grown rap-idly since it was established in the early years of independence. The sector's foundations were laid during the late 1960s and early 1970s with the establishment of:

- Chartered Industries of Singapore (CIS) in 1967 to produce small arms ammunition. The initial project to establish CIS was codenamed Operation Doberman and relied heavily on advice from Sir Laurence Hartnett, an Australian industrial consultant. CIS soon branched out into manufacturing mortar bombs, medium- and large-calibre ammunition, demolition materials and licence-producing M-16 rifles.[40] In 1973, CIS set up Ordnance Development and Engineering (ODE) to manufac-ture heavier weapons and ammunition such as machine-guns, grenade launchers and mortars.[41]
- Singapore Shipbuilding and Engineering (SSE) in 1968 as a specialist shipyard for maintaining and building naval vessels. In 1969, SSE entered into a technology transfer agreement with the German firm Lürssen, which provided training and technical advice. In the same year, the SSE–Lürssen joint venture won a contract to build six MGBs for the RSN.[42]
- Singapore Electronic and Engineering Limited (SEEL) in 1969 to provide electronic engineering services for the air force.
- Singapore Automotive Engineering (SAE) in 1971 to maintain, modify and upgrade military vehicles.

- The Allied Ordnance Company of Singapore (AOS) in 1973 as a joint venture with the Swedish Bofors company, initially to produce naval and anti-aircraft guns and ammunition.

In 1974 the government set up Sheng-Li ('Victory') Holdings to coordinate the activities of these companies, which were owned by the Ministry of Finance (except for AOS, in which Bofors held a 40 per cent stake) but directed by MINDEF. Subsequently the Sheng-Li group expanded and diversified rapidly, and its subordinate units were restructured several times:

- Two major new functional units were created under Sheng-Li in 1982: the Singapore Technology Corporation, which grouped the ordnance and vehicle companies including CIS, ODE and SAE; and Singapore Aircraft Industries (SAI), created by merging SEEL with the Singapore Aircraft Maintenance Company (SAMCO, set up in 1976). SSE constituted a third unit. These three units became known collectively as Singapore Defence Industries (SDI).[43]
- In 1989, Sheng-Li was re-styled Singapore Technologies (ST) Holdings, indicating extensive diversification towards non-military activities, particularly in high-technology electronics and engineering. There were four divisions under ST: CIS; Singapore Aerospace (SAe, as SAI was retitled); SSE; and the new Singapore Technologies Industrial Corporation (STIC), which subsumed 21 civil-focused companies. In a major corporate reform during the early 1990s, SAe, SSE, STIC and CIS subsidiary SAE became publicly listed companies, though the state retained controlling shareholdings.[44] According to then Second Defence Minister (Services) Lee Hsien Loong, public listing was aimed particularly at providing the companies with 'more flexibility to enter strategic alliances and partnerships with overseas firms and thus establish themselves as technology-based global firms'.[45] However, it was also part of a general move to reduce the government's direct role in business following the mid-1980s recession, with the aim of strengthening the private sector and deepening and broadening the local stock market.[46]
- In 1995 most ST Holdings assets—including those of its already listed companies—were vested in a new operational headquarters known as Singapore Technologies Pte Ltd, mainly to facilitate the group's expansion into regional and international markets. Simultaneously, the names of many ST companies were changed: SAe became ST Aerospace (STAero),

SAE became ST Automotive (STA) and SSE became ST Ship-building & Engineering (STSE).[47]

- In 1997, four core ST businesses—ST Aero, STA, STSE and ST Electronic & Engineering—were grouped under a new publicly listed company, ST Engineering (STEngg). The merger's main aim was to create the critical mass for a listed company which would be more attractive to investors because of its size and smoother revenue stream, and which would benefit from cross-fertilisation and rationalisation of R&D operations.[48]

Singapore Technologies' defence activities

Although ST companies have to compete against international suppliers for some major SAF contracts, they effectively remain MINDEF's favoured suppliers because of the leeway given to Acquisition Management Teams at the third stage of the procurement process to opt for local production or upgrading programmes, combined with the heavy weighting apparently routinely assigned in the analytical hierarchy process to local industrial participation. Senior SAF officers frequently assume positions in ST companies on retirement from active military service, ensuring that the defence industry remains closely attuned to military requirements.[49]

ST activities which support the SAF can be grouped into five main categories. At the most basic level, ST continues to perform its original two roles of providing routine logistic support and depot-level maintenance, and supplying an extensive range of munitions (from 5.56 mm ammunition for infantry weapons up to 155 mm artillery shells and 500 lb bombs) to all three services. These munitions include both licence-produced and locally developed types.

ST's support role was expanded during the 1990s as the SAF—motivated by personnel shortages as well as the desire for efficiency gains—commercialised more of its service, support and logistic functions to the benefit of local industry.[50] A typical example was the complete contractorisation of the SAF's food supplies. ST's comprehensive support is integral to the SAF's potential for sustained operations in time of crisis or war and provides a key strategic advantage over other regional states.

A third type of activity has involved the licence production and assembly of weapons systems and other equipment, ranging from M-16 rifles to naval vessels. Though locally developed systems have superseded some items originally produced under licence, in

1999 local industry was due to start producing Russian Igla manportable SAMs.[51]

In the fourth category, ST companies have—in close collaboration with DMO—upgraded the operational capabilities of many SAF weapon systems since the 1980s. Notable programmes have included:

- refitting the RSAF's large fleet of A-4S strike aircraft (originally purchased second-hand from the US Navy), successively to A-4S-1 and A-4SU standard, the former including a new avionics package and the latter the installation of a new engine providing 30 per cent more thrust and substantially improved performance;[52]
- modifying the RSAF's F-5 fighters to upgrade their capabilities as interceptors, and the conversion of some into RF-5E Tigereye reconnaissance platforms;[53]
- modernising the army's AMX-13 light tanks, involving the installation of turbo-charged diesel engines with automatic transmission, more effective shock-absorbing suspension, and an ergonomically-designed interior. The resulting AMX-13SM1 is faster, more fuel-efficient and has greater operational range;[54]
- converting 300 of the army's M-113A1 APCs into Ultra armoured IFVs, with more powerful engines and new weapons;[55]
- upgrading M71 155 mm gun-howitzers to M71S standard by fitting an engine to drive hydraulic systems and installing firing spades able to harness the gun's recoil to embed it firmly in the ground. The new weapon can be deployed by eight men in two minutes, whereas it took 12 men ten minutes to set up the original M71; and[56]
- retrofitting the RSN's MGBs with Harpoon anti-ship missile launchers. New navigation systems were also installed, and a structural life extension programme was implemented in the mid-1990s.[57]

Finally, ST has itself developed and produced a range of new equipment for the SAF. It would be erroneous to call most of these 'indigenous' systems, as they have relied heavily on imported design expertise. However, over time the systems produced have become increasingly sophisticated, reflecting the ST companies' expanding confidence and capabilities. As with the upgrade projects, close collaboration with DMO has characterised these programmes.

The earliest locally produced weapons, in the late 1970s and early 1980s, were the Ultimax 100 light machine-gun (designed by the noted US weapons expert James Sullivan) and the SAR 80 assault rifle (based on a design purchased from the British Sterling company).[58] From the beginning, the SAF demonstrated that it was by no means a 'captive market' for local products: it was only interested if they were of the required quality. While CIS sold the Ultimax—claimed to be the world's lightest machine-gun—to the SAF in large numbers, the SAR 80—which was intended to replace the M-16 rifle—was never adopted as standard issue equipment because of reliability problems; nor did a follow-up version, the SR 88A, find favour with the SAF. Ultimately, it was not until the high-tech SAR 21, equipped with a laser-aiming device, was developed in the late 1990s that the SAF found a suitable local successor to the M-16.[59] Nevertheless, two other CIS products entered series production for the SAF in the late 1980s and early 1990s: the CIS 50MG heavy machine-gun and the CIS 40AGL automatic grenade launcher.[60] The development, production and export of such weapons led *Jane's Defence Weekly* to list CIS as one of the world's 'top ten' small-arms companies in 1992.[61]

In 1983, ODE began development of a 155 mm gun-howitzer, a far more ambitious and risky project. While it was recognised that buying new artillery 'off-the-shelf' from a foreign supplier would have been simpler, MINDEF calculated that an indigenous project was worthwhile because of the gains for the local defence industry in terms of experience and confidence.[62] The basic design for the weapon was reputedly acquired from SRC International, the Belgian company allegedly involved in helping Iraq to build a super-long-range gun during the 1980s. Singapore's programme resulted in the 30 km-range FH-88 and 40 km-range FH 2000, the world's first towed 52-calibre 155 mm artillery piece.[63]

In the 1990s, SAE developed the Bionix infantry fighting vehicle, which MINDEF claimed was designed to meet the SAF's specific needs: one unique feature is a hydro-pneumatic suspension system to improve rough terrain performance.[64] SAE plans to use the Bionix as the basis for developing further new vehicles, possibly including a light tank, in conjunction with foreign partners.[65]

During the 1970s and 1980s, SSE built larger combat vessels for the RSN under licence. Following the pattern set with its construction of 45-metre MGBs in the early 1970s, between 1988 and 1991 SSE built five 62-metre (595-tonne) MCVs under licence from Lürssen; the first of the class was produced in Germany. SSE's next major project for the RSN, in the mid-1990s, involved building three Landsort-class minehunters under licence from the Swedish company Kockums; again the first-of-class was built in the country of origin. During the 1990s, SSE graduated to building to its own warship designs, as well as integrating C³ and weapons systems into the vessels. The first two such programmes involved the 12 'Fearless' class patrol vessels, including six with sonars and torpedoes for ASW,[66] and the four 'Endurance' class 8500-tonne landing ships.

The major naval programme between 2000 and 2009 will involve construction of a class of French-designed 3000-tonne frigates. The first of six ships will be built in France and the rest in Singapore. This project's announcement in early 2000 came as a surprise: it had been widely expected that the next naval programme after the LSTs would involve developing a 1000- to 1500-tonne 'stealth' corvette, possibly with a trimaran hull.[67] During the late 1990s, there was already close collaboration with Kockums on this project.[68] However, it remains possible that this project, involving greater local technological input than in the case of the frigates, will proceed in order to provide a replacement for the RSN's existing MCVs, which will be 20 years old by 2010.

By the late 1990s, STEngg was developing the Blue Horizon and Firefly high-altitude, high-speed UAVs, using Israeli technology. In the first instance, Firefly could fill an RSAF requirement for a high-altitude, high-speed reconnaissance platform but in the longer-term it could be converted into a cruise missile by fitting a warhead.[69] This programme is likely to draw on the strengths of all major components of STEngg, with ST Aero responsible for the UAV platform, ST Electronics for command and control systems and ST Automotive and ST Marine integrating the system with vehicles and—possibly—warships.[70]

These are the most obvious, high-profile programmes, but behind the scenes ST is undoubtedly closely involved with DSO and SOC in a range of highly confidential high-technology projects, only hinted at in official statements, in the areas of command, control, communications and computer-processing as well as sensor systems. These projects are likely to be pivotal in maintaining the SAF's 'information dominance' on the battlefield.[71] Other key areas of research involve developing computerised wargaming and simulation, and information security systems. Many of these programmes draw on dual-use technology, such as using COTS computers in real-time command and control systems.

The civilianisation of Singapore Technologies

Over the years, and particularly during the 1990s, Singapore Technologies' diversification has dramatically reduced its overall dependence on defence business, and particularly MINDEF contracts. Even in its early years, the Sheng-Li group was never concerned exclusively with military maintenance and production: for example, from its beginnings in 1967 CIS was assigned responsibility for minting coins, and during the mid-1970s the absence of construction orders from Singapore's navy forced SSE to diversify into the construction of civil tug-boats, barges, tankers and container vessels.[72] The various aerospace subsidiaries were heavily involved in servicing civil as well as military aviation in Singapore from the early 1970s. By the time that STIC was created in 1989, ST civil-oriented enterprises included companies concerned with electronics and information technology, precision engineering, industrial leasing, construction and infrastructural development, food processing and distribution and travel and leisure.[73] In 1998, STIC merged with another government-linked corporation, Sembawang (originally a shipyard but more recently a highly diversified conglomerate), to form SembCorp Industries, the largest infrastructure and engineering business in Southeast Asia.[74]

By 1989, non-defence business accounted for 55 per cent of Singapore Technologies' overall turnover; the share had increased to 73 per cent by 1995 and was expected to expand to 80 per cent by 1999.[75] Military business remained central to the activities of STEngg, which in the late 1990s still derived nearly 70 per cent of its sales from MINDEF contracts.[76] Nevertheless, even here there was a determination to expand civil operations: ST Aero aims ultimately to reduce its dependence on military contracts to 30 per cent.[77]

Having benefited from large-scale government investment since the late 1960s, access to the cream of Singapore's engineers and scientists (recruited particularly through the Defence Technology Training Awards scheme) and important transfusions of foreign technology connected with defence contracts, ST companies form the core of Singapore's high-technology industries and perform the 'critical role of grooming engineering and technological skills for the country'.[78] ST has played a vital, catalytic role in Singapore's development as a high-technology oasis in Southeast Asia. Even ST's 'civilian' activities may indirectly help to enhance Singapore's military capabilities, due to the expanding military applications of dual-use innovations and COTS products.

Singapore's arms exports

There has been an important international dimension to ST's diversification. Since the 1980s, the group has aimed to become a multinational company, deriving considerable earnings from overseas and particularly from elsewhere in Asia. Much of ST's overseas activity has been essentially non-military, such as STIC's involvement in developing industrial and high-technology parks in China, India and Indonesia. However, the still defence-oriented businesses within STEngg have also tried hard to reduce their dependence on MINDEF by pursuing export opportunities.

Independent Singapore's earliest arms exports, which began around 1969–70, consisted essentially of CIS-manufactured small arms ammunition and mortar bombs supplied to New Zealand, Australia, Thailand and the Philippines. SSE built fast attack craft for Thailand. In addition, during the 1970s and 1980s the now-defunct Singapore branch of the British-owned Vosper company exported small naval vessels.

As Singapore's state-owned defence industry became more sophisticated, in the late 1970s the government decided to encourage arms exports more actively as a means of subsidising production for the SAF. In 1978, an organisation called Unicorn International was established as Sheng-Li's international marketing arm. In 1983, ST's managing director revealed that the corporation was attempting to increase its export of arms and other products to approximately 50 per cent of production.[79] Thailand remained a particularly important importer of Singapore's defence products, ranging from SAR 80 rifles to licence-manufactured Bofors 40 mm L/70 anti-aircraft guns during the 1980s. A joint venture factory was also established to produce grenade-launchers.[80] Another widely reported contract during the 1980s was India's purchase of SSE-built fast attack craft for its Coast Guard.

During the 1990s ST Aero secured contracts to upgrade F-5 combat aircraft for Venezuela and, in conjunction with Israel Aircraft Industries and Elbit, for Turkey and Brazil; it has also converted Taiwanese F-5s into reconnaissance aircraft.[81] At the same time, Singapore continued to export small arms, other army weapons and various types of ammunition to a wide variety of customers, including Cambodia, Indonesia, Pakistan, the Philippines, Sri Lanka and Zimbabwe. Indonesia began manufacturing grenade launchers under licence from CIS. SSE sold landing and supply craft to Kuwait.

At the end of the 1990s, STEngg entered into a strategic alliance with the British company, Vickers Defence Systems (VDS). Almost certainly linked to the sale of Vickers 105 mm artillery to the SAF, the alliance has involved VDS in attempting to sell modified versions of ST's Bionix IFV to the US and British armies.

Overall though, Singapore has remained a relatively minor defence exporter, successful only in small niche markets. There is considerable evidence that the competitiveness of the international defence market has sometimes pushed Singapore towards the margins of the arms trade and involvement in highly politically sensitive, clandestine deals. On occasion, the republic reportedly acted as an intermediary between western suppliers and clients embargoed by western governments.

Singapore's alleged role in supplying arms to the Middle East has twice provoked international repercussions. In the first case, it was alleged that RBS-70 missiles supplied in component form by the Swedish Bofors company to the Allied Ordnance joint venture for assembly in Singapore in 1979–81 were re-exported to Bahrain, Dubai and possibly Iran, countries to which Swedish arms exports were banned due to the Iran–Iraq war. As a result of these allegations, Sweden froze arms exports to Singapore (the Swedish defence industry's largest overseas customer between 1977 and 1986) for short periods in 1985 and 1987. At the same time, Bofors relinquished its 40 per cent holding in AOS, which became wholly owned by Sheng-Li.[82] However, Sweden ultimately exonerated Singapore's government from responsibility for the illegal exports to the Middle East and Singapore prosecuted the General Manager of AOS for accepting bribes from Bofors and abetting the forgery of end-user certificates.[83]

Although the conclusion to the Bofors affair suggested that a single errant senior defence industry employee may have been culpable on the Singapore side, revelations in Britain in 1995 concerning the 'BMARC scandal' suggested that ST may actually have been more deeply involved in diverting arms imports to third parties. The allegation, which contributed to the downfall of British Cabinet minister Jonathan Aitken, was that 220 naval guns (together with spares sufficient to manufacture a further 100) supplied by the British company BMARC on behalf of the Swiss Oerlikon firm to CIS between 1986 and 1989 were—after assembly in Singapore—re-exported to Iran, contrary to both UK government policy and a United Nations embargo. Other military supplies allegedly transferred from the UK to Iran via Singapore included large quantities of artillery shells and mortar fuses. It was reportedly 'common knowledge among arms dealers that Singapore was a conduit for embargo-busting deals with Iran and Iraq in the 1980s'.[84]

Singapore is also believed to have concluded secret arms export deals during the 1980s and 1990s with Burma (Myanmar); in this case the exports were mainly manufactured in the republic. In late 1988 Foreign Minister Wong Kan Seng tentatively denied that Singapore was exporting arms to Burma,[85] but independent sources claim that subsequently the republic became one of the SLORC regime's major suppliers, transferring mortars, automatic rifles, ammunition, computers, communications and electronic warfare equipment, information technology and radars to Rangoon's armed forces.[86] Singapore may also have transferred its British-supplied Bloodhound SAMs when these became surplus to requirements in the early 1990s.[87] CIS is also reported to have helped modernise Burma's defence industry, for example by supplying a prefabricated factory capable of making small arms and ammunition.[88]

CONCLUSION

By the end of the 1990s Singapore was Southeast Asia's largest arms importer, procuring defence equipment through an efficient, competitive, uncorrupt process aimed at securing the most effective systems at the lowest price. However, it had also developed the most sophisticated defence industry and defence-related R&D in the ASEAN region.

There has been an extremely close triangular relationship between the SAF, MINDEF's DTG (DSTA from April 2000) and ST companies. In other political settings such incestuous links might have engendered corruption and inefficiency, but this has not been the case in Singapore. To the extent that there is a 'military–industrial complex' in Singapore, it seems to have ensured that the armed forces derive good value from their procurement spending in terms of enhanced operational capability, as well as the promise of operational sustainability through first-class maintenance and logistic support in the event of conflict. Though MINDEF sees ST as a strategic partner and as a national resource to be nurtured, the procurement process is broadly competitive. Local solutions to SAF procurements have to be justified in terms of cost-effectiveness. Foreign suppliers find that MINDEF drives a hard bargain in reaching a final price. Similarly, since the corporatisation of DSO National Laboratories, basic defence R&D may now be contracted out to other bodies.

Singapore's diverse range of locally developed arms programmes, many based on assiduously cultivated technology transfer, underlines the extent to which the republic's defence industry and R&D are more advanced in most areas than their Southeast Asian counterparts. One particularly important capability largely missing elsewhere in Southeast Asia is Singapore's ability to integrate and adapt systems from a wide variety of sources—including locally generated dual-use technologies—to produce militarily credible weapons. This capacity was originally developed in relation to upgrade projects, but has increasingly been applied in new-build programmes.

Recognising Singapore's determination to develop its defence R&D as well as its defence industry still further, during the 1990s some western governments (most prominently Sweden and France) decided to promote long-term prospects for arms exports to Singapore by supporting not only industrial cooperation programmes, but also collaboration between their own and Singapore's defence R&D establishments.

Despite its defence–industrial sophistication, Singapore's arms exports have been largely restricted to fairly basic products and services, which have from time to time been sold in national markets embargoed or otherwise ruled out by western exporters. While this has sometimes brought Singapore considerable political opprobrium in return for relatively little direct financial benefit, the republic may have hoped to gain indirect but still tangible diplomatic and economic advantages from such deals.

9

Regional and international links

Many of the SAF's regional and international connections can be traced back to the late 1960s and early 1970s but since the 1980s MINDEF has assigned 'defence diplomacy' a considerably heightened profile as a key activity for Singapore's military. There appear to be several main reasons for this emphasis on developing and maintaining close relations with other states' armed forces and defence establishments, both within Southeast Asia and further afield:

- to encourage benign outside powers (notably the United States and the extra-regional members of the FPDA) to maintain their interest in the security of Southeast Asia, and particularly Singapore;
- to provide a broad context of defence cooperation to facilitate access to extra-territorial training facilities, as well as up-to-date military doctrine and defence technology,[1] while in some cases incidentally improving the prospects for selling Singapore-made defence equipment;
- to develop interoperability with the armed forces of friendly states;
- to facilitate functional security cooperation (for example, joint naval patrols with Indonesia against piracy in regional waters);
- to underpin political and economic relations with military-dominated regimes (such as Suharto's New Order in Indonesia and Myanmar's SLORC/SPDC); and
- to mitigate tensions with potential regional adversaries (most obviously Malaysia), through exercises and other military exchanges aimed essentially at confidence-building.

Beyond exercises, training and exchanges, the SAF's overseas activities have also included minor contributions to UN observer missions and UN-backed military coalitions, as well as disaster relief and the evacuation of Singaporean and friendly states' nationals from crisis zones.

THE ISRAELI CONNECTION

Israel provided crucial military advice and training through its military mission to Singapore between 1966 and 1974. Also during the late 1960s, the Israeli Defence Force (IDF) trained SAF pioneers, such as the 36 original Singapore Armour officers, in its own specialist schools.[2] Subsequently, the two states have maintained an extremely close and multifaceted military relationship. Notwithstanding the early doubts of some SAF personnel concerning the relevance of Israel's military experience to Singapore's tropical environment,[3] the IDF has been one of the most important influences on the development of the SAF. Israel has also been a key source of defence equipment and technology.

The SAF's Israeli connection has been shrouded in secrecy from its beginnings, largely out of fear of exacerbating already sporadically tense relations with Singapore's predominantly Muslim neighbours. MINDEF does not hide the fact that military cooperation with Israel continues, but admits only to the existence of 'several joint projects with the Israeli Ministry of Defence'.[4] Nevertheless, it is clear that Israel's most intimate military link in Southeast Asia is with Singapore, which was the Jewish state's most important defence export market during the 1990s.[5] While the United States has been a more important supplier of major defence equipment (particularly aircraft), Israel has consistently provided Singapore with systems and technology which have enabled the SAF to maintain its superiority over likely regional adversaries. One particular advantage of Israeli-supplied equipment has been Israel's willingness—which has sometimes contrasted with the United States' reluctance—to supply Singapore with source codes enabling the modification and improvement of system software for local requirements.[6]

During the 1970s, Israel supplied Gabriel anti-ship missiles for the navy's fast attack craft and 155 mm howitzers for the artillery. In the 1980s, MINDEF purchased Israeli-built Scout UAVs. Israel's arms exports to Singapore expanded appreciably during the 1990s, and included:

- signals intelligence and electronic warfare systems for MCVs and maritime patrol aircraft;
- Barak naval SAMs;
- radar warning receivers and tactical datalink terminals for combat aircraft;
- air combat training systems, including a Hotshot simulator, an air combat manoeuvring range (ACMR) located in Indonesia and an EHUD air combat manoeuvring instrumentation (ACMI) system;
- systems integration for upgraded F-5 fighters;
- installation of additional avionics, including electronic counter-measures equipment, in F-16D strike aircraft;
- Searcher UAVs and technological assistance in developing more advanced UAVs;
- Spike anti-tank missiles, which are to be manufactured in Singapore, possibly alongside the larger NT-D.[7]

Israel may also have supplied Python 3 and Python 4 short-range infra-red guided AAMs.

Like other suppliers, by the late 1990s Israel's defence industry was increasingly stressing its willingness to transfer technology through industrial participation programmes in order to maintain its share of Singapore's defence market.[8]

Israel has continued to provide advice on a wide array of military topics, ranging from night operations to aviation psychology, and there are understood to be routine exchanges of information between the two countries' intelligence establishments. A small number of IDF officers serves in staff appointments within MINDEF.

TRAINING IN TAIWAN

Singapore entered into a second important new defence relationship after independence, with Taiwan. Since the early 1970s, the essence of the connection has been Singapore's use of Taiwan as the site for its army's most extensive and important overseas training programme (Project Starlight), which has encompassed infantry, armour and artillery training facilities, all attached to Republic of China (ROC) army bases. Heavy SAF equipment kept in Taiwan on a long-term basis, at least until the mid-1990s, included modernised Centurion MBTs, AMX-13 light tanks, M728 combat engineer vehicles and M-71S 155 mm artillery.[9] There is also an air force helicopter detachment, operating Super Pumas.

While Singapore has paid for the construction of purpose-built infrastructure, Taiwan—seeking to enhance its international links wherever possible—has provided the SAF with access to its training areas free of charge.

At their height during the 1980s, Singapore army manoeuvres in Taiwan were codenamed Exercise (Ex) Starlight, Ex Bright Star and Ex Ulysses for battalion-, brigade- and division-level exercises respectively. Ex Firelight involved air defence artillery units. All these exercises offered the SAF opportunities for training in much larger areas than was possible in Singapore, as well as for live-firing of weapons. The biennial Ex Ulysses, which pitted two SAF divisions against each other, was particularly important as it provided senior officers with invaluable 'experience' in the command and control of formations at the operational level of warfare. More than 150 000 SAF troops had trained in Taiwan by 1995. However, for reasons of political sensitivity—Singapore has never maintained diplomatic relations with Taiwan and has no wish to offend the Chinese government in Beijing—MINDEF, the SAF and Singapore's media have seldom acknowledged the existence of Project Starlight. It is an extremely low-profile operation, with SAF conscripts and reservists being flown to Taiwan on clandestine SIA charter flights. Once in Taiwan, SAF troops wear ROC uniforms, distinguishable only by 'Starlight' insignia.

There is also the Sealight series of annual bilateral exercises with Taiwan's navy. Relations between the Singapore and ROC navies have been close since 1975 when Colonel Khoo Eng An, a Singapore-born Taiwanese officer, became RSN Commander, a post he held for ten years.[10] The Sealight exercises usually involve two RSN MCVs and continued despite the high tension between Taiwan and China in the mid- and late 1990s. In addition, the ROC Navy's Training Squadron visits Singapore each year.[11]

On two occasions Singapore's leaders have felt it necessary to discuss the SAF's training in Taiwan publicly. In the first instance, after Indonesia normalised its relations with the People's Republic in 1990, Prime Minister Lee Kuan Yew stressed the importance of the SAF's Taiwanese facilities in the context of Project Starlight being the only possibly significant obstacle remaining in the way of establishing diplomatic links with Beijing. At the same time, though, Chinese Premier Li Peng indicated that Beijing understood and was not 'too disturbed' by Singapore's military training in Taiwan.[12]

Second, at the time of the early 1996 'Straits crisis', which precipitated a degree of popular concern in Singapore over the

safety of SAF personnel in Taiwan, Defence Minister Tony Tan
made it clear that SAF training there would continue.[13] During
1996, the SAF staged brigade and division Command Post Exercises (CPXs) in Taiwan. However, Chinese pressure (which may
have included an offer of facilities for the SAF on the island of
Hainan or elswhere in the People's Republic), combined with the
availability of alternative training areas in Australia and New
Zealand, led to some reduction in Singapore's military activities
in Taiwan. Significantly, it is believed that the SAF armour
training camp closed in 1996. Artillery, infantry and Commando
training has continued on a reduced scale, and during the late
1990s included company-level exercises with ROC troops such as
Marines and Special Forces.

COMMONWEALTH LINKS

Singapore's search for fresh sources of military advice and training
assistance after 1965 was not paralleled by any severance of
defence links with the UK, Australia and New Zealand. Indeed,
Singapore retained close defence relations with all three countries,
even after they withdrew their forces from the republic, through
bilateral links as well as the Five Power Defence Arrangements
(FPDA).

Five Power Defence Arrangements (FPDA)

Apart from the notional earmarking of air force units to the
Integrated Air Defence System (IADS) for the joint defence of
Malaysian and Singaporean airspace in the event of a jointly
perceived threat materialising, Singapore's main FPDA-related
activities involve participation in and hosting joint exercises.
Every year, there are normally three air defence exercises (Adex):
two Minor Adex involving only forces from Singapore and Malaysia, though directed by the Australian Air Vice-Marshal who
commands the IADS, supported by a five-nation staff, from the
Malaysian air base at Butterworth; and one Major Adex which
also involves Australian, New Zealand and British forces. Singapore regularly contributes virtually every type of combat and
support aircraft in the RSAF's order of battle, as well as air defence
missile and 35 mm gun units, to the Adex series.

The most important annual exercise, held in August–September,
is known as Stardex and combines the former second Major Adex
of the year with a naval exercise (the former Ex Starfish), involving

forces from all five members. Since the early 1980s, these exercises have expanded considerably in terms of numbers of units participating, duration and sophistication.[14] In 1997, a larger-scale combined naval and air exercise, Ex Flying Fish, was staged for the first time: it is scheduled to be held every third year.[15] Singapore contributes a wide range of RSN warships, including MCVs, MGBs, MCMVs and landing ships, to the Stardex and Flying Fish exercises. There is also a small-scale annual five-nation army command post exercise (CPX), Ex Suman Warrior, for which the Singapore army usually deploys approximately 50 officers and men from an infantry unit. Malaysia's decision in September 1998 to withdraw temporarily from participation in FPDA exercises led to the cancellation of scheduled manoeuvres, but exercises resumed in early 1999.[16]

Other FPDA activities, sometimes hosted by Singapore, include a biennial Defence Chiefs' Conference and occasional Air Defence Seminars and Joint Operations Forums. Since 1990, small numbers of officers from the extra-regional FPDA partners have been allowed to attend the Singapore Command and Staff College.[17]

Australia

Mutual interests, as well as the context for cooperation provided by the FPDA, have ensured that Singapore's bilateral defence relations with Australia, New Zealand and Britain have remained close despite the withdrawal of their forces from the republic. The most significant of these bilateral connections is with Australia, and is founded on similar strategic outlooks set within the context of a broader bilateral political, economic and technological nexus. The Singapore–Australia New Partnership, which included establishing a bilateral ministerial committee, was announced in early 1996 and survived the electoral defeat of Australia's Labor government shortly afterwards.[18] The bilateral relationship—including its security dimension—continued to broaden and deepen during the late 1990s.[19]

In relation to regional security, Singapore and Australia share an interest in encouraging the United States to remain closely involved in the region's security while attempting to engage China in the regional security dialogue.[20] At the end of the decade, mutual concern over Indonesian developments strengthened the strategic concurrence between Singapore and Australia.[21] By late 1999, following the collapse of the 1995 Agreement on Maintaining Security with Indonesia as a result of Australia's leading role in the international intervention in East Timor, the link with Singapore constituted Australia's closest Asian defence relationship.

During the 1970s and 1980s Singapore benefited from small amounts of Australian military aid, including the provision of flying instructors for the RSAF, under Canberra's defence cooperation program (DCP). With the heightening of regional tensions following the Vietnamese occupation of Cambodia and the Soviet invasion of Afghanistan, Australia not only attempted to resuscitate the FPDA but at the same time to intensify its bilateral defence relationships in Southeast Asia. Because of its perception that any threat to Australia would almost certainly come through Southeast Asia, Canberra has been keen to strengthen the military capabilities of regional states. In the early 1980s, DCP assistance to Singapore was increased significantly (though it still amounted to little over A$1 million annually) and Singaporean army and air force units were granted greater access to training facilities in Australia. RSAF A-4 strike aircraft and Hunter fighters began training detachments to the Royal Australian Air Force (RAAF) base at Williamtown, New South Wales, in 1982, taking advantage of its relatively uncrowded airspace and range facilities.[22] The Matilda series of bilateral Australia–Singapore armour exercises continued, but in addition Singapore troops held their first unilateral exercise in the Shoalwater Bay Training Area (SWBTA) near Rockhampton, Queensland.[23] SWBTA is at least twice the size of Singapore, and features varied and rugged terrain which is ideal for armoured units to train in.

Similar training detachments continued through the 1980s and, in the RSAF's case, broadened to include deployment of F-5 fighters, the use of the Amberley air base in Queensland and live-fire exercises for the Rapier SAM squadron. In 1990, the RSAF joined the hitherto bilateral US–Australian air exercise, Ex Pitch Black, for the first time. Singapore's contingent included F-5s, KC-130 in-flight refuelling tankers and Rapiers: according to the RSAF, the exercise provided 'excellent opportunities to develop strategies and tactics for strike missions in realistic conditions'.[24] The RSAF has participated in all subsequent Pitch Black exercises, which have often involved logistically challenging deployments to various bases in northern Australia. Since 1993, Singapore has also contributed warships and RSAF strike, air defence and maritime patrol aircraft to the biennial Kakadu series of multilateral naval exercises hosted by Australia and also involving other FPDA and ASEAN members.[25] A small Singapore army contingent took part, with other foreign contingents, in the major Kangaroo 95 joint-service exercise rehearsing the defence of northern Australia.[26] The 1990s also saw the inauguration of several alternately hosted annual bilateral exercise series, aimed essentially at enhancing the interoperability of SAF and Australian Defence Force units:

- Ex Flaming Arrow, an infantry exercise involving live-firing (since 1992);[27]
- Ex Singaroo, a naval and maritime air exercise which includes joint training in ASW, anti-air warfare and over-the-horizon targeting (since 1995);[28]
- Ex MCM Hunter, a mine countermeasures exercise (since 1996);[29]
- Ex Axolotl, an annual explosive ordnance disposal exercise involving the RSN's NDU and Australian navy clearance diving teams.[30]

Agreements signed in October 1996 signalled a deepening bilateral defence nexus, covering personnel exchanges and air-to-air refuelling (AAR).[31]

Singapore's unilateral training activities in Australia also intensified during the 1990s, as the republic took advantage of Canberra's eagerness to become more closely-engaged in security partnerships with Asian, and particularly Southeast Asian, governments. Under a 1992 MoU, the RSAF was allowed to deploy combat aircraft to the air bases at Darwin and Amberley, and C-130 transports to Richmond, for up to ten-and-a-half months annually. A further MoU in 1993 covered the wholesale relocation of the RSAF's basic flying training to RAAF Pearce in Western Australia. Prompted by increasing congestion in Singapore's airspace, this agreement runs for 15 years with an option to renew for a further ten years, and involves the basing at Pearce of 160 RSAF personnel (together with 60 civilian technical staff and a total of 200 dependants) and 27 S-211 training aircraft. The Pearce facility allows access to airspace 'two to three times' larger than the RSAF's South China Sea training area.[32]

Singapore's doubts over the future of its defence links with Taiwan precipitated interest in ensuring the future of its unilateral army training programme at SWBTA. A new agreement in February 1995 provided for not only the SAF's continued use of SWBTA for up to 45 days annually until the end of 1999, but also the construction of facilities at Rockhampton Airport (80 kilometres from SWBTA) for storing training equipment during the intervals between annual exercises. The new facilities, managed by British Aerospace Australia, opened in December 1995 and accommodate, *inter alia*, more than 140 vehicles including AMX-13 SM1 tanks and APCs.[33] During the late 1990s, SAF exercises at SWBTA (such as Wallaby 3/96, Wallaroo 97, Wallaroo 98 and Wallaby 4/99) were brigade-scale, involving up to 2000 troops at any one time and as many as 4000 in total, including both NS and NSF units. Up to 230 vehicles (including 90 armoured) were involved in 1995, 1997 and 1998, and as many as 400 (150 armoured) in 1996 and 1999. From 1996, the exercises involved infantry as well as armoured units. In 1998, an ATEC evaluation was carried out on a unit training at SWBTA for the first time. The RSAF provides support with strike and air defence aircraft as well as transports and helicopters.[34] A new agreement signed in September 1999 extended the SAF's use of SWBTA until December 2004 and permitted larger exercises involving up to 6600 troops.[35]

In the longer term, Singapore may become involved in the joint development of a major new army training area in the Northern Territories. This facility will be four times the size of Singapore.[36]

Partially meeting a long-felt MINDEF requirement for an expansion of air force training facilities in Australia, an agreement signed in October 1996 allows the RSAF to station a squadron of up to 12 helicopters and 66 accompanying personnel (plus dependants) at the Australian Army Aviation Centre at Oakey, Queensland, until December 2012.[37] Construction of infrastructure to support the deployment began in November 1997 and the Super Puma helicopters arrived at Oakey in September 1998. The detachment was formally opened in August 1999.[38] As well as conducting advanced and operational flying training, the Oakey-based RSAF helicopters began supporting exercises at SWBTA, approximately 575 kilometres away, almost as soon as they arrived in Queensland.[39]

Under a further agreement, signed in August 1999, the RSAF relocated its air-grading programme, which screens potential pilots for aptitude, to the British Aerospace Flight Training College at Tamworth, New South Wales. The contract, which commenced in December 1999, will be for three years in the first instance, with a seven-year extension option. Thirteen RSAF instructors will be based at Tamworth to screen up to 240 pilot candidates annually.[40]

Singapore's defence relations with Australia are undoubtedly highly beneficial to the city-state, but they have not always run perfectly smoothly. In 1996, during a period of political controversy in Australia over Asian immigration, and embarrassingly coincident with the first meeting of the Singapore–Australia Joint Ministerial Committee, it was reported that SAF personnel and their families had been 'assaulted, robbed and spat at' in Rock-hampton.[41]

More significantly, though, the fact that the economic benefits for Australia of Singapore's Flying Training School (FTS) at Pearce were at least initially disappointing prompted substantial criticism of the republic's attitude, especially by the West Australian state government, particularly in view of the fact that Australia makes no charge for the use of its facilities. It was reported in early 1995 that 'local industry has yet to see any benefits' from the arrangement.[42] STAero was heavily involved in a joint venture established to support the FTS from January 1996.[43] Apparently partly as a result of this dissatisfaction, Singapore has been at pains to ensure that Australian companies benefit more substantially from subsequent arrangements. In December 1997, MINDEF awarded the contract for a three-year, A$25 million Commercial Support Package for the first-line maintenance, scheduled servicing and general technical support of the Oakey helicopter detachment to a local company, Bristow Helicopters Australia. This was the first time that a RSAF maintenance contract had been awarded to a private company in a host nation.[44] MINDEF also emphasised that A$20 million had been spent on building infrastructure at Oakey and that the detachment was expected to inject A$5 million into the local community annually.[45] A less direct benefit for Australian industry of closer bilateral defence relations has been the sale of defence equipment to the SAF. Australia has remained a relatively minor supplier, but significant contracts in the late 1990s included two for a total of approximately 80 Flyer light strike/reconnaissance vehicles produced by Australian Defence Industries.[46]

Although agreement was reached on the basing of RSAF helicopters, Singapore's hope to establish an advanced jet flying training school, equipped with 20 A-4SUs and TA-4SUs, was frustrated. The RSAF's preferred location was Amberley, already host to temporary detachments. However, local complaints over the noise of existing A-4 operations led Canberra to offer alternative sites including the remote base at Woomera (500 kilometres from Adelaide). Other possibilities included building facilities at Rockhampton Airport or constructing a new dedicated base from scratch.[47] Economic and environmental issues aside, negotiations over the proposed jet training facility may have been complicated by a new problem which had arisen by early 1996: Australian defence and intelligence officials claimed privately that, following a serious but unspecified 'incident', Canberra was concerned over apparent Singaporean efforts to collect intelligence on Australia's military capabilities. Ultimately, agreement proved impossible and in July 1997 Singapore opted instead to relocate the RSAF's advanced flying training operation to France.

In the medium-term, however, Singapore may still choose to relocate its advanced flying training to Australia, according to its Chief of Air Force.[48] One possibility is that Singapore could use a proposed commercially operated advanced school equipped with British Aerospace Hawks, similar to the NATO-sponsored programme in Canada which the RSAF joined in 2000.[49]

New Zealand

Although the 740–strong New Zealand Force in Southeast Asia, consisting mainly of an infantry battalion, was withdrawn from Singapore in 1989, a strong bilateral defence relationship has persisted in addition to New Zealand's continued participation in FPDA activities. A New Zealand–Singapore Defence Coordinating Group was set up in 1995 to promote cooperation.

Bilateral interaction forms an important part of the defence relationship, and expanded during the 1990s to include:

- Ex Silver Cobra and Ex Kiwi Cobra, brigade-level army CPXs hosted in alternate years by Singapore and New Zealand respectively, involving the command and control of combined operations;
- Ex Lionwalk, an infantry battalion live-fire exercise;
- Ex Skytrain, a tactical air-drop exercise involving both air forces' C-130 transports;
- Ex Singkiwi, an air force combat exercise inaugurated in 1998;
- Ex Lion Zeal, a biennial navy wargaming exercise scheduled to commence in 1999;
- company-level special forces exercises involving Singapore's Commandos and New Zealand's Special Air Service Regiment;
- an 'affiliation' between air force maritime patrol units.[50]

Like Australia, New Zealand has helped to satisfy some of Singapore's requirements for unilateral army training in wide open spaces. Since 1997, Singapore's artillery has conducted Ex Thunder Warrior, involving the firing of 155 mm guns, at New Zealand's Waioru exercise area. The exercise series began inauspiciously in 1997, when two accidents, including a breach explosion, killed three SAF soldiers.[51] Nevertheless, having commenced at battery strength, in 1999 Ex Thunder Warrior expanded to include a whole artillery battalion of 12 guns.[52] Singapore has also conducted unilateral Commando and UAV training in New Zealand.[53]

New Zealand continues to maintain a Defence Support Unit, consisting of about 12 personnel and tasked primarily with facilitating visits by New Zealand forces, in Singapore. It is also believed to have an intelligence-gathering role.

United Kingdom

Since the withdrawal of British forces during the 1970s, Singapore's most important defence contacts with the UK have taken place in the context of the FPDA. However, during the 1990s the UK not only contributed significantly to FPDA exercises (most notably Ex Flying Fish in 1997), but also strengthened bilateral defence ties with Singapore. Cynics have asserted that the UK's intention to increase its defence sales to Singapore underpinned these efforts, but it is clear that Singapore has remained an important anchor for Britain's residual concern to contribute to Southeast Asian regional stability and protect its regional interests. Despite the withdrawal of all its operational units from Singapore by 1976, the UK left behind a Royal Navy (RN) Supply and Transport Office to maintain and manage two berths at Sembawang for use by visiting RN, United States, Australian and New Zealand warships.

Even during the 1970s and 1980s, UK bilateral military assistance was well-received, despite its small scale. According to one senior MINDEF official:

> The debt of friendship that the SAF owes to the United Kingdom for its assistance is . . . very considerable. Without fanfare, the British have over the years been quietly giving valuable advice, places at Sandhurst, Camberley and other renowned British military schools and colleges, training courses, training for pilots and ground crews, the training of bomb disposal personnel and assistance in many other areas.[54]

During the 1970s, British support for Singapore's fledgling air force was especially important and included the supply of loan personnel to fill key command and staff positions.[55] An RSAF detachment flying Hunter fighters was co-located with the RAF's tactical weapons training units in the UK, first at Chivenor and later Brawdy from 1972 until 1976.

During the 1990s, defence links between Britain and Singapore took the form of collaboration between more equal partners and were set in the context of mutual efforts to intensify bilateral relations across the board, exemplified in the Singapore–UK 'Action Agenda' announced in 1997.[56] The run-up to the return of Hongkong to China in 1997 and the closure of the British garrison and naval facilities there focused the UK defence ministry's thinking on the future role of Britain's armed forces in Asia, providing an additional rationale for closer defence links with Singapore. Rumours that the UK might base a RN warship or even a battalion of Gurkhas in Singapore proved unfounded. However, in 1996 a visiting British Admiral suggested that RN ship visits to Singapore would increase and, in April 1997, the RN and RSN signed an MoU intended to 'strengthen bilateral relations, enhance mutual cooperation and develop common doctrine' and to 'facilitate more regular exercises and formalise training exchanges'.[57] During the same month, Singapore Commandos and British Royal Marines trained together in the first of a new exercise series, Ex Lion City.[58]

Malaysia's temporary withdrawal from FPDA exercises at short notice in September 1998 unexpectedly provided the RSN with an opportunity to exercise bilaterally with an RN frigate which had expected to participate in the annual FPDA Stardex maritime and air defence exercise.[59] The first of a series of annual naval operational planning and war-gaming exercises, Ex Lion Heart 1/99, was staged in June 1999.[60]

Singapore's renewed importance for the RN was demonstrated when it was used as a 'base for forward engineering support and a source of dedicated supplies' during four visits by HMS *Glasgow* during her deployment to the region between April and October 1999. The destroyer participated in two major FPDA exercises, and subsequently joined the flotilla supporting the Australian-led international intervention in East Timor.[61]

DEFENCE RELATIONS WITH THE UNITED STATES: A QUASI-ALLIANCE

During the 1990s, Singapore came to play a key role in keeping the United States deeply involved in regional security and the ever-closer bilateral security relationship began to resemble a quasi-alliance, notwithstanding the lack of a mutual defence treaty obliging the US to defend Singapore.

Singapore's defence relationship with the United States dates from the late 1960s, when it actively supported Washington's war effort during the Vietnam conflict, particularly by providing support for United States Navy (USN) operations in the region in the form of maintenance and resupply, as well as allowing 'rest and recreation' visits. In 1969, a local USN Office (USNO) was set up to administer support for visiting ships. During the 1970s, the United States became Singapore's main defence equipment supplier and small-scale bilateral naval exercises began in 1975. In early 1978, it was disclosed that the USN was using Tengah Air Base for long-range patrol flights over the Indian Ocean. Closer collaboration during the 1980s included the commencement in 1981 of Ex Tiger Balm, an annual joint brigade-level CPX between the Singapore and US armies. The United States Air Force (USAF) was allowed to maintain a facility at Paya Lebar Air Base in support of transiting transport aircraft.

Fears that the US might be forced by nationalist pressure in the Philippines to withdraw its forward-based military presence from Southeast Asia led to a 1990 MoU in which Singapore agreed to allow the expanded use of local facilities for US naval repairs and air force training.[62] This agreement led to more frequent USN visits, the deployment of USAF fighters to Singapore several times annually and an increase in the number of locally based US military support personnel from 20 to 95. The USNO was expanded into a Naval Regional Contracting Office, and the USAF established the 497th Tactical Fighter Training Squadron at Paya Lebar air base to support visiting detachments.

The Philippine Senate's rejection of a proposed new bases treaty with the United States in 1991 led Singapore to agree in January 1992 to allow the transfer of an important USN support unit to the city-state. Consequently, the COMLOG WESTPAC (Commander, Logistics Group, Western Pacific) headquarters was established in Singapore later in the same year with the task of providing logistic support for the US Seventh Fleet and coordinating bilateral exercises throughout Southeast Asia.[63] Greater access to facilities in Singapore soon proved invaluable to the US armed forces in operational terms: for example, Singapore was a key transit point for American ships and aircraft during the 1990–91 Gulf War.[64] In 1998, Singapore further agreed—in an addendum to the 1990 MoU—to allow US Navy ships, including aircraft carriers and submarines, access to the new Changi Naval Base following its completion in 2000. In March 2000, MINDEF and the US Department of Defense signed an Acquisition and Cross-Servicing Agreement, providing for reciprocal logistics support.[65]

This increasingly close relationship, which by the late 1990s saw more than 100 USN vessels visiting annually, together with an average of six one-month deployments by USAF fighter detachments, has benefited Singapore's security not only by helping to maintain a favourable regional balance of power and by complicating the calculations of potential regional aggressors. It has also allowed SAF involvement in increasingly comprehensive and complex bilateral—and indeed multilateral—exercises. The Commando Sling series of exercises began in 1991, and pits visiting USAF fighters (F-16s or F-15s) against RSAF F-16s, F-5s and A-4s in dissimilar air combat training. Occasionally, similar exercises have involved US Marine Corps AV-8B Harriers. In 1998, a Commando Sling exercise included Australian air force participation for the first time.[66] The RSAF also takes part in the annual trilateral Ex Cope Tiger with the US and Thai air forces. In May 2000, the SAF participated for the first time in the large-scale, joint-service Cobra Gold exercise, previously a bilateral US–Thai affair, contributing a small contingent to its CPX phase.

Since 1995, Singapore has been the hub for a new series of bilateral exercises between the USN's Seventh Fleet and Southeast Asian partners. These CARAT (Cooperation Afloat Readiness and Training) exercises, which are planned and coordinated by COMLOG WESTPAC, each comprises a series of sub-exercises. For example, Ex CARAT-Singapore 97 included Ex Mercub (involving combined Task Group-level operations including a maritime air dimension), Ex Mergate (anti-submarine and anti-surface warfare) and Ex Miata (explosive ordnance disposal and damage control).[67] Apart from the CARAT series, each year there is also a bilateral MCM exercise (Ex Mercury) and a trilateral explosive ordnance disposal exercise (Ex Tri-Crab) involving Australia.[68] Future cooperation with the USN may include collaboration in submarine operations and training.[69]

Other examples of closer interaction between the SAF and the US armed forces during the 1990s included the inauguration in 1991 of the usually annual Valiant Mark infantry exercises with the US Marine Corps and a smaller-scale annual bilateral exercise, Ex Lightning Strike, with the US Army from 1996.[70] Though Washington turned down Singapore's requests for a division-level CPX, in 1997 the US Army upgraded its participation in Ex Tiger Balm by deploying an active rather than National Guard brigade headquarters.[71] The SAF's Special Operations Force has conducted joint training with US special forces.[72] By the early 1990s, a small number of US officers (including two USAF pilots and an army staff officer) had been appointed to posts inside the SAF. Annual Staff Talks between senior SAF and US Pacific Command officers commenced in 1995 with the aim of identifying potential areas of further cooperation.[73]

The relationship's most crucial dimension in terms of its impact on the SAF's capabilities, however, has been the extensive range of long-term training opportunities provided for Singapore's air force in the USA. The first such programme, Peace Carvin I, commenced in early 1988 and saw the RSAF's first F-16 fighter unit based at Luke Air Force Base (AFB) in Arizona, where it could take advantage of the local Air Combat Manoeuvring Range (ACMR) and extensive air-to-ground ranges as well as the vast airspace available to the USAF for training. After building up the operational readiness of pilots and groundcrew, culminating in participation in Red Flag (the USAF's most demanding tactical fighter exercise), the squadron departed for Singapore in late 1989.

Recognising the inadequacy of Singapore's airspace and tactical training facilities if the RSAF's front-line fighter force was to maintain a sufficient edge over likely adversaries, in the early 1990s MINDEF secured US agreement to host an F-16 training unit on a longer-term basis. In a move which foreshadowed the expansion of the RSAF's F-16 force, in 1993 a new 10-year programme of RSAF training on F-16s commenced at Luke AFB.[74] This programme, Peace Carvin II, initially used early model F-16A/Bs leased from the USAF, but by 1996 these had been superseded by leased F-16C/Ds. In 1996, Peace Carvin II was extended to a 25-year programme, allowing the RSAF to remain at Luke until 2018. The 130-strong RSAF detachment, composed of personnel on two-year tours, is fully integrated into USAF operational training schedules and is designated as the USAF's 425th Fighter Squadron. The squadron practices live-firing of AAMs (in Ex Combat Archer), deploys throughout the US for dissimilar air combat training, exercises in an anti-shipping role in California and regularly takes part in Red Flag.[75]

In 1996, the RSAF began training personnel for its CH-47D Chinook medium-lift helicopters (ordered in 1994), under the auspices of the Texas Army National Guard at Dallas Naval Air Station. In late 1996, the US Defense Department agreed to a 30–40 per cent increase in the size of this 'Peace Prairie' Detachment to approximately 150 personnel.[76] Although the detachment's original personnel and six helicopters began to return to Singapore during 1999, additional Chinooks had been ordered in the meantime and in 1997 the US government approved Singapore's request for the continuation of Peace Prairie on a long-term basis.

Singapore and the US also agreed in 1997 on a 25-year training programme, known as 'Peace Guardian', in support of the RSAF's purchase of refurbished and upgraded KC-135 in-flight refuelling aircraft from the USAF. As a result, a KC-135 training detachment was established under the USAF's 22nd Air Refuelling Wing at McConnell AFB, Kansas in July 1998. The RSAF's KC-135R aircraft were scheduled for delivery during 1999; in the meantime Singapore leased KC-135 flying hours from the USAF. Approximately 40 RSAF personnel are based at McConnell.[77]

A further training detachment was established in the US in November 1998, with the inauguration of another Singapore F-16C/D unit within the USAF, under the Peace Carvin III programme: the 428th Fighter Squadron at Cannon AFB, New Mexico with 140 RSAF personnel. The Cannon detachment goes through a similar training programme to the unit at Luke and, in early 1999, during Ex Combat Archer became the first RSAF unit ever to fire a radar-guided AAM (an AIM-7 Sparrow). Later that year, the 428th Fighter Squadron joined other USAF, RSAF, Thai and Japanese units in a multilateral exercise, Ex Cape Thunder 99-4, in Alaska.[78]

There is no doubt that the RSAF's close links with the operationally experienced US armed forces have contributed extremely significantly to the development of its own capabilities: existing RSAF training arrangements in the US will remain vital for many years and may be supplemented by others (such as one supporting the AH-64D Apache attack helicopters ordered in 1999). Nevertheless, mainly because of the Pentagon's occasionally restrictive attitude towards the transfer of key technologies and weapons, in the late 1990s there was a degree of unease in MINDEF and the SAF regarding the potential dangers of over-dependence on Washington, particularly in the air power sphere.

INTRA-ASEAN DEFENCE COOPERATION

Since the 1980s, Singapore's leaders have called for closer defence collaboration between ASEAN members. However, recognising the absence of strongly held common threat perceptions, the continued existence of tensions amongst ASEAN members, and the likely military weakness of even ASEAN's combined military capabilities, Singapore has never favoured the Association's transformation into a military alliance, emphasising instead the value of enhancing bilateral links, as provided for in the 1976 Declaration of ASEAN

Concord. Singapore has certainly never seen closer intra-ASEAN defence arrangements as an alternative to continued reliance on the reassurance provided by continued links with the United States and the extra-regional parties to the FPDA.

During the Cold War, the ostensible motive for closer bilateral defence cooperation within ASEAN was to enhance non-communist Southeast Asia's security in the face of a perceived threat from Soviet-backed Vietnam. During the 1990s the declaratory focus has been on building confidence among regional states: according to Tony Tan, joint military exercises are the 'foundation of trust and honesty among neighbouring countries in Southeast Asia'.[79] However, in some cases defence relations with ASEAN partners have served a variety of additional purposes for Singapore.

Malaysia

Although Singapore and Malaysia are partners in the FPDA as well as in ASEAN, frequently poor political relations have prevented bilateral defence links from moving beyond superficial exchanges. Building mutual confidence may have been a significant intention of Singapore–Malaysia defence relations, but joint military activities seem to have reflected, rather than inspired, confidence at the political level: the first casualty of political disagreements has often been military cooperation. By the end of the 1990s, the three main bilateral defence cooperation elements (the Singapore–Malaysia Defence Forum, the Semangat Bersatu army exercise and the Malapura naval exercise), each of which was supposed to take place annually, were all in abeyance. The most substantial recorded bilateral contact between the Singaporean and Malaysian armed forces during 1999 was a golf game between teams of senior officers.[80]

Indonesia

Singapore's defence relations with Indonesia have undoubtedly been its closest within Southeast Asia. In tandem with the blossoming of Singapore's wider relationship with Jakarta during the late 1980s and 1990s, particularly in relation to the economic development of the Riau islands, these military links became increasingly substantial, serving the multiple roles of not only reducing mutual suspicions, cementing Singapore's relations with Indonesia's politically powerful military elite and securing military training facilities for the SAF, but also helping to control low-intensity maritime security threats. As Defence Minister Lee

Boon Yang said in 1994, defence cooperation had become an 'extremely valuable and extremely important facet of Singapore's overall ties with Indonesia'.[81]

Though biennial joint naval (Eagle) and air (Elang Indopura) exercises had been conducted since 1974 and 1980 respectively, there was a marked upswing in defence relations from the late 1980s. Notably, in mid-1987 Jakarta offered Singapore the use of military training facilities for the first time and, as a result, a joint air weapons range was opened at Siabu close to Pekan Baru air base in central Sumatra in March 1989.[82] An MoU was also signed to provide for bilateral army exercises, leading to the first annual Safkar Indopura CPX in December 1989.[83] A Joint Training Committee (JTC) to guide the further development of bilateral military links was established in 1990.

During the 1990s, defence relations did indeed intensify. In terms of exercises and joint training, Safkar Indopura was expanded from a battalion command post/wargame exercise to a brigade-level field manoeuvre in 1995, involving live-firing from 1997 and combined arms training in 1998.[84] The Eagle naval exercises widened in scope to include maritime patrol aircraft and MCMVs. In 1997, the first Joint Minex bilateral mine-clearance exercise took place. The Elang Indopura air exercises became more sophisticated, using the Siabu air-to-ground range, and by 1998 involved C-130 transport aircraft supporting ground troops, and helicopters operating in a search and rescue role. In August 1999, the first exercise in the Camar Indopura bilateral maritime air surveillance series was held in the Natuna Islands; a second followed in January 2000.[85] Air force cooperation also included 'goodwill' visits by Indonesian fighter aircraft to Singapore, an SAR agreement in 1994 leading to regular SAR exercises and a joint fighter weapons instructor course in 1998.[86] Exchanges between officer cadet schools and staff colleges became routine.

In deference to Indonesian nationalist sensibilities, the two countries' armed forces always stressed the 'joint' benefits of Singapore's increasing access to Indonesian military facilities during the 1990s, but much of the training conducted by the SAF in Indonesia was effectively unilateral. An ACMR, built at Singapore's expense with Israeli technical assistance, was opened in the vicinity of the Siabu range in 1994.[87] Singapore also made infrastructural improvements at Pekan Baru air base, including the provision of aircraft shelters, to permit longer-term RSAF training deployments: these facilities were opened in 1998 with the promise that they would eventually be transferred to Indonesia's air force.[88] The RSAF deploys aircraft to Pekan Baru six times a year for three to four weeks at a time. The Indonesian navy made available its naval gunfire range at Pulau Kayu Ara in the South China Sea for use by Singapore's navy and facilities there were developed jointly.[89]

In the late 1990s, the SAF seemed to be on the brink of winning even greater access to training facilities in Indonesia. In 1996, it was reported that the JTC had agreed on joint development of an army training ground in West Kalimantan.[90] This may not have been accurate, but the issue of 'land-training areas' for the SAF remained on the JTC's agenda.[91] In 1997, Indonesia leased 700 hectares to the SAF for use as a helicopter training base close to Tanjungpandan on the island of Belitung (between Sumatra and Kalimantan), where the two air forces had already developed a joint air weapons range.[92]

Cooperation between the two states' navies and marine police was particularly important in practical terms for Singapore. The 1992 Indonesia–Singapore Coordinated Patrol agreement, overseen by an Indonesia–Singapore Joint Coordinating Committee co-chaired by the the SAF's Director JOPD and the Indonesian armed forces' Chief of Staff, brought tangible operational cooperation in the form of highly successful joint patrols against piracy in the Singapore Straits and Phillip Channel. Within a year, these 'Indo-Sin' patrols—which make use of communications hotlines established under a 1992 agreement on naval radio links—had reduced piracy to 'almost zero'.[93] Cooperation against piracy became even more important for Singapore with the escalation in attacks on commercial shipping which accompanied Indonesia's economic recession at the end of the decade.

Reflecting the mutually perceived importance of their cooperation, in 1997 the Indonesian and Singapore defence ministries inaugurated annual policy talks to exchange views on regional security and defence matters as well as future directions for bilateral defence cooperation.[94]

Although Indonesia's economic and political turmoil following the financial crisis of 1997 caused serious tensions between Singapore and Jakarta, the strong military-to-military links built up over the previous decade provided an unbroken thread of continuity in the bilateral relationship. This contrasted with the attenuation of Singapore's bilateral defence cooperation with Malaysia and the suspension of FPDA exercises in 1998 because of political disagreements. If Indonesia maintains its geopolitical cohesion and there is no overwhelming nationalist backlash against foreign influences as a result of the country's economic problems and its perceived humiliation by the international intervention in East Timor, MINDEF and the SAF are likely to continue building on existing links. However, this is by no means assured and either Indonesia's disintegration or an eruption of xenophobia could cause defence relations to unravel.

Thailand

Singapore's relations with Thailand have a particularly strong strategic dimension. There have been relatively few diplomatic disputes between Singapore and Thailand, which have strong bilateral economic relations. Their wider international outlooks are similar: both have close security and links with the United States and both have developed important relationships with China. At the same time, both have unstable political relationships with Malaysia. According to Tony Tan, 'Singapore has a special and enduring defence relationship with Thailand'.[95]

Thailand provides the SAF with some of its most important overseas training facilities. Commando officers and NCOs first trained with Thai special forces at Lopburi in 1973.[96] Artillery and Combat Engineer training has been undertaken at Ban Yai Sok in Kanchanaburi province (about 100 kilometres west of Bangkok) since 1979, under a programme codenamed Crescendo. A 1997 MoU on RSAF training in Thailand formalised the deployment, usually twice annually, of combat aircraft to Korat air base (where they use the local ACMI and air-to-ground ranges) and helicopters to Kokekathiam (the army aviation centre at Lopburi).[97]

Other military cooperation includes air, naval and army exercises. An annual bilateral air exercise, Ex Air Thaising, was held from 1983 to 1993, but from 1994 was superseded by the trilateral Ex Cope Tiger, which also involves US participation. Ex Cope Tiger comprises a CPX phase in Singapore followed by a flying component at Korat, to which the RSAF contributes fighter and strike aircraft and SAM and radar units.[98] A joint naval exercise, Ex Sing Siam, is staged every two years. Following an agreement in 1996 to expand defence ties, an annual bilateral army CPX, Ex Kocha Singa, commenced in 1997 and in 2000 Singapore decided to join the annual US–Thai Cobra Gold exercise. Other innovations included a junior naval officer exchange programme and air force flight safety cooperation.[99]

The Philippines

Singapore's relations with the Philippines have generally been cordial, but bilateral military links have been limited. Until the early 1990s, the most substantial cooperation took the form of the RSAF basing training detachments of combat aircraft (F-5s, A-4s and Hunters) at the USAF's Clark Air Base, which was permitted by a 1979 Singapore–Philippines agreement. RSAF detachments used the Crow Valley ACMR and bombing ranges, and participated in multilateral Cope Thunder exercises organised by the USAF.[100] These detachments continued until the eruption of nearby Mt Pinatubo forced the evacuation of Clark in 1991, prompting the RSAF to sponsor the construction of the ACMR at Pekan Baru to make up for the loss of access to Crow Valley.

Following the United States' total military withdrawal from the Philippines in 1992, Singapore responded to Manila's efforts to establish bilateral defence links with other ASEAN members to compensate for the loss of the American presence. Joint exercises commenced with Ex Anoa-Singa, involving infantry manoeuvres, in 1993: this was the Philippines' first bilateral exercise with any state other than the US.[101] In August 1994 the RSN and the Philippine Navy approved an Exercise Procedure Document for the planning and conduct of joint exercises, the first of which was scheduled for July 1995.[102] The third Ex Anoa-Singa, in early 1995, involved helicopter and armoured units for the first time.[103] However, a serious diplomatic dispute following Singapore's execution of a Filipina domestic servant convicted of murder resulted in the two states withdrawing their ambassadors in March 1995; military contacts including the planned naval exercise were suspended.

Relations had improved considerably by early 1996 and the first Ex Dagat Singa, which included live-firing at sea, was held in July 1996, soon after the fourth Ex Anoa-Singa.[104] Defence cooperation was one component of the Philippine–Singapore Action Plan signed in December 1998 and aimed at enhancing the overall bilateral relationship.[105] The possibility of benefits for its own defence industry from the Philippines' planned large-scale military modernisation programme may partially have explained Singapore's continuing interest in cultivating defence links.[106] However, the lack of a status of forces agreement between the two countries prevented the staging of more bilateral exercises: during the 1997–99 period military contacts were restricted to passage exercises at sea, visits by senior officers and the attendance of Philippine officers on SAF courses.[107] The Philippine Senate's ratification of the Visiting Forces Agreement with the US in May 1999 may clear the way for a similar accord with Singapore, allowing exercises to resume.

Brunei

Singapore maintains an extremely close all-round political and economic relationship with Brunei, and their defence connection is mutually beneficial: the Sultanate provides the republic with its main jungle-training facility while the SAF provides the Royal Brunei Armed Forces (RBAF) with a comprehensive range of bilateral training opportunities.

The SAF began its jungle warfare training programme—codenamed Lancer—in Brunei's Temburong District (which is separated from the main part of the Sultanate by Malaysian territory) in 1977. Initially based in former Gurkha barracks at Kilong Camp, in 1983 Lancer moved to custom-built facilities at Lakiun.[108] At Lakiun, a 100-strong long-term training and support cadre provides comprehensive jungle training for both NSF and NS infantry and Guards battalions in three-week courses.[109] When still prime minister, Lee Kuan Yew highlighted the importance of Lakiun, claiming that 'the jungle training school we have here is the most valuable single facility which will be difficult to duplicate elsewhere'.[110]

There is a HQ and transit camp at Jalan Aman, on the outskirts of Brunei's capital, Bandar Seri Begawan, as well as a permanent RSAF detachment operating UH-1H helicopters from the international airport. Also located in the main part of Brunei is a joint RBAF–SAF armour live-firing range at Binturan, where the SAF has based an Armour Detachment with AMX-13 light tanks and M-113 APCs since 1983.[111] Since the mid-1990s, a small number of Centurion MBTs has also been deployed to Binturan.

The first SAF–RBAF joint exercises involved the two navies. Ex Pelican, first staged in 1979, became increasingly sophisticated during the 1990s. Reflecting the widening opportunities for Singapore's navy to engage in exercises with regional partners, however, from the late 1990s a sea-going Pelican exercise was held only biennially, with a CPX in alternate years.[112]

In 1983 an SAF–RBAF Interaction Programme was established, leading to a sustained widening of annual bilateral training contacts between branches of the two armed forces:

- Ex Flaming Arrow has brought together an SAF infantry battalion (sometimes a reservist unit) and an RBAF infantry company in a live-fire exercise since 1985;
- Ex Bold Sabre, inaugurated in 1992, involves an SAF armoured battalion and the RBAF's Armoured Reconnaissance Squadron or one of its mechanised infantry companies;
- Ex Bold Castle, established in 1993, is a Combat Engineer exercise, focused on activities such as obstacle clearance, bridging and demolition;
- Ex Airguard has exercised SAF and RBAF air defence units equipped with Rapier SAMs since 1994;
- Ex Maju Bersama is a combined arms battalion-strength manoeuvre exercise, first held in 1995; and
- SAF units training at Lakiun also occasionally exercise with the RBAF.[113]

Greater interaction also involved the SAF in training individual RBAF personnel. A particularly important SAF contribution in this respect has been the routine training of RBAF officers, including both helicopter and fixed-wing pilots.

Singapore's Vosper yard supplied the RBAF with fast attack and coastal patrol craft during the 1970s, but the republic is not known to have sold any other significant defence equipment to Brunei. However, in 1996 Tony Tan offered 'Singapore's expertise' to assist the RBAF's modernisation programme.[114] In the 1998 Maju Bersama exercise, Bruneian infantrymen operated from SAF Bionix IFVs, possibly presaging a contract to supply these vehicles to the RBAF.[115]

Burma

During the 1990s, Singapore's defence relationship with Burma—which paralleled the city-state's growing economic stake there, as well as its policy of constructive engagement with the SLORC regime—expanded beyond the supply of defence equipment to include the provision of specialised training, particularly in information technology. From the mid-1990s, RSAF transport aircraft on navigational training flights visited Rangoon *en route* to Bangladesh and Singapore Artillery units may have undertaken training on Burmese ranges.[116] The appointment of the Director of MINDEF's Joint Intelligence Directorate, a senior serving SAF officer, as ambassador in Rangoon in 1996 underlined the importance of the defence dimension to bilateral relations.[117]

Vietnam

Despite having played a leading role in opposing Vietnam's military role in Cambodia during the 1980s, even before Hanoi joined ASEAN in July 1995 Singapore was exploring the possibility of developing bilateral defence links in the context of burgeoning economic ties and a thaw in political relations. A visit by Vietnam's defence minister in March 1995 formally established defence ties, with Singapore perceiving opportunities for both defence sales and securing access to additional training facilities (including access to Vietnamese air bases).[118] Further visits and discussions followed, but by the end of the decade little had been achieved in terms of concrete collaboration. In early 1999, Washington's opposition prevented STA from securing a contract to refurbish and upgrade 100 of Vietnam's US-supplied M-113 APCs in partnership with a company controlled by Vietnam's defence ministry.[119]

NEW INTERNATIONAL HORIZONS

During the 1990s, MINDEF has also sought to enhance previously existing defence relationships with more distant partners, while simultaneously establishing several entirely new defence links outside the region. Some of these partnerships have yielded substantial benefits for the SAF, particularly in the form of improved training opportunities, but others—notably with Japan and China—have constituted little more than exercises in defence diplomacy, defined fairly narrowly.

India

Singapore's defence relations with India intensified during the 1990s, but have focused exclusively on naval cooperation. The Lion King series of annual bilateral ASW exercises began in 1993, involving RSN MCVs training with Indian Navy frigates and submarines in the Andaman Sea, Bay of Bengal or Indian Ocean. Over time, these exercises' duration and complexity have increased. The 1998 exercise lasted 12 days and involved RSN ASW patrol vessels for the first time.[120] Cooperation with India also allowed RSN personnel to train on board Indian Navy Foxtrot-class submarines, providing valuable 'hands-on' experience before Singapore acquired its own submarines from Sweden in the late 1990s.[121]

It was reported in late 1998 that the Indian and Singapore navies would 'soon' sign an MoU on ASW training and cooperation in protecting sea lanes in the eastern Indian Ocean.[122]

Bangladesh

In 1993, the RSAF began one-week training deployments of transport aircraft and helicopters to Bangladesh's Bashar Air Base, near Dhaka.[123] In February 1994, an MoU formalised such training on a long-term basis, allowing the RSAF to send 'a number of aircraft' to Bangladesh air bases for 'several months' annually.[124] Bangladesh Air Force transport aircraft have also visited Singapore.[125]

South Africa

Following a series of reciprocal visits by ministers and senior military officers since 1994, in November 1997 Singapore and South Africa signed an Agreement on Military Cooperation, which provided a framework for cooperation in areas such as 'military training, exchange of expertise and knowledge, defence technology and industrial cooperation, military medical services and peacekeeping operations'.[126] From Singapore's viewpoint defence relations with South Africa opened up important new training possibilities. In 1997, the RSAF conducted the first of a series of SAM live-firing exercises, using RBS 70 and Mistral missiles, at the Overberg Toetsbann instrumented range.[127] In its June 1999 exercise at the range the RSAF fired Igla missiles for the first time.[128] In December 1998, the RSAF deployed a UAV training detachment of 60 personnel to Hoedspruit Air Base, near Pretoria, for six weeks.[129]

Canada

In December 1997, Singapore and Canada signed an MoU allowing the RSAF to deploy aircraft, equipment and personnel to Canadian air bases for training. The MoU included provisions for RSAF fighter, transport and air defence artillery units to join multilateral exercises in Canada, further widening the training opportunities available to US-based RSAF detachments. In May 2000, the RSAF deployed 10 F-16s from Cannon AFB to Ex Maple Flag, a large-scale multilateral air combat exercise at Cold Lake, Alberta.[130] Singapore's participation in the NATO Flying Training in Canada scheme will see RSAF fast jet pilot trainees undertaking advanced and operational flying training at Moose Jaw, Saskatchewan and Cold Lake, respectively.

France

The SAF's French connection dates from the late 1960s, when RSAF rotary-wing pilots were trained in France following Singapore's purchase of Alouette III helicopters. During the 1970s and 1980s Singapore acquired some significant defence equipment from France, including second-hand T-33 jet trainers, AMX-13 tanks and Ecureuil and Super Puma helicopters. In the early 1990s, a major deal involved armoured vehicles, light artillery, short-range SAMs and more helicopters. However, although there was some low-level interaction between the SAF and the French armed forces, including operational training for RSAF helicopter crews in France and occasional passage exercises between the two navies,[131] there was no substantial defence cooperation before the late 1990s.

France has stressed its strategic interest in developing security links with Singapore in view of the latter's geostrategic position (particularly her proximity to the Malacca Straits).[132] French interest in closer cooperation with the SAF, however, was at least partially motivated by a desire to cultivate Singapore as a customer for further major defence sales, particularly naval vessels, the new Rafale fighter and the Tiger attack helicopter. In January 1997, a consultative French Air Force–RSAF Air Group was established, with the aim of promoting cooperation and the 'sharing of information in professional military matters'.[133] In June 1997, a two-year agreement allowed the exchange of helicopter pilots between the RSAF and France's army aviation.[134] A bilateral Army Working Group met for the first time in September 1998.[135]

Several months of negotiation through the Air Group resulted in a highly significant agreement in July 1997 which allowed the RSAF to deploy aircraft and personnel to French air bases for training.[136] As a result of this agreement, an Advanced Jet Training detachment of approximately 100 personnel and 10 A-4SU and TA-4SU aircraft was deployed to Cazaux air base in southwest France in June 1998.[137] Following the signing of a Defence Cooperation and Status of Forces Agreement in October 1998, allowing the RSAF to remain at Cazaux for up to 20 years, the size of the detachment—which MINDEF still described as 'temporary'—was increased to approximately 200 personnel and 18 aircraft by April 1999.[138] Another dimension of the RSAF's training in France may have involved its aircrew flying in French air force Mirage 2000s for electronic warfare training.[139] In May 2000, RSAF aircraft from Cazaux participated in ODAX 2000, a French-led multilateral exercise also involving other NATO air forces.

In a display of determination to bolster defence cooperation with Singapore, in early 1998 the French air force sent six Mirage 2000 fighters, as well as its Chief of Staff, to the island for Ex Eastern Arc, a two-week long dissimilar air combat training exercise.[140] The second Ex Eastern Arc involved a similar deployment in February 2000.[141]

In June 1999, the two states' defence ministers signed a General Security Agreement covering the exchange of classified information, and the following month a French Armed Forces—SAF Joint Committee was established to explore further possibilities for cooperation.[142] The order for six French-designed frigates led to the establishment in April 2000 of a bilateral Navy Working Group.

Sweden

Despite interruptions to the bilateral defence–industrial relationship and a temporary souring of the bilateral political relationship during the mid-1980s as a result of Singapore's alleged unreliability as an end-user of its military imports,[143] during the 1990s the SAF again became a major customer for Swedish defence products, mainly in the naval sphere. The bilateral defence relationship has focused particularly on providing the RSN with training in support of its defence procurement from Sweden.

The Lejon-Singa exchange programme, which has involved an annual, alternately hosted bilateral MCM exercise since 1996, is an extension of cooperation relating to Singapore's purchase of four Swedish-designed Landsort-class MCM vessels (three of which were built in Singapore).[144]

In September 1995, Tony Tan announced that Singapore would purchase a second-hand Sjoormen-class (A12 type) submarine from Sweden. The boat would be refurbished and the Swedish navy would provide a two- to four-year training programme for RSN crews, including sea training on A12 type boats and other, more modern submarines. The first 33 RSN personnel were sent to Sweden in March 1996 and were awarded their submarine insignia in December 1997. They remained in Sweden for advanced training and to take part in sea trials of the RSN's first submarine.[145] Meanwhile, it was announced in July 1997 that three additional A12 type submarines would be purchased; a navy-to-navy agreement covering an enlarged, longer-term training programme was signed in February 1998.[146]

Japan

Despite sharing important strategic interests with Japan, particularly in terms of sea lane security, for historical reasons and because of fears over potential Sino-Japanese confrontation, Singapore has attempted to discourage Japan from extending its military activities beyond its established self-defence posture. Nevertheless, bilateral defence cooperation increased during the 1990s as the Japan Defence Agency (JDA) became more assertive in seeking regional links.

Japanese warships on training cruises began making occasional 'goodwill' visits to Singapore during the 1970s, but these visits had become annual by the early 1990s.[147] According to MINDEF, defence links with Japan were 'growing steadily' by the mid-1990s; in March 1996 the RSN and Japan's Maritime Self Defence Force conducted a 'goodwill exercise'—the first of an annual series—in the Singapore Straits.[148] In December 1997, MINDEF and the JDA established an annual dialogue on defence and security matters; in early 1999 the two defence ministers agreed to discuss the specifics of bilateral defence cooperation in these MINDEF–JDA Policy Talks. They also agreed to increase naval and air force exchanges. In May 2000 the two sides decided to augment their policy discussions with military staff talks.[149]

In May 1998, the SAF provided facilities for Japan's second largest military deployment to Southeast Asia since 1945, when Tokyo sent six transport aircraft and 200 military personnel, as well as two large Maritime Safety Agency (coast guard) ships, to Singapore in readiness to evacuate Japanese nationals from Indonesia at the time of the violent demonstrations against President Suharto.

China

Mainly because of a wish to avoid alienating its immediate neighbours and the United States, and possibly also because of lingering concerns over subversion inspired by Beijing, Singapore's defence collaboration with China has remained extremely limited. Nevertheless, in October 1997 Singapore agreed to a 'more regular' exchange of reciprocal visits by senior defence officials and military officers with a view to promoting 'better mutual understanding and confidence'.[150] China's Minister for National Defence, Chi Haotian, visited Singapore in December 1998.[151]

Defence seminars and conferences

Apart from its bilateral defence cooperation, the SAF has attempted to broaden its links with other Asia-Pacific armed forces through its senior officers' involvement in the US-sponsored Western Pacific Naval Symposium and the Pacific Army Chiefs' Conference (which Singapore co-hosted in 1999). In February 2000, the RSAF organised a Millennium Air Power Conference to coincide with the Asian Aerospace 2000 exhibition in Singapore.

SINGAPORE AS INTERNATIONAL GOOD CITIZEN: UN AND COALITION OPERATIONS

The SAF's reliance on conscripts and reservists has prevented Singapore from allocating forces to UN peacekeeping operations as such. However, since 1989 it has contributed military observers, election monitors, and medical and air support to various UN activities in Namibia (UNTAG, 1989), Angola (UNAVEM II, 1991–92), Cambodia (UNTAC, 1993), South Africa (UNOMSA, 1994), Guatemala (MINUGUA, 1997), Afghanistan (UNSMA, 1997–98) and on the Iraq–Kuwait border (UNIKOM, since 1991).[152] Singapore has played a continuous, long-term role in UNIKOM, and despatched its ninth team of four officers to the mission in April 1999. Reservist as well as regular SAF officers have served with UNIKOM.

Singapore's increasing involvement in UN-sponsored military activities during the 1990s reflected not just its general 'commitment as a responsible member of the international community and . . . firm belief in the principles of the UN Charter',[153] but also a more specific interest in securing a non-permanent Security Council seat for 2001–2. Since 1995, the SAF has contributed three staff officers at any one time to the Directorate of Peacekeeping Operations at UN Headquarters in New York.[154] In 1997, Singapore pledged a quick-reaction force including two teams of four military observers, 15 medical personnel and planning officers, as well as small numbers of RSAF C-130 transports and Super Puma helicopters, to the United Nations Standby Arrangements.[155]

Coalition operations: the Gulf War and Interfet

Singapore has also contributed minor elements to two UN-authorised coalition operations led by western powers. Both operations related to the liberation of small territories which had been violated by larger powers.

In 1991, in Operation Nightingale, the SAF sent a 35-strong medical team, including conscripts and reservists as well as regulars, to form part of a British army General Hospital in Saudi Arabia during the Gulf War.[156]

The SAF's second coalition involvement began in September 1999, when it despatched a 250-strong contingent consisting of a medical detachment, military observers and two RSN landing ships to join the Australian-led multinational force, INTERFET, in East Timor. The tri-service, 26-strong medical team was attached to an Australian Forward Surgical Troop, while the landing ships were used to ferry supplies from Darwin to Dili.[157] A third LST and an RSAF C-130 transport aircraft were deployed in January 2000 to assist in the transfer of responsibility for the territory's security from INTERFET to the UN Transitional Administration in East Timor (UNTAET).

The SAF continued to play a role in East Timor after UNTAET took over in February 2000, Singapore's contribution comprising a 21-strong medical team, and eight military observers and staff officers. A team of 40 police officers was also deployed.

Humanitarian missions

The SAF has been sending personnel and emergency supplies to Asian countries affected by natural disasters since 1970. The first mission—in which a medical team was despatched to Bangladesh following a devastating cyclone—depended on the British RAF for air transport. However, the RSAF has transported subsequent missions, beginning with the medical team sent to Bali after the earthquake there in 1976.

With the increased availability of air transport following the expansion of the RSAF's C-130 fleet during the 1980s and the accumulation of disaster relief experience, such emergency aid has become a significant aspect of the SAF's defence diplomacy. Missions have included: Philippines, 1987 (Typhoon Nina); Nepal, 1988 (earthquake); Philippines, 1990 (Baguio earthquake); Philippines, 1991 (Mt Pinatubo eruption); Indonesia, 1992 (Flores earthquake); Indonesia, 1995 (Jambi earthquake); Laos, 1997 (flooding); and Taiwan, 1999 (earthquake).[158]

RSAF aircraft have also been used in several other international missions:

- in a joint operation with Brunei to deliver emergency aid to Jordan and to evacuate from Amman Sri Lankan refugees expelled from Iraq in 1990;
- to evacuate ASEAN, Sri Lankan and Indian nationals from Saudi Arabia in 1991;
- to evacuate 450 Singaporeans from Cambodia during political instability there in July 1997; and
- assist the Indonesian air force in the airborne diffusion of chemicals intended to disperse 'haze' over southern Sumatra in October 1997.[159]

In August 1998, Singapore's government used RSAF aircraft and a navy landing ship to deliver humanitarian aid supplies (rice and medicines) to Indonesia. RSN participation in Indonesian navy 'socio-civic programmes' became routine during the late 1990s; the sixth such Surya Bhaskara Jaya (SBJ) mission took place in February 2000.[160]

CONCLUSION

Singapore's range of international military links and activities is undoubtedly the most extensive of any Southeast Asian state. A claim by Singapore's defence minister in 1998 that he and his MINDEF colleagues gave 'daily attention' to regional and wider defence relations is inherently credible,[161] for during the 1990s these relations became more crucial than ever to the continuing enhancement of the SAF's capabilities. The SAF has benefited not just through access to realistic overseas training, but also from widespread exposure to combat-experienced western armed forces' operational doctrine. The extremely close collaboration between the RSAF and the US armed forces is the most obvious example of this.

Increasingly close defence relations with the US, Australia, New Zealand, the UK and France have helped to anchor these friendly powers' regional security presence in Singapore, improving the city-state's security by complicating the calculations of likely aggressors. At the same time, the SAF has developed high levels of interoperability with not only these countries' armed forces, but also those of some ASEAN members (notably Thailand and Brunei), increasing the potential for joint military operations.

Defence diplomacy, including humanitarian operations, has served a confidence-building role in relation to some regional states. Even in the case of defence links with Malaysia, which seem to have suffered as a result of bilateral political tension, it may be argued that the existence of channels of communication between the Singapore and Malaysian armed forces—both bilaterally and through the FPDA—could in some circumstances prevent deteriorating relations from spiralling out of control.

However, despite the great breadth and depth of Singapore's regional and international defence connections, none of these relationships constitutes an alliance in the sense of providing a security guarantee. In the last resort, Singapore must still be prepared to defend itself using its own resources.

10

Political and administrative roles

Even taking into account its important but essentially low-profile background role of nation-building, the SAF's non-military activities have been minimal compared with those of most other Southeast Asian armed forces. Because of the relative unimportance of internal security considerations and the absence of the rural socioeconomic deprivation so prevalent elsewhere in the region, the SAF has not exercised a civic action role apart from assisting small-scale community projects such as bridge-building and road-repairing during the late 1960s and early 1970s.[1] Moreover, until the 1980s it was common for the SAF to be grouped with the Malaysian Armed Forces (MAF) as one of the least politically oriented national military forces in Southeast Asia.

AN APOLITICAL POSTURE?

Over the years, several explanations have been suggested for the SAF's posture of political non-involvement. In the first place, the successful separation of Singapore from Malaysia in 1965 owed nothing to the SAF, which did not yet exist as an entity distinct from the MAF. So unlike some of its Southeast Asian counterparts, the SAF's officer corps has never had grounds for claiming even a degree of political legitimacy based on a role in national liberation.

A related point is that the SAF can trace its origins to various colonial armed forces set up under British auspices from the mid-nineteenth century onwards. In the first instance, the SAF closely followed the British military pattern in matters of organisation, terminology and custom. The SAF also imbibed the

British armed forces' traditional posture of apolitical profession-alism, involving full subservience to the civilian political authority. This is not to suggest that the British military heritage of the SAF automatically led to its adoption of an apolitical posture: there are too many examples of British-pattern armed forces intervening in politics (as in Pakistan, Bangladesh, Nigeria, Ghana and Fiji) to support any such notion. It is clear though, that the residual influence of the apolitical British military style reinforced other reasons for the SAF's lack of interest in becoming politically involved. Later influences on the SAF—resulting from close military relationships with the United States and Israel—almost certainly further bolstered the SAF's professionalism, in the sense of political disinterestedness as well as technical com-petence in the military art.

More importantly, however, in Singapore after 1965 there was an effective civilian government formed by a political party which had secured widespread popular support. There was no political vacuum for the military to fill. As local academic Chan Heng Chee wrote:

> . . . the development and expansion of the SAF have taken place in the midst of strong, complex political structures which enjoy high legitimacy; in no sense does the island state under the PAP government manifest the conditions of a praetorian society. The strong identification with and approval of the populace towards the existing government give no grounds for military intervention.[2]

The 'economic miracle' which transformed Singapore into one of East Asia's four 'little dragons' during the 1970s constituted an extremely important element in the PAP's legitimacy. This eco-nomic success yielded highly tangible benefits for the SAF: the allocation of substantial resources to defence helped to create conditions in which SAF officers could develop their military professionalism: generous pay and conditions of service, excellent opportunities for both general education and technical training and a modern technological environment.

THE SAF AND THE 'ADMINISTRATIVE STATE'

In what was by Singaporean standards a strikingly forthright article, in 1975 Chan Heng Chee contended that Singapore had become an 'administrative state', in which 'the meaningful political arena is shifting, or has shifted to the bureaucracy'. Chan pointed out that:

> ... whilst this is a universal trend and problem, the bureaucracy in Singapore plays a . . . pre-eminent role because of the vast deployment of governmental development activities in non-conventional areas. It is the extension into an entirely new range of activities in the charge of civil servants that a greater awareness of the bureaucrats' role and its consequences must be grasped as they run important ministries, statutory institutions and private companies.[3]

She went on to argue that:

> The growth of government activities through the statutory boards and private companies has increased the scope of power of the civil servants who are placed in charge . . . In any real life situation, the traditional dichotomy between politics and administration is academic. Administrators are politicians in their own way. In Singapore, the division between the administrator and the politician is particularly blurred because it is unstated official policy to politicise the administrators and entrust them with major power in decision-making . . .[4]

Chan expressed concern that while 'the bureaucrats have not usurped power because the political leadership is strong', there was 'no assurance that the next generation of political leaders will possess the same authority and control over the bureaucrats'.[5] There was, in her view, a danger that the civil servants—wielding 'power and privilege without accountability to the public'—might become Singapore's 'real rulers'.[6] Another aspect of the blurring of the dichotomy between administration and politics in Singapore was the transfer of a number of senior civil servants into parliament and ministerial positions during the 1970s and 1980s: the civil service was 'the favoured recruiting ground for future PAP political leaders'.[7]

Although the 1980s witnessed a significant resurgence of organised political opposition to the dominance of the PAP, the ruling party's hold on power has remained unshaken. In November 1990, an important stage in the transition to the second-generation PAP leadership was completed when Goh Chok Tong replaced Lee Kuan Yew as prime minister. Despite alterations to governmental style under Goh's leadership, however, there has been no significant change in the substance of PAP rule. While there is no evidence that Goh and his cohort have less control over the bureaucracy than did Lee Kuan Yew and his first-generation

PAP leadership, neither was there any sign that Singapore during the 1990s was less of an administrative state than it had been during the 1970s.

Writing in 1975, Chan Heng Chee referred in passing to 'the problem of the military-industrial-administrative complex'[8] but neither then nor in her later work on civil–military relations in Singapore did she anticipate that such a complex would ever be a significant factor in Singapore's politics.[9] By the 1990s, however, Singapore was not only an 'administrative state': it was an administrative state in which senior active and reservist SAF officers came to fill key bureaucratic and political positions. Because of virtually universal conscription since 1967, by the end of the 1990s most adult male Singaporeans below the age of 50 were former SAF conscripts and present-day SAF reservists. So it should not be surprising that, increasingly, PAP politicians and senior civil servants were also middle-ranking reservist SAF officers. It was noticeable, however, during the 1980s that high-ranking officers, usually reservists but sometimes still on the active list, began to assume significant influence over governmental decision-making in a wide variety of spheres, as the result of initiatives which brought them into the centre of the policy-making arena— principally the SAF Scholarship and 'dual-career' schemes. The significance of this development, though, is open to debate.

THE 'DUAL-CAREER SCHEME'

In 1981, MINDEF introduced a 'dual-career scheme' under which middle- or high-ranking SAF officers who were Scholars could be seconded to positions in the civil service or statutory boards, and would ultimately have the opportunity to transfer to the elite Administrative Service on a permanent basis.[10] In 1993, the head of the civil service revealed that Administrative Service personnel included 26 SAF dual-career officers (about 10 per cent of the total).

The dual-career scheme has involved SAF officers in several types of non-traditional activity. Middle-ranking and senior SAF officers have assumed a broader and more influential role within MINDEF since the late 1980s, taking on posts previously held by civil servants, particularly in the policy directorate and the Defence Technology Group.[11] In addition, serving SAF officers have been seconded to diplomatic posts: in 1999, Singapore's ambassadors to China, the Republic of Korea and Myanmar were all seconded Brigadier-Generals.

The dual-career scheme has also seen senior serving SAF officers (mainly Colonels and Brigadier-Generals) playing part-time roles as members of statutory boards and of councils of institutions of higher learning. The number of serving officers on such boards and councils generally totalled 12 or 13 during the mid-1980s, then rose to around 20–25 during the 1990s. The institutions involved include the Maritime and Port Authority of Singapore, the Public Utilities Board, the Telecommunication Authority of Singapore, the Housing and Development Board, the Construction Industry Development Board, the National Heritage Board, the Sentosa Development Corporation and the Urban Redevelopment Authority.[12] The official rationale for these placements, which are as important an element in the career patterns of many SAF Scholars as they are for civilian Administrative Service high-flyers, is that they provide a 'more macro perspective of how Singapore works'.[13]

The most crucial aspect of the dual-career scheme is that on retirement from active service in the SAF, usually in their mid- to late thirties, Scholars can expect to be appointed to senior positions in the public sector, while retaining reservist military status. Many Scholars who have served on one or other board or council later transferred out of the SAF into political or public sector positions on a full-time basis. Indeed, the particular board appointments held by certain SAF Scholars before their retirement suggests that their subsequent public sector careers were planned years in advance. For example, as a serving officer, Major-General Han Eng Juan was a member of the Land Transport Authority's Board before becoming the Authority's chief executive in 1998.[14] Officially, the idea behind such transfers is that SAF Scholars constitute a national resource, in which a considerable investment has been made and which the armed forces should not be allowed to monopolise. However, transferring Scholars out of the regular SAF not only benefits the government and the public sector: it also provides careers which are sufficiently challenging and lucrative to maintain the credibility of the SAF Scholarship schemes as attractive alternatives to the lure of the Administrative Service or the private sector.

Since the early 1980s, high-ranking Scholars—and occasionally other senior SAF officers—have transferred with increasing frequency into the civil service and other parts of the public sector, although almost as many have opted for post-SAF careers in the private sector.[15] In 1982, the SAF's Deputy Chief of General Staff (the second most senior serving officer), Brigadier-General (BG)

Table 10.1   Reservist and retired senior officers in civil service and parastatal posts, 2000

Rank and name	Post
MG (NS) Han Eng Juan	CEO, Land Transport Authority
MG (NS) Lim Neo Chian	Chairman, Jurong Town Corporation and CEO, Suzhou Project
BG (NS) Lam Joon Khoi	Deputy Secretary (Services), Ministry of Finance
BG (Retd) Tan Chin Tiong	Permanent Secretary, Ministry of Foreign Affairs
BG (NS) Lee Hsien Yang	President and CEO, Singapore Telecommunications Ltd
BG (NS) Boey Tak Hap	President and CEO, Singapore Power Ltd
BG (NS) Tan Yong Soon	Deputy Secretary (Revenue), Ministry of Finance
RADM (NS) Kwek Siew Jin	Managing Director, Singapore Mass Rapid Transit Ltd
COL (Retd) Peter Ho Hak Ean	Permanent Secretary (Defence Development), Ministry of Defence
COL (Retd) Ho Meng Kit	Deputy Secretary (Industry & Planning), Ministry of Trade and Industry
COL (NS) Pek Beng Choon	Director (Budget), Ministry of Finance
COL (NS) Koh Tin Fook	Deputy Chief Executive Officer, Singapore Broadcasting Authority
COL (NS) Chen Chin Chi	Executive Director, Singapore International Foundation

Sources: *Singapore Government Directory*, July 1999; 'Former army officer set to take over reins at SIF', *Strait Times*, 28 June 1996; 'He's no newcomer to transport' *Straits Times*, 2 July 1998; 'Nine receive SAF Overseas Scholarships', MINDEF Internet Webservice, 5 August 1999.

Tan Chin Tiong, left active service to became second permanent secretary at the Ministry of Home Affairs. In 1986 he was appointed permanent secretary,[16] exercising administrative control over *inter alia* the police, the civil defence force and the Internal Security Department. In 1996 BG Tan transferred to the Ministry of Foreign Affairs as one of two permanent secretaries there. Several other middle-ranking and senior officers followed Tan into traditionally civilian areas of government during the mid- and late 1980s.[17] During the 1990s, the transfer of SAF Scholars into the state apparatus became routine, which should have been no surprise in light of the clarification of government policy on this matter provided in August 1990 by Major-General (MG) Winston Choo, then CDF: 'If an officer is seen to be capable of filling an appointment which is important nationally, then that officer will be moved to that appointment'.[18] Table 10.1 lists former senior officers holding posts in the civil service and parastatal organisations in 2000.

Though the number of personnel involved was hardly large, it is notable that, during the 1990s, former senior SAF officers filled positions where they could influence strategic decision-making and decision-taking in key areas of national policy. This was particularly true in relation to Singapore's critical national infrastructure (energy, transport and telecommunications) as well as economic development and finance. By 1999, both deputy secretaries and the director (Budget) in the Ministry of Finance were senior SAF reservists, and that ministry's permanent secretary had previously been MINDEF's permanent secretary. Other former SAF officers, such as former air force chief MG Goh Yong Siang who joined Singapore Technologies Industrial Corporation in 1998, have dominated the strategic direction and management of the ST defence-industrial conglomerate since the 1980s.[19]

SAF OFFICERS IN THE GOVERNMENT

The widening administrative role of SAF officers potentially has significant implications, but the transfer of senior SAF officers to *political* positions has received considerably greater publicity. The first officer to make such a move was BG Lee Hsien Loong, the then prime minister's elder son, who resigned from his SAF appointment as chief of staff (General Staff), joined the reserve list and took up a political career at the age of 32. Elected as a PAP MP in the December 1984 general election, BG Lee was made a junior minister in both MINDEF and the Ministry of Trade and Industry in 1985. In 1986, he joined the Cabinet as minister for Trade and Industry, while retaining his secondary post in MINDEF. Lee was also appointed chairman of the PAP's Youth Wing when it was set up in 1987.

A second senior officer soon joined Lee in government. Just before the September 1988 general election, BG George Yeo, then 34, left his military appointment as director, JOPD for politics, and after election as a government MP quickly became minister of state (Finance and Foreign Affairs) as well as vice-chairman— and subsequently chairman, replacing Lee Hsien Loong—of the PAP's Youth Wing.[20] Lee and Yeo, both of whom had held President's as well as SAF Scholarships, subsequently assumed even higher political profiles. In February 1989 BG Lee was elected to a senior post within the main PAP organisation, becoming second assistant secretary-general. In the Cabinet reshuffle which followed Goh Chok Tong's accession to the premiership in November 1990 Lee was appointed second deputy prime minister (while remaining minister for Trade and Industry). BG Yeo placed himself firmly at the centre of a number of important political debates including those concerning the supposed need for a 'national ideology' and the government's language policy; in November 1990 he joined the Cabinet as acting minister of Arts and Culture and senior minister of state for Foreign Affairs. In a Cabinet reorganisation in July 1991, Yeo's status increased as he was confirmed in his primary post and was also appointed second minister for Foreign Affairs.

In November 1992, the government suffered a crushing blow when it was discovered that both deputy prime ministers, Ong Teng Cheong and BG Lee, were suffering from cancer. Although the prognosis for BG Lee was that he had a 90 per cent chance of being cured, the fact that he required intensive chemotherapy necessitated that he temporarily relinquish his Trade and Industry portfolio. He remained a deputy prime minister and 'economic adviser' to the prime minister.[21] Prime Minister Goh Chok Tong persuaded S. Dhanabalan (who had resigned from the government only three months previously) to return to the Cabinet with responsibility for Lee's portfolio.[22] Goh also admitted that there were plans to recall Tony Tan, who had left the Cabinet at the end of 1991, if BG Lee's condition deteriorated.[23]

It was clear that the PAP was facing a crisis. Lee had been the jewel in the crown of the PAP's younger generation of politicians: it had been widely anticipated since he entered politics that he would eventually succeed to the prime ministership, and Goh had acknowledged that he himself was effectively an interim leader. Although in May 1993 Lee Kuan Yew said that his son's health problem did not rule out the possibility that he could become prime minister ('. . . if he doesn't get a relapse, it should not affect him'),[24] in late 1992 and early 1993 it seemed possible that long-term concerns over Lee's health might disqualify him from succeeding Goh. The day before the public announcement of the deputy prime ministers' illnesses, Goh had told a meeting of PAP cadres that 'the most important . . . but also the most urgent' of his objectives as prime minister was to find people of ministerial calibre to renew the membership of the Cabinet. He pointed out that the average age of the Cabinet was already 50.3 years.[25] The resignations of several more ministers during 1993 reinforced this concern with leadership renewal.[26] Indeed, by late 1994 Goh was warning that Singapore's government might fall into mediocre hands, as it faced 'a serious succession problem by 2000'.[27]

Notwithstanding his eventual recovery, over-reliance on Lee Hsien Loong's potential as prime minister was the most obvious reason for the perceived succession crisis. But it was also clear that the government had failed to replenish its ranks during the 1980s with able young recruits from the traditional recruiting grounds for PAP politicians—the civil service, the business community, academe, and the trade union movement. There appeared to be a particular problem in attracting civilian Scholars from the Administrative Service into politics: if they left the service it was almost always to go into the private sector.[28] The PAP had no recent tradition of cultivating future MPs and Ministers from among either its mass base (numbering tens of thousands) or its cadre membership (around 500 strong).[29] Still wary of the potential disruption which might arise if activism or democracy was allowed within the party, even 30 years after the traumatic internecine conflict of 1961, which had split the movement between 'pro-communists' and 'moderates' (social democrats), the PAP was—as Chan Heng Chee put it—'a cadre party in a mass party guise'.[30]

Whatever the cause of the problem, one consequence was that Scholars from the SAF had become a vital source of new blood for the government. Even Lim Hng Kiang, a civil servant who relinquished his post as chief executive of the Housing & Development Board to contest the August 1991 general election, was actually an SAF Scholar who had left active service as an RSAF Lieutenant-Colonel only five years previously. Once elected, he was immediately appointed minister of state for National Development and, in 1994, joined the Cabinet, initially as acting minister for National Development.

The pre-eminence of SAF Scholars among third-generation PAP leaders was underscored again when the government called a by-election in the prime minister's own Marine Parade 'GRC' (Group Representation Constituency)[31] in December 1992. According to Goh, the 'big issue' in the by-election was that of political self-renewal in terms of bringing fresh faces into the Cabinet. But the only new face in Goh's constituency team was that of Commodore Teo Chee Hean, who had relinquished his post as Chief of Navy in order to stand for election. Goh claimed that he himself had recruited Teo, who had held both SAF Overseas and President's Scholarships and was previously 'being groomed to be the Chief of Defence Force', 'before the two DPMs' illnesses'.[32] With 73 per cent of the vote, Goh and his colleagues easily won the by-election. Goh immediately appointed Commodore Teo as minister of state for both Finance and Communications, saying that he expected the new minister 'to develop into a very important member of the Cabinet'.[33] In 1995, Teo joined the Cabinet as

Table 10.2 Reservist senior officers in the Cabinet, 2000

Rank and name	Post
BG (NS) Lee Hsien Loong	Deputy prime minister
BG (NS) George Yeo	Minister for Trade and Industry
RADM (NS) Teo Chee Hean	Minister for Education and second minister for Defence
LTC (NS) Lim Hng Kiang	Minister for Health and second minister for Finance

acting minister for the Environment and was confirmed in this post in 1996.

Although Lim Boon Heng, a 45–year old junior minister with a civilian background, was elevated to the Cabinet in July 1993— effectively as a replacement for Deputy Prime Minister Ong Teng Cheong (who stood successfully for election as president the following month)—by the mid-1990s the four youngest members of the Cabinet were all former senior SAF officers: Lee Hsien Loong, George Yeo, Lim Hng Kiang and Teo Chee Hean. In June 1996, Goh named these four ministers as part of the 'core for the next generation of leaders'.[34] All of them maintained a high political profile into the late 1990s and it seems likely that they will dominate Singapore's government for at least the first decade of the twenty-first century. Table 10.2 shows their positions in government in 2000. Lee Hsien Loong, who in his secondary role as chairman of the Monetary Authority of Singapore has played a leading role in liberalising Singapore's financial sector in response to the regional economic recession which began in 1997, is widely expected to become prime minister at some stage after the general election due by 2002.[35]

Goh's admission that, of the three potential new candidates identified by the PAP for the 1992 by-election, only Teo Chee Hean could 'come on board at the moment'[36] further underlined the seriousness of the leadership succession problem. Reliance on the pool of SAF Scholars as a source of ministerial talent could evidently not provide the whole answer to the problem. While the SAF Scholars were undoubtedly individually well-qualified in many ways to contribute to Singapore's government and administration, potential dangers accompanied their increasing prominence in Singapore's public life. First, there was a general concern that a Cabinet increasingly composed of Scholars—let alone specifically SAF Scholars—might lead the government's thinking to become 'type-cast' in an inflexible and conservative mould.[37] When Tony Tan rejoined the Cabinet in 1995, he expressed concern that 'most of the ministers have actually had very little experience of working in the private sector, particularly the younger ministers who have been either from the Singapore Armed Forces or from various arms of government'.[38] In Tan's view, the PAP had retained power for so long 'because it had always inducted people from all areas of society': the implication was that it needed to continue recruiting widely if it wished to remain in power.[39] A more specific worry was the danger of a 'military mind-set' coming to dominate governmental decision-making, with the implication that defence and security considerations might assume an unwarranted priority in official policies, perhaps receiving disproportionate budgetary allocations.[40] There was also the question of whether the pre-eminence of SAF Scholars in the national leadership risked future problems of legitimacy in relation to Singapore's ethnic minorities and female voters: although SAF Merit Scholarships have been awarded to women as well as men since 1993, SAF Scholars are almost exclusively Chinese; only a handful of Merit Scholarships and, as far as is known, no Overseas Scholarships have been awarded to ethnic Indians or Malays.[41]

These indications that future PAP leaders needed to be drawn from a wider cross-section of the elite was clearly not lost on the government, particularly as Goh Chok Tong became more firmly established and respected as prime minister and party leader during the early 1990s. Under Goh's leadership, the government renewed its efforts to recruit candidates for the next general election, due to be held by April 1997. In contrast to the traditionally highly-centralised system of selecting parliamentary candidates, much of the responsibility for finding new political talent in the run-up to the 1997 election was delegated to PAP-run Town Councils, chaired by backbench MPs. Particular emphasis was placed on identifying potential Cabinet members, with possible candidates being drawn both from the private sector and ethnic minorities. At the same time, however, the SAF harboured considerable potential talent in the form of its expanding pool of Scholars and it would not have been surprising if more SAF Scholars had been brought into politics at this time. As it turned out, however, this was not to be the case. Although roughly half of the 24 new PAP candidates fielded in the January 1997 general election were from the public sector, including a number of Scholars, only one was an SAF Scholar. This was Lim Swee Say, who had left the SAF with the rank of Major on completion of his eight-year bond in 1984, transferring first to the Administrative Service and subsequently to the para-political National

Trades Union Congress.[42] The leadership clearly saw Lim as a high-flier with ministerial potential—in May 1999 he was appointed minister of state in the ministries of Defence and Information and the Arts.[43]

THE POSSIBILITY OF MILITARY INTERVENTION

While the government has claimed that the growing involvement of senior SAF officers in politics and administration during the 1980s and 1990s reflects its determination to exploit fully the pool of highly educated and capable technocrats in the SAF officer corps (particularly as a result of the SAF Scholarship scheme), this may not constitute the full explanation. A fuller rationale for the expanded role of SAF officers (at least in its early stages) might be found in the concern of Lee Kuan Yew and his Old Guard colleagues (particularly Goh Keng Swee and S. Rajaratnam) during the early 1980s to ensure that their legacy—in terms of Singapore's prosperity and security—was not frittered away once they had left the scene by weak leadership on the part of the successor generation of politicians. By using the SAF Scholarship and dual-career schemes to create a network of senior reservist officers possessing proven moral backbone and decision-making ability throughout the apparatus of government and state, Lee Kuan Yew and the Old Guard may have been attempting to implant potential leaders competent to assume a central role in running Singapore should future generations of PAP politicians prove unequal to the task.[44] The fact that Lee Kuan Yew encouraged both his sons to pursue military careers indicates the extent to which he saw the SAF as being one of Singapore's key institutions of the future.[45]

Giving SAF officers political and administrative roles may also have been intended as a way of dispersing power in order to maintain political stability and continuity in the face of potential threats from opposition movements.[46] Even before the dual-career and Scholarship schemes had any significant impact, local political scientist Shee Poon Kim had argued that '. . . one should not rule out the possibility of the military elite entering the political arena to compete with the civilian politicians . . . If Singapore suffers a major economic crisis and the present PAP second generation leadership fails to overcome it, then an alternative to the PAP government under the tutelage of the military could become possible'.[47] At around the same time that Shee Poon Kim pointed to this danger, Rajaratnam claimed that a central reason for planning to bring SAF officers into the Cabinet was the perceived need to make them 'part of the ruling class'. By giving the military direct representation at 'the highest levels of decision-making' it was intended to pre-empt the 'remote' possibility that SAF officers could be influenced by the vogue for political inter-vention on the part of armed forces elsewhere in Southeast Asia.[48]

By the 1990s, though, it was hard to conceive of SAF officers attempting to mount a coup. Even in a crisis, it seems virtually inconceivable that serving senior SAF officers could intervene, not only because of those factors which have in the past militated against the military's corporate involvement in Singa-pore's politics, but also due to the complex checks and balances which the command and control system imposes on the SAF. Any military attempt to intervene politically would almost certainly require former SAF officers in government to take a leading role. In other words, it would amount to what has become known in Latin America as an *autogolpe*, a 'self-coup' in which a faction within the government uses the military to fulfil its own ends.

However, even an *autogolpe* led from within the government seems an unlikely prospect in the light of new factors which have arisen since the 1980s. In the first place, the SAF officer corps is far from unified. While it is not exactly faction-ridden, the very mechanism which has been largely responsible for introducing senior officers into politics and policy-making—the Scholarship scheme—has damaged its cohesiveness. By the early 1990s, this problem had crystallised into a divide within the officer corps between Scholars and Farmers.[49] These tensions suggest that the Farmers, who are more oriented towards a purely military role, might be unwilling to lend their support if the Scholars' widening role eventually inclined them towards political assertiveness *en bloc*. Despite the increasing numbers of Scholars in the SAF, even during the 1990s they by no means monopolised senior appoint-ments: many key command positions remained in the hands of Farmers; in other cases, Scholars in such posts were shadowed by deputies who were Farmers.

Another factor reducing the likelihood of intervention is the lack of precise political uniformity among even those SAF Scholars who have joined the government. Although his image had soft-ened somewhat by the late 1990s,[50] Lee Hsien Loong has been widely perceived by both his supporters and his detractors as the leading hardliner within the Cabinet—indeed, as his father's true political heir. George Yeo, however, has emphasised that the government must respond to social change: Singaporeans were now more prosperous, better-educated and more aware of the world outside.[51] He has called for a 'lively democracy' tolerating a 'diversity of views' and for a more active 'civic society'.[52] Though he banned films made by political parties during his time as Arts and Information minister (1991–99), Yeo continued to encourage a strengthening of Singapore's civil society.[53] By the PAP's stand-ards, Yeo is a liberal. Teo Chee Hean has spoken of the need for 'an open, consultative style of government which focuses on national issues and builds consensus'.[54] Lim Hng Kiang reputedly 'takes pride in his conservatism'.[55] Unlike these first four SAF Scholars who are all essentially English-educated (in terms of their schooling in Singapore), Lim Swee Say spent the first ten years of his education in Chinese-medium schools, with consequences for his social and political outlook.[56] While these differences might amount to little more than nuances, there is no indication that the SAF Scholars have developed a set of non-military corporate objectives and have become a cohesive, let alone hardline, faction within the government.

Even if there was no fault-line in the SAF officer corps dividing Scholars from Farmers, and the Scholars possessed more closely identical political outlooks, other important obstacles to greater political assertiveness would remain. Serving SAF officers, like civil servants, are debarred from membership of political parties (including the PAP), but the political relation-ships between senior civilian politicians and senior SAF Scholars in government are close, with the former cast in the role of patrons and the latter as clients. Like other government ministers, backbench MPs and even senior civil servants, all the SAF Scholars in government are 'followers' (clients) of civilian political leaders, which during the 1990s implied alle-giance to one of the two recognisable power centres at the centre, one of which is dominated by Goh Chok Tong and the other by Lee Kuan Yew and Lee Hsien Loong. It is also well-known within the SAF that George Yeo's military and political career benefited from the patronage of Dr Yeo Ning Hong (no relation), who became second minister for Defence in 1983 and minister for Defence in 1991. By 1993, however, it was widely rumoured in Singapore that Lee Kuan Yew, concerned about the shadow cast over the future leadership succession by his son's illness, had adopted George Yeo as a protégé. Teo Chee Hean is known to 'follow' Goh Chok Tong, who has spoken publicly of his strenuous and ultimately successful efforts to recruit the former.[57] Lim Hng Kiang and Lim Swee Say, though, are believed to be more closely affiliated with Lee Kuan Yew and Lee Hsien Loong than with Goh.

Like most recruits to the government since independence, the SAF Scholars have commenced their political lives with bases of support in neither the PAP nor the population as a whole. Only in the longer-term, once they have proven themselves politically and their civilian patrons have left the scene, would the ex-SAF clients be in a position to assert themselves with a degree of autonomy. It is true that by the end of the 1990s, Lee Hsien Loong appeared increasingly ready to assume the premiership. However, a transfer of power was by no means imminent and it was clear that Lee would need broad support from within the PAP's 'inner group'—which in the late 1990s included several senior civilian politicians (Tony Tan, S. Jayakumar and Wong Kan Seng) as well as Lee Kuan Yew, Goh Chok Tong and the four SAF Scholars—if he was to become prime minister.[58] The implication of all these constraints on the SAF Scholars' willingness and ability to act autonomously and as a bloc is that an *autogolpe* would almost certainly only be feasible if it was seen as desirable by the majority of PAP's core leaders. Given that the imposition of a military-dominated regime would probably seriously undermine the PAP's credibility, not only with the domestic electorate but also with foreign investors and hitherto friendly western governments (particularly in Washington, where support for such regimes has been out of fashion since the end of the Cold War), only the direst of national emergencies could make such a scenario feasible. However, even without activating a military-dominated regime, the network of serving, reservist and retired SAF officers in the state's administrative structure could still serve the government well in the event of a severe national crisis. Indeed, this network—which includes ministers and senior bureaucrats in all key ministries—could bolster Singapore's ability to continue functioning effectively in the face of external threat or internal disorder, in effect supervising the implementation of the non-military aspects of Total Defence.

DEFENDING THE SAF'S CORPORATE INTERESTS?

Rather less tenuous than this speculation concerning the potential for military intervention is the notion that the political ascendancy of ex-SAF men has served to preserve and enhance both the military effectiveness and the social status of the SAF. It seems likely that men who have played key roles in creating and leading the SAF since the 1980s would be extremely reluctant to acquiesce in policy decisions—such as to reduce defence spending or the length of conscription—which might damage Singapore's military capability. Indeed, at least some of the officers who have transferred into politics and the public sector may have retained a special attachment to the institution which has nurtured them in the formative stages of their careers. Two retiring Brigadier Generals' farewells to the army expressed such sentiments clearly: 'My heart is with the military and always will be. I learnt everything there . . . My friends are all there' (Chin Siat Yoon); 'The SAF has and will always be a part of me' (Boey Tak Hap).[59] Goh Chok Tong even played on such attachment to the SAF's corporate professional interests when attempting to persuade Teo Chee Hean to leave his 'rewarding job in the Navy':

> . . . I told him that the job may be rewarding, but if Singapore had a weak Cabinet which does not put emphasis on the security of Singapore and defence expenditure is cut down, your job is not going to be satisfying. So you had better come in to join us at the centre.[60]

The longer-term durability of senior SAF officers' loyalty to the military institution once they become ministers with necessarily wider perspectives on Singapore's national interests and proper priorities may be less certain. However, in some cases, an interest in the wellbeing of the military has led to policy initiatives. For example, after joining the government George Yeo (in his capacity as president of the SAF Reservists' Association) argued that 'national servicemen and reservists deserve a lot more recognition than they are getting for their contribution to the nation's defence'.[61] BG Yeo translated this argument into policy by providing the impetus for the establishment of both RECORD and the SAF Veterans' League. RECORD helped the government formulate policies aimed at minimising the disruption which their military commitments inflict on reservists' occupational and family lives, as well as substantially improving the subsidised recreational facilities provided for reservists.[62] Over time, the attachment of SAF Scholars in government to SAF interests may attenuate, but it is unlikely to dissipate entirely.

CONCLUSION

The military—or at least a caucus of senior military officers, both serving and reservist—has played an important political and administrative role in Singapore since the 1980s. The impetus for this role has come from the government rather than from within the SAF. The Scholarship scheme has been used to create an elite of highly educated young officers who have been appointed to important posts (mainly outside the defence sector) on their resignation from active service in the SAF. While the official rationale emphasises the need to maximise the state's exploitation of scarce top-level manpower in which it had invested heavily, it appears that the PAP Old Guard has also attempted to create a reliable alternative power structure in case subsequent generations of civilian leaders prove insufficiently resilient in the face of future crises.

During the 1990s, the increasingly common transfers of SAF officers—particularly Scholars—into the civil service, statutory boards and government-linked companies effectively transformed what Chan Heng Chee had called an 'administrative state' into a military–administrative state. Given that most SAF officers leaving active service still had at least 20 years of working life ahead of them, their cumulative medium- to long-term impact on the culture of Singapore's public sector could be substantial. Whether this impact will be entirely beneficial is open to debate. Many Singaporeans, particularly in the private sector, question the effectiveness of men whom they see as lacking sufficient drive, business sense and technological expertise to manage Singapore in the twenty-first century. However, these doubts do not relate solely to SAF Scholars: they are also expressed in relation to government Scholars more generally.[63]

In the formal political sphere, the SAF Scholars became a source of recruits for renewing the ranks of the PAP government during the 1980s and early 1990s. But the choice of new PAP candidates for the 1997 general election made it clear that the government—in which Goh Chok Tong had evidently secured the upper hand—recognised the need to draw on a wider cross-section of Singapore's elite to provide the future leadership.

Despite the earlier forebodings of some observers when the SAF Scholars first began to transfer into politics and civil administration during the 1980s, by the end of the 1990s it seemed extremely unlikely that these former officers possessed either the will or the capacity to intervene directly in politics of their own

accord. It is also difficult to conceive of Singapore's government
acquiescing in the establishment of a military-dominated regime.
However, the presence of numerous former senior officers in
politics and the bureaucracy would facilitate national mobilisation and the implementation of Total Defence in a crisis.

Parallels may be drawn between the non-military role of
Singapore's officer corps and civil–military relations in certain
other political systems. The comparison which `the Singapore
government prefers is with Switzerland. The difference is that
senior reservist officers who hold important political, administrative or—as is more often the case—business positions in
Switzerland are not, as in Singapore, retired regular officers especially selected for educational sponsorship and extraordinary
career opportunities with their long-term bureaucratic potential
in mind. In the Swiss army, part-time reservists hold all senior
command and staff appointments below the level of divisional
commander; it is these men and their reservist subordinates who
simultaneously occupy prominent positions in civilian life.[64] While
'networking' among reservist officers is undoubtedly a fact of life
in Switzerland, these officers are ordinary citizens with a reservist
military role rather than military men who have been co-opted
into a civilian role.

Another comparison might perhaps be made with the pattern
of civil–military relations prevalent in other countries governed by
a Leninist party—for this is what the PAP remains in organisational terms—such as the former Soviet Union, China and Taiwan.
One interesting comparison in Singapore's immediate region is
with Vietnam, where there is, superficially, a rather similar close
relationship between the Party, the state bureaucracy and the
armed forces, with the Party dominant.[65] But important differences undermine this comparison: in Singapore, a form of
democracy remains intact and regular elections affirm the popular
legitimacy of the Party's dominance, whereas in communist Vietnam,
recent fundamental economic reforms have not been matched by
any significant political reforms in the direction of democracy.
Moreover, the Vietnamese armed forces' central role in the struggles
for independence and national unification has legitimised their
political role; this contrasts with the situation in Singapore, where
the SAF has no historically based institutional legitimacy in
political terms. In Vietnam, the armed forces' rank-and-file have
increasingly over time provided the bulk of the Party's membership;
in Singapore, active SAF personnel are prohibited from joining any
political party—even the PAP.

There would also be important weaknesses in comparisons which might be drawn with South Korea, Israel and other cases of civil–military relations which may manifest superficial similarities to Singapore's. Like so many aspects of contemporary Singapore's development, the non-military role of SAF's officer corps is essentially unique.

Conclusion

Singapore's armed forces are one of the many features which distinguish the city-state from its Southeast Asian neighbours. The SAF's development has been driven by the pessimistic outlook of Singapore's PAP leadership, particularly its dominant figure, Lee Kuan Yew, who during the 1970s rated the chance of Singapore being drawn into conflict as '50:50' during the active lifetime of his sons, then about to embark on military careers.[1] Singapore's government has always taken defence against external threats extremely seriously and has developed armed forces which are highly credible as a deterrent to threats from within the Southeast Asian region. These forces incidentally provide a basis for wide-ranging defence cooperation with friendly powers—most importantly the United States, and the non-Southeast Asian partners in the FPDA. Singapore's strategy, though, is based primarily on nationally self-reliant deterrence and, if necessary, self-reliant defence.

The SAF's capabilities have developed in the context of a wider programme of enhancing Singapore's overall resilience in the face of potential external threats. This programme, known since the 1980s as Total Defence, involves plans for the thorough-going mobilisation of Singapore's society and economy to ensure national survival in a crisis or war. This comprehensive approach to national security includes efforts to reduce Singapore's medium- to long-term dependence on external sources of water and food, as well as to provide civil defence protection for the civilian population. This Total Defence effort has meshed with the SAF's growing capabilities to support a more sophisticated version of the earlier defence doctrine, which had been based on the strategic pre-emption of adversaries (most probably Malaysia

248

or Indonesia). Singapore now envisages the possibility of absorbing an enemy's first strike before using the SAF to strike back hard and decisively.

Singapore's defence strategy has not only attempted to negate the likelihood of a direct attack on the city-state. It is also designed to deter military, political or economic pressure from other regional states. Specifically, it ensures that the Malaysian and Indonesian governments treat the republic with a degree of respect which might otherwise be absent. Singapore's neighbours understand only too well that any direct interference with its vital interests (such as its water supply or its sea lanes) would court a military response. Singapore is not the 'Israel of Southeast Asia', but it has sent strong signals since the late 1960s that it is willing, *in extremis*, to risk assuming that status.

THE SAF'S STRENGTHS AND WEAKNESSES

It is often claimed that armed forces reflect the strengths and weaknesses of the societies from which they spring. This truism certainly applies to Singapore. Consequently, while the SAF is in many ways the most impressive military force in contemporary Southeast Asia, it suffers from some key weaknesses which could be critical in time of crisis or war.

Singapore's status as one of the world's wealthiest independent political units, on a *per capita* basis, has permitted sustained high levels of defence spending. Though buffeted by the regional recession of the late 1990s, Singapore was quick to recover from the economic slowdown and it is likely that defence spending will continue to rise as economic growth resumes. If the government felt it necessary, in the event of a particularly acute further deterioration in Singapore's strategic circumstances, defence spending could be increased substantially and still remain within the '6 per cent of GDP' limit. If the republic's economic circumstances deteriorated simultaneously, the government could draw on the huge national financial reserves to increase the allocation to defence.

Singapore is renowned for its industrial, commercial and governmental efficiency and productivity. These qualities also characterise the SAF's use of the defence budget and scarce personnel resources, as well as their well-rehearsed mobilisation procedures. The low incidence of corruption—another national characteristic—is reflected in MINDEF's procedures for procurement on behalf of the SAF, which are probably the cleanest of any Southeast Asian state.

Like Singapore as a whole, the SAF relies heavily on technology to provide an 'edge' over regional competitors, while minimising personnel-intensive activities. In the SAF's case, the extent to which high-technology weapons systems and C⁴I systems are seen as force multipliers able to provide decisive advantages over potential adversaries (in the process avoiding SAF casualties) is particularly striking. The SAF's technological advantages rest, to a large extent, on the capabilities of the local defence industry and MINDEF's R&D establishment, both of which derive much of their strength from Singapore's status as a high-technology centre in more general terms. Singapore's sophisticated defence–industrial capabilities also provide a high degree of assurance that the SAF's logistic systems would function effectively in wartime.

As the result of governmental policies since the 1960s, the republic's population is now one of the most highly educated in Asia. This yields benefits in terms of operational capability: high levels of education allow even conscripts to operate sophisticated, modern military equipment effectively. This factor in itself provides a key advantage over other Southeast Asian states' armed forces.

Singapore's economic success owes much to its wide (rather than narrowly regional) international connections. The SAF similarly derives much of its strength from its international links: the growth of Singapore's military capability has been paralleled, particularly during the 1990s, by an expanding range of cooperative defence activities, mainly but not exclusively bilateral in nature. Access to extensive training grounds and facilities in numerous friendly states has allowed the SAF to escape the constraint imposed by Singapore's small land area on the extent to which it can train realistically at home. Deepening relations with western countries' armed forces—most importantly those of the United States, Australia, New Zealand, the UK, Sweden and France—has benefited the SAF by providing access to their operational doctrines and, in some cases, to their operational experience.

The majority of Singaporeans take great pride in their city-state's rapid development since 1965. Most—particularly those who have been through the formative experience of NS—are imbued with at least a modicum of patriotism and would almost certainly be willing to defend their country and their families against clear external threats. In any case, Singapore is a highly disciplined society and there can be little doubt that there would be a rapid and full response to any mobilisation call in the context of an imminent external threat.

While the SAF has derived many positive features from the republic's social and economic strengths, conversely the military has also helped to mould modern Singapore. First, since the late 1960s, the institution of universal NS has produced not only a huge force of military reservists, but also a considerably healthier and more disciplined male workforce than would otherwise have been the case. Second, NS has also helped to integrate Singapore's ethnically, linguistically and culturally diverse society. Moreover, through the SAF Scholarship system and the dual-career scheme, senior military officers have increasingly been integrated into Singapore's administrative and political systems. The long-term impact of these officers' roles in civilian arenas remains to be seen, but at the very least it seems likely to ensure that defence continues to be a high priority for the government long after Lee Kuan Yew's eventual passing from the political scene. In a crisis, former SAF officers in civilian posts would play key parts in mobilising Singapore's critical national infrastructure (including the defence industry) to support Total Defence.

However, though the SAF's technological superiority in the region owes much to the nature of modern Singapore's society and economy, and while the SAF has undoubtedly influenced Singapore's development, the military–society relationship is not entirely synergistic. Indeed, Singapore's inherent characteristics also impose some serious constraints on its armed forces. Although it has been somewhat dented by the recession of the late 1990s, Singapore's sustained economic success has bred an overweening confidence which has tended to colour many of its citizens' comparisons of the republic with other countries, particularly those in its immediate region. In consequence, Singapore's defence planners need to beware of falling into the trap (which proved the undoing of Britain's position in Southeast Asia prior to the Japanese onslaught in 1941–42) of overestimating their own armed forces' potential performance and underestimating the capabilities of likely adversaries.

After more than 30 years of NS, conscription and reservist service are still only grudgingly accepted as necessary evils by Singapore's predominantly ethnic Chinese population. Geopolitically Singapore is clearly vulnerable, but on a day-to-day level there is no sense of living Israeli-style, 'on the brink': relations with neighbours may be neuralgic, but they are not unremittingly hostile. One consequence is that there is little evidence within the SAF of the sort of 'fighting spirit', based on the notion of 'no alternative', which has characterised the Israeli Defence Force since 1948.[2] Moreover, Singapore is a young state and there is little popular sense of national history or heritage: it is a society without historical heroes and SAF units lack the histories, traditions and sense of identity which contribute to *esprit de corps* in even the reservist elements of many longer-established armed forces.[3]

Though mobilisation exercises routinely generate reassuringly high and prompt turnouts, any prolonged run-up to conflict might—in the worst case—provoke significant numbers of Singaporeans and permanent residents (particularly those retaining strong family ties to their countries of origin) to leave, sapping the strength and morale of reservist units. Even if this were not the case, there are reasons for doubting the motivation of NSmen after their first few years of ICT. How well and for how long they could fight effectively, particularly when deployed offensively on enemy territory against professional defending forces protecting their homeland, remain open questions.

A major drawback to having worked effectively as a deterrent since the late 1960s is that the SAF remains utterly untested in combat. The handful of officers and NCOs with operational experience dating from Confrontation has retired, and only small numbers of their successors have experienced even UN observer missions. There should be particular concern over the extent to which the SAF's regular officers are technocratic managers rather than military leaders and, more specifically, the degree to which they possess the attributes of daring, initiative and flexibility necessary to prevail in combat. SAF regular officers in command and staff positions are generally decidedly young and inexperienced compared with their western (or indeed, Malaysian and Indonesian) counterparts: when appointed as Singapore's Chief of Defence Force in April 2000, Major-General Lim Chuan Poh was aged only 38.[4] Moreover, observers from other armed forces sometimes question SAF officers' commitment to their military careers, particularly in the case of SAF Scholars, who sometimes appear to be 'marking time' before moving into more powerful or lucrative civilian posts.

Another weakness is that although the SAF has undoubtedly assisted the government's nation-building project since the late 1960s, MINDEF's policies with regard to Singapore's 14 per cent Malay minority population have accentuated social cleavages, with lasting repercussions for not only society as a whole but also the SAF. The marginalised status of the Malay community is magnified within the armed forces, and the government's continuing distrust of this ethnic group undermines the SAF's status as a truly national institution.

Finally, the SAF's extensive international links with the outside world potentially bring problems as well as benefits. Though Singapore's heavy dependence on international cooperation in the defence sphere (particularly for equipment procurement) might largely be mitigated in a crisis by the existence of sophisticated local defence–industrial capabilities, the stationing outside the island of significant forces, including combat aircraft, helicopters and armoured vehicles, could complicate the SAF's mobilisation for war. There might be significant logistical or political obstacles to the timely repatriation of equipment and personnel from Taiwan, Australia, the United States and elsewhere in time of crisis.

SINGAPORE'S STRATEGIC FUTURE

At the end of the 1990s, the SAF possessed important advantages over likely adversaries, particularly in terms of its high-quality equipment and training, and its growing capability for combined arms and joint-service operations. However, there was no room for the defence establishment to become complacent. Quite apart from the SAF's intrinsic weaknesses in some areas, Singapore's strategic environment had deteriorated significantly since 1997, with few signs that it would improve in the foreseeable future. Although relations with Kuala Lumpur stabilised during the 1990s, and Dr Mahathir's UMNO-led coalition government prevailed in the November 1999 general election in the context of an apparent economic recovery, it seemed likely that continuing political instability in Malaysia would inject uncertainty into bilateral relations. At the same time, the economic upswing had encouraged Malaysia to resuscitate extensive plans for modernising its armed forces.[5]

Developments in Indonesia posed a different type of challenge. Despite the establishment of a reformist civilian government there in late 1999, continuing social, economic and political instability, perhaps leading to intensifying secessionist struggles around the country's periphery, raised the possibility of a 'complex emergency' on Singapore's doorstep. The fact that ASEAN, which had traditionally helped to mitigate tensions between its members, was weakened by the economic recession and the collapse of

Indonesia's traditional role as *primus inter pares* within the organisation, threatened to further complicate Singapore's relations with its near neighbours.

In these uncertain circumstances, Singapore's leaders have repeatedly emphasised the continuing importance of the republic's military instrument as a deterrent and it is clear that MINDEF's defence planners will continue to do their best to ensure that the SAF retains its advantages over likely adversaries. National Service will remain central to Singapore's defence posture, though calls for a reduction in the length of conscription may become louder as the economy grows and if the political system eventually loosens up. Nevertheless, a continuing low birth rate implies that conscript and reservist manpower will still be in short supply.[6]

In a speech in October 1999, Minister of State for Defence David Lim revealed that the SAF has developed secret capabilities, which he called 'silver bullets', for use only in 'extreme conditions'.[7] This apparently confirmed the long-rumoured existence of MINDEF's 'black programmes', based on clandestine local defence R&D. Uncorroborated reports suggest that Singapore may have experimented with binary artillery shells and air-delivered bombs suitable for use with chemical agents, and in the mid-1990s allegedly showed interest in 120 km-range Russian SS-21 surface-to-surface missiles.[8] However, bearing in mind Singapore's close relations with western powers and its signatory status in relation to international agreements such as the Non-Proliferation Treaty, Biological Warfare Convention and Convention on Chemical Weapons, it is highly unlikely that the republic has either developed or acquired weapons of mass destruction. It would not be surprising, however, if the SAF's inventory includes highly destructive conventional weapons such as fuel-air explosives, capable of producing a blast effect comparable to that of a small nuclear weapon.

Less speculatively, MINDEF's heavy investment in electronic warfare (EW)—which *Defending Singapore in the 21st century* explicitly identified as a 'silver bullet'[9]—and in SIGINT systems, as well as its evidently deep interest in information warfare, highlight the fact that Singapore is seriously attempting to take part in the 'revolution in military affairs' (RMA). As early as 1992, it was reported that the SAF planned operations based on a 'radio electronic combat' doctrine, which integrated EW with reconnaissance, physical disruption and deception.[10] Electronic support measures, electronic countermeasures, electronic counter-countermeasures and communications and electronic intelligence systems constitute vital elements in the SAF's technological edge over possible regional adversaries.[11] The ability of Singapore's armed forces, in conjunction with its defence science establishment and industry, to continue developing such systems and to integrate them with the modern information and communications technologies extensively employed for command and control, other surveillance systems (including AEW, maritime patrol and tactical reconnaissance aircraft, UAVs, and ground-based radars) and, ultimately, precision-guided weapons, will be key to the SAF's continuing military superiority in the early twenty-first century. The aim will be to allow the SAF (particularly the air force, navy and artillery) to locate, target and destroy targets more effectively in the context of round-the-clock combined arms and joint-service operations. At the same time, greater emphasis on criteria of range and endurance in selecting major platforms (primarily ships and aircraft) is intended to provide Singapore with an artificial form of strategic depth by allowing the SAF to fight at a greater distance from its homeland.

Malaysian defence procurement plans at the end of the 1990s appeared to mimic the SAF's efforts to develop RMA-style capabilities. The MAF's potential acquisition, during the first decade of the twenty-first century, of advanced weapons such as multiple launch rocket systems, long-range anti-tank missiles, airborne laser target designators, and medium-range SAMs,[12] on top of the new air force and naval equipment already purchased during the late 1990s, suggest that maintaining the SAF's precious technological edge may become an increasingly expensive business. However, taking into account Malaysia's educational and technological shortcomings and Singapore's impressive defence–industrial and R&D capabilities, there seems little doubt that, providing defence spending recovers from the recession-induced stagnation which began in 1998, the SAF will be able to retain the upper hand.

Like their counterparts in other states engaging in the RMA, Singapore's security planners face the need to deal with possible asymmetric responses to their probable conventional military superiority. These responses might include various combinations of terrorism, the use of weapons of mass destruction (particularly chemical or biological agents) or information attacks, aimed primarily at Singapore's civilian population and national infrastructure. Chemical contamination of Singapore's water supply, for example, could be a particular effective asymmetric weapon. Although countering such asymmetric threats would largely be the responsibility of non-military agencies under the Ministry of

Home Affairs, MINDEF claims that the SAF has a range of capabilities relevant to such contingencies (for example, the SOF in the anti-terrorist role).[13]

While there is no evidence that either of Singapore's immediate neighbours has offensive non-conventional capabilities, it is conceivable that the SAF might in future have to operate under chemical or biological warfare conditions on the battlefield. However, although MINDEF and the SAF evidently focused attention on the potential chemical threat during the 1990s,[14] the level of chemical protection within the armed forces was probably still only rudimentary by the end of the decade.

The SAF's increasing dependence on advanced technology systems (for example, the highly automated frigates due to come into service from 2005) has increased its potential vulnerability to information warfare. Although MINDEF claims that DSO has developed a significant capability to protect the 'military communications and computing infrastructure from external attack',[15] the concern of western states' armed forces over threats from cyber-warfare suggests that there is no room for complacency in this area.

Another form of asymmetric response to the SAF's technological superiority could involve an adversary sapping Singapore's strength through persistent political or military provocation, sufficiently serious to trigger mobilisation, but insufficient to justify the operational deployment of the SAF. Such a 'phoney war' strategy could inflict severe damage on Singapore's economy (through lost productivity, declining business confidence and increased defence spending) and might undermine national morale to the point of encouraging migration.

There is also the question of how relevant Singapore's high-technology military capabilities are to the type of diffuse, low-intensity operations which the SAF might be drawn into (in the Indonesian islands to Singapore's south, for example). Such contingencies might call essentially for the long-term deployment of infantry-based ground forces, well-supported by engineering, logistics, medical and intelligence units. While the continuing development of rapid deployment capabilities—including enhanced airlift and amphibious transport for the army's 21st Division—will increase the SAF's intervention capabilities, the suitability of NS and NSF forces for prolonged operations outside Singapore will remain questionable. It would be difficult for Singapore's government to deploy major army units operationally except in the event of a direct threat to either national survival or national interests, particularly if there was a risk of casualties. The limited forces which Singapore was able to deploy to Interfet and UNTAET in East Timor in 1999–2000 highlighted this problem.

However, though it is clear that its military strength does not provide a panacea for its security problems, there can be little doubt that, for the foreseeable future, Singapore's continued existence as a fully sovereign state will remain dependent to a large extent on its fielding armed forces which provide military advantages over likely regional opponents. In the very long-term, far-reaching political accommodation with neighbouring states (as Lee Kuan Yew tentatively advocated in relation to Malaysia in 1996) might render such a calculation irrelevant but, at the turn of the century, such a positive diplomatic development seemed less likely than at any time since the 1960s. From the viewpoint of Singapore's government, the political and social impact of economic recession has underlined the SAF's role as a 'stabilising force'.[16]

Appendix 1

Summary of forces

In 1999 there were approximately 20 000 regular personnel (including 4000+ women), 40 000 NSFs (conscripts) and 300 000 NSmen (reservists with training obligations) in the armed forces.[1] According to the government, the SAF's total strength is roughly 350 000.

ARMY

Army personnel total approximately 310 000, comprising 15 000 regular officers and NCOs, 35 000 NSFs and 260 000 or more NSmen.

The spearhead army formations, combining active and reservist components, are:

- three combined arms divisions (3rd, 6th and 9th), each including two infantry brigades, an armoured brigade, an artillery group, combat engineer, signals and air defence battalions and a divisional logistic support command;
- one rapid deployment division (21st), comprising three Guards brigades (including one airmobile and one amphibious), artillery, combat engineer, signals and air defence battalions and a divisional logistic support command;
- one independent armoured brigade (4 SAB), which may form the core of a mechanised or armoured division in the future; and
- two Commando battalions (one active, one reservist).

The main second-line formations, made up of reservists, are:

- two People's Defence Force Commands (1st and 2nd), controlling a total of 12 light infantry brigades; and

- one 'army operational reserve' division (25th) composed of infantry brigades and other units which have completed their 13-year NS training cycle.

The main active units are: nine infantry (including three Guards), four armoured and reconnaissance; four artillery (including one locating); four Combat Engineer, and one Commando battalions. Reservist units include approximately 60 infantry (including Guards), 12 artillery; eight armour; eight Combat Engineer; and one Commando battalions.

Divisions and PDF Commands are commanded by regular Colonels or Brigadier-Generals, brigades by regular or reservist Lieutenant-Colonels. Active battalions are led by regular Majors or Lieutenant-Colonels, and reservist battalions by reservist (or, exceptionally, regular) Captains or Majors. Regular officers in command of reservist units usually simultaneously hold positions in training units or centres.

Major army equipment

- 80–100 Tempest (modernised Centurion) MBTs.
- 350 AMX-13SM1 light tanks.
- Approximately 1000 other AFVs: 450(+) M-113 (to be reduced) and 300 M-113 Ultra, 300(+) Bionix 25 and Bionix 40/50 (being delivered), 22 AMX-10PAC90, 22 AMX-10P, 250 V-150/V-200 Commando.
- 108 155 mm howitzers: 18 FH-2000, 52 FH-88, 38 M-71S. Older 155 mm artillery (16 M-114 and 45 M-68) may have been retained in storage.
- 37(+) LG1 Mk1 105 mm light guns.
- 12 160 mm and 50 120 mm mortars.
- Artillery locating systems, including AN/TPQ-36 and -37 radars.
- Anti-tank weapons: NT-S Spike and 30(+) Milan missile systems, 200 Carl Gustav 84 mm recoilless rifles; Armbrust rocket-launchers.

Major Combat Engineer equipment includes 12 M-60 AVLB armoured bridge-layers, Leguan tactical bridges, M-728 CEVs, and 36 FV180S CETs.

AIR FORCE

RSAF personnel number 13 500, comprising 3000 regulars, 3000 NSFs and 7500 NSmen.

RSAF flying units operate from four air bases and one other location in Singapore:

Tengah Air Base

- 111 Squadron   E-2C   (AEW and control)
- 140 Squadron   F-16A/B/C/D   (air defence and strike)
- 142 Squadron   A-4SU/TA-4SU   (strike)
- 145 Squadron   A-4SU/TA-4SU   (strike)

Murai Camp (near Tengah Air Base)

- 128 Squadron   Malat Searcher 2 (UAV)
                  Malat Scout (UAV)
                  Chukar III (target drone)

Paya Lebar Air Base

- 122 Squadron   C-130H, KC-130B/H (transport and tanker)
- 141 Squadron   RF-5S; F-5T   (reconnaissance)
- 144 Squadron   F-5S/T   (air defence and strike)
- 149 Squadron   F-5S/T   (air defence and strike)
- Flight Test Centre

Sembawang Air Base (helicopters)

- 120 Squadron   UH-1H   (transport)
- 123 Squadron   AS550A2 Fennec   (reconnaissance and training)
- 124 Squadron   AS550C2 Fennec   (anti-armour)
- 125 Squadron   AS332M Super Puma (transport and SAR)
                  AS532UL Cougar   (transport)
- 127 Squadron   CH-47D   (transport)

Changi Air Base

- 121 Squadron   Fokker 50 (maritime patrol and transport)

Air Force squadrons are usually commanded by Majors, Air Bases by Colonels.

Overseas detachments

Approximately one-third of the RSAF's aircraft are deployed for training overseas on a long-term basis. The main training detachments are:

- 120 Squadron Detachment, Brunei (UH-1H)
- 126 Squadron, Oakey, Queensland (AS332M and AS532UL)
- 130 Squadron (Flying Training School), Pearce, Western Australia (S211)
- Flying Grading Centre, Tamworth, New South Wales
- 150 Squadron, Cazaux, France (A-4SU and TA-4SU)
- 425th Fighter Squadron, Luke AFB, Arizona (F-16C/D)
- 428th Fighter Squadron, Cannon AFB, New Mexico (F-16C/D)
- 'Peace Prairie' Detachment, Grand Prairie, Texas (CH-47D)
- Detachment with 22nd Air Refuelling Wing, McConnell AFB, Kansas (KC-135R).

Missile and radar units

Air Defence Systems Division controls the RSAF's missile and radar units through its three subsidiary brigades:

Divisional Air Defence Artillery Brigade (DAB)
- 3 Air Defence Battalion (equipped with RBS70 and Igla SAM, Super Giraffe radar: attached to 3rd Division)
- 6 Air Defence Battalion (RBS70 SAM, Super Giraffe radar: attached to 6th Division)
- 9 Air Defence Battalion (RBS70 SAM, Super Giraffe radar: attached to 9th Division)
- 18 Air Defence Battalion (Mistral SAM, P-STAR radar: attached to 21st Division)

Air Defence Brigade (ADB)
- 160 Squadron (Oerlikon 35 mm AA guns: headquartered at Seletar, with detachments at air bases)
- 163 Squadron (I-HAWK SAM: based at Lim Chu Kang)
- 165 Squadron (Rapier SAM and Blindfire radar: based at Lim Chu Kang)
- 201 Squadron (FPS-117 radar and mobile operations control centre: based at Gombak)

Air Force Systems Brigade (AFSB)
- 203 Squadron (military element of Singapore Air Traffic Control Centre, Changi, operating Thomson-CSF LORADS II and Westinghouse AN/TPS-43 radar systems)

Major air force equipment

- 165+ combat aircraft (including 42 overseas): 42 F-16C/D (24 in the USA), 7 F-16A/B, 60–70 A-4SU and TA-4SU (18 in

France), 40 F-5S/T, 8 RF-5S; 5 Fokker 50 Enforcer. An additional 20 F-16C/Ds are on order.
- 4 E-2C AEW and control aircraft.
- 4 KC-135R tanker aircraft (two to remain in USA).
- 5 C-130H, 1 KC-130H and 4 KC-130B transport, tanker and ELINT aircraft.
- 4 Fokker 50 transport aircraft.
- 69 helicopters: 18 UH-1H (transport), 19 Super Puma (transport and SAR), 12 Cougar (transport), 6 CH-47D (transport); 10 AS550A2 Fennec (armed reconnaissance and training); 10 AS550C2 Fennec (anti-armour). Of these totals, 5 UH-1Hs are based in Brunei, 12 Super Pumas and Cougars in Australia and some of the CH-47Ds in the USA. There are also 8 AH-64D Apache attack helicopters and 6 CH-47SDs on order.
- 27 S211 basic trainers (in Australia).
- 40 Malat Searcher Mk2 UAV and 24 Chukar III target drones. A small number of Malat Scout UAV may also remain in service.

NAVY

Navy personnel total 9600, comprising 3600 regulars (including 250+ women), 1000 NSFs and 5000 NSmen.

The RSN's vessels are organised into type-based squadrons, most of which are grouped into two Flotillas (constituting the Fleet) and Coastal Command:

- The First Flotilla operates six Sea Wolf-class (FPB-45) MGBs (185 Squadron), six Victory-class (MGB-62) MCVs (188 Squadron) and six Fearless-class APVs (189 Squadron).
- The Third Flotilla operates one ex-Royal Navy LSL and two County-class LSTs (being replaced in 191 Squadron by five new Endurance-class LSTs), six ramp-powered launches and a hundred or more 'fast craft' (landing craft) (195 Squadron). 192 and 193 Squadrons operate requisitioned CR vessels when mobilised.
- Coastal Command deploys six Resilience-class PVs (182 Squadron), four Bedok-class (Landsort) MCM vessels, a diving support vessel and fast boats (194 Squadron). The command also includes the NDU and Giraffe 100 radar sites at Bedok, Pedra Branca, Raffles Lighthouse, Sultan Shoal and St John's Island.

The Submarine Project Office at Karlskrona in Sweden and 171 Squadron, under HQ Fleet in Singapore, operate the navy's A12–type submarines, which will eventually total four. During 2000, these boats began to transfer to Singapore, although the training arrangement with Sweden is likely to continue into the long-term.

The Fleet and other naval commands are commanded by Colonels, Squadrons by Lieutenant-Colonels and ships usually by Majors.

Appendix 2

Paramilitary forces

Singapore's paramilitary forces, broadly defined, comprise four elements: the Singapore Civil Defence Force (SCDF), the Singapore Police Force (SPF) (which includes branches with internal security and coastguard functions), the National Cadet Corps (NCC), and the Youth Flying Club (YFC).

SINGAPORE CIVIL DEFENCE FORCE

Though it is unarmed and administered by the Ministry of Home Affairs, the SCDF deserves classification as a paramilitary organisation for two reasons. First, it plays an important part in Total Defence. Singapore's extremely high population density and the close proximity of housing estates to military installations mean that its people are particularly vulnerable in the event of war.[1] As a result, Singapore's government has prioritised civil defence (CD) to a greater degree than most other countries', apart from Sweden's and Switzerland's. It has taken CD particularly seriously since the mid-1980s, partly apparently in order to add flexibility to its deterrent posture. Second, the SCDF relies on NSFs and NSmen to provide a large proportion of its personnel. By the late 1990s, the SCDF had a total strength of more than 82 000, comprising 1600 regulars, 3200 NSFs, 23 000 NSmen (many of them former SAF reservists, transferred at the end of their 13-year training cycle in the army) and 54 000 volunteers.[2]

The SCDF—which subsumed Singapore's Fire Service in 1989 after major disasters (the Hotel New World Collapse in 1986 and an oil rig fire in 1988) revealed inefficient duplication of effort by the two services—controls the Disaster Assistance and Rescue

Team (DART), four CD divisions, 12 fire stations and two training schools. A Construction Brigade is trained to repair damaged roads and buildings. The Force also possesses its own supply and maintenance bases. Under the CD divisions, there are rescue battalions and companies (including paramedics) at political constituency and residential zone levels. In 1997, the SCDF established a Hazardous Materials Unit to combat the threat from chemical contamination.[3]

The most dramatic sign of the government's commitment to CD has been the integration of shelter facilities into major new public buildings and other infrastructure. Every Housing and Development Board (HDB) block of flats built since 1987 has incorporated a community shelter and, in 1997, the first HDB flats with individual household shelters were handed over to their owners.[4] Shelters have also been built into underground railway stations, schools and community centres. By 1998, there were sufficient shelters for 300 000 people, and the coverage was expected to grow significantly by 2003. Extensive R&D by both DTG's Lands and Estates Organisation and Protective Technology Centres at Singapore's two universities has supported the shelter-building programme.

SINGAPORE POLICE FORCE

The SPF, like the SCDF, depends on NS to provide much of its manpower, which includes 3500 NSFs and more than 21 000 NSmen. In a national security crisis, this large reserve could be mobilised for public order duties.

The bulk of the SPF is employed on routine policing duties, which it performs with exemplary efficiency. However, it does include some paramilitary elements. The 750-strong Singapore Gurkha Contingent guards key installations (such as the Istana, the government's nerve centre) and prisons and, importantly, provides an ethnically neutral riot squad. Its senior officers are still British, either recruited on contract or on loan service from the British Army. The heavily armed police Special Operations Command includes the Police Task Force (also used for crowd control) and the Special Tactics and Rescue Unit (trained for rescuing hostages).

The Special Operations Command contributed heavily to Singapore police contingents sent to UN peacekeeping missions in

Namibia (1989) and Cambodia (1992–3 and 1998).[5] An SPF team joined UNTAET in East Timor in early 2000.

The renaming of the former Marine Police as the Police Coast Guard (PCG) in the early 1990s reflected its expanding roles and capabilities. Between 1993 and 1998 the PCG inherited the RSN's 12 Coastal Patrol Craft, which were considerably larger than any of its previous boats. The RSN trained police crews for the CPCs and loaned personnel to ease their induction into service. Responsible for patrolling Singapore's territorial waters, in close collaboration with the navy's Coastal Command, the PCG is organised into the Coastal Patrol Squadron (operating the CPCs), the Port Squadron (PT and PX class boats) and the Interceptor Squadron (PC class boats). In all it operates approximately 90 craft, ranging from two to 46 tonnes. In 1998, the PCG ordered 20 new Australian-built 18-metre fast boats to replace the PX class.[6]

NATIONAL CADET CORPS

The NCC is organised through Singapore's secondary schools, 104 of which had cadet units by 1997, with 11 000 members. At that time, MINDEF and the Ministry of Education decided to increase funding for the NCC with the aim of establishing another 25 units and raising total membership to 14 000 by the year 2000. MINDEF had come to see NCC training (which includes basic military skills such as shooting and fieldcraft) as important because NSFs who were former cadets were better prepared for BMT, both mentally and physically.[7] NCC units, which include specialist Air and Sea branches, are affiliated with nearby SAF formations (such as infantry brigades and naval and air bases); the NCC 21 masterplan, announced in May 1999, attempts to encourage even closer links by attaching SAF officers to cadet units as advisers.[8]

YOUTH FLYING CLUB

The YFC was established as the Junior Flying Club in the early 1970s. Although it has a town headquarters, its flying unit (which has a 'shadow' identity as the RSAF's 151 Squadron) operates 12 MINDEF-owned, but civil-registered Piper Warrior II light aircraft and is based at Seletar Airport, where it provides air experience and primary flying training to Private Pilot's Licence standard for pre-university, university and polytechnic students aged from 16 years. Familiarisation flights in RSAF aircraft are also arranged for members of the club.[9] The YFC's main objective—in which it has been highly successful—is to encourage students to pursue RSAF careers, particularly as pilots.

Notes

Abbreviated references relate to books or book chapters, journal and newspaper articles, official documents and publications and Internet sources listed in the Bibliography.

Abbreviated titles: *ADJ (Asian Defence Journal)*, *AFM (Air Forces Monthly)*, *APDR (Asia-Pacific Defence Reporter)*, *FEER (Far Eastern Economic Review)*, *IDR (International Defense Review)*, *JDW (Jane's Defence Weekly)*, MIW (MINDEF Internet Webservice), *PDS (Parliamentary Debates Singapore)*, *Pointer (Pointer. Journal of the Singapore Armed Forces)*, *PRO (Public Record Office)*, *ST (Straits Times)*, *STWE (Straits Times Weekly Edition)*, *STWOE (Straits Times Weekly Overseas Edition)*, SWB (BBC Summary of World Broadcasts).

INTRODUCTION

1 Quoted in 'Majulah Singapura', *Pioneer*, August 1990, p. 31.
2 Quoted in *ADJ*, June 1987, p. 5.
3 *Singapore 1998*, p. 51.
4 See, for example, Murfett, Miksic, Farrell and Chiang 1999.
5 One of the few substantial, published official sources on the SAF's early years is Gill 1990.

1 THE SINGAPORE ARMED FORCES' ORIGINS AND EARLY YEARS

1 'The fixed political objectives of our party', People's Action Party 1960, p. 6.
2 Gill 1990, p. 27.
3 Chandran 1975, p. 8.

4 See Hawkins 1972, pp. 15–18.
5 David Lee 1984, pp. 183–9.
6 *Malaysia Agreement* 1963.
7 *Colony of Singapore Annual Report 1957*, p. 276.
8 Gill 1990, pp. 7–28.
9 *Our security. Keselamatan kita* 1969, pp. 13–14.
10 ibid., pp. 15–16.
11 ibid., p. 12.
12 Gill 1990, pp. 25–6.
13 Hawkins 1972, pp. 24–5.
14 ibid., pp. 39–51.
15 *Our security. Keselamatan kita* 1969, p. 14.
16 Lee Kuan Yew 1998, p. 657.
17 ibid., p. 636.
18 ibid., pp. 636–7.
19 Independence of Singapore Agreement, 1965, in Boyce 1968, p. 32.
20 Lee Kuan Yew 1998, p. 663.
21 Gill 1990, p. 54.
22 *Singapore Year Book 1965*, p. 156.
23 ibid., p. 157.
24 Gill 1990, p. 57.
25 *Our security. Keselamatan kita* 1969, p. 21.
26 Gill 1990, pp. 57–8.
27 ibid., p. 57.
28 Chiang 1997, p. 22.
29 ibid., pp. 57–61; Gill 1990, p. 60; Wilson 1972, p. 62; Chan 1991, pp. 162–3, 180; Menon 1995, pp. 25–6.
30 PRO, WO32/21398.
31 Darby 1973, pp. 316–20.
32 Statement by the Prime Minister, *PDS*, vol. 26, no. 3 (8 September 1967), col. 173.
33 See interview with defence minister Yeo Ning Hong, *ADJ*, February 1992, p. 7.
34 Gill 1990, pp. 54–6; Hawkins 1972, p. 27.
35 Chiang 1997, pp. 23–4; Gill 1990, p. 63.
36 See the debate on the National Service (Amendment) Bill, *PDS*, vol. 25, no. 17 (14 March 1967), cols 1197–258.
37 *Singapore Year Book 1967*, pp. 184–5.
38 Chiang 1997, p. 35; Menon 1995, p. 32.
39 *PDS*, vol. 25, no. 17 (14 March 1967), col. 1253.
40 Hawkins 1972, pp. 40–3; Darby 1973, p. 325.
41 *Singapore Year Book 1969*, p. 138.
42 *Singapore 1973*, pp. 105–6.
43 Lee Kuan Yew 1998, pp. 556–69.
44 Chiang 1997, pp. 79–81.
45 See Lee Kuan Yew's speech, 'Why Singapore is ready to pay a high premium for security', *ST*, 3 July 1987.
46 *Defence of Singapore 1994–95*, p. 5.

47 Parliamentary statement by S. Jayakumar, minister of Home Affairs, *ST*, 14 March 1987.
48 *Singapore 1971*, p. 106.
49 'Two-day internal security exercise', *ST*, 30 April 1986.
50 Menon 1995, p. 49.
51 *The Singapore Artillery. 100th Anniversary Commemorative Book*, 1988, pp. 96–120.
52 Headquarters Armour homepage, MIW.
53 'Combat Engineers—advance and overcome', *Pioneer*, June 1992, pp. 10–11.
54 'A memorable finale', *Pioneer*, February 1984, p. 28.
55 'Singapore Armed Forces forms first combined arms division', *ST*, 22 March 1991.
56 *Q & A on defence. 1—Defence policies and organisation* 1985, pp. 26–7.
57 *Singapore 1971*, p. 102; Lim 1992, pp. 31–2; Chiang 1997, pp. 84–8.
58 See Schofield 1998, pp. 81, 91.
59 Lim 1992, pp. 35, 37.
60 ibid., pp. 37, 41; *Defending Singapore in the 21st century*, p. 52.
61 PRO, WO32/21398.
62 Chew 1993, pp. 20–5.
63 Chiang 1997, pp. 90–1.
64 Chew 1993, p. 25; Pocock 1986, pp. 62–4, 90–92.
65 Pocock 1986, p. 64; 'Keeping Singapore safe', *Pioneer*, September 1995, p. 5.
66 Pocock 1986, pp. 61, 64, 90, 92; Fricker 1994, p. 215.
67 Boey 1993, p. 244.
68 'Strong air defence will deter aggressors: Dr Yeo', *ST*, 30 March 1994.

2 DEFENCE POLICY, THREAT PERCEPTIONS AND STRATEGY

1 *Defending Singapore in the 21st century*, p. 12.
2 Kwa 1998, pp. 129–30.
3 *Defence of Singapore 1994–95*, p. 5.
4 ibid.
5 ibid., pp. 13–16.
6 ibid., p. 13.
7 ibid., pp. 13–14.
8 'Do you know what happened 32 years ago?', *ST*, 22 July 1996.
9 'Teachers witness capability of the SAF', MIW, 21 May 1998.
10 See Vasil 1995.
11 'Beware foreign elements: Dr Yeo', *ST*, 6 May 1988.
12 'Singapore group buys tanker to stockpile oil', *ST*, 24 August 1990.
13 *Defending Singapore in the 21st century*, p. 13.
14 'Dr Hu unveils prudent budget', *STWE*, 28 February 1998; 'FY99 expenditure estimates', *ST*, 26 February 1999.

15 Speech by Dr Tony Tan, deputy prime minister and minister for Defence, MIW, 7 January 1998.

16 Interview with Defence Minister Lee Boon Yang, *Defense News*, 5–11 December 1994, p. 38.

17 *Defence of Singapore 1994–95*, pp. 63–7.

18 Huxley and Boey 1996, pp. 174–5; Boey 1996a, pp. 318–19.

19 'Information technology. Giving the SAF a strategic edge', *Pioneer*, March 1990, pp. 14–17.

20 Huxley and Boey 1996, p. 34; *Defence of Singapore 1994–95*, p. 21.

21 For a typical exposition of Singapore's vulnerabilities, see interview with Dr Yeo Nin Hong, second minister for Defence, in Southeast Asia supplement, *IDR*, December 1986, p. 10.

22 Speech by Prime Minister Lee Kuan Yew, *ST*, 3 July 1987.

23 See comments by Prime Minister Goh Chok Tong, 'Singapore must not be another Kuwait', *ST*, 13 August 1990; Defence Minister Yeo Ning Hong, 'Nation's security depends on strong defence: Dr Yeo', *Singapore Bulletin*, April 1991, p. 1.

24 Teo 1991, p. 54.

25 Leifer 1995, p. 30.

26 Quoted in Chan 1971, p. 45.

27 Leifer 1989, p. 968.

28 Wu 1972, p. 662.

29 Ul Haq 1987, p. 290.

30 ibid., p. 667.

31 Lee Khoon Choy 1976, p. 110.

32 Leifer 1989, pp. 973–4.

33 See *From Phnom Penh to Kabul* 1980.

34 See, for example, the interview with Defence Minister Lee Boon Yang, *ADJ*, July 1995, p. 6.

35 Interview with Defence Minister Tony Tan, 'Attracting, keeping the best as SAF regulars a key concern', *ST*, 1 February 1996.

36 Leifer 1989, p. 978.

37 Interview with Senior Minister Lee Kuan Yew, *ST*, 9 June 1996.

38 'Singapore seeks defence pact', *Age*, 16 October 1980; 'Singapore seeks new defence umbrella', *Canberra Times*, 6 July 1981.

39 'The FPDA: commitment to regional stability', *Pioneer*, February 1990, p. 9.

40 Methven 1992, p. 115.

41 See, for example, interview with Defence Minister Yeo Ning Hong, *ADJ*, March 1994, p. 25.

42 '5–power group "more relevant now"', *ST*, 16 April 1997; 'Security challenges and responses in the Asia-Pacific', Keynote address by Dr Tony Tan at the First General Meeting of the Council for Security Cooperation in the Asia-Pacific, MIW, 4 June 1997.

43 Interview with Defence Minister Yeo Ning Hong, *Armed Forces Journal International*, May 1992, p. 38.

44 Leifer 1989, p. 971.

45 See, for example, 'It's the right decision says Goh', *ST*, 2 July 1975.

46 da Cunha 1991, p. 62.

47 Simon 1992, pp. 112–14; Stubbs 1992, pp. 397–410.
48 Emmerson 1996, p. 83.
49 Ganesan 1994, pp. 458–60.
50 'NS period and defence budget will not be cut', *Singapore Bulletin*, January 1992, pp. 1, 8.
51 Ganesan 1998a, p. 591.
52 Leifer 1995, pp. 147–8.
53 Leifer 1989, p. 969.
54 'BG defends cautious approach', *ST*, 18 March 1987.
55 Speech by Prime Minister Lee Kuan Yew, 'Why Singapore is ready to pay a high premium for security', *ST*, 3 July 1987.
56 *ST*, 18 March 1997.
57 See, for example, interview with Lieutenant-General Winston Choo, Singapore's Chief of Defence Force, in *ADJ*, March 1989, p. 47.
58 Pillai 1990, p. 34.
59 Methven 1992, pp. 69–91.
60 Aznam 1989, pp. 20–21; Pillai 1990, p. 34.
61 *STWOE*, 17 February 1990.
62 Methven 1992, p. 140.
63 Huxley and Boey 1996, p. 175.
64 Shamira 1998, pp. 24–47; interviews, Singapore, July 1996.
65 *PDS*, vol. 67, no. 2 (2 June 1997), col. 76.
66 Interview with Lee Boon Yang, *ADJ*, July 1995.
67 'PM Goh, Mahathir to work for closer ties', *Singapore Bulletin*, April 1998.
68 'KL's water promises not enough', *ST*, 21 April 1998.
69 'Relocating our CIQ—facts of the case', *Singapore Bulletin*, August 1998, pp. 1–2.
70 *ST*, 5 August 1998; *Financial Times* (London), 5 August 1998.
71 'Singaporean visit eases tensions with Malaysia', *International Herald Tribune*, 6 November 1998.
72 'Tok Mat: we want to regain what's ours', *Star*, 10 August 1998.
73 Jayasankaran 1998, p. 20.
74 'KL curbs airspace use by RSAF jets', *STWE*, 19 September 1999.
75 TV3 television (Kuala Lumpur), 17 September 1998, SWB FE/3336 B/6, 19 September 1998.
76 *Utusan Malaysia* (Kuala Lumpur), 11 November 1998, SWB FE/3382 B/6, 12 November 1998.
77 'Aid for KL will be "on basis of win-win"', *ST*, 9 November 1998.
78 'S'pore, KL to settle issues as a package', *ST*, 18 December 1998.
79 'CIQ: S'pore's sovereignty at stake', *ST*, 21 January 1999.
80 See statement by Foreign Minister S. Jayakumar, *PDS*, vol. 67, no. 14 (30 July 1997), col. 1352.
81 Desker 1991, p. 109.
82 'Singapore, Indonesia sign pact to develop water resources in Bintan', *Singapore Bulletin*, April 1992, p. 13; Ganesan 1998b, p. 26.
83 Singh 1994, pp. 108–9, 122.
84 'Singapore to get piped gas from Indonesia', *ST*, 1 May 1997.
85 Interviews, Singapore, July–August 1996.

86 'S'pore's third round of aid', *ST*, 7 January 1999.
87 'Habibie, Golkar chief take offence at SM's remarks', *ST*, 12 February 1998.
88 'Habibie unhappy with S'pore: AWSJ', *ST*, 5 August 1998.
89 'Malay leaders in Singapore hit back at Habibie', *STWE*, 13 February 1999.
90 'Indonesia tests Singapore', *STWE*, 6 March 1999.
91 'S'pore, Indon navies help Indonesian villagers', *Pioneer*, August 1998, p. 18.
92 'More patrols in waterways', *STWE*, 8 May 1999.
93 'US$8b deal signed', *Singapore Bulletin*, September 1998, p. 2; 'Landmark Natuna gas deal signed', *Singapore Bulletin*, February 1999, p. 1.
94 'Water deal with Jakarta is possible, says Philip Yeo', *ST*, 16 January 1999.
95 Dolven 1999, p. 31.
96 'Growth- and Asean-driven Jakarta good for region, says BG Lee', *ST*, 30 March 1999.
97 'Gus Dur gets warm welcome', *STWE*, 13 November 1999; 'PM Goh's $1.2 billion plan for Indonesia', *ST*, 14 January 2000.
98 'Southeast Asians fear a breakup of Indonesia', *International Herald Tribune*, 16 November 1999.
99 See Lee Kuan Yew's 1967 comments on this theme, cited in Josey 1980, p. 376; and more recent remarks by Rear Admiral Teo Chee Hean, second defence minister, in 'Singaporeans should be willing to fight to keep country's independence', *Pioneer*, December 1997, p. 11.
100 *Singapore: the next lap*, 1991, p. 141.
101 'A conversation with BG Lee Hsien Loong', *Asean Forecast*, vol. 4, no. 10 (October 1984), p. 164 cited in Singh 1992, p. 123.
102 See, for example, *Defence of Singapore 1994–95*, p. 17.
103 Statement by Matthias Yao, Minister of State for Defence, at the Singapore Combat Engineers' 30th anniversary parade-cum-commissioning of the Combat Engineering Tractor, MIW, 11 April 1997.
104 Chin 1987, pp. 199–200.
105 See Huxley 1994, p. 26.
106 'New hardware will help Navy to be "balanced force"', *ST*, 5 May 1993. See also interview with Defence Minister Yeo Ning Hong, *ST*, 1 July 1993.
107 'Australia, Singapore prepare to defend Malaysia', *Canberra Times*, 10 May 1977.
108 An article by a senior SAF operational commander in 1986 foreshadowed such relatively small-scale *Blitzkrieg* operations. See Ng 1986.
109 Dillon 1994, p. 60.
110 Vatikiotis, Dolven and Tasker 1998, p. 22.
111 Interview with Abdul Razak Abdullah Baginda, 'Singapore expands overseas basing, training', *Defense News*, 31 March 1997.
112 Andrew Tan 1997, p. 15.
113 *ST*, 4 November 1998.

114 Speech by Dr Tony Tan, deputy prime minister and minister for Defence, 13 February 1999, MIW.

115 See Huxley 1993a, pp. 50–8.

116 *New Straits Times*, 16 September 1991 and 1 February 1993; Saw 1992, pp. 32–3.

117 *PDS*, vol. 37, no. 9 (14 March 1978), cols 770–1.

118 'Air force takes aim at AMRAAM', *ADJ*, October 1998, p. 63.

119 *ST*, 12 March 1993.

120 'Attacks by pirates double in Indonesia', *ST*, 22 October 1999.

121 'Troops sent to Batam as 20 die in clashes', *STWE*, 31 July 1999; 'Mob protests on Bintan contained by police', *ST*, 16 January 2000; 'Riau's main parties call for secession', *ST*, 2 February 2000.

122 See 'Batam at risk' (editorial), *ST*, 31 July 1999.

123 See Ho 1993, p. 53.

124 'Three water plants by 2011', *STWE*, 9 May 1998.

125 'Rice pact with Thailand soon', *Singapore Bulletin*, April 1999, p. 3; 'Move to boost local fish and vegetable supply', *Singapore Bulletin*, September 1999, p. 16.

126 See speeches by Deputy Prime Minister and Defence Minister Tony Tan, MIW, 1 July 1999 and 28 July 1999.

3 COMMAND AND CONTROL

1 In his first speech to the Malaysian parliament in December 1963, Lee had argued that 'in Asia, particularly in Southeast Asia, armies when expanded have a tendency ultimately to take over . . .' . Cited in Josey 1980, p. 191.

2 See Robert Tilman 1989, pp. 53–8.

3 ibid., p. 60.

4 Han, Fernandez and Tan 1998, p. 96; Chan 1976, p. 171.

5 Chiang 1997, p. 72; 'Former SAF Director of General Staff passes away', *Pioneer*, November 1989, p. 43.

6 'B-G: Elected President's role is to balance the powers of ministers', *STWOE*, 20 August 1988.

7 See, for example, the photograph of Goh inspecting a passing-out parade at Beach Road Camp in November 1966, in Chiang 1990, p. 38.

8 'Singapore's fate depends on 300 men', speech by Lee Kuan Yew, 28 April 1971, cited in Han, Fernandez and Tan 1998, p. 90.

9 Boey 1995, p. 68; 'Singapore puts force integration into place', *JDW*, 30 April 1997, p. 25.

10 For fuller discussion of the Scholarship scheme, see Chapter 4, 'Singapore's military scholars' and Chapter 10, 'The dual-career scheme'.

11 'Achievements of five state award recipients', *Pioneer*, September 1983, p. 8.

12 *STWOE*, 12 December 1992.

13 See Chapter 10, 'SAF officers in the government' for a discussion of the wider implications of these officers' moves into politics.

14 'COL (NS) Peter Ho is now PS (DD)', *Pioneer*, November 1995, p. 25; 'RADM Richard Lim to assume new appointment in MINDEF', *Pioneer*, September 1999, p. 7.

15 'New permanent secretary (Defence)', *Pioneer*, June 1994, p. 18.

16 *STWOE*, 20 August 1988.

17 *ST*, 31 August 1990. In 1996, further legislation circumscribed the President's powers to veto appointments by allowing Parliament to over-ride the veto in some circumstances. 'Bill seeks changes to powers of Elected President', *STWE*, 5 October 1996.

18 Speech by Dr Tony Tan Keng Yam, deputy prime minister and minister for Defence, in the Budget Debate, *PDS*, vol. 65, no. 11 (13 March 1996), col. 1078.

19 Evidence of this knowledge is to be found in the discussions among SAF reservists in Internet discussion groups such as 'soc.culture. Singapore' since the mid-1990s.

20 Ho 1976; *FEER*, 11 February 1977, p. 15.

21 Chan 1989, p. 85.

22 *PDS*, vol. 68, no. 7 (11 March 1998), cols 926–32.

23 'Accord changeover ceremony at Tuas naval base', MIW, 26 May 1999.

24 *Singapore 1998*, p. 94.

25 'Singapore Armed Forces Act', in *The Statutes of the Republic of Singapore* 1995.

26 'Amendments to SAF Act', *Pioneer*, February 1994, p. 24.

27 Worthington 1999, pp. 269–72; Baker 1999, p. 92; Tai 2001.

28 *Defence of Singapore 1994–95*, pp. 19–20; *The MINDEF/SAF Fact Book*, p. 2; 'Inauguration of the Defence Science and Technology Agency', MIW, 29 March 2000.

29 'Change in nomenclature', *Pioneer*, June 1990, p. 2.

30 *Our security. Keselamatan kita* 1969, p. 22.

31 'SAF should be the concern of every Singaporean', speech by Defence Minister Goh Chok Tong, *ST*, 16 April 1983; Sengupta 1999a, p. 14; *Defending Singapore in the 21st century*, p. 28.

32 Sengupta 1999a, p. 16.

33 'SAF Signals formation shows Admiral Teo operational capability and readiness', MIW, 30 November 1996.

34 'Communication technology—the vital link in warfare', *Pioneer*, March 1993, p. 13.

35 'Towards new era in military communications', *Pioneer*, October 1990, p. 39; 'Signals provides vital link', *Pioneer*, April 1991, pp. 23–5.

36 'SAF signallers—providing the vital link', *Pioneer*, February 1997, p. 5.

37 *ADJ*, May 1991, p. 76.

38 Boey 1996b, p. 48.

39 *Defence of Singapore 1994–95*, p. 60.

40 Boey 1995, pp. 67–8; 'Regional maritime air power evolves', *APDR*, February–March 1999, p. 19.

41 'Singapore's first satellite to launch in May', *Singapore Bulletin*, March 1998, p. 17; 'S'pore's first satellite blasts off into space', *STWE*, 29 August 1998, p. 24.

42 'SingTel pulls out of $1b Asia-Pac satellite venture', *STWE*, 9 May 1998.

43 'Hughes loses Asian satellite contract', *Flight International*, 21 April 1999, p. 6.

44 'Plans for home-made micro-satellites', *STWE*, 11 April 1998; 'NTU launches first satellite successfully', *ST*, 22 April 1999.

45 'SAF to widen use of info technology', *ST*, 20 January 1990.

46 Speech by Dr Tony Tan Keng Yam, deputy prime minister and minister for Defence, MIW, 4 October 1996.

47 Gwee 1992, p. 34.

48 'Millennium force', *Flight International*, 16 June 1999, p. 67.

49 *FEER*, 21 December 1989, pp. 20–1.

50 Ball 1995a, pp. 15–16.

51 ibid., pp. 19–25.

52 ibid., p. 30.

53 'Crisp pictures from S'pore's eye in the sky', *ST*, 15 May 1997; 'New eye in sky for close look at region', *ST*, 25 March 1998.

54 'Plans for home-made micro-satellites', *STWE*, 11 April 1998 'Detroit airport pictured by UK satellite', *Flight International*, 2 June 1999, p. 30; 'Israel, Singapore to sign satellite deal', *JDW*, 5 July 2000, p. 2.

55 Speech by Dr Tony Tan, deputy prime minister and minister for Defence, MIW, 3 November 1997.

56 Ball, 1995a, p. 19; *Singapore Government Directory*, July 1999, pp. 222–3.

57 Speech by Dr Tony Tan, MIW, 3 November 1997.

58 Worthington 1999, p. 269–72.

4 PERSONNEL

1 'NS the very basis for Singapore's continued existence', *Pioneer*, November 1995, p. 26.

2 *Q & A on defence. 2—Manpower* 1985, pp. 6–7.

3 See, for example, statements by second defence minister (Services), Brigadier-General Lee Hsien Loong, *STWOE*, 17 March 1990; and by Minister of State for Defence Matthias Yao Chih, Committee of Supply, 11 March 1998, *PDS*, vol. 68, no. 7, col. 925.

4 Speech by the minister of Defence, Howe Yong Chong, 16 October 1979, Singapore Government Press Release, MC/OCT/20/79 (Defence).

5 Seah 1989, pp. 951–2; Chiang 1997, pp. 48–53.

6 Menon 1995, pp. 12, 15.

7 Leong 1978.

8 'SAF should be the concern of every Singaporean', *ST*, 16 April 1983.

9 'Lt-Gen Choo: enlisted men today are more positive', *Sunday Times* (Singapore), 12 August 1990.

10 'Attitudes towards NS more positive', *Singapore Bulletin*, August 1992, p. 11.
11 'Voluntary early enlistment', *Pioneer*, February 1992, p. 27.
12 'For your info: financial help for servicemen', *Pioneer*, December 1993, p. 25.
13 *Amnesty International Report 1998*, p. 302.
14 Hanna 1973, pp. 2–3.
15 Boey 1996a, p. 317.
16 'Shorter NS for fit recruits', *Pioneer*, May 1993, p. 15; 'Commercialising to save manpower', ibid., May 1994, p. 8; 'Better educated NSFs to provide higher levels of service', ibid., July 1994, p. 18.
17 Goh Keng Swee, minister of Defence, Addendum to Presidential address at opening of the second session of the fourth parliament, 26 December 1978, Singapore Government Press Release.
18 'We must stop danger trend', *ST*, 14 September 1987.
19 Statement by minister of state for Defence, Matthias Yao Chih, Committee of Supply, 23 July 1997, *PDS*, vol. 67, no. 1, col. 723.
20 ibid., cols 723–4; Comments by the minister for the Environment and second minister for Defence, RADM (NS) Teo Chee Hean, at the visit to Headquarters, SAF Signals formation, MIW, 30 November 1996; 'Commercialising to save manpower', *Pioneer*, May 1994, p. 8; 'Greater responsibility for NSF armourers', ibid., July 1996, p. 8; 'More NSFs to fill mid-level Specialist posts', ibid., September 1996, p. 15.
21 'Gearing up students for the rigours of military life', *ST*, 10 January 1987.
22 'Obese NS men will have basic training extended', *STWOE*, 2 June 1990.
23 'SAF responds to rising national obesity trend to maintain operational readiness', MIW, 5 December 1997.
24 'Parents prefer direct enlistment', MIW, 1 April 1998.
25 'SAF training resumes after three-day suspension' , *STWE*, 12 April 1997; 'Army accidents to prompt SAF review', *Jane's Pointer*, June 1997, p. 10.
26 'Seeing comrades die may affect some soldiers', *ST*, 16 April 1997.
27 'A shoulder on stand-by', *Army News*, April 1998, p. 2.
28 'Chosen to lead', *Pioneer*, March 1997, pp. 8–9.
29 'With pride we lead—the making of the SAF's specialists', *Pioneer*, June 1997, pp. 2–6.
30 According to second minister for Defence, RADM Teo Chee Hean, Committee of Supply, 13 March 1996, *PDS*, vol. 65, no. 11, col. 1082.
31 Menon 1995, pp. 127–8.
32 'A salute to the SAF', *Pioneer*, July 1993, p. 2.
33 Chiang 1997, pp. 84, 103, 126.
34 ibid., pp. 89–91, 107, 130–2.
35 Speech by Howe Yoon Chong, minister of Defence, 16 May 1979, Singapore Government Press Release, MC/May/27/79 (Defence).
36 *Singapore 1973*, p. 104.
37 'Overcoming the vulnerabilities of a small nation', speech by George Yeo, minister for Information and the Arts, MIW, 7 November 1996.

38 'Four tell why it's hard to brainwash men who've done NS', *ST*, 22 June 1987.
39 According to Deputy Prime Minister and Defence Minister Tony Tan. 'Dr Tan outlines his vision for the SAF', *ST*, 1 February 1996.
40 See Chiang 1997, pp. 185–8.
41 It has nevertheless been alleged—notably through the medium of the Internet discussion group soc.culture.singapore ('How much do we know about SAF', 16 May 1996)—that special privileges are granted to NSFs with wealthy or influential parents, who are known in the SAF as 'White Horses'.
42 Chiang 1997, pp. 43, 45.
43 'Education in the SAF', *Pioneer*, March 1983, p. 12.
44 Bedlington 1981, pp. 257–61.
45 *PDS*, vol. 36, no. 8 (23 February 1977), cols 398–9.
46 Li 1989, pp. 108–9; Peled 1998, p. 118.
47 *ST*, 23 February 1987.
48 'This is a Singapore problem. We will solve it ourselves . . .', *ST*, 18 March 1987.
49 See 'Malay Singaporeans want to belong—in all ways', *ST*, 9 August 1996.
50 'No quick solution to ethnic, religious issues', *STWE*, 2 October 1999.
51 See 'SAF reservists lack morale and discipline', *ST*, 8 February 1981; Chiang 1997, p. 94.
52 'SAF fights the flab', *Pioneer*, February 1991, p. 33.
53 'Reservist officers' course revamped', *Pioneer*, December 1992, p. 22.
54 'Reservist upgrading scheme', *Pioneer*, October 1983, pp. 18–19.
55 'Bill to allow for extension of reserve service', *ST*, 10 December 1986.
56 'New policies for reservists', *Pioneer*, December 1983, p. 8; 'Bigger allowance for reservist key appointment holders', *Pioneer*, September 1991, p. 5.
57 In 1990, the three-day BCTC course was compacted into a two-day session. 'Bigger allowance for reservist key appointment holders', *Pioneer*, September 1991, p. 5.; 'Reservists as front-line troopers', *Mirror* (Singapore), vol. 21, no. 15 (1 August 1985), pp. 2–3; *Q & A on defence. 3—Training and discipline* 1986, p. 15; 'Training more reservists in shorter time', *Pioneer*, January 1990, p. 13.
58 'Operationally Ready National Service', MIW.
59 'Reservists are getting fitter', *ST*, 14 December 1985.
60 'Frontline: the development of reservist training', *Pioneer*, July 1986, pp. 18–19.
61 '"Reservists" now called "Operationally Ready National Servicemen"', *Pioneer*, January 1994, p. 18.
62 Speech by President Benjamin Sheares at the opening of the fifth parliament, *ST*, 4 February 1981.
63 'Frontline: the development of reservist training', *Pioneer*, July 1986, p. 20; 'Reservists as front-line troopers', *Mirror* (Singapore), vol. 21, no. 15 (1 August 1985) p. 3.
64 'Reservists and their employers', *Pioneer*, April 1993, pp. 7–9.

65 Chiang 1997, pp. 178–9; 'RECORD II', *Pioneer*, November 1996, p. 7.
66 'Attracting, keeping the best as SAF regulars a key concern', *ST*, 1 February 1996.
67 'Recession helps SAF recruit men', *ST*, 26 February 1986.
68 Chan 1991, p. 145.
69 'Scholars urged to go for double degrees', *STWE*, 7 November 1999.
70 Chan 1991, p. 146; *Q & A on defence. 4—Personnel affairs and services* 1986, pp. 17–18; '1PS meets Merit scholars', *Pioneer*, November 1990, p. 15.
71 Brigadier-General (Reservist) Lee Hsien Loong, second minister for Defence (Services), quoted in *STWOE*, 18 March 1989.
72 'Kirpa Wong bin Rahim', 'Fashioning Singapore's tough armed forces', *Pacific Defence Reporter*, 1982, p. 32.
73 'Manpower Policies' supplement, *Pointer*, February 1982, p. 10.
74 ibid.
75 *FEER*, 13 January 1983, p. 27.
76 'Manpower Policies' supplement, p. 8.
77 Tai 1991, p. 15.
78 'Groomed for the top', *ST*, 9 August 1993.
79 Tai 1991, p. 16.
80 For a description of the promotion process, see 'How officers move up the ranks', *ST*, 29 June 1994.
81 'Manpower Policies' supplement, p. 4.
82 *Singapore Government Directory, July 1999*, pp. 215–25, 412–30.
83 'SAF military officers given recognition for contributions', *MIW*, 26 June 1998.
84 'Retiring SAF officers to get new career as teachers', *ST*, 29 June 1994; 'Ex-SAF men to take up jobs in school operations', *STWE*, 6 December 1997.
85 'Dr Tan's announcement at the SAF Day dinner for senior officers', *MIW*, 4 July 1997.
86 ibid.
87 Speech by Dr Tony Tan, deputy prime minister and minister for Defence, *MIW*, 12 January 1998.
88 'Continuing professional education for SAF officers', *Pioneer*, April 1997, pp. 8–10.
89 'Officers from the army, navy and air force to train together', *ST*, 7 October 1998.
90 'Continuing professional education for SAF officers', *Pioneer*, April 1997, pp. 10–11.
91 *Defence of Singapore 1994–95*, p. 71.
92 *Singapore Government Directory, July 1999*, pp. 215–25, 412–30.
93 'Malay body sends protest note to Habibie', *ST*, 23 February 1999.
94 'Challenges of a battalion commander's job', *Pioneer*, September 1996, p. 14.
95 'Why are so many Chinese Christians in leading positions?', *ST*, 7 May 1997.
96 'SAF wants parents to encourage sons to join', *ST*, 3 March 1986.
97 'SAF offers 300 poly scholarships', *ST*, 20 January 1986.

98 'Singapore Polytechnic—Singapore Armed Forces Diploma Scheme', *Singapore Polytechnic Prospectus,1990–91*, p. 223.
99 'SAF WOSEs—towards excellence', *Pioneer*, March 1997, p. 16.
100 'Keen interest shown in new NCO scheme', *STWOE*, 28 April 1990; 'Recruiting higher calibre combat NCOs', *Pioneer*, June 1990, p. 23.
101 '"A" level study programme: combat NCOs of high calibre', *Pioneer*, April 1991, p. 19.
102 'New professional Corps of WOs and Corps of Specialists', *Pioneer*, March 1992, pp. 21–3.
103 'Higher responsibilities for Warrant Officers', *Pioneer*, September 1994, p. 13; 'From strict disciplinarians to skilled middle managers: Warrant Officers in the SAF', ibid., February 1996, p. 11.
104 Cyber Pioneer, MIW, 6 July 1996.
105 'From strict disciplinarians to skilled middle managers', *Pioneer*, September 1994, p. 12.
106 'Savings plan for SAF's "backbone"', *ST*, 23 February 2000.
107 'Chance for reservist NCOs to study and be officers', *STWOE*, 6 May 1989.
108 *Defence of Singapore 1994–95* , p. 71.
109 Koh 1993, p. 79.
110 Ang 1988, pp. 10–14.
111 'Women in green', *Pioneer*, April 1990, p. 24.
112 'Female trainees choose technical career in army', *Pioneer*, July 1988, p. 17.
113 'First woman SWO is a model soldier', *ST*, 30 September 1987.
114 Cheah 1992, p. 117.
115 'In a class of her own', *Army News*, February 1998, p. 2.
116 'SAF awards merit scholarships to women for the first time', *STWE*, 12 August 1993; *Defence of Singapore 1994–95*, p. 72.
117 'She earned her SAF wings, and now she's top in class too', *ST*, 19 September 1997.
118 'Three generals promoted', *STWE*, 3 July 1999.
119 'RSAF's first female chopper pilot', *Pioneer*, May 1994, p. 25.
120 Lim 1992, p. 104.
121 'The navy's most valuable asset—people', *Naval Forces*, vol. 18, no. 2 (1997) 'Republic of Singapore Navy' Special Issue, p. 24.
122 Goh Keng Swee, minister of Defence, Addendum to Presidential Address at the opening of the second session of the fourth parliament, 26 December 1978, Singapore Government Press Release.
123 Statement by Matthias Yao, minister of state for Defence, Committee of Supply, *PDS*, vol. 68, no. 7 (11 March 1998), cols 924–5.

5 SINGAPORE'S ARMY

1 On the importance of FIBUA training, see 'NS Men operationally ready for home defence', MIW, 16 December 1997.
2 'Building the 21st century warrior—Army 21', *Pioneer*, May 1999, p. 13; *Defending Singapore in the 21st century*, p. 30.

3 Chiang 1997, pp. 112–13.
4 'An old warrior revitalized', *Pioneer*, January 1991, p. 18.
5 Headquarters Armour homepage, MIW.
6 'New reservist divisions in SAF', *Pioneer*, April 1991, p. 17.
7 'Combined arms divisions', *Pioneer*, February 1995, pp. 2–6.
8 'SAF: achieving the best mix', *ST*, 26 February 1995.
9 Sengupta 1992, p. 76.
10 'Iron and steel—the SAF Commandos', *Pioneer*, January 1995, p. 7.
11 'Elite Red Berets display high state of readiness', MIW, 21 February 1997.
12 'SAF Commandos storm hijacked plane', *Pioneer*, April 1991, p. 3.
13 'SAF unveils Special Operations Force', *Pioneer*, April 1997.
14 'Brigade gets vital support', *Pioneer*, February 1986; 'Army support arm enhances combat effectiveness', MIW, 14 July 1999.
15 'Mobile field hospital', *Pioneer*, April 1998, pp. 12–15; 'RADM (NS) Teo experiences healthcare in the field', MIW, 27 July 1999.
16 '"Housecalls" to fix equipment', MIW, 23 June 1997.
17 'Commercialising to save manpower', *Pioneer*, May 1994, pp. 8–9.
18 'MINDEF constructs first underground ammunition facility', MIW, 12 August 1999.
19 Chiang 1997, p. 71.
20 'Launch of new assault rifle at opening ceremony of Army Open House '99', MIW, 11 September 1999.
21 Huxley and Boey 1996, p. 177.
22 See, for example, 'Singapore fighting Kites', *IDR*, May 1987.
23 'Deadly aim. The SSG 69 Steyr sniper rifle', *Pioneer*, October 1989, pp. 10–11; 'More versions of the SAR 21 rifle', *JDW*, 3 May 2000, p. 29.
24 'Tank busters', *Pioneer*, October 1993, pp. 1–4.
25 'Fact sheet—Spike anti-tank guided missile (ATGM)', MIW, 13 July 1999.
26 'It's light but armed to strike', MIW, 2 April 1998; 'ADI profits down but outlook good', *JDW*, 10 March 1999, p. 46.
27 *The Singapore Artillery* 1988, pp. 116–20.
28 'Singapore puts force integration into place', *JDW*, 30 April 1997, p. 26.
29 'Training on the TPQ-37' , *Pioneer*, October 1992, p. 2.
30 'Mark Berent's Washington report', *ADJ*, November 1988, p. 124.
31 'Singapore considers two artillery bids', *JDW*, 30 October 1996, p. 5.
32 Sengupta 1999b, p. 20; Gill and Mak 1997, p. 124.
33 Saaid 1987, p. 10.
34 'SAF adds 600 versatile M113s to its armour', *ST*, 16 August 1986.
35 'Singapore poised to roll out new fighting vehicle', *JDW*, 9 April 1997, p. 12.
36 Sengupta 1992, p. 75.
37 ibid., p. 76.
38 Sengupta 1999b, p. 20.
39 Saaid 1987, p. 18.
40 Sengupta 1992, p. 76.

41 'Stingray light tanks for Singapore?', *ADJ*, April 1991, pp. 89–90.
42 'SAF's first Ultra battalion is operational', MIW, 17 June 1998.
43 See Sengupta 1992, p. 76; 'AFVs for ASEAN armies', *ADJ*, August 1994, p. 54; 'The Singapore Armed Forces: some future growth trends', *ADJ*, July 1995, p. 10; Spellman 1991, p. 32; Gill and Mak 1997, p. 126.
44 'Singapore poised to roll out new fighting vehicle', *JDW*, 9 April 1997, p. 12; Foss 1999, pp. 37–9.
45 'Singapore army sets its sights on new light tank', *JDW*, 7 January 1998, p. 13.
46 'Combat Engineers—advance and overcome', *Pioneer*, June 1992, pp. 10–14; 'MVs in service: Singapore', *Wheels and Tracks*, no. 43 (1993), p. 38; 'Enter the Leguan', *Pioneer*, June 1993, pp. 14–15; 'Singapore orders Eurobridge systems', *JDW*, 19 April 2000, p. 15.
47 Zulkarnen 1995, p. 69.
48 'New all-terrain vehicles for Singapore', *ADJ*, April 1993, p. 84; Huxley and Boey 1996, p. 180; 'Singapore launches new tracked vehicle', *JDW*, 5 April 2000, p. 30.
49 'The History of HQ Infantry', HQ Infantry website.
50 'Guards show off might in heliborne exercise', MIW, 1 March 1999.
51 'ATEC's 100th evaluation celebration' and 'The Aggressors—the army's key to training realism', *Army News*, November 1998, p. 5.
52 *The Singapore Artillery* 1988, pp. 150–2; 'Trajectory, load, fire!', *Pioneer*, March 1995, p. 4.
53 'The Singapore Armed Forces' best units', MIW, 24 June 1999.
54 Statement by Matthias Yao Chih, minister of state for Defence, *PDS*, vol. 67, no. 9 (23 July 1997), col. 726.
55 'Operational readiness of reservist units very high, says Dr Yeo', *ST*, 30 September 1993.
56 'SAF to train in more non-traditional areas', *Pioneer*, January 1991, p. 11.
57 COL Andrew Tan, 'Improving the efficiency of the army training system', *Pointer*, vol. 21, no. 3 (July–September 1995), p. 13.
58 See Chapter 9.
59 'First FIBUA exercise on homeground', *Pioneer*, September 1988, p. 24; 'SAF troops train in Pulau Sudong: maximising land usage', *Pioneer*, September 1990, pp. 4–5.
60 COL Andrew Tan 1995, p. 13; 'Pulau Tekong to double in size as training ground', *ST*, 15 December 1997.
61 'Weapons simulators for SAF to improve training', *ST*, 29 April 1987; 'Readiness and reality—simulator training in the SAF', *Pioneer*, July 1998.
62 'SAF goes for more realistic exercises', *ST*, 21 July 1989.
63 'SAF planning to use electronic battlefield for training of troops', *ST*, 15 December 1997.
64 'Fighting an electronic war', *Army News*, July 1998, p. 8.
65 Chiang 1997, p. 97.
66 *Singapore Armed Forces Reservist Handbook* 1989, pp. 6–7;

'Mobilisations', *Pioneer*, February 1991, pp. 10–15; Boey 1996a, pp. 318–19.

67 'Nee Soon Driclad Centre', *Army News*, February 1998, p. 8.

68 'Daytime recalls of reservists may be next', *Sunday Times* (Singapore), 10 November 1985.

69 'Response time to be halved', *ST*, 15 April 1989.

70 'NSmen to get own personal equipment', *Pioneer*, October 1994, p. 19.

71 'NSmen's operational readiness impresses Dr Lee', *Pioneer*, May 1995, p. 12.

72 See speech by BG (NS) George Yeo, minister for Information and the Arts and second minister for Foreign Affairs, 'S'pore: a competitive city-state that sails with the rising tide', *ST*, 21 August 1992 and interview with BG Lim Neo Chian, Chief of Army, '3 battle-ready divisions "within hours of activation"', *ST*, 5 June 1994.

6 THE REPUBLIC OF SINGAPORE AIR FORCE (RSAF)

1 *The Air Force*, pp. 22–3; Chew 1993, pp. 30, 65.

2 'The Republic of Singapore Air Force at twenty-five', *Asian Military Review*, December 1993, 35; 'Millennium force', *Flight International*, 16 June 1999, p. 67.

3 'Singapore to modify F-5E for recce role', *IDR*, July 1990, p. 810.

4 'Python 4 heads for Chile and Singapore air forces', *Flight International*, 12 March 1997, p. 11.

5 'STAero F-5 upgrade', *AFM*, April 1998, p. 11; 'RSAF's F-5S squadrons now fully operational', MIW, 3 April 1999.

6 'Singapore leases F-16s from US Air Force', *Flight International*, 29 July 1992.

7 'Singapore pilots stay in U.S. to train', *Defense News*, 7 October 1996, pp. 26, 28 and 'Singapore to fortify forces with F-16s', *Defense News*, 10 November 1997, p. 5.

8 Speech by Lt-Gen Bey Soo Khiang, Forth Worth, Texas, MIW, 9 April 1998.

9 'RSAF to get F-16C/Ds', MINDEF News Release, 9 July 1994.

10 'US, Singapore seek compromise on AMRAAM sale', *Defense News*, 6 March 2000, p. 1.

11 'F-16C/Ds boost RSAF's fighting capability', MIW, 14 August 1998.

12 'Singaporean F-16D Block 52s reveal Israeli design heritage', *Flight International*, 22 April 1998.

13 'News briefs', *AFM*, April 1998, p. 13.

14 'Holding the fort', *Flight International*, 1 December 1999, p. 33; 'RSAF replaces ageing A-45U Super Skyhawks', MIW, 14 July 2000.

15 'Eurofighter aims for Singapore sale', *Flight International*, 10 December 1997, p. 8; 'RSAF fighter choice hinges on support', *Flight International*, 4 March 1998, p. 10; 'Singapore considers new fighter jets', *Pioneer*, December 1998, p. 15.

16 'Singapore joins Joint Strike Fighter programme', *Flight International*, 28 April 1999, p. 6.

17 'Future fighter needs', *Flight International*, 18 February 1998.

18 'RSAF 30th anniversary. Into the new millennium', *ST*, 4 September 1998.

19 'Israeli UAV hits requirements snag in Singapore', *Defense News*, 7 April 1997; 'Singapore invites bids for unmanned aerial vehicle', *Defense News*, 15 December 1997, p. 11; Speech by Rear-Admiral (NS) Teo Chee Hean, Minister for Education and Second Minister for Defence, MIW, 3 March 1998.

20 'Singapore company in UAV deal with Israel', *JDW*, 2 December 1998, p. 6.

21 'RSN looking for maritime patrol aircraft', *ADJ*, January 1991, p. 93.

22 'RSAF introduces Enforcer Mk2', *Jane's Navy International*, September/October 1995, p. 8; 'The poison shrimp matures', *APDR*, December 1999, p. 17.

23 'Singapore boosts SIGINT using C-130 transports', *JDW*, 17 September 1997, p. 19.

24 *Defending Singapore in the 21st century*, p. 65; 'The poison shrimp matures', *APDR*, December 1999, p. 17; 'AEW on the attack', *Flight International*, 15 February 2000, p. 84.

25 'RSAF receives its first KC-135 aircraft', MIW, 13 September 1999; 'The poison shrimp matures', *APDR*, December 1999, p. 17.

26 'Singapore boosts SIGINT using C-130 transports', *JDW*, 17 September 1997, p. 19.

27 'Modified Fokker 50s fly in', *JDW*, 5 February 1994, p. 11.

28 'RSAF Fennecs', *AFM*, June 1992, p. 6.

29 'Airscene headlines: Military affairs: Singapore', *Air International*, December 1997, p. 326; 'Singapore wants more Chinooks', *Flight International*, 30 June 1999, p. 19.

30 '127 Squadron inaugurated', *Pioneer*, July 1999, p. 14.

31 'USA clears Singapore for Longbow attack radar', *Flight International*, 6 January 1999, p. 12; 'Singapore's Apaches will be first for SE Asia', *JDW*, 10 March 1999, p. 8; 'Israel, Singapore sign for Apache deals', *JDW*, 1 March 2000, p. 6.

32 'SBAB and 7 SIB form special bond', *Pioneer*, October 1986, p. 29.

33 'FLASH for Singapore', *IDR*, April 1996, p. 9.

34 'Holding the fort', *Flight International*, 1 December 1999, p. 33.

35 Chew 1993, pp. 56–60; Chiang 1997, pp. 90–1.

36 'S'pore to boost FPDA further with 48 I-Hawk missiles', *STWOE*, 5 May 1990.

37 'Singapore in talks to buy Russian missiles', *JDW*, 4 September 1999, p. 3.

38 '35mm AA gun upgrade', *Air Force News*, November 1993.

39 'Defence Minister visits 18 SADA', *Air Force News*, January 1994, p. 1; 'Mistral, P-STAR systems now fully operational', *Pioneer*, August 1997, p. 11; 'PSTAR attains full operational capability', *Pioneer*, October 1999, p. 20.

40 Saw 1996, p. 21.

41 'RSAF acquires Russian made Igla air defence missile system', MIW, 15 October 1997.

42 *APDR*, April–May 1993, p. 25.

43 'Better radar for the air force', *Pioneer*, September 1998, p. 8.

44 'New formation for the RSAF', *Pioneer*, June 1995, p. 8.

45 'Enhanced national air defence capability', MIW, 13 July 1998.

46 'In full control', *Pioneer*, September 1991, pp. 14–15; Chew 1993, p. 67.

47 Farrer 1999, p. 33.

48 'Reply to media queries on Malaysian newspaper reports', MIW, 19 September 1998.

49 Speech by Howe Yoon Chong, minister of Defence, 9 March 1979, Singapore Government Press Release, MC/March/23/79 (Defence).

50 'Air force relaxes eyesight rule', *ST*, 16 December 1986.

51 'RSAF to produce pilots in shorter time', *Pioneer*, July 1994, p. 16.

52 Stijger 1999, p. 48; 'RSAF to participate in NATO flying training in Canada', MIW, 23 February 2000.

53 'Flight simulators get bigger role in RSAF', *ST*, 1 May 1987; 'More realistic air combat training with the ACMI', *Air Force News*, September 1995, pp. 10–11; 'Simulator trains C-130 pilots', *Singapore Bulletin*, June 1992, p. 14; 'Dr Lee unveils RSAF's first helicopter simulator', *ADJ*, June 1995, p. 70; 'Singapore tries UAV simulator', *Defense News*, 2 March 1998, p. 16.

54 'RADM Teo's visit to Systems Command Training School', MIW, 24 March 1998; 'SADA's new all-in-one simulator', *Pioneer*, August 1994, pp. 18–19.

55 Boey 1993, pp. 244–5.

56 'Airfield maintenance crucial to RSAF operations', MIW, 8 January 1999.

57 Boey 1993, p. 245; 'RSAF Emergency Runway Exercise', *Air Force News*, April 1998, pp. 6–7.

58 'Field Defence Squadrons show firepower', *Pioneer*, December 1996, p. 13.

59 Boey 1993, p. 245; Chew 1993, pp. 93, 96.

60 Chew 1993, pp. 94–5.

61 'Air force reservists', *Pioneer*, October 1989, pp. 26–9; 'On the ground', *Pioneer*, December 1995, p. 14.

62 'RSAF mobilises light aircraft', *Pioneer*, January 1988, p. 33.

63 'RSAF civil resource vehicles requisition exercise', *Air Force News*, January 1999. p. 7; Chew 1993, p. 98.

64 'Broader horizons', *Flight International*, 15 February 2000, p. 79.

7 THE REPUBLIC OF SINGAPORE NAVY (RSN)

1 'In the pursuit of excellence', *Naval Forces*, 2/1999, p. 20.

2 'COSCOM takes over coastal defence', *Pioneer*, December 1991, p. 33.

3 'Coast Guard takes over command of 4 RSN vessels', *ADJ*, March 1993.

4 Boey 1995, pp. 67–8.

5 'Missiles fitted to intercept hostile aircraft', *ST*, 16 June 1994; 'Navy buys Barak anti-missile system', *ST*, 23 April 1996.

6 'Diving support vessel for Singapore', *IDR*, October 1990, p. 1181.

7 'Navy's "made-to-measure" minesweeper', *ST*, 19 July 1993.

8 'Operational readiness of patrol vessels impresses Dr Tan', MIW, 30 July 1997; '182 Sqn family is complete', *Navy News*, October 1998, p. 1.

9 'Navy studying need for submarines', *Singapore Bulletin*, July 1995, p. 11.

10 'S'pore to buy second-hand submarine', *ST*, 24 September 1995.

11 'Navy buys three more Sjöormen submarines', *Pioneer*, September 1997, p. 11.

12 'Singapore navy launches two more submarines', MIW, 28 May 1999.

13 'Singapore leads region in naval modernization drive', *Defense News*, 7 June 1999, p. 6.

14 'Our titans of the sea', *Pioneer*, May 1999, pp. 2–7.

15 'MINDEF news release, 3 Mar 2000', MIW, 3 March 2000.

16 'Singapore steps up search for naval stealth', *JDW*, 19 May 1999, p. 8.

17 *APDR Annual Reference Edition 1999*, p. 83.

18 'Republic of Singapore Navy: missions, roles and organisation', *Naval Forces*, Special Issue 2/97, p. 19.

19 'Diving to new depths—improved training with NDU's new camp', *Pioneer*, August 1997, pp. 14–15.

20 'Changi Naval Base to enhance protection of S'pore's territorial waters', *Pioneer*, March 1998, p. 17; 'Foundation laid for navy's nerve centre', *ST*, 12 January 2000.

21 'DPM visits navy's new Training Command', MIW, 23 September 1995.

22 ibid.; 'New minehunting simulators offer effective training', *Pioneer*, November 1996, p. 24.

23 'Official opening of RSN's Institute of Maritime Warfare', MIW, 13 April 1998.

24 'Rear-Admiral Teo inaugurates two RSN training institutes', MIW, 17 September 1999.

25 'Navy's Gabriel missile hits right on target', *ST*, 2 September 1998.

26 'In the pursuit of excellence', *Naval Forces*, 2/1999, p. 19.

27 'Ready, aim, fire . . . and missile is on target', *ST*, 26 August 1997.

28 'Automated Storage & Retrieval System (ASRS)', MIW, 26 May 1999.

29 'Steering forward with logistics', *Pioneer*, December 1991, pp. 16–17.

30 'In the pursuit of excellence', *Naval Forces*, 2/1999, p. 24.

31 Huxley and Boey 1996, p. 175.

32 'Building tomorrow's navy', *Naval Forces*, Special Issue 2/97, p. 21.

33 'Navy reservists conduct CR requisition exercise', *Pioneer*, May 1991, p. 17.

34 'RSN delivers food aid to Indonesia', *Navy News*, October 1998, p. 6.

8 DEFENCE PROCUREMENT, R&D AND INDUSTRY

1 'An SAF that strives for excellence', speech by Defence Minister Yeo Ning Hong, 26 March 1994 in *ST*, 1 July 1994.

2 'Dr Tony Tan makes introductory visit to the United States', Cyber Pioneer, MIW, 28 September 1996.

3 See Boey 1996b, pp. 22–3.

4 The major restructuring of MINDEF's technology arm in March 2000 significantly affected some of the organisational nomenclature relating to defence procurement and R&D (particularly because of the absorption of DTG into the new Defence Science and Technology Agency) and is likely to lead to thoroughgoing changes in the management of the SAF's technological development. However, as full details of how the new system will work remained unclear at the time of writing, the analysis here is based on the situation of early 2000, before the creation of the DSTA.

5 Defence Procurement Division 1998, Section 1.

6 'Applying Life Cycle Management', *Pioneer*, December 1991, p. 35.

7 Defence Procurement Division 1998, Section 7.

8 'Country Briefing: Singapore—state sector thrives in commercial arena', *JDW*, 30 April 1997, p. 31; 'ST Aero's plans for 2000', *AFM*, March 2000, p. 13.

9 'MINDEF launches first Internet-based trading system', MIW, 17 April 1998.

10 Defence Procurement Division, 'Tender Results 1996', MIW.

11 Defence Procurement Division 1998, Section 4.

12 *Defence of Singapore 1994–95*, p. 58.

13 Speech by Dr Tony Tan, MIW, 4 October 1996.

14 'An SAF that strives for excellence', *ST*, 1 July 1994.

15 *Singapore Government Directory*, July 1999, pp. 218–20.

16 Sengupta 1999c, p. 26.

17 'They build buildings only to blow them up', *ST*, 28 November 1997.

18 'Constructing for defence. The Lands & Estates Organisation', *Pioneer*, November 1997, pp. 3–4.

19 'Singapore sets up defence laboratory', *JDW*, 14 October 1998, p. 14.

20 Speech by David Lim, minister of state for Defence and Information and the Arts, MIW, 2 August 1999.

21 'MINDEF's new weapon: ice machines', 'MINDEF to plug into solar power in big way' and '"Smart" buildings and solar power', all *ST*, 18 February 1999.

22 'Resource Planning Office: harnessing national resources to support the SAF', *Pioneer*, November 1989, p. 33; Sengupta 1999c, p. 27.

23 'Defence Science Organisation. Defence R&D at its best', *Pioneer*, November 1989, p. 18; speech by Deputy Prime Minister BG (NS) Lee Hsien Loong, MIW, 3 October 1997.

24 Speech by Dr Tony Tan, minister of Defence, MIW, 4 November 1998.

25 Speech by Deputy Prime Minister BG (NS) Lee Hsien Loong, MIW, 3 October 1997.

26 'DSO National Laboratories. Revolutionising defence through technology', *Pioneer*, January 1999, pp. 3–4; 'The lab's job', *Singapore Bulletin*, March 1999, p. 12; *Defending Singapore in the 21st century*, p. 66.

27 'Communication technology—the vital link in warfare', *Pioneer*, March 1999, p. 13; 'Corporatisation of DSO', Media releases, MIW, 14 March 1997; *Defending Singapore in the 21st century*, pp. 66–7.

28 'Corporatisation of DSO', ibid.

29 'DSO National Laboratories. Revolutionising defence through technology', *Pioneer*, January 1999, pp. 4–5.

30 'DSO, as a national resource, is uniquely suited to build up technologies for both military and commercial applications', MIW, 3 October 1997.

31 *The MINDEF/SAF Fact Book*, p. 21.

32 *Defending Singapore in the 21st century*, p. 70; 'Inauguration of the Defence Service and Technology Agency', MIW, 29 March 2000.

33 'US and Singapore in talks to block hi-tech leakages', *Financial Times*, 16 August 1985; 'RSAF plan to update Skyhawks blocked by Pentagon', *Business Times* (Singapore), 27 March 1986.

34 'Singapore joins JSF, Australia stays out', *Defense News*, 10 May 1999.

35 'Singapore, Sweden will market defense to undersea threats', *Defense News*, 11 April 1994.

36 'Singapore, Sweden set up US$5m research fund', *Pioneer*, November 1997, p. 10.

37 'Dr Tony Tan visits France', MIW, 12 June 1999.

38 'Partners in defence science and technology', *Pioneer*, May 1993, p. 23; 'Chief of Defence Force's visit to France', MIW, 12 September 1998; 'Tony Tan in S. Africa to discuss defence ties', *ST*, 10 November 1997; 'German-Singapore accord could boost Mako', *Defense News*, 6 March 2000, p. 4.

39 See Singh 1990, pp. 13–27; 38–44.

40 ibid., p. 15; 'The CIS story', *Pioneer*, July 1983, pp. 10–11.

41 Singh 1990, p. 18.

42 'Made in Singapore—Part One', *Pioneer*, February 1992, p. 8.

43 Singh 1990, pp. 14–15.

44 See Chuang 1990, pp. 28–36.

45 ibid., p. 32.

46 'Singapore's government-linked companies report', Embassy of the United States of America, 1994.

47 'S'pore Technologics Group announces major restructuring', *ST*, 13 February 1995.

48 'Newcomer with a bulging order book', Singapore Survey, *Financial Times*, 31 March 1998; Sengupta 1999d, pp. 22–5.

49 For examples, see Huxley 1993b, p. 11.

50 'Country Briefing: Singapore—state sector thrives in commercial arena', *JDW*, 30 April 1997, p. 31.

51 'Igla MANPADS for Asia-Pacific', *ADJ*, October 1999, p. 25.

52 'Launch of Super Skyhawks', *ST*, 26 January 1988.

53 'Singapore's F-5 fleet is brought up to date', *Jane's IDR*, April 1998, pp. 68–9.
54 'Upgrading the AMX-13 light tank the SAE way', *ADJ*, August 1987, pp. 52–8.
55 'SAF's first Ultra battalion is operational', MIW, 17 June 1998.
56 'M71. Licence renewed', *Pioneer*, April 1993, pp. 14–15.
57 'The RSN's missile gun boats', *Pioneer*, August 1995, pp. 18.
58 'Marching to self-sufficiency in arms as well as defence', *FEER*, 13 January 1983, pp. 29–30.
59 'Lethal weapon, made in Singapore', *Sunday Times* (Singapore), 12 September 1999.
60 *Defence & Foreign Affairs Weekly*, 4–10 August 1986, p. 3; Tillman 1989, pp. 1681–3.
61 'S'pore's arms-making firm in top 10 list', *ST*, 19 June 1992.
62 'Armed Forces to be equipped with more made-in-Singapore arms', *STWOE*, 26 November 1988.
63 'Singapore's FH 2000—a world first', *Pioneer*, July 1995, pp. 44–5.
64 'Locally produced indigenous IFV rolls out', MIW, 6 September 1997; 'Singapore now armed with Bionix', *JDW*, 25 August 1999, p. 14.
65 'Singapore army sets its sights on new light tank', *JDW*, 7 January 1998, p. 13; Foss 1999, pp. 37–9.
66 'Navy launches twelfth patrol vessel', MIW, 18 April 1998.
67 'Singapore steps up search for naval stealth', *JDW*, 19 May 1999, p. 8.
68 *Jane's Fighting Ships 1998–99*, p. 622.
69 'Singapore company in UAV deal with Israel', *JDW*, 2 December 1998, p. 6.
70 'Singapore solutions', *Flight International*, 21 January 1998, p. 53.
71 *Defending Singapore in the 21st century*, p. 46.
72 'The CIS story', *Pioneer*, July 1983, p. 10; Singh 1990, p. 27.
73 'STIC biodata', Singapore Technologies Industrial Corporation Pte Ltd press release, 10 February 1993.
74 'Who said bailout?', *FEER*, 11 June 1998, p. 62.
75 Interview with Lee Boon Yang, minister of Defence, *ADJ*, July 1995, p. 7.
76 'ST Engineering shares soar on safe status', *Business Times* (Singapore), 22 January 1998.
77 'ST Aero will expand leasing business', *Flight International*, 15 January 1997, p. 12.
78 Singh 1990, p. 57.
79 'Coming out of the closet', *FEER*, 30 June 1983, pp. 13–14; Robertson 1984.
80 'Budget for arms venture', *Bangkok Post*, 22 September 1978.
81 'Singapore's F-5 fleet is brought up to date', *Jane's IDR*, April 1998, p. 69.
82 'Singapore protests to Sweden over arms export freeze', *ST*, 4 April 1987; 'Bofors implicates Singapore in illegal arms exports to the Gulf', *JDW*, 11 April 1987, p. 619.

83 'Sweden satisfied S'pore not at fault' and 'Arms firm GM on graft charge', *ST*, 17 July 1987.

84 'MoD knew of Singapore arms connection', *Independent* (London), 7 July 1995; 'Royal Ordnance linked to arms for Iran', *The Times*, 7 July 1995.

85 '"No arms shipments to Burma from S'pore"', *STWOE*, 19 November 1988.

86 'Myanmar', in *Jane's Sentinel Southeast Asia 1997*, section 6.15.10; Ball 1998, p. 235; Ashton 1998, p. 33.

87 *Asian Aviation*, June 1994, p. 36.

88 'Exposed: Burma's weapons industry', *Jane's Pointer*, December 1998, p. 9.

9   REGIONAL AND INTERNATIONAL LINKS

1 Singapore's international collaboration in defence R&D is examined in Chapter 8.

2 Chiang 1997, p. 76.

3 Kwa 1994, p. 123.

4 'Singapore pilots stay in U.S. to train', *Defense News*, 7 October 1998.

5 'Israel seeks new money in Asia', *JDW*, 17 November 1999, p. 21.

6 'RSAF turns to Israel for EW', *JDW*, 10 October 1992, p. 5.

7 Ball 1995b, pp. 16–17; 'Python 4 heads for Chile and Singapore air forces', *Flight International*, 12 March 1997, p. 11; 'Singaporean F-16D Block 52s reveal Israeli design heritage', *Flight International*, 22 April 1998, p. 15; 'Singapore company in UAV deal with Israel', *JDW*, 2 December 1998, p. 6; 'Singapore Link 16 move angers USA', *Flight International*, 24 February 1999, p. 6; 'Rafael to help build missile plant in Singapore', *Flight International*, 25 August 1999, p. 19.

8 'Israel seeks new money in Asia', *JDW*, 17 November 1999, p. 21.

9 'Singapore prepares for mechanized warfare', *Jane's IDR*, 4/1996, p. 6.

10 'A tribute to the late Col (Ret) Khoo Eng An', *Navy News*, March 1999, p. 1.

11 Central News Agency, Taipei, 25 May 1998, in SWB, FE/3237 B/7, 27 May 1998.

12 'S'pore to carry on training troops in Taiwan, says PM Lee', *ST*, 14 August 1990.

13 'Not true SAF will stop training in Taiwan', *ST*, 1 February 1996.

14 'FPDA defence chiefs' conference visit joint naval and air exercises', MIW, 14 September 1996.

15 'Biggest-ever five-power exercise starts', *ST*, 15 April 1997.

16 'Major Adex 99–2', MIW, 10 April 1999.

17 'SAF's Command and Staff College opens its door to FPDA officers', *Singapore Bulletin*, March 1990, p. 15.

18 'Singapore and Australia in new partnership', *Singapore Bulletin*,

February 1996; 'Panel to strengthen S'pore-Australia ties', *ST*, 6 March 1995.

19 'S'pore-Aussie talks reaffirms strong partnership', *Singapore Bulletin*, March 1999, p. 2.

20 Radio Australia, 31 October 1996, in SWB, FE/2758 B/6, 1 November 1996.

21 'S'pore-Aussie talks focus on security', *ST*, 23 February 1999.

22 'Regional co-operation boosts two-way security', *Australian*, 1 October 1982.

23 'Singapore army exercise in Australia', Defence News Release (Canberra), 23/82, 3 March 1982.

24 'Ex Pitch Black', *Pioneer*, October 1990, p. 12.

25 'Navy's MCVs in multilateral naval exercise', *Pioneer*, May 1995, p. 15; 'Kakadu IV', *AFM*, December 1999, pp. 56–7.

26 '40 SAR in multilateral exercise in Darwin', *Pioneer*, October 1995, p. 18.

27 'S'pore, Australian troops in live-firing exercise', *Pioneer*, May 1997, p. 10.

28 'Australia and Singapore conduct naval exercises', MIW, 6 May 1999.

29 'Ex MCM Hunter 3/98', *Navy News*, August 1998, p. 6.

30 'Ex Axolotl', *Navy News*, April 1998.

31 'S'pore, Australia sign three new agreements', *ST*, 22 October 1996.

32 'Partial relocation of Flying Training School to Australia', *Pioneer*, May 1993, pp. 22–3.

33 'New warehouse for SAF vehicles in Rockhampton', *Pioneer*, October 1995, p. 19; 'Singapore Armed Forces', British Aerospace Australia website.

34 'Of "war" and Wallaby', *Pioneer*, December 1996, pp. 6–7; '41 SAR training in Australia', *Army News*, November 1998, p. 8; 'SAF conducts Ex Wallaby 4/99 in Australia', MIW, 4 November 1999.

35 'Agreement between the Government of Australia and the Government of the Republic of Singapore concerning the use of Shoalwater Bay Training Area and the associated use of storage facilities, done at Singapore on 15 September 1999'.

36 'SAF keen on more areas for training in Australia', *ST*, 25 October 1996.

37 'Dr Tony Tan signs agreement to base RSAF helicopters in Australia for training', MIW, 22 October 1996.

38 'Opening ceremony of the RSAF helicopter detachment in Oakey, Australia', MIW, 20 August 1999.

39 'Ex Wallaroo', *Air Force News*, January 1999, p. 7.

40 'Singapore outsources pilot screening to Australia', *Flight International*, 1 September 1999, p. 23.

41 Radio Australia external service, 30 October 1996, in SWB, FE/2757 B/3, 31 October 1996; 'Singapore MPs say prejudice issue put at rest', *Australian*, 1 November 1996.

42 'Singapore/Australian air force plan in doubt', *Flight International*, 12 April 1995, p. 14.

43 'ST Aerospace partners Australian company to maintain RSAF aircraft at Pearce', *Pioneer*, January 1996, p. 19.
44 'Contract commencement date at Oakey', *Air Force News*, January 1999, p 6.
45 'Singapore choppers take up Australian residence', MIW, 1 September 1998.
46 'ADI profits down but outlook good', *JDW*, 10 March 1999, p. 46.
47 'Singapore studies bases', *Flight International*, 27 August 1997, p. 24.
48 'Future fighter needs', *Flight International*, 18 February 1998, p. 63.
49 'BAe eyes Asian training facility with Australian expansion plans', *Flight International*, 30 September 1998, p. 18.
50 'Joint Singapore/New Zealand army exercise', MIW, 25 November 1998; 'Ex Lionwalk 1998', *Army News*, May 1998, p. 8; 'New Zealand defence minister calls on Dr Tony Tan', MIW, 17 April 1997; 'Ex Singkiwi', *Air Force News*, January 1999, p. 7; 'New Zealand, S'pore navies sign arrangement', *Pioneer*, April 1998, p. 10.
51 'Fatal blast baffles army', *Dominion* (Wellington), 10 March 1997.
52 'Thunder Warrior '99', *Army News*, February/March 1999, p. 4.
53 'Tony Tan on four-day visit to New Zealand', *ST*, 23 January 1998.
54 Chiang 1990, p. 223.
55 *The Air Force*, p. 96.
56 'Action plan for British-Singapore ties', *Singapore Bulletin*, March 1997, p. 3.
57 'The Royal Navy—Republic of Singapore Navy', MIW, 11 April 1997.
58 'Elite Singapore and United Kingdom Commandos in Action', MIW, 29 April 1997.
59 'Training activities between the RSN and the RN', MIW, 21 September 1998.
60 'Navies of United Kingdom and Singapore in inaugural bilateral exercise', MIW, 14 June 1999.
61 'Five star accommodation', *Warships. International Fleet Review*, Autumn 1999, p. 6.
62 'Port in a storm', *FEER*, 22 November 1990, pp. 10–11.
63 'USA takes Singapore option in hunt for new SE Asian home', *JDW*, 18 January 1992, p. 83.
64 'Tony Tan on three-day visit to US', *ST*, 29 September 1996.
65 'Singapore, US formalise berthing pact', *Singapore Bulletin*, December 1998, p. 2; 'US Pacific Commander-in-Chief calls on DPM Tan', MIW 1 April 2000.
66 'Singapore in air exercise with Australia and US', MIW, 4 May 1998.
67 'Spin-offs from training with the best', *ST*, 26 August 1997.
68 'United States and Singapore navies in annual bilateral exercise', MIW, 7 July 1997; 'Australia–Singapore–U.S. EOD exercise: Tri-Crab 98', *Asia-Pacific Defense Forum*, Winter 1998–99, pp. 35–9.
69 'USA-Singapore submarine links', *JDW*, 20 January 1999, p. 16.
70 'Joint exercise with US Marines', *Pioneer*, August 1996, p. 16; '4 SIR exercises with US Army', *Pioneer*, May 1996, p. 21.
71 'United States Assistant Secretary of State calls on Dr Tony Tan', MIW, 25 August 1997.

72 'United States Special Operations Commander-in-Chief calls on Dr Tony Tan', MIW, 19 May 1997.

73 'SAF holds first annual talks with US military', *Singapore Bulletin*, February 1996, p. 17.

74 'RSAF personnel to train at Luke Air Force Base in US', *Pioneer*, April 1993, p. 14.

75 'RSAF airmen in US enjoy best of both worlds', *ST*, 16 October 1994; 'More RSAF men for copter training in US', *Singapore Bulletin*, November 1996, pp. 15–16; 'Singapore air force pilots train in U.S. skies', *Asia-Pacific Defense Forum*, Summer 1999, pp. 26–8.

76 'More RSAF men for copter training in US', *Singapore Bulletin*, November 1996, pp. 15–16.

77 'Inauguration of RSAF KC-135 detachment', MIW, 28 July 1998.

78 'RSAF News' (2nd Quarter 1999), Unofficial RSAF Website, 24 May 1999; 'Cooperative Cope Thunder 99–4', *Asia-Pacific Defence Forum*, Winter 1999–2000, pp. 30–5.

79 'Lee calls for closer Asean defence ties', *Age* (Melbourne), 19 December 1981; 'Military links in Asean important', *ST*, 17 March 1988; 'Asean must boost military ties', *ST*, 5 August 1994; Dr Tony Tan, quoted by Micool Brooke, 'Do joint military exercises enhance security in ASEAN?', *ADJ*, September 1999, p. 7.

80 'MAF invites senior SAF officers for golf', *Pioneer*, September 1999, p. 11.

81 'S'pore-Indonesian defence ties extremely valuable: Boon Yang', *ST*, 13 August 1994.

82 'Promoting bilateral co-operation between Singapore and Indonesia', *Pioneer*, April 1989, pp. 2–3.

83 'Safkar Indopura', *Pioneer*, February 1990, pp. 2–5.

84 'Dr Tan confers prestigious award on Indonesian army chief', MIW, 27 February 1996; 'Army holds joint live-firing exercise with Indonesians', *ST*, 15 November 1997; 'Training in Batu Raja, Indonesia', *Army News*, November 1998.

85 'Singapore and Indonesia begin eight-day air exercise today', *ST*, 6 July 1994; 'S'pore-Abri exercise goes on', *ST*, 25 August 1998; 'Broader horizons', *Flight International*, 15 February 2000, p. 79.

86 'Taking it one step closer—1st ABRI-SAF SAREX', *Pioneer*, May 1995, p. 14; 'Singapore and Indonesia conduct first combined fighter weapons instructor course', MIW, 3 September 1999.

87 Boey 1994, p. 22.

88 'Singapore and Indonesian defence chiefs jointly commission joint detachment facilities', MIW, 29 August 1998; 'Asia-Pacific News: Newsbriefs', *AFM*, December 1998, p. 13.

89 'ABRI-SAF Joint Training Committee (JTC) meeting', MIW, 15 July 1998.

90 Radio Republic of Indonesia, 11 July 1996 in SWB FE/2663 B/3, 13 July 1996.

91 'Jakarta may offer more training areas', *ST*, 7 August 1998.

92 'Airscene headlines: Military affairs: Singapore', *Air International*,

May 1997, p. 260; 'Helicopter training in Indonesia', *Singapore Bulletin*, May 1997, p. 17; 'Military medals for two', *ST*, 26 July 1997.

93 'Joint patrols reduce sea robberies', *Pioneer*, August 1994, p. 23.

94 'Inaugural Indonesia–Singapore defence policy talks', MIW, 17 March 1997.

95 'Thailand, S'pore agree to expand defence ties', *ST*, 23 July 1996; 'Ex Kocha Singa', *Army News*, December 1997/January 1998.

96 Conboy 1991, p. 46.

97 'Dr Tan confers prestigious military award on Royal Thai Air Force Commander-in-Chief', MIW, 15 August 1997.

98 'Singapore joins Thailand and the US in air exercise', MIW, 28 October 1996.

99 'Thailand, S'pore agree to expand defence ties', *ST*, 23 July 1996; 'S'pore to join Cobra Gold exercise this year', *ST*, 14 January 2000.

100 *Flight International*, 19 January 1980; Dantes 1992, p. 62.

101 'S'pore and Philippines start their first bilateral army exercise', *ST*, 16 June 1993.

102 'First bilateral exercise for Singapore and Philippines', *Pioneer*, October 1994, p. 25.

103 'SAF, Philippine army begin joint exercise', *ST*, 9 March 1995.

104 'S'pore, Philippines in first joint naval exercise', *Pioneer*, July 1996, p. 19.

105 'Philippine navy chief visits Singapore', MIW, 4 December 1999.

106 'Singapore: Manila says Singapore to help modernise army', Reuters, 20 August 1996.

107 'Ties with Manila will be strong: Tony Tan', *ST*, 14 June 1998; 'Chief of Navy receives honorary Command at Sea badge', MIW, 13 January 1999.

108 'Lakiun Camp', *Pioneer*, November 1983, pp. 19–20.

109 'Jungle training in Brunei', *Pioneer*, April 1998, pp. 2–5.

110 'Why Brunei training is so valuable', *ST*, 22 August 1986.

111 'PM sees our troops training in Brunei', *Pioneer*, October 1986.

112 'Brunei and Singapore conduct naval exercise', MIW, 7 December 1998.

113 'Singapore and Brunei combat engineers in bilateral exercise', MIW, 7 November 1996; 'Singapore and Brunei in joint armour exercise', MIW, 27 August 1997; 'Brunei and Singapore in joint infantry live-firing exercise', MIW, 4 December 1997; 'Ex Maju Bersama (Progress Together)', *Army News*, September 1998, p. 8; 'Singapore and Brunei in joint air defence exercise', MIW, 25 November 1998.

114 Radio Corporation of Singapore, 10 April 1996 in SWB FE/2587 B/3, 16 April 1996.

115 'Ex Maju Bersama (Progress Together)', *Army News*, September 1998, p. 8.

116 Ashton 1998, p. 33.

117 'New ambassador to Myanmar appointed', *ST*, 18 September 1996.

118 'Milestone in Singapore–Vietnam defence ties', *Pioneer*, April 1995, p. 25.

119 'Singapore halted in tracks to update Vietnamese APCs', *JDW*, 14 April 1999, p. 17.
120 'Ex Lion King 5/98', *Navy News*, April 1998, p. 3.
121 Preston 1995, p. 22.
122 Sengupta 1998, p. 18.
123 'RSAF aircraft now train in Bangladesh as well', *Sunday Times* (Singapore), 20 June 1993.
124 'RSAF pilots can train in Bangladesh', *Singapore Bulletin*, April 1994, p. 14.
125 'Chief of Air Force visits Bangladesh', *Pioneer*, September 1997, p. 12.
126 'S Africa offers to extend Singapore link', *Flight International*, 4 January 1995; 'S'pore signs military cooperation agreement with South Africa', *Pioneer*, January 1998, p. 16.
127 'S'pore signs military cooperation agreement with South Africa' *Pioneer*, January 1998, p. 16.
128 'RSAF scores direct hits with Igla missiles', *Pioneer*, September 1999, p. 16.
129 'Mr Matthias Yao visits South Africa', MIW, 30 November 1998.
130 'Singapore to train air force pilots in Canada', *JDW*, 10 December 1997, p. 11; 'RSAF participates in multilateral exercises in France and Canada', MIW, 19 May 2000.
131 'Thailand and French navies ended joint exercise', *ADJ*, January 1994, p. 96.
132 'France's "natural partner"', *ST*, 24 February 1999.
133 'French Air Force–Republic of Singapore Air Force Air Group formed', MIW, 29 January 1997.
134 'RSAF can now train at French air bases', *ST*, 26 July 1997.
135 'French Chief of Army Staff calls on Dr Tan', MIW, 28 September 1998.
136 ibid.
137 AFP news agency, 7 June 1998 in SWB FE/3248 B/5, 9 June 1998.
138 'Visit to France', *Air Force News*, January 1999; Stijger 1999, pp. 48–9.
139 'Airscene headlines: Military affairs: Singapore', *Air International*, April 1998, p. 196.
140 'Exercise Eastern Arc', *Air Force News*, April 1998, p. 2.
141 'French and Singapore airforces in bilateral exercise', MIW, 22 February 2000.
142 'S'pore, France sign General Security Agreement', *Pioneer*, August 1999, p. 37; 'French armed forces chief visits Singapore', MIW, 26 July 1999.
143 'Sweden gets the chop for halting arms sales', *ADJ*, May 1987, p. 115.
144 'S'pore, Sweden sign MCM exchange programme document', *Pioneer*, January 1996, p. 18.
145 'RSN sends men for submarine training in Sweden', *Pioneer*, November 1995, p. 6; 'Submariners earn their badge', *Navy News*, February 1998, p. 8.
146 'Navy buys three more Sjöormen submarines', *Pioneer*, September 1997, p. 11; 'RSwN and RSN deepen relations', *Navy News*, March 1998.

147 'Two Japanese warships here on visit', *ST*, 10 October 1985; 'Japanese ships here on goodwill visit', *ST*, 19 July 1994.
148 'Japanese Joint Staff Council Chairman calls on Dr Tony Tan', MIW, 2 December 1996.
149 'Permanent Secretary (Defence) visits Japan', MIW, 30 September 1998; 'Dr Tan visits Japan', *Pioneer*, February 1999, p. 12; 'Singapore and Japan to step up defence dialogue interactions and exchanges', MIW, 2 May 2000.
150 'Fostering better defence relations with China', *Pioneer*, December 1997, p. 15.
151 Xinhua news agency (Beijing), 29 November 1998 in SWB FE/3397 B/6, 30 November 1998.
152 'Making a difference in the international community', *Pioneer*, December 1998, p. 8.
153 'SAF Overseas Service Medal for 10 who served in UN peacekeeping operations', MIW, 23 August 1999.
154 Speech by Dr Tony Tan, 27 March 1998, MIW.
155 'Singapore offers quick-reaction force for UN', *Singapore Bulletin*, May 1997, p. 4.
156 Tan Chi Chiu 1992, pp. 2–17.
157 'SAF pledges continued support', *ST*, 20 October 1999; 'Homecoming of RSAF C-130', MIW, 23 February 2000.
158 'Samaritans of the RSAF', *Pioneer*, October 1991, p. 22; 'Singapore's medical team returns from Taiwan', MIW, 3 October 1999.
159 'Operation Flying Eagle', *Pioneer*, December 1990, p. 14; 'Better than any SAF advertisement', *ST*, 21 July 1997; 'Assistance to Indonesia to fight the haze', MIW, 8 October 1997.
160 'RSN ship participates in socio-civic activities with TNI-AL', MIW, 28 February 2000.
161 *PDS*, vol. 68, no. 7 (11 March 1998), col. 907.

10 POLITICAL AND ADMINISTRATIVE ROLES

1 Bedlington 1981, pp. 255–6.
2 Chan 1985, p. 153.
3 Chan 1975, p. 62.
4 ibid., p. 63.
5 ibid., p. 67.
6 ibid., p. 68.
7 Chan 1985, p. 138.
8 Chan 1975, p. 61.
9 Chan 1985, pp. 136–56.
10 'Who wields the real power?', *Singapore Business*, November 1990, p. 52.
11 Huxley 1993b, pp. 9–11.
12 *Singapore Government Directory, July 1999*.
13 'Groomed for the top', *ST*, 9 August 1993.
14 'He's no newcomer to transport', *ST*, 2 July 1998.

15 For details, see Huxley 1993b, pp. 8–9.
16 'Who wields the real power?', *Singapore Business*, November 1990, p. 52.
17 Huxley 1993b, p. 8.
18 *Sunday Times* (Singapore), 12 August 1990.
19 Huxley 1993b, pp. 10–11.
20 *STWOE*, 20 August 1988 and 17 December 1988.
21 ibid., 21 November 1992.
22 ibid., 5 December 1992.
23 ibid., 20 December 1992. In the event, Tan was recalled in 1995 even though Lee Hsien Loong's health had by then recovered.
24 '"It was a bolt from the blue. But that is life"', *STWOE*, 15 May 1993, pp. 4–5.
25 STWOE, 21 November 1992.
26 'PM concerned over "so many ministers" wishing to quit', *STWE*, 18 December 1993, p. 1.
27 'Singapore sees Cabinet woe', *Financial Times* (London), 1 November 1994.
28 'Looking for Mandarins' (editorial), *ST*, 6 August 1993.
29 *ST*, 20 March 1993; 'PAP to recruit more members', *STWE*, 27 November 1999, p. 24.
30 Chan 1985, p. 159.
31 A GRC is a parliamentary constituency in which electors cast a single vote for one of a number of 'teams' of candidates, each team being from one party. The official explanation for the system stressed that it would enable members of ethnic minorities—one candidate in each team—to be elected without reliance on non-communal voting by Chinese electors. However, the implementation of the system clearly also made it harder for the small, factionalised political opposition to present credible alternative representatives to the electorate. See Mulliner and The-Mulliner 1991, p. 62.
32 'I felt like I had been hit by lightning twice: PM', *STWOE*, 12 December 1992, p. 4.
33 'Finance Communications posts for Cdre Teo', *STWOE*, 26 December 1992, p. 1.
34 'PM Goh prepared to call a GE after National Day rally', *ST*, 10 June 1996.
35 'PM Goh to step down "some time after next GE"', *STWE*, 27 November 1999, p. 3.
36 *ST*, 10 December 1992.
37 See 'Schooled for leadership', *ST*, 13 August 1994; 'The third generation: a conscript leadership', *ST*, 17 June 1996.
38 'Dr Tan hopes to inject private sector perspective', *Business Times* (Singapore), 30 June 1995.
39 ibid.
40 'Schooled for leadership', *ST*, 13 August 1994.
41 'SAF awards merit scholarships to women for the first time', *STWE*, 12 August 1993; 'Men of merit', *Pioneer*, January 1997, p. 8; 'A citizen and a scholar', *STWE*, 15 August 1998, p. 3.

42 'Minorities represented well in slate of new faces', *STWE*, 23 November 1996; 'PAP election candidate Lim Swee Say: Western mind, Chinese heart', *ST*, 5 November 1996.
43 'PM announces Cabinet reshuffle', *ST*, 15 May 1999.
44 See Rodan 1993, pp. xx–xxi.
45 'A father's advice', *STWOE*, 27 August 1988.
46 Vasil 1988, pp. 188–9.
47 Shee 1983, p. 195.
48 ibid., p. 188.
49 See Chapter 4, 'Singapore's military scholars'.
50 'Reinventing the heir', *FEER*, 15 July 1999, pp. 8–11.
51 *Singapore Bulletin*, January 1991, p. 4.
52 *STWOE*, 28 January 1989 and 'Anchoring people to S'pore', *STWOE*, 22 June 1991, p. 1.
53 See, for example, 'BG Yeo sends "strong signal" to civic groups', *ST*, 8 May 1998.
54 *ST*, 26 February 1993.
55 'Reinventing the heir', *FEER*, 15 July 1999, p. 11.
56 'PAP election candidate Lim Swee Say: Western mind, Chinese heart', *ST*, 5 November 1996.
57 *ST*, 10 December 1992.
58 According to Lee Kuan Yew. See 'S'pore will survive me: SM', *STWE*, 8 June 1996.
59 See 'Is there a Mindef mafia?', *Singapore Business*, November 1990, p. 52.
60 *ST*, 10 December 1992.
61 *STWOE* , 27 January 1990.
62 ibid., 17 March 1990 and 16 June 1990; *Pioneer*, July 1990, p. 5; 'Recognising Veterans', *Pioneer*, November 1990, p. 43.
63 'Will a foreigner take over Philip Yeo's job?', *STWE*, 3 July 1999.
64 Kurz 1983, p. 15.
65 Thayer 1985, pp. 234–66.

CONCLUSION

1 'A father's advice', *STWOE*, 27 August 1988.
2 Tay 1996, pp. 68–75.
3 Lim 1996, pp. 37, 41–2.
4 'Changes of Chief of Defence Force and Chief of Army', MIW, 22 January 2000.
5 Sengupta 1999e, pp. 14–18.
6 'S'pore is short of 200 000 babies', *STWOE*, 23 October 1999.
7 Speech by David Lim, minister of state for Defence and Information, MIW, 29 October 1999.
8 'Singapore in talks to buy Russian missiles', *JDW*, 4 September 1999, p. 3.
9 *Defending Singapore in the 21st century*, p. 63.
10 Sengupta 1992, p. 73.

11 See Ball 1995b, pp. 16–18.
12 Sengupta 1999e, pp. 14–18.
13 *Defending Singapore in the 21st century*, pp. 48–9.
14 See, for example, Khoo 1991, pp. 27–9; Ho 1993, p. 21.
15 *Defending Singapore in the 21st century*, p. 66.
16 Speech by Lee Yock Suan, minister for Information and the Arts and minister for the Environment, MIW, 2 October 1999.

APPENDIX 1: SUMMARY OF FORCES

1 The data in this Appendix is derived from numerous published sources, including *The Military Balance 1999–2000*, pp. 203–4.

APPENDIX 2: PARAMILITARY FORCES

1 Boey 1996a, pp. 318–20.
2 *Singapore 1998*, p. 104.
3 'SCDF gets new tool to fight toxic spills', *ST*, 10 September 1997.
4 *Singapore 1998*, p. 104.
5 'S'pore police to join UN team for Cambodian polls', *ST*, 20 July 1998.
6 'Police Coast Guard orders 20 fast boats', *ST*, 8 January 1998.
7 Speech by Matthias Yao, minister of state for Defence, MIW, 8 March 1997.
8 'NCC21 masterplan unveiled', *Pioneer*, June 1999, p. 19.
9 'Young flying aces soar in RSAF F-5 aircraft, MIW, 12 December 1998.

Bibliography

BOOKS AND BOOK CHAPTERS

Amnesty International Report 1998, Amnesty International Publications, London, 1998

Ball, Desmond, *Burma's military secrets*, White Lotus Press, Bangkok, 1998

Bedlington, Stanley S., 'Ethnicity and the armed forces in Singapore' in *Ethnicity and the military in Asia*, (eds) DeWitt C. Ellinwood and Cynthia H. Enloe, Transaction Books, New Brunswick, NJ, 1981

Chan Heng Chee, *Singapore: the politics of survival, 1965–1967*, Oxford University Press, Singapore, 1971

——, 'Politics in an administrative state: where has the politics gone?', in *Trends in Singapore*, (ed.) Seah Chee Meow, Singapore University Press, 1975

——, *The dynamics of one party dominance. The PAP at the grass-roots*, Singapore University Press, 1976

——, 'Singapore', in *Military-civilian relations in South-East Asia*, (eds) Zakaria Haji Ahmad and Harold Crouch, Oxford University Press, Singapore, 1985

——, 'The structuring of the political system', in *Management of success. The moulding of modern Singapore*, (eds) Kernial Singh Sandhu and Paul Wheatley, Institute of Southeast Asian Studies, Singapore, 1989

——, 'Political developments, 1965–1979' in *A history of Singapore*, (eds) Ernest C. T. Chew and Edwin Lee, Oxford University Press, Singapore, 1991

Chandran, Jeshurun, *The growth of the Malaysian Armed Forces 1963–77: some foreign press reactions*, Institute of Southeast Asian Studies, Singapore, 1975

Chew, Melanie, *The sky our country. 25 years of the Republic of Singapore Air Force*, Republic of Singapore Air Force, Singapore, 1993

Chiang, Mickey, *Fighting fit. The Singapore Armed Forces*, Times Editions, Singapore, 1990

——, *SAF and 30 years of national service*, MINDEF Public Affairs, Singapore, 1997

Chin Kin Wah, 'Singapore: threat perceptions and defence spending in a city-state' in *Defence spending in Southeast Asia*, (ed.) Chin Kin Wah, Institute of Southeast Asian Studies, Singapore, 1987

Conboy, Ken, *South-East Asian Special Forces*, Osprey Publishing, London, 1991

Darby, Philip, *British defence policy east of Suez 1947–1968*, Oxford University Press for the Royal Institute of International Affairs, London, 1973

Desker, Ambassador Barry, 'Developments in Indonesia-Singapore bilateral relations: politics' in *Singapore-Indonesia relations: problems and prospects*, (eds) Lau Teik Soon and Bilveer Singh, Singapore Institute of International Affairs, 1991

Emmerson, Donald K., 'Indonesia, Malaysia, Singapore: a regional security core?' in *Southeast Asian security in the new millennium*, (eds) Richard Ellings and Sheldon W. Simon, ME Sharpe, Armonk, NY, 1996

Ganesan, Narayanan, 'Singapore. Realist cum trading state' in *Asian security practice. Material and ideational influences*, (ed.) Muthiah Alagappa, Stanford University Press, Stanford, CA, 1998a

Gill, Bates and J. N. Mak, (eds), *Arms, transparency and security in South-East Asia*, Oxford University Press for Stockholm International Peace Research Institute, Oxford, 1997

Han Fook Kwang, Warren Fernandez and Sumiko Tan, *Lee Kuan Yew. The man and his ideas*, Times Editions, Singapore, 1998

Hawkins, David, *The defence of Malaysia and Singapore: from AMDA to ANZUK*, Royal United Services Institute for Defence Studies, London, 1972

Huxley, Tim, *Insecurity in the Asean region*, Whitehall Paper 23, Royal United Services Institute for Defence Studies, London, 1993a

Jane's Fighting Ships 1998–99, Jane's Information Group, Coulsdon, 1998

Jane's Sentinel Southeast Asia, Jane's Information Group, Coulsdon, 1997

Josey, Alex, *Lee Kuan Yew. The crucial years*, Times Books International, Singapore, 1980

Kurz, Dr Hans-Rudolf, 'The Swiss Militia System' in *The defence forces of Switzerland*, AQ & DJ Publications, Tavistock, 1983

Kwa Chong Guan, 'Singapore' in *Asia Pacific security outlook*, (ed.) Charles E. Morrison, Japan Centre for International Exchange, Tokyo, 1998

Lau Teik Soon and Bilveer Singh, (eds) *Singapore–Indonesia relations: problems and prospects*, Singapore Institute of International Affairs, 1991

Lee, Air Chief Marshal Sir David, *Eastward. A history of the Royal Air Force in the Far East, 1945–1972*, Her Majesty's Stationery Office, London, 1984

Lee Khoon Choy, 'Foreign policy' in *Socialism that works . . . the Singapore way*, (comp. and ed.) C. V. Devan Nair, Federal Publications, Singapore, 1976

Lee Kuan Yew, *The Singapore story. Memoirs of Lee Kuan Yew*, Times Editions and ST Press, Singapore, 1998

Leifer, Michael, 'The conduct of foreign policy' in *Management of success. The moulding of modern Singapore*, (eds) Kernial Singh Sandhu and Paul Wheatley, Institute of Southeast Asian Studies, Singapore, 1989

——, *Dictionary of the modern politics of South-East Asia* Routledge, London, 1995

Leong, C. C., *Youth in the army*, Federal Publications, Singapore, 1978

Li, Tania, *Malays in Singapore. Culture, economy and ideology*, Oxford University Press, Singapore, 1989

Lim, Peter H. L., *Navy. The vital force*, Republic of Singapore Navy, Singapore, 1992

Menon, Col (Ret) R., *To command. The SAFTI Military Institute*, Landmark Books, Singapore, 1995

Methven, Philip, *The Five Power Defence Arrangements and military cooperation among the Asean states. Incompatible models for security in Southeast Asia? Canberra Papers on Strategy and Defence no. 92*, Strategic and Defence Studies Centre, Australian National University, Canberra, 1992

Mulliner, K. and Lian The-Mulliner, *Historical Dictionary of Singapore*, Scarecrow Press, Metuchen, NJ and London, 1991

Murfett, Malcolm H., John N. Miksic, Brian P. Farrell and Chiang Ming Shun (eds), *Between two oceans. A military history of Singapore from first settlement to final British withdrawal*, Oxford University Press, Singapore, 1999

Peled, Alon, *A question of loyalty. Military manpower policy in multi-ethnic states*, Cornell University Press, Ithaca and London, 1998

Rodan, Garry, 'Introduction. Challenges for the new guard and directions for the 1990s', in *Singapore changes guard. Social, political and economic directions in the 1990s*, (ed.) Garry Rodan, Longman Cheshire, Melbourne, 1993

Sandhu, Kernial Singh and Paul Wheatley (eds), *Management of success. The moulding of modern Singapore*, Institute of Southeast Asian Studies, Singapore, 1989

Seah Chee Meow, 'National security' in *Management of success. The moulding of modern Singapore*, (eds) Kernial Singh Sandhu and Paul Wheatley, Institute of Southeast Asian Studies, Singapore, 1989

Shamira Bhanu Abdul Azeez, *The Singapore-Malaysia 'remerger' debate of 1996, Monographs on South-East Asian Politics and International Relations no. 3*, Centre for South-East Asian Studies, University of Hull, Hull, 1998

Shee Poon Kim, 'Political leadership and succession in Singapore', in *Singapore development policies and trends*, (ed.) Peter S. J. Chen, Oxford University Press, Singapore, 1983

Singh, Bilveer, *Singapore's defence industries, Canberra Papers on Security and Defence no. 70*, Strategic and Defence Studies Centre, Australian National University, Canberra, 1990

——, 'A small state's quest for security. Operationalizing deterrence in Singapore's strategic thinking' in *Imagining Singapore*, (eds) Ban Kah Choon, Anne Pakir and Tong Chee Kiong, Times Academic Press, Singapore, 1992

Tai Yong Tan, 'Singapore: civil-military fusion', in *State and soldier in Asia*, (ed.) Muthiah Alagappa, Stanford University Press, forthcoming 2001

——, *ABRI and the security of Southeast Asia. The role and thinking of General L. Benny Moerdani*, Singapore Institute of International Affairs, Singapore,1994

Thayer, Carlyle, 'Vietnam' in *Military-civilian relations in South-East Asia*, (eds) Zakaria Haji Ahmad and Harold Crouch, Oxford University Press, Singapore, 1985

The Air Force, Headquarters Republic of Singapore Air Force, nd

The Military Balance 1999–2000, International Institute for Strategic Studies, London, 1999

Tilman, Robert O., 'The political leadership. Lee Kuan Yew and the PAP team' in *Management of success. The moulding of modern Singapore*, (eds) Kernial Singh Sandhu and Paul Wheatley, Institute of Southeast Asian Studies, Singapore, 1989

Ul Haq, Obaid, 'Foreign policy' in *Government and politics of Singapore*, (eds) Jon S. T. Quah, Chan Heng Chee and Seah Chee Meow, Oxford University Press, Singapore, 1987

Vasil, Raj, *Governing Singapore. Interviews with the new leaders*, Times Books international, Singapore, (rev. edn) 1988

——, *Asianising Singapore. The PAP's management of ethnicity*, Heinemann Asia, Singapore, 1995

Wilson, Dick, *The future role of Singapore*, Royal Institute of International Affairs, London, 1972

JOURNAL ARTICLES AND RESEARCH PAPERS

Baker, Nicola, 'The dynamics of contested spaces: the defence policies of Malaysia, Singapore and Indonesia', PhD thesis, Australian National University, Canberra, December 1999

Ball, Desmond, 'Signals intelligence (SIGINT) in Singapore', unpublished paper, 1995a

——, *Developments in signals intelligence and electronic warfare in Southeast Asia, Working Paper no. 290*, Strategic and Defence Studies Centre, Australian National University, Canberra, 1995b

Boey, David, 'Defending Singapore: a fragile city-state's approach to defence and security', MA dissertation, University of Hull, 1996b

Cheah Swee Nee, LTA Patricia, 'Feminine mystique and the SAF(W) officer', *Pointer*, vol. 18, no. 2, April–June 1992

da Cunha, Derek, 'Major Asian powers and the development of the Singaporean and Malaysian armed forces', *Contemporary Southeast Asia*, vol. 13, no. 1, June 1991

Dillon, Dana, 'A Southeast Asian scenario', *Military Review*, September 1994

Ganesan, N., 'Malaysia-Singapore relations: some recent developments', *Asian Affairs, an American Review*, vol. 25, no. 1, Spring 1998b

——, 'Taking stock of post-cold war developments in Asean', *Security Dialogue*, vol. 25, 1994

Gill, Maj Mejar Singh, 'History of the Singapore Infantry Regiment 1945–1967', supplement to *Pointer*, September 1990

Gwee Choon Lin, Maj Peter, 'Auftragstaktik. A philosophy for management, training and war', *Pointer*, vol. 18, no. 4, October–December 1992

Hanna, Willard A., 'The Singapore Infantry Regiment. A metropolitan force prepares for the jungle', American Universities Field Staff, Southeast Asia Series, vol. XII, no. 12 (Malaysia), nd

——, 'The new Singapore Armed Forces', American Universities Field Staff, Southeast Asia Series, vol. XXI, no. 1, 1973

Ho Kong Wai, Maj, 'Chemical warfare. Trends and implications', *Pointer*, vol. 19, no. 2, April–June 1993

Ho Kwon Ping, Maj (NS), 'MNCs and Singapore's development and security', *Pointer*, October–December 1993

Huxley, Tim, 'Singapore and Malaysia: a precarious balance?', *Pacific Review*, vol. 4, no. 3, 1991

——, *The political role of the Singapore Armed Forces: towards a military-administrative state?*, *Working Paper no. 279*, Strategic and Defence Studies Centre, Australian National University, Canberra, 1993b

Khoo Hock Hee, Cpt Augustine, 'Chemical warfare. Its implications for Singapore', *Pointer*, vol. 17, no. 4, October–December 1991

Koh Chi Wee, Cpt Kelvin, 'Sex integration in the military', *Pointer*, vol. 19, no. 4, October–December 1993

Kwa Chong Guan, Ltc (NS), 'Discipline in the SAF', *Pointer*, vol. 20, no. 4, October–December 1994

Lim Fung Gan, Lta Colin, 'History and the SAF', *Pointer*, vol. 22, no. 2, April–June 1996

'Manpower Policies' supplement, *Pointer*, February 1982

Schofield, Julian, 'War and punishment. The implication of arms purchases in maritime Southeast Asia', *Journal of Strategic Studies*, vol. 21, no. 2, June 1998

Simon, Sheldon W., 'The regionalization of defence in Southeast Asia', *Pacific Review*, vol. 5, no. 2, 1992

Stubbs, Richard, 'Subregional security co-operation in ASEAN: military and economic imperatives and political obstacles', *Asian survey*, vol. 32, 1992

Tan, Col Andrew, 'Improving the efficiency of the army training system', *Pointer*, vol. 21, no. 3, July–September 1995

Tan, Andrew, *Problems and issues in Malaysia-Singapore relations*, *Working Paper no. 314*, Strategic and Defence Studies Centre, Australian National University, Canberra, 1997

Tan Chi Chiu, Maj (Dr), 'The Operation Nightingale experience' in 'SAF Medical Mission to the Gulf', supplement to *Pointer*, May 1992

Tay Swee Yee, LTA, 'The fighting spirit—do we have it?', *Pointer*, vol. 22, no. 2, April–June 1996

Teo Chee Hean, Cdre, 'Maritime powers in South-East Asia', *Pointer*, vol. 17, no. 4, October–December 1991

Worthington, Ross Ronald, 'An Asian core executive: aspects of contemporary governance in Singapore', PhD thesis, Australian National University, Canberra, December 1999

Wu, Yuan-li, 'Planning security for a small nation: lessons from Singapore', *Pacific Community*, vol. 3, no. 4, July 1972

NEWSPAPER, NEWS SERVICE AND MAGAZINE ARTICLES

'A citizen and a scholar', *STWE*, 15 August 1998

'A father's advice', *STWOE*, 27 August 1988

'"A" level study programme: combat NCOs of high calibre', *Pioneer*, April 1991

'A memorable finale', *Pioneer*, February 1984

'A salute fo the SAF', *Pioneer*, July 1993

'A shoulder on stand-by', *Army News*, April 1998

'A tribute to the late Col (Ret) Khoo Eng An', *Navy News*, March 1999

'Achievements of five state award recipients', *Pioneer*, September 1983

'Action plan for British-Singapore ties', *Singapore Bulletin*, March 1997

'ADI profits down but outlook good', *JDW*, 10 March 1999

'AEW on the attack', *Flight International*, 15 February 2000

AFP news agency, 7 June 1998 in SWB FE/3248 B/5, 9 June 1998

'AFVs for ASEAN armies', *ADJ*, August 1994

'Aid for KL will be "on basis of win-win"', *ST*, 9 November 1998

'Air force relaxes eyesight rule', *ST*, 16 December 1986

'Air force reservists', *Pioneer*, October 1989

'Air force takes aim at AMRAAM', *ADJ*, October 1998

'Airscene headlines: Military affairs: Singapore', *Air international*, May 1997

'Airscene headlines: Military affairs: Singapore', *Air international*, December 1997

'Airscene headlines: Military affairs: Singapore', *Air international*, April 1998

'Amendments to SAF Act', *Pioneer*, February 1994

'An old warrior revitalized', *Pioneer*, January 1991

'An SAF that strives for excellence', speech by Defence Minister Yeo Ning Hong, 26 March 1994 in *ST*, 1 July 1994

'Anchoring people to S'pore', *STWOE*, 22 June 1991

Ang Lay Wah, 'From penpushers to combat instructors', *Woman Now*, February–March 1988

'Applying Life Cycle Management', *Pioneer*, December 1991

'Armed Forces to be equipped with more made-in-Singapore arms', *STWOE*, 26 November 1988

'Arms firm GM on graft charge', *ST*, 17 July 1987

'Army accidents to prompt SAF review', *Jane's Pointer*, June 1997

'Army holds joint live-firing exercise with Indonesians', *ST*, 15 November 1997

'Asean must boost military ties', *ST*, 5 August 1994

Ashton, William, 'Burma receives advances from its silent suitors in Singapore', *JIR*, March 1998

'Asia-Pacific news: Newsbriefs', *AFM*, December 1998

'ATEC's 100th evaluation celebration', *Army News*, November 1998

'Attacks by pirates double in Indonesia', *ST*, 22 October 1999

'Attitudes towards NS more positive', *Singapore Bulletin*, August 1992

'Attracting, keeping the best as SAF regulars a key concern', *ST*, 1 February 1996

'Australia, Singapore prepare to defend Malaysia', *Canberra Times*, 10 May 1977

'Australia-Singapore-U.S. EOD exercise: Tri-Crab 98', *Asia-Pacific Defense Forum*, Winter 1998–99

Aznam, Suhaini, 'Neighbourly interest', *FEER*, 21 December 1989

'BAe eyes Asian training facility with Australian expansion plans', *Flight International*, 30 September 1998

'Batam at risk' (editorial), *ST*, 31 July 1999

'Better educated NSFs to provide higher levels of service', *Pioneer*, July 1994

'Better radar for the air force', *Pioneer*, September 1998

'Better than any SAF advertisement', *ST*, 21 July 1997

'Beware foreign elements: Dr Yeo', *ST*, 6 May 1988

'BG defends cautious approach', *ST*, 18 March 1987

'B-G: Elected President's role is to balance the powers of ministers', *STWOE*, 20 August 1988

'BG Yeo sends "strong signal" to civic groups', *ST*, 8 May 1998

'Bigger allowance for reservist key appointment holders', *Pioneer*, September 1991

'Biggest-ever five-power exercise starts', *ST*, 15 April 1997

'Bill seeks changes to powers of Elected President', *STWE*, 5 October 1996

'Bill to allow for extension of reserve service', *ST*, 10 December 1986

Boey, David, 'Keeping airpower airborne. Singapore's airbase defences', *IDR*, 3/1993

——, 'ABRI-SAF commission ACMR facility', *Aerospace (Asia-Pacific)*, April 1994

——, 'Singapore's fleet gets boost from Navy 2000', *IDR*, 12/1995

——, 'Singapore: a fragile nation toughens up', *Jane's Intelligence Review*, July 1996a

'Bofors implicates Singapore in illegal arms exports to the Gulf', *JDW*, 11 April 1987

'Brigade gets vital support', *Pioneer*, February 1986

'Broader horizons', *Flight International*, 15 February 2000

'Budget for arms venture', *Bangkok Post*, 22 September 1978

'Building the 21st century warrior—Army 21', *Pioneer*, May 1999

'Building tomorrow's navy', *Naval Forces*, Special Issue 2/97

Central News Agency, Taipei, 25 May 1998, in SWB FE/3237 B/7, 27 May 1998

'Challenges of a battalion commander's job', *Pioneer*, September 1996

'Chance for reservist NCOs to study and be officers', *STWOE*, 6 May 1989

'Change in nomenclature', *Pioneer*, June 1990

'Changi Naval Base to enhance protection of S'pore's territorial waters', *Pioneer*, March 1998

'Chief of Air Force visits Bangladesh', *Pioneer*, September 1997

'Chosen to lead', *Pioneer*, March 1997

Chuang Peck Ming, 'Defence group takes the offensive', *Singapore Business*, July 1990

'CIQ: S'pore's sovereignty at stake', *ST*, 21 January 1999

'Coast Guard takes over command of 4 RSN vessels', *ADJ*, March 1993

'COL (NS) Peter Ho is new PS (DD)', *Pioneer*, November 1995

'Combat Engineers—advance and overcome', *Pioneer*, June 1992

'Combined arms divisions', *Pioneer*, February 1995

'Coming out of the closet', *FEER*, 30 June 1983

'Commercialising to save manpower', *Pioneer*, May 1994

'Communication technology—the vital link in warfare', *Pioneer*, March 1993

'Constructing for defence. The Lands & Estates Organisation', *Pioneer*, November 1997

'Continuing professional education for SAF officers', *Pioneer*, April 1997

'Contract commencement date at Oakey', *Air Force News*, January 1999

'Cooperative Cope Thunder 99–4', *Asia-Pacific Defense Forum*, Winter 1999–2000

'COSCOM takes over coastal defence', *Pioneer*, December 1991

'Country Briefing: Singapore—state sector thrives in commercial arena', *JDW*, 30 April 1997

'Crisp pictures from S'pore's eye in the sky', *ST*, 15 May 1997

Dantes, Edmond, 'Tactics and dissimilar air combat development centres in Asia-Pacific', *ADJ*, September 1992

'Daytime recalls of reservists may be next', *Sunday Times* (Singapore), 10 November 1985

'Deadly aim. The SSG 69 Steyr sniper rifle', *Pioneer*, October 1989

'Defence Minister visits 18 SADA', *Air Force News*, January 1994

'Defence Science Organisation. Defence R&D at its best', *Pioneer*, November 1989

'Detroit airport pictured by UK satellite', *Flight International*, 2 June 1999

'Diving support vessel for Singapore', *IDR*, October 1990

'Diving to new depths—improved training with NDU's new camp', *Pioneer*, August 1997

'Do joint military exercises enhance security in ASEAN?', *ADJ*, September 1999

'Do you know what happened 32 years ago?', *ST*, 22 July 1996

Dolven, Ben, 'Friend or foe?', *FEER*, 25 March 1999

'Dr Hu unveils prudent budget', *STWE*, 28 February 1998

'Dr Lee unveils RSAF's first helicopter simulator', *ADJ*, June 1995

'Dr Tan hopes to inject private sector perspective', *Business Times* (Singapore), 30 June 1995

'Dr Tan outlines his vision for the SAF', *ST*, 1 February 1996

'Dr Tan visits Japan', *Pioneer*, February 1999

'DSO National Laboratories. Revolutionising defence through technology', *Pioneer*, January 1999

'Education in the SAF', *Pioneer*, March 1983

'Enter the Leguan', *Pioneer*, June 1993

'Eurofighter aims for Singapore sale', *Flight International*, 10 December 1997

'Ex Axolotl', *Navy News*, April 1998

'Ex Kocha Singa', *Army News*, December 1997/January 1998

'Ex Lion King 5/98', *Navy News*, April 1998

'Ex Lionwalk 1998', *Army News*, May 1998

'Ex Maju Bersama (Progress Together)', *Army News*, September 1998

'Ex MCM Hunter 3/98', *Navy News*, August 1998

'Ex Pitch Black', *Pioneer*, October 1990

'Ex Singkiwi', *Air Force News*, January 1999

'Ex Wallaroo', *Air Force News*, January 1999

'Exercise Eastern Arc', *Air Force News*, April 1998

'Exposed: Burma's weapons industry', *Jane's Pointer*, December 1998

'Ex-SAF men to take up jobs in school operations', *STWE*, 6 December 1997

'F-16s kept in US for two years "to avoid a misunderstanding"', *STWOE*, 10 February 1990

Farrer, Mark, 'Uneven impacts—economic crisis and regional airpower', *APDR 1999 Annual Reference Edition*

'Fatal blast baffles army', *Dominion* (Wellington), 10 March 1997

'Female trainees choose technical career in army', *Pioneer*, July 1988

'Field Defence Squadrons show firepower', *Pioneer*, December 1996

'Fighting an electronic war', *Army News*, July 1998

'Finance, Communications posts for Cdre Teo', *STWOE*, 26 December 1992

'First bilateral exercise for Singapore and Philippines', *Pioneer*, October 1994

'First FIBUA exercise on homeground', *Pioneer*, September 1988

'First woman SWO is a model soldier', *ST*, 30 September 1987

'Five star accommodation', *Warships. International Fleet Review*, Autumn 1999

'FLASH for Singapore', *IDR*, April 1996

'Flight simulators get bigger role in RSAF', *ST*, 1 May 1987

'For your info: financial help for servicemen', *Pioneer*, December 1993

'Former SAF Director of General Staff passes away', *Pioneer*, November 1989

Foss, Christopher F., 'Singapore drives Bionix IFV to new limits', *Jane's IDR*, October 1999

'Fostering better defence relations with China', *Pioneer*, December 1997

'Foundation laid for navy's nerve centre', *ST*, 12 January 2000

'Four tell why it's hard to brainwash men who've done NS', *ST*, 22 June 1987

'France's "natural partner"', *ST*, 24 February 1999

Fricker, John, 'Singapore's citizen air force', *Air Pictorial*, May 1994

'Friend or foe?', *FEER*, 25 March 1999

'From strict disciplinarians to skilled middle managers: Warrant Officers in the SAF', *Pioneer*, February 1996

'Frontline: the development of reservist training', *Pioneer*, July 1986

'Future fighter needs', *Flight International*, 18 February 1998

'FY99 expenditure estimates', *ST*, 26 February 1999

'Gearing up students for the rigours of military life', *ST*, 10 January 1987

'German-Singapore accord could boost Mako', *Defense News*, 6 March 2000

'Greater responsibility for NSF armourers', *Pioneer*, July 1996

'Groomed for the top', *ST*, 9 August 1993

'Growth- and Asean-driven Jakarta good for region, says BG Lee', *ST*, 30 March 1999

'Gus Dur gets warm welcome', *STWE*, 13 November 1999

'Habibie, Golkar chief take offence at SM's remarks', *ST*, 12 February 1998

'Habibie unhappy with S'pore: AWSJ', *ST*, 5 August 1998

'Helicopter training in Indonesia', *Singapore Bulletin*, May 1997

'Helping each other', *FEER*, 25 June 1998

'He's no newcomer to transport', *ST*, 2 July 1998

'Higher responsibilities for Warrant Officers', *Pioneer*, September 1994

Ho Kwon Ping, 'Washington aids ASEAN build-up', *FEER*, 23 July 1976

'Holding the fort', *Flight International*, 1 December 1999

'How officers move up the ranks', *ST*, 29 June 1994

'Hughes loses Asian satellite contract', *Flight International*, 21 April 1999

Huxley, Tim, 'Singapore forces shape up', *JDW*, 19 November 1994

Huxley, Tim and David Boey, 'Singapore's army—boosting capabilities', *Jane's Intelligence Review*, April 1996

'I felt like I had been hit by lightning twice: PM', *STWOE*, 12 December 1992

'Igla MANPADS for Asia-Pacific', *ADJ*, October 1999

'In a class of her own', *Army News*, February 1998

'In full control', *Pioneer*, September 1991

'In the pursuit of excellence', *Naval Forces*, 2/1999

'Indonesia tests Singapore' (editorial), *STWE*, 6 March 1999

'Information technology. Giving the SAF a strategic edge', *Pioneer*, March 1990

Interview with Defence Minister Lee Boon Yang, *Defense News*, 5–11 December 1994

Interview with Defence Minister Lee Boon Yang, *ADJ*, July 1995

Interview with Defence Minister Yeo Ning Hong, *ADJ*, February 1992

Interview with Defence Minister Yeo Ning Hong, *Armed Forces Journal International*, May 1992

Interview with Defence Minister Yeo Ning Hong, *ST*, 1 July 1993

Interview with Defence Minister Yeo Ning Hong, *ADJ*, March 1994

Interview with Dr Yeo Ning Hong, second minister for Defence, *IDR*, Southeast Asia supplement, December 1986

Interview with Senior Minister Lee Kuan Yew, *St*, 9 June 1996

'Iron and steel—the SAF Commandos', *Pioneer*, January 1995

'Is there a MINDEF mafia?', *Singapore Business*, November 1990

'Israel seeks new money in Asia', *JDW*, 17 November 1999

'Israel, Singapore sign for Apache deals', *JDW*, 1 March 2000

'Israel, Singapore to sign satellite deal', *JDW*, 5 July 2000

'Israeli UAV hits requirements snag in Singapore', *Defense News*, 7 April 1997

'It's the right decision says Goh', *ST*, 2 July 1975

' "It was a bolt from the blue. But that is life"', *STWOE*, 15 May 1993

'Jakarta may offer more training areas', *ST*, 7 August 1998

'Japanese ships here on goodwill visit', *ST*, 19 July 1994

Jayasankaran, S., 'Under the gun', *FEER*, 3 September 1998

'Joint exercise with US Marines', *Pioneer*, August 1996

'Joint patrols reduce sea robberies', *Pioneer*, August 1994

'Jungle training in Brunei', *Pioneer*, April 1998

'Kakadu IV', *AFM*, December 1999

'Keen interest shown in new NCO scheme', *STWOE*, 28 April 1990

'Keeping Singapore safe', *Pioneer*, September 1995

'Kirpa Wong bin Rahim', 'Fashioning Singapore's tough armed forces', *Pacific Defence Reporter*, May 1982

'KL curbs airspace use by RSAF jets', *STWE*, 19 September 1999

'KL's water promises not enough', *ST*, 21 April 1998

'Lakiun Camp', *Pioneer*, November 1983

'Landmark Natuna gas deal signed', *Singapore Bulletin*, February 1999

'Launch of Super Skyhawks', *ST*, 26 January 1988

'Lee calls for closer Asean defence ties', *Age* (Melbourne), 19 December 1981

'Lethal weapon, made in Singapore', *Sunday Times* (Singapore), 12 September 1999

'Looking for Mandarins' (editorial), *ST*, 6 August 1993

'Lt-Gen Choo: enlisted men today are more positive', *Sunday Times* (Singapore), 12 August 1990

'Made in Singapore—Part One', *Pioneer*, February 1992

'MAF invites senior SAF officers for golf', *Pioneer*, September 1999

'Majulah Singapura', *Pioneer*, August 1990

'Making a difference in the international community', *Pioneer*, December 1998

'Malay body sends protest note to Habibie', *ST*, 23 February 1999

'Malay leaders in Singapore hit back at Habibie', *STWE*, 13 February 1999

'Malay Singaporeans want to belong—in all ways', *ST*, 9 August 1996

'Malaysia targets vehicles, copters', *Defense News*, 20 December 1999

'Marching to self-sufficiency in arms as well as defence', *FEER*, 13 January 1983

'Mark Berent's Washington report', *ADJ*, November 1988

'Men of merit', *Pioneer*, January 1997

'Milestone in Singapore-Vietnam defence ties', *Pioneer*, April 1995

'Military links in Asean important', *ST*, 17 March 1988

'Military medals for two', *ST*, 26 July 1997

'Millennium force', *Flight International*, 16 June 1999

'MINDEF's new weapon: ice machines', *ST*, 18 February 1999

'MINDEF to plug into solar power in big way', *ST*, 18 February 1999

'Minorities represented well in slate of new faces', *STWE*, 23 November 1996

'Missiles fitted to intercept hostile aircraft', *ST*, 16 June 1994

'Mistral, P-STAR systems now fully operational', *Pioneer*, August 1997

'Mob protests on Bintan contained by police', *ST*, 16 January 2000

'Mobile field hospital', *Pioneer*, April 1998

'Mobilisations', *Pioneer*, February 1991

'MoD knew of Singapore arms connection', *Independent* (London), 7 July 1995

'Modified Fokker 50s fly in', *JDW*, 5 February 1994

'More NSFs to fill mid-level Specialist posts', *Pioneer*, September 1996

'More patrols in waterways', *STWE*, 8 May 1999

'More realistic air combat training with the ACMI', *Air Force News*, September 1995

'More RSAF men for copter training in US', *Singapore Bulletin*, November 1996

'More versions of SAR 21 rifle', *JDW*, 3 May 2000

'Move to boost local fish and vegetable supply', *Singapore Bulletin*, September 1999

'MVs in service: Singapore', *Wheels and Tracks*, no. 43, 1993

'M71. Licence renewed', *Pioneer*, April 1993

'Nation's security depends on strong defence: Dr Yeo', *Singapore Bulletin*, April 1991

'Navy buys Barak anti-missile system', *ST*, 23 April 1996

'Navy buys three more Sjöormen submarines', *Pioneer*, September 1997

'Navy reservists conduct CR requisition exercise', *Pioneer*, May 1991

'Navy studying need for submarines', *Singapore Bulletin*, July 1995

'Navy's Gabriel missile hits right on target', *ST*, 2 September 1998

'Navy's "made-to-measure" minesweeper', *ST*, 19 July 1993

'Navy's MCVs in multilateral naval exercise', *Pioneer*, May 1995

'NCC21 masterplan unveiled', *Pioneer*, June 1999

'Nee Soon Driclad Centre', *Army News*, February 1998

'New all-terrain vehicles for Singapore', *ADJ*, April 1993

'New ambassador to Myanmar appointed', *ST*, 18 September 1996

'New eye in sky for close look at region', *ST*, 25 March 1998

'New formation for the RSAF', *Pioneer*, June 1995

'New hardware will help Navy to be "balanced force"', *ST*, 5 May 1993

'New minehunting simulators offer effective training', *Pioneer*, November 1996

'New permanent secretary (Defence)', *Pioneer*, June 1994

'New policies for reservists', *Pioneer*, December 1983

'New professional Corps of WOs and Corps of Specialists', *Pioneer*, March 1992

'New reservist divisions in SAF', *Pioneer*, April 1991

'New warehouse for SAF vehicles in Rockhampton', *Pioneer*, October 1995

'New Zealand, S'pore navies sign arrangement', *Pioneer*, April 1998

'Newcomer with a bulging order book', Singapore Survey, *Financial Times*, 31 March 1998

'News briefs', *AFM*, April 1998

Ng Jui Ping, Brigadier-General, 'Emerging trends in the organization of armies in the immediate region', *The Pointer*, vol. 13, no. 1, October–December 1986

'"No arms shipments to Burma from S'pore"', *STWOE*, 19 November 1988

'No quick solution to ethnic, religious issues', *STWE*, 2 October 1999

'Not true SAF will stop training in Taiwan', *ST*, 1 February 1996

'NS period and defence budget will not be cut', *Singapore Bulletin*, January 1992

'NS the very basis for Singapore's continued existence', *Pioneer*, November 1995

'"NSmen to get own personal equipment', *Pioneer*, October 1994

'NSmen's operational readiness impresses Dr Lee', *Pioneer*, May 1995

'NTU launches first satellite successfully', *ST*, 22 April 1999

'Obese NS men will have basic training extended', *STWOE*, 2 June 1990

'Of "war" and Wallaby', *Pioneer*, December 1996

'Officers from the army, navy and air force to train together', *ST*, 7 October 1998

'On the ground', *Pioneer*, December 1995

'Operation Flying Eagle', *Pioneer*, December 1990

'Operational readiness of reservist units very high, says Dr Yeo', *ST*, 30 September 1993

'Our titans of the sea', *Pioneer*, May 1999

'Panel to strengthen S'pore—Australia ties', *ST*, 6 March 1995

'PAP election candidate Lim Swee Say: Western mind, Chinese heart', *ST*, 5 November 1996

'PAP to recruit more members', *STWE*, 27 November 1999

Parliamentary statement by S. Jayakumar, Minister of Home Affairs, *ST*, 14 March 1987

'Partial relocation of Flying Training School to Australia', *Pioneer*, May 1993

'Partners in defence science and technology', *Pioneer*, May 1993

Pillai, M.G.G., 'Chill winds in the Straits of Johore', *Pacific Defence Reporter*, February 1990

'Plans for home-made micro-satellites', *STWE*, 11 April 1998

'PM announces Cabinet reshuffle', *ST*, 15 May 1999

'PM concerned over "so many ministers" wishing to quit', *STWE*, 18 December 1993

'PM Goh, Mahathir to work for closer ties', *Singapore Bulletin*, April 1998

'PM Goh prepared to call a GE after National Day rally', *ST*, 10 June 1996

'PM Goh to step down "some time after next GE"', *STWE*, 27 November 1999

'PM Goh's $1.2 billion plan for Indonesia', *ST*, 14 January 2000

'PM sees our troops training in Brunei', *Pioneer*, October 1986

Pocock, Chris, 'Singapore sting', *Air International*, August 1986

'Police Coast Guard orders 20 fast boats', *ST*, 8 January 1998

'Port in a storm', *FEER*, 22 November 1990

Preston, Antony, 'The submarine threat to Asian navies', *ADJ*, October 1995

'Promoting bilateral co-operation between Singapore and Indonesia', *Pioneer*, April 1989

'PSTAR attains full operational capability', *Pioneer*, October 1999

'Pulau Tekong to double in size as a training ground', *ST*, 15 December 1997

'Python 4 heads for Chile and Singapore air forces', *Flight International*, 12 March 1997

Radio Australia, 31 October 1996 in SWB, FE/2758 B/6, 1 November 1996

Radio Australia external service, 30 October 1996 in SWB, FE/2757 B/3, 31 October 1996

Radio Corporation of Singapore, 10 April 1996 in SWB FE/2587 B/3, 16 April 1996

Radio Republic of Indonesia, 11 July 1996 in SWB FE/2663 B/3, 13 July 1996

'RADM Richard Lim to assume new appointment in MINDEF', *Pioneer*, September 1999

'Rafael to help build missile plant in Singapore', *Flight International*, 25 August 1999

'Readiness & reality—simulator training in the SAF', *Pioneer*, July 1998

'Ready, aim, fire . . . and missile is on target', *ST*, 26 August 1997

'Recession helps SAF recruit men', *ST*, 26 February 1986

'Recognising Veterans', *Pioneer*, November 1990

'RECORD II', *Pioneer*, November 1996

'Recruiting higher calibre combat NCOs', *Pioneer*, June 1990

'Regional co-operation boosts two-way security', *Australian*, 1 October 1982

'Regional maritime air power evolves', *APDR*, February–March 1999

'Reinventing the heir', *FEER*, 15 July 1999

'Relocating our CIQ—facts of the case', *Singapore Bulletin*, August 1998

'Republic of Singapore Navy: missions, roles and organisation', *Naval Forces*, Special Issue, 2/97

'Reservist officers' course revamped', *Pioneer*, December 1992

'Reservist upgrading scheme', *Pioneer*, October 1983

'Reservists and their employers', *Pioneer*, April 1993

'Reservists are getting fitter', *ST*, 14 December 1985

'Reservists as front-line troopers', *Mirror* (Singapore), vol. 21, no. 15 (1 August 1985)

'"Reservists" now called "Operationally Ready National Servicemen"', *Pioneer*, January 1994

'Resource Planning Office: harnessing national resources to support the SAF', *Pioneer*, November 1989

'Response time to be halved', *ST*, 15 April 1989
'Retiring SAF officers to get new career as teachers', *ST*, 29 June 1994
'Riau's main parties call for secession', *ST*, 2 February 2000
'Rice pact with Thailand soon', *Singapore Bulletin*, April 1999
Robertson, Frank, 'Singapore's billion dollar aerospace show', *Pacific Defence Reporter*, February 1984
'Royal Ordnance linked to arms for Iran', *The Times*, 7 July 1995
'RSAF aircraft now train in Bangladesh as well', *Sunday Times* (Singapore), 20 June 1993
'RSAF airmen in US enjoy best of both worlds', *ST*, 16 October 1994
'RSAF can now train at French air bases', *ST*, 26 July 1997
'RSAF civil resource vehicles requisition exercise', *Air Force News*, January 1999
'RSAF Emergency Runway Exercise', *Air Force News*, April 1998
'RSAF Fennecs', *AFM*, June 1992
'RSAF fighter choice hinges on support', *Flight International*, 4 March 1998
'RSAF's first female chopper pilot', *Pioneer*, May 1994
'RSAF introduces Enforcer Mk2', *Jane's Navy International*, September/October 1995
'RSAF mobilises light aircraft', *Pioneer*, January 1988
'RSAF personnel to train at Luke Air Force Base in US', *Pioneer*, April 1993
'RSAF pilots can train in Bangladesh', *Singapore Bulletin*, April 1994
'RSAF plan to update Skyhawks blocked by Pentagon', *Business Times* (Singapore), 27 March 1986
'RSAF scores direct hits with Igla missiles', *Pioneer*, September 1999
'RSAF 30th anniversary. Into the new millennium', *ST*, 4 September 1998
'RSAF to produce pilots in shorter time', *Pioneer*, July 1994
'RSAF turns to Israel for EW', *JDW*, 10 October 1992
'RSN delivers food aid to Indonesia', *Navy News*, October 1998
'RSN looking for maritime patrol aircraft', *ADJ*, January 1991
'RSN sends men for submarine training in Sweden', *Pioneer*, November 1995
'RSwN and RSN deepen relations', *Navy News*, March 1998
Saaid, M. Shuhud, 'The Singapore Army', *ADJ*, June 1987
'S Africa offers to extend Singapore link', *Flight International*, 4 January 1995
'SADA's new all-in-one simulator', *Pioneer*, August 1994
'SAF: achieving the best mix', *ST*, 26 February 1995.
'SAF adds 600 versatile M113s to its armour', *ST*, 16 August 1986
'SAF awards merit scholarships to women for the first time', *STWE*, 12 August 1993
'SAF Commandos storm hijacked plane', *Pioneer*, April 1991
'SAF fights the flab', *Pioneer*, February 1991
'SAF goes for more realistic exercises', *ST*, 21 July 1989
'SAF holds first annual talks with US military', *Singapore Bulletin*, February 1996
'SAF keen on more areas for training in Australia', *ST*, 25 October 1996
'SAF offers 300 poly scholarships', *ST*, 20 January 1986
'SAF, Philippine army begin joint exercise', *ST*, 9 March 1995
'SAF planning to use electronic battlefield for training of troops', *ST*, 15 December 1997

'SAF pledges continued support', *ST*, 20 October 1999

'SAF reservists lack morale and discipline', *ST*, 8 February 1981

'SAF should be the concern of every Singaporean', speech by Defence Minister Goh Chok Tong, *ST*, 16 April 1983

'SAF signallers—providing the vital link', *Pioneer*, February 1997

'SAF to train in more non-traditional areas', *Pioneer*, January 1991

'SAF to widen use of info technology', *ST*, 20 January 1990

'SAF training resumes after three-day suspension', *STWE*, 12 April 1997

'SAF troops train in Pulau Sudong: maximising land usage', *Pioneer*, September 1990

'SAF unveils Special Operations Force', *Pioneer*, April 1997

'SAF wants parents to encourage sons to join', *ST*, 3 March 1986

'SAF WOSEs—towards excellence', *Pioneer*, March 1997

'Safkar Indopura', *Pioneer*, February 1990

'SAF's Command and Staff College opens its door to FPDA officers', *Singapore Bulletin*, March 1990

'Samaritans of the RSAF', *Pioneer*, October 1991

'Savings plan for SAF "backbone"', *ST*, 23 February 2000

Saw, David, 'Malaysia looks beyond its deal of the decade', *Armed Forces Journal International*, June 1992

——, 'Air defence in Singapore', *Asian Military Review*, February/March 1996

'SBAB and 7 SIB form special bond', *Pioneer*, October 1986

'SCDF gets new tool to fight toxic spills', *ST*, 10 September 1997.

'Scholars urged to go for double degrees', *STWE*, 7 November 1999

'Schooled for leadership', *ST*, 13 August 1994

'Seeing comrades die may affect some soldiers', *ST*, 16 April 1997

Sengupta, Prasun K., 'Singapore and the Army 2000 plan', *Military Technology*, 7/1992

——, 'A builder's navy takes shape', *ADJ*, December 1998

——, 'Total defence and the Singaporean Armed Forces', *ADJ*, July 1999a

——, 'SAF geared for integrated warfare', *ADJ*, July 1999b

——, 'Investments in defence R&D pay off', *ADJ*, July 1999c

——, '"We have an integrated capability"', *ADJ*, July 1999d

——, 'Malaysia's force modernisation plans back on stream', *ADJ*, December 1999e

'She earned her SAF wings, and now she's top in class too', *ST*, 19 September 1997

'Shorter NS for fit recruits', *Pioneer*, May 1993

'Signals provides vital link', *Pioneer*, April 1991

'Simulator trains C-130 pilots', *Singapore Bulletin*, June 1992

'Singapore air force pilots train in U.S. skies', *Asia-Pacific Defense Forum*, Summer 1999

'Singapore and Australia in new partnership', *Singapore Bulletin*, February 1996

'Singapore and Indonesia begin eight-day air exercise today', *ST*, 6 July 1994

'Singapore Armed Forces forms first combined arms division', *ST*, 22 March 1991

'Singapore army exercise in Australia', Defence News Release (Canberra) 23/82, 3 March 1982

'Singapore army sets its sights on new light tank', *JDW*, 7 January 1998
'Singapore/Australian air force plan in doubt', *Flight International*, 12 April 1995
'Singapore boosts SIGINT using C-130 transports', *JDW*, 17 September 1997
'Singapore company in UAV deal with Israel', *JDW*, 2 December 1998
'Singapore considers new fighter jets', *Pioneer*, December 1998
'Singapore considers two artillery bids', *JDW*, 30 October 1996
'Singapore expands overseas basing, training', *Defense News*, 31 March 1997
"Singapore fighting Kites', *IDR*, May 1987
'Singapore forces shape up', *JDW*, 19 November 1994
'Singapore group buys tanker to stockpile oil', *ST*, 24 August 1990
'Singapore halted in tracks to update Vietnamese APCs', *JDW*, 14 April 1999
'Singapore in talks to buy Russian missiles', *JDW*, 4 September 1999
'Singapore, Indonesia sign pact to develop water resources in Bintan', *Singapore Bulletin*, April 1992
'Singapore invites bids for unmanned aerial vehicle', *Defense News*, 15 December 1997
'Singapore joins Joint Strike Fighter programme', *Flight International*, 28 April 1999
'Singapore joins JSF, Australia stays out', *Defense News*, 10 May 1999
'Singapore launches new tracked vehicle', *JDW*, 5 April 2000
'Singapore leads region in naval modernization drive', *Defense News*, 7 June 1999
'Singapore leases F-16s from US Air Force', *Flight International*, 29 July 1992
'Singapore Link 16 move angers USA', *Flight International*, 24 February 1999
'Singapore: Manila says Singapore to help modernise army', Reuter News Service, 20 August 1996
'Singapore MPs say prejudice issue put at rest', *Australian*, 1 November 1996
'Singapore must not be another Kuwait', *ST*, 13 August 1990
'Singapore now armed with Bionix', *JDW*, 25 August 1999
'Singapore offers quick-reaction force for UN', *Singapore Bulletin*, May 1997
'Singapore orders Eurobridge systems', *JDW*, 19 April 2000
'Singapore outsources pilot screening to Australia', *Flight International*, 1 September 1999
'Singapore pilots stay in U.S. to train', *Defense News*, 7 October 1996
'Singapore poised to roll out new fighting vehicle', *JDW*, 9 April 1997
'Singapore prepares for mechanized warfare', *Jane's IDR*, 4/1996
'Singapore protests to Sweden over arms export freeze', *ST*, 4 April 1987
'Singapore puts force integration into place', *JDW*, 30 April 1997
'Singapore sees Cabinet woe', *Financial Times*, 1 November 1994
'Singapore seeks defence pact', *Age* (Melbourne), 16 October 1980
'Singapore seeks new defence umbrella', *Canberra Times*, 6 July 1981
'Singapore sets up defence laboratory', *JDW*, 14 October 1998
'Singapore solutions', *Flight International*, 21 January 1998
'Singapore steps up search for naval stealth', *JDW*, 19 May 1999
'Singapore studies bases', *Flight International*, 27 August 1997
'Singapore, Sweden set up US$5m research fund', *Pioneer*, November 1997
'Singapore, Sweden will market defense to undersea threats', *Defense News*, 11 April 1994

'Singapore Technologies Aerospace F-16 upgrade', *AFM*, April 2000

'Singapore to fortify forces with F-16s', *Defense News*, 10 November 1997

Singapore to get piped gas from Indonesia', *ST*, 1 May 1997

'Singapore to modify F-5E for recce role', *IDR*, July 1990

'Singapore to train air force pilots in Canada', *JDW*, 10 December 1997

'Singapore tries UAV simulator', *Defense News*, 2 March 1998

'Singapore, US formalise berthing pact', *Singapore Bulletin*, December 1998

'Singapore wants more Chinooks', *Flight International*, 30 June 1999

'Singaporean F-16D Block 52s reveal Israeli design heritage', *Flight International*, 22 April 1998

'Singaporean visit eases tensions with Malaysia', *International Herald Tribune*, 6 November 1998

'Singaporeans should be willing to fight to keep country's independence', *Pioneer*, December 1997

'Singapore's Apaches will be first for SE Asia', *JDW*, 10 March 1999

'Singapore's F-5 fleet is brought up to date', *Jane's IDR*, April 1998

'Singapore's FH 2000—a world first', *Pioneer*, July 1995

'Singapore's first satellite to launch in May', *Singapore Bulletin*, March 1998

'SingTel pulls out of $1b Asia-Pac satellite venture', *STWE*, 9 May 1998

'"Smart" buildings and solar power', *ST*, 18 February 1999

'Soldiers and Scholars', *FEER*, 5 December 1991

'Southeast Asians fear a breakup of Indonesia', *International Herald Tribune*, 16 November 1999

Speech by President Benjamin Sheares at the opening of the fifth parliament, *ST*, 4 February 1981

Speech by Prime Minister Lee Kuan Yew, *ST*, 3 July 1987

Spellman, Anthony, 'Singapore, Thailand want scout vehicles', *Armed Forces Journal International*, June 1991

'Spin-offs from training with the best', *ST*, 26 August 1997

'S'pore: a competitive city-state that sails with the rising tide', *ST*, 21 August 1992

'S'pore-Abri exercise goes on', *ST*, 25 August 1998

'S'pore and Philippines start their first bilateral army exercise', ST, 16 June 1993

'S'pore-Aussie talks focus on security', *ST*, 23 February 1999

'S'pore-Aussie talks reaffirms strong partnership', *Singapore Bulletin*, March 1999

'S'pore, Australia sign three new agreements', *ST*, 22 October 1996

'S'pore, Australian troops in live-firing exercise', *Pioneer*, May 1997

'S'pore, France sign General Security Agreement', *Pioneer*, August 1999

'S'pore, Indon navies help Indonesian villagers', *Pioneer*, August 1998

'S'pore-Indonesian defence ties extremely valuable: Boon Yang', *ST*, 13 August 1994

'S'pore is short of 200 000 babies', *STWDE*, 23 October 1999

'S'pore, KL to settle issues as a package', *ST*, 18 December 1998

'S'pore, Philippines in first joint naval exercise', *Pioneer*, July 1996

'S'pore police to join UN team for Cambodian polls', *ST*, 20 July 1998

'S'pore signs military cooperation agreement with South Africa', *Pioneer*, January 1998

'S'pore, Sweden sign MCM exchange programme document', *Pioneer*, January 1996

'S'pore Technologies Group announces major restructuring', *ST*, 13 February 1995

'S'pore to boost FPDA further with 48 I-Hawk missiles', *STWOE*, 5 May 1990

'S'pore to buy second-hand submarine', *ST*, 24 September 1995

'S'pore to carry on training troops in Taiwan, says PM Lee', *ST*, 14 August 1990

'S'pore to join Cobra Gold exercise this year', *ST*, 14 January 2000

'S'pore will survive me: SM', *STWE*, 8 June 1996

'S'pore's arms-making firm in top 10 list', *ST*, 19 June 1992

'S'pore's first satellite blasts off into space', *STWE*, 29 August 1998

'S'pore's third round of aid', *ST*, 7 January 1999

'ST Aero F-5 upgrade', *AFM*, April 1998

'ST Aero will expand leasing business', *Flight International*, 15 January 1997

'ST Aero's plans for 2000', *AFM*, March 2000

'ST Aerospace partners Australian company to maintain RSAF aircraft at Pearce', *Pioneer*, January 1996

'ST Engineering shares soar on safe status', *Business Times* (Singapore), 22 January 1998

'Steering forward with logistics', *Pioneer*, December 1991

Stijger, Eric, 'Singapore in France', *AFM*, August 1999

'Stingray light tanks for Singapore?', *ADJ*, April 1991

'Strong air defence will deter aggressors: Dr Yeo', *ST*, 30 March 1994

'Strong SAF the best deterrent', *ST*, 10 October 1999

'Submariners earn their badge', *Navy News*, February 1998

'Sweden gets the chop for halting arms sales', *ADJ*, May 1987

'Sweden satisfied S'pore not at fault', *ST*, 17 July 1987

Tai Ming Cheung, 'Soldiers and scholars', *FEER*, 5 December 1991

'Taking it one step closer—1st ABRI-SAF SAREX', *Pioneer*, May 1995

'Tank busters', *Pioneer*, October 1993

'Thailand and French navies ended joint exercise', *ADJ*, January 1994

'Thailand, S'pore agree to expand defence ties', *ST*, 23 July 1996

'The Aggressors—the army's key to training realism', *Army News*, November 1998

'The CIS story', *Pioneer*, July 1983

'The citizen soldier', *FEER*, 13 January 1983.

'The FPDA: commitment to regional stability', *Pioneer*, February 1990

'The lab's job', *Singapore Bulletin*, March 1999

'The navy's most valuable asset—people', 'Republic of Singapore Navy' Special Issue, *Naval Forces*, vol. 18, no. 2, 1997

'The poison shrimp matures', *APDR*, December 1999

'The Republic of Singapore Air Force at twenty-five', *Asian Military Review*, December 1993

'The RSN's missile gun boats', *Pioneer*, August 1995

'The Singapore Armed Forces: some future growth trends', *ADJ*, July 1995

'The third generation: a conscript leadership', *ST*, 17 June 1996

'They build buildings only to blow them up', *ST*, 28 November 1997

'This is a Singapore problem. We will solve it ourselves . . .', *ST*, 18 March 1987

'Three generals promoted', *STWE*, 3 July 1999

'Three water plants by 2011', *STWE*, 9 May 1998

'Thunder Warrior '99', *Army News*, February/March 1999

'Ties with Manila will be strong: Tony Tan', *ST*, 14 June 1998

Tillman, Andrew C., 'Singapore's automatic grenade launcher', *IDR*, December 1989

'Tok Mat: we want to regain what's ours', *Star* (Kuala Lumpur), 10 August 1998

'Tony Tan in S. Africa to discuss defence ties', *ST*, 10 November 1997

'Tony Tan on four-day visit to New Zealand', *ST*, 23 January 1998

'Tony Tan on three-day visit to US', *ST*, 29 September 1996

'Towards new era in military communications', *Pioneer*, October 1990

'Training in Batu Raja, Indonesia', *Army News*, November 1998

'Training more reservists in shorter time', *Pioneer*, January 1990

'Training on the TPQ-37', *Pioneer*, October 1992

'Trajectory, load, fire!', *Pioneer*, March 1995

'Troops sent to Batam as 20 die in clashes', *STWE*, 31 July 1999

'Two-day internal security exercise', *ST*, 30 April 1986

'Two Japanese warships here on visit', *ST*, 10 October 1985

'Upgrading the AMX-13 light tank the SAE way', *ADJ*, August 1987

'US and Singapore in talks to block hi-tech leakages', *Financial Times*, 16 August 1985

'US, Singapore seek compromise on AMRAAM sale', *Defense News*, 6 March 2000

'USA clears Singapore for Longbow attack radar', *Flight International*, 6 January 1999

'USA-Singapore submarine links', *JDW*, 20 January 1999

'USA takes Singapore option in hunt for new SE Asian home', *JDW*, 18 January 1992

'US$8b deal signed', *Singapore Bulletin*, September 1998

Vatikiotis, Michael, Ben Dolven and Rodney Tasker, 'Friends indeed', *FEER*, 8 October 1998

'Visit to France', *Air Force News*, January 1999

'Voluntary early enlistment', *Pioneer*, February 1992

'Water deal with Jakarta is possible, says Philip Yeo', *ST*, 16 January 1999

'We must stop danger trend', *ST*, 14 September 1987

'Weapons simulators for SAF to improve training', *ST*, 29 April 1987

'Who said bailout?', *FEER*, 11 June 1998

'Who wields the real power?', *Singapore Business*, November 1990

'Why are so many Chinese Christians in leading positions?', *ST*, 7 May 1997

'Why Brunei training is so valuable', *ST*, 22 August 1986

'Why Singapore is ready to pay a high premium for security', *ST*, 3 July 1987

'Will a foreigner take over Philip Yeo's job?', *STWE*, 3 July 1999

'With pride we lead—the making of the SAF's specialists' *Pioneer*, June 1997

'Women in green', *Pioneer*, April 1990

Xinhua news agency (Beijing), 29 November 1998 in SWB FE/3397 B/6, 30 November 1998

Zulkarnen, Isaak, 'Trucks and soft-skinned vehicles', *ADJ*, September 1995

'1PS meets Merit scholars', *Pioneer*, November 1990

'3 battle-ready divisions "within hours of activation"', *ST*, 5 June 1994

'4 SIR exercises with US Army', *Pioneer*, May 1996

'35 mm AA gun upgrade', *Air Force News*, November 1993
'5–power group "more relevant now"', *ST*, 16 April 1997
'40 SAR in multilateral exercise in Darwin', *Pioneer*, October 1995
'41 SAR training in Australia', *Army News*, November 1998
'127 Squadron inaugurated', *Pioneer*, July 1999
'182 Sqn family is complete', *Navy News*, October 1998

OFFICIAL DOCUMENTS

'Agreement between the Government of Australia and the Government
    of the Republic of Singapore concerning the use of Shoalwater Bay
    Training Area and the associated use of storage facilities, done at
    Singapore on 15 September 1999', *Review of treaties tabled on
    12 October 1999* (Canberra: Parliament of Australia, Joint Standing
    Committee on Treaties, 1999)
Colony of Singapore Annual Report 1957, Her Majesty's Stationery Office,
    London, 1959
Defence of Singapore 1994–95, Ministry of Defence, Singapore, 1994
Defence Procurement Division, *Doing business with MINDEF*, Ministry
    of Defence, Singapore, 3rd edn, 1998
Defending Singapore in the 21st century, Ministry of Defence, Singapore, 2000
Financial Statements for the Financial Year, 1966–1993/94, Singapore
    Government
From Phnom Penh to Kabul, Ministry of Foreign Affairs, Singapore, 1980
Goh Keng Swee, Minister of Defence, Addendum to Presidential address
    at opening of the second session of the fourth parliament, 26 Decem-
    ber 1978, Singapore Government Press Release
Government Finance Statistics Yearbook 1998, International Monetary
    Fund
'Independence of Singapore Agreement' in *Malaysia and Singapore in
    international diplomacy. Documents and commentaries*, Peter Boyce,
    Sydney University Press, Sydney, 1968
International Financial Statistics Yearbook 1998, International Monetary
    Fund
*Malaysia: Agreement concluded between the United Kingdom of Great
    Britain and Northern Ireland, the Federation of Malaya, North
    Borneo, Sarawak and Singapore*, Cmd 22, Government Printing
    Office, Singapore, 1963
Our security. Keselamatan kita, Ministry of the Interior and Defence,
    Singapore, 1969
Parliamentary Debates Singapore (PDS), vols 25, 36–6, 65, 67–8 (1967,
    1977–8, 1996–8)
Public Record Office (London) (PRO), WO32/21398, 'Brief from Com-
    monwealth Relations Office to the PM', original file ref. 9/1/1A
Q&A on defence. 1—Defence policies and organisation, Public Affairs
    Department, Ministry of Defence, Singapore, 1985
Q&A on defence. 2—Manpower, Public Affairs Department, Ministry of
    Defence, Singapore, 1985

Q&A on defence. 3—Training and discipline, Public Affairs Department, Ministry of Defence, Singapore, 1986

Q&A on defence. 4—Personnel affairs and services, Public Affairs Department, Ministry of Defence, Singapore, 1986

'RSAF to get F-16C/Ds', Ministry of Defence News Release, 9 July 1994

Singapore 1971, Ministry of Culture, Singapore, 1971

Singapore 1973, Ministry of Culture, Singapore, nd

Singapore 1997, Ministry of Information and the Arts, Singapore, 1997

Singapore 1998, Ministry of Information and the Arts, Singapore, 1998

'Singapore Armed Forces Act', in *Statutes of the Republic of Singapore*, rev. edn 1995

Singapore Armed Forces Reservist Handbook, Public Affairs Department, Ministry of Defence, Singapore

Singapore Government Directory, July 1999, Times Trade Directories for Ministry of Information and the Arts, Singapore, 1999

Singapore Polytechnic Prospectus, 1990–91

Singapore: the next lap, Government of Singapore,1991

Singapore Year Book 1965, Government Printing Office, Singapore, nd

Singapore Year Book 1967, Government Printing Office, Singapore, 1968

Singapore Year Book 1969, Government Printing Office, Singapore, 1970

'Singapore's government-linked companies report', prepared by Economic/Political Section, Embassy of the United States of America, Singapore, January 1994

Speech by Howe Yoon Chong, minister of defence, 9 March 1979, Singapore Government Press Release, MC/March/23/79 (Defence)

——, 16 May 1979, Singapore Government Press Release, MC/May/27/79 (Defence)

——, 16 October 1979, Singapore Government Press Release, MC/Oct/20/79 (Defence)

The Budget for the financial year, 1994/95—1997/98, Singapore Government

'The fixed political objectives of our party' in *People's Action Party 6th anniversary celebration souvenir*, People's Action Party, Singapore, 1960

The MINDEF/SAF Fact Book Ministry of Defence, Singapore, nd (*circa* 1999)

The Singapore Artillery. 100th year commemorative book, Headquarters Singapore Artillery and Public Affairs Department, Ministry of Defence, Singapore, 1988

The Statutes of the Republic of Singapore, Government Printer, Singapore, rev. edn 1995

'STIC biodata', Singapore Technologies Industrial Corporation Pte Ltd press release, 10 February 1993

INTERNET SOURCES

'ABRI-SAF Joint Training Committee (JTC) meeting', MIW, 15 July 1998

'Accord changeover ceremony at Tuas naval base', MIW, 26 May 1999

'Airfield maintenance crucial to RSAF operations', MIW, 8 January 1999

'Army support arm enhances combat effectiveness', MIW, 14 July 1999

'Assistance to Indonesia to fight the haze', MIW, 8 October 1997

'Australia and Singapore conduct naval exercises', MIW, 6 May 1999

'Automated Storage & Retrieval System (ASRS)', MIW, 26 May 1999

'Brunei and Singapore conduct naval exercise', MIW, 7 December 1998

'Brunei and Singapore in joint infantry live-firing exercise', MIW, 4 December 1997

'Change of Chief of Defence Force and Chief of Army', MIW, 22 January 2000

'Chief of Defence Force's visit to France', MIW, 12 September 1998

'Chief of Navy receives honorary Command at Sea badge', MIW, 13 January 1999

Comments by the minister for the Environment and second minister for defence, RADM (NS) Teo Chee Hean, MIW, 30 November 1996

'Corporatisation of DSO', MIW, 14 March 1997

Cyber Pioneer, MIW, 6 July 1996

Defence Procurement Division, 'Tender Results 1996', MIW

'DPM visits navy's new Training Command', MIW, 23 September 1995

'Dr Tan confers prestigious award on Indonesian army chief', MIW, 27 February 1996

'Dr Tan confers prestigious military award on Royal Thai Air Force Commander-in-Chief', MIW, 15 August 1997

'Dr Tan's announcement at the SAF Day dinner for senior officers', MIW, 4 July 1997

'Dr Tony Tan makes introductory visit to the United States', Cyber Pioneer, MIW, 28 September 1996

'Dr Tony Tan signs agreement to base RSAF helicopters in Australia for training', MIW, 22 October 1996

'Dr Tony Tan visits France', MIW, 12 June 1999

'DSO, as a national resource, is uniquely suited to build up technologies for both military and commercial applications', MIW, 3 October 1997

'Elite Red Berets display high state of readiness', MIW, 21 February 1997

'Elite Singapore and United Kingdom Commandos in Action', MIW, 29 April 1997

'Enhanced national air defence capability', MIW, 13 July 1998

'Fact sheet—Spike anti-tank guided missile (ATGM)', MIW, 13 July 1999

'FPDA defence chiefs' conference visit joint naval and air exercises', MIW, 14 September 1996

'French Air Force—Republic of Singapore Air Force Air Group formed', MIW, 29 January 1997

'French and Singapore air forces in bilateral exercise', MIW, 22 February 2000

'French armed forces chief visits Singapore', MIW, 26 July 1999

'French Chief of Army Staff calls on Dr Tan', MIW, 28 September 1998

'F-16C/Ds boost RSAF's fighting capability', MIW, 14 August 1998

'Guards show off might in heliborne exercise', MIW, 1 March 1999

Headquarters Armour homepage, MIW

'Homecoming of RSAF C-130', MIW, 23 February 2000

'"Housecalls" to fix equipment', MIW, 23 June 1997

'Inaugural Indonesia-Singapore defence policy talks', MIW, 17 March 1997

'Inauguration of RSAF KC-135 detachment', MIW, 28 July 1998

'Inauguration of the Defence Science and Technology Agency; MIW, 29 March 2000

'It's light but armed to strike', MIW, 2 April 1998

'Japanese Joint Staff Council Chairman calls on Dr Tony Tan', MIW, 2 December 1996

'Joint Singapore/New Zealand army exercise', MIW, 25 November 1998

'Launch of new assault rifle at opening ceremony of Army Open House '99', MIW, 11 September 1999

'Locally produced indigenous IFV rolls out', MIW, 6 September 1997

'Major Adex 99-2', MIW, 10 April 1999

'MINDEF constructs first underground ammunition facility', MIW, 12 August 1999

'MINDEF launches first Internet-based trading system', MIW, 17 April 1998

'MINDEF news release, 3 Mar 2000', MIW, 3 March 2000

'Mr Matthias Yao visits South Africa', MIW, 30 November 1998

'Navies of United Kingdom and Singapore in inaugural bilateral exercise', MIW, 14 June 1999

'Navy launches twelfth patrol vessel', MIW, 18 April 1998

'New Zealand defence minister calls on Dr Tony Tan', MIW, 17 April 1997

'NSmen operationally ready for home defence', MIW, 16 December 1997

'Official opening of RSN's Institute of Maritime Warfare', MIW, 13 April 1998

'Opening ceremony of the RSAF helicopter detachment in Oakey, Australia', MIW, 20 August 1999

'Operational readiness of patrol vessels impresses Dr Tan', MIW, 30 July 1997

'Operationally Ready National Service', MIW

'Overcoming the vulnerabilities of a small nation', speech by George Yeo, minister for Information and the Arts, MIW, 7 November 1996

'Parents prefer direct enlistment', MIW, 1 April 1998.

'Permanent Secretary (Defence) visits Japan', MIW, 30 September 1998

'Philippine navy chief visits Singapore', MIW, 4 December 1999

'RADM (NS) Teo experiences healthcare in the field', MIW, 27 July 1999

'RADM Teo's visit to Systems Command Training School', MIW, 24 March 1998

'Rear-Admiral Teo inaugurates two RSN training institutes', MIW, 17 September 1999

'Reply to media queries on Malaysian newspaper reports', MIW, 19 September 1998

'Republic of Singapore Navy's submarine returns to Singapore', MIW, 2 May 2000

'RSAF acquires Russian-made Igla air defence missile system', MIW, 15 October 1997

'RSAF News' (2nd Quarter 1999), Unofficial RSAF Website, 24 May 1999

'RSAF participates in multilateral exercises in France and Canada', MIW, 19 May 2000

'RSAF receives its first KC-135 aircraft', MIW, 13 September 1999

'RSAF replaces ageing A-4SU Super Skyhawks', MIW, 14 July 2000

'RSAF to participate in NATO flying training in Canada', MIW, 23 February 2000

'RSAF's F-5S squadrons now fully operational', MIW, 3 April 1999

'RSN ship participates in socio-civic activities with TNI-AL', MIW, 28 February 2000

'SAF conducts Ex Wallaby 4/99 in Australia', MIW, 4 November 1999

'SAF military officers given recognition for contributions', MIW, 26 June 1998

'SAF Overseas Service Medal for 10 who served in UN peacekeeping operations', MIW, 23 August 1999

'SAF responds to rising national obesity trend to maintain operational readiness', MIW, 5 December 1997

'SAF Signals formation shows Admiral Teo operational capability and readiness', MIW, 30 November 1996

'SAF's first Ultra battalion is operational', MIW, 17 June 1998

'Security challenges and responses in the Asia-Pacific', Keynote address by Dr Tony Tan at the First General Meeting of the Council for Security Cooperation in the Asia-Pacific, MIW, 4 June 1997

'Singapore and Brunei combat engineers in bilateral exercise', MIW, 7 November 1996

'Singapore and Brunei in joint air defence exercise', MIW, 25 November 1998

'Singapore and Brunei in joint armour exercise', MIW, 27 August 1997

'Singapore and Indonesia conduct first combined fighter weapons instructor course', MIW, 3 September 1999

'Singapore and Indonesian defence chiefs jointly commission joint detachment facilities', MIW, 29 August 1998

'Singapore and Japan to step up defence dialogue interactions and exchanges', MIW, 2 May 2000

'Singapore Armed Forces', British Aerospace Australia website.

'Singapore choppers take up Australian residence', MIW, 1 September 1998

'Singapore in air exercise with Australia and US', MIW, 4 May 1998

'Singapore joins Thailand and the US in air exercise', MIW, 28 October 1996

'Singapore navy launches two more submarines', MIW, 28 May 1999

'Singapore's medical team returns from Taiwan', MIW, 3 October 1999

Speech by Deputy Prime Minister BG (NS) Lee Hsien Loong, MIW, 3 October 1997

Speech by David Lim, minister of state for Defence and Information and the Arts, MIW, 2 August 1999

Speech by David Lim, MIW, 29 October 1999

Speech by Dr Tony Tan, deputy prime minister and minister for Defence, MIW, 4 October 1996

——, MIW, 3 November 1997

——, MIW, 7 January 1998

——, MIW, 12 January 1998

——, MIW, 27 March 1998

——, MIW, 4 November 1998

——, MIW, 13 February 1999

——, MIW, 1 July 1999

——, MIW, 28 July 1999

Speech by Lee Yock Suan, minister for Information & the Arts and minister for the Environment, MIW, 2 October 1999

Speech by Lt-Gen Bey Soo Khiang, MIW, 9 April 1998

Speech by Matthias Yao, minister of state for Defence, 8 March 1997

Speech by Rear-Admiral (NS) Teo Chee Hean, minister for Education and second minister for Defence, 3 March 1998, MIW

Statement by Matthias Yao, minister of state for Defence, MIW, 11 April 1997

'Teachers witness capability of the SAF', MIW, 21 May 1998

'The History of HQ Infantry', HQ Infantry website, MIW

'The Royal Navy—Republic of Singapore Navy', MIW, 11 April 1997

'The Singapore Armed Forces' best units', MIW, 24 June 1999

'Training activities between the RSN and the RN', MIW, 21 September 1998

'United States and Singapore navies in annual bilateral exercise', MIW, 7 July 1997

'United States Assistant Secretary of State calls on Dr Tony Tan', MIW, 25 August 1997

'United States Special Operations Commander-in-Chief calls on Dr Tony Tan', MIW, 19 May 1997

'US Pacific Commander-in-Chief calls on DPM Tan', MIW, 1 April 2000

'Young flying aces soar in RSAF F-5 aircraft', MIW, 12 December 1998

Index